Indian Banking

Technology, Innovations and Key Concerns

Indian Banking

Technology, Innovations and Key Concerns

Dr. Deepak Tandon

Dr. Neelam Tandon

Dr. Kanhaiya Ahuja

KUNAL BOOKS

New Delhi-110002, India

KUNAL BOOKS
4596/1A, First Floor,
11, Daryaganj, New Delhi-110002
Phones: 9811043697, 011-30125412
E-mail: *Kunalbooks@gmail.com*

Indian Banking: Technology, Innovations and Key Concerns

First Published 2011

Published in India by Prem Singh Bisht for Kunal Books, and printed at **Asian Offset Press**, Delhi.

About Book

The Indian banking industry has been undergoing major changes, reflecting a number of underlying developments. Advancement in communication and information technology has facilitated growth in internet-banking, ATM Network, electronic transfer of funds and quick dissemination of information. Structural reforms in the banking sector have improved the health of the banking sector, Deregulation, new rules, of the game (Universal Banking) Efficiency, Diffused customer loyalty, misaligned mindset, competency have called for Opportunities and Challenges. Investing in state of the art technology as the back bone to ensure reliable service delivery, leveraging the branch network and sales structure to mobilize low cost current and savings deposit, Making aggressive forays in the retail advances segment of home and personal loans, implementing organization wide initiatives involving people, process and technology to reduce the fixed costs and cost per transaction, focusing on fee based income to compensate for squeezed spread, is key concern Innovating Products to capture 'mind share' to begin with and later the wallet Share improving the asset quality as per Base II norms and need for Basle. III are some key concerns in the todays arena. Changed mindset from the conventional Banking to specialized Banking such as Retail Banking, Financial inclusion, Technological products and performance, Forex Trading & Risk Management, Reducing Gross Nonperforming Assets, Need based viable Asset quality/Credit disbursement are some grave areas of concerns other than the Hedging tools Derivatives, Convergence to new Accounting IFRS pathway.

The Current book is a resource for Indian Banking with an abundance of real-world examples. A few of the new areas of concerns have been discussed:

* Technological transformation, Diversification, Upgradation, allocative efficiency analysis of PSU and Private sector Banks
* Opportunities and challenges in areas of Risk Management, Basle II aftermaths and Basle III
* Credit Management, Credit default Risk Modeling and NPA Management in Banks
* Forex Management and Exposures
* Abbreviations and objectives in the Indian Banking
* The book is designed for a Course in Management of Banks & Financial Institutions (MBA/PGDM Cou, Banker, Researchers and practicing Risk Managers, Professionals

About Authors

Dr. Deepak Tandon, Professor, Accounting and Finance and the Programme Coordinator-(Post Graduate Programme Executive Programme (PGMAX) at the Lal Bahadur Shastri Institute of Management, Dwarka, New Delhi, is having 32 years work experience (Academics - 20 years and Industry Experience - 12 years) He has taught at all leading B- schools in Mumbai, Delhi/NCR in recent years and has worked in Punjab National Bank, Vysya Bank Ltd, The J & K Bank Ltd, Indusind Bank ltd, Oriental bank of Commerce in Scale I to Scale V majorly in areas of Operations, Forex and Credit, He is Ph.D., M.Sc., L.L.B., C.A.I.I.B, M.B.A (Finance)-FMS Delhi University, Diploma in International Trade-Exports Teaching and research interests are in Corporate Risk Management, Stock Market Operations, Corporate Taxation, Derivatives, International Financial Management, Security Analysis and Portfolio Management, Banking, Customer Relationship Management & Banking, Risk Management-Credit, Operational and Market Risk Management, Taxation & Auditing, International Financing - Trade Financing & Arbitrages International Finance - Arbitrages, Trade Finance. He is the author of 3 title books, 4 book reviews, 65 research papers & 3 international publication published and has been recently awarded "Jewel of India Award" from Ex Tamil Nadu Governor on behalf of Indian Solidarity Council and "Vidya Gaurav Gold Medal Award" from International Institute of Education & Management Mumbai and Member of Indian Institute of Banking & Finance Mumbai - Life Member, Foreign Exchange Dealers Association of India - FEDAI, He is a Corporate Trainer in MDP workshops, Jadavpur University Faculty of Arts (Phd thesis Evaluator) and a Professional Risk Managers' International Association (PRMIA), Wilmington, DE, USA (Kolkata Chapter Registered member)

Dr. Neelam Tandon, Associate Professor- Economics & Finance at JIMS Kalkaji, Dew Delhi. She is Ph.D., M.Phil, (Economics), M.A from DAVV Indore, PGHRM, Diploma in Internationl Trade Exports. She has worked as a visting Faculty (Economics) for PGDM & MBA programmes at JIMS Mathura Road, New Delhi, National Institute of Adverting Noida, IIPM New Delhi & Gurgaon, Amity University, ICFAI, Delhi Business School, Asia Pacific Institute of Management and other Management Institutes of repute, She has over 15 research papers published and has an accredited recognition at National & International conferences, She has also authored 2 books namely Excel in Economic & Elementary Statistics. She Teaches Banking, Economics, Market Research, International Trade & Business Procedures, E-Commerce at Postgraduate level.

Dr. Kanhaiya Ahuja, Associate Professor, School of Economics is an eminent economist of Devi Ahilya University, Indore, Having done his Master's degree and Ph.D. in Economics, MBA from DAVV, he has significantly contributed to the growth of school of Economics. Dr. Ahuja has a rich 16 years of teaching experience at post graduate level. Given his valuable experience of 15 years of research, he has been a party to many conferences and seminars and has 36 research publications and 2 books to his credit. He also has a wide experience in coordinating & organizing numerous workshops, seminars, conferences & other academic discussions and has successfully completed many research projects. He has taken up 5 Major Research Projects which have been sponsored by bodies like UGC and ICSSR, New Delhi. His research interest lies in the field of Business Economics, Macro Economics, Rural Marketing/ Finance, International Business, Quantitative Techniques & Environmental Economics. Many research scholars have achieved their doctorate under his guidance.

ACKNOWLEDGEMENTS

A large number of individuals have contributed to preparation of the book. Academicians, practitioners, top Bankers, students of various B- schools, have given valuable suggestions which have been incorporated in the book. We are thankful to all of them for their help and encouragement.

We sincerely thank the opportunity and express the sense of gratitude to the Department of Economics, DAVV, Indore particularly Dr Ganesh Kawadia -Head & Professor for his expert guidance, meticulous attention, inspiration & valuable suggestions in carrying the research aspects in this book.

We sincerely thank Shri Anil Shastri, Chairman & (BOD) LBSIM, Dr KC Mishra, Director Lal Bahadur Shastri Institute of Management and Dr G.L Sharma Professor & Advisor-Corpororate Interface, LBSIM, New Delhi for giving an opportunity to do the research.

We also thank Dr Amit Gupta, Chairman, Shri Manish Gupta, Dr (Cdr) Satish Seth, Director, Dr RP Maheshwari DG, Jagannath International Business School Kalkaji and Rohini, New Delhi and Ms Namrta Suri, Chairman, National Institute of Advertising for their ongoing inspirational support .

We also express our gratitude to all our Colleagues from various B- schools, Universities, Professional Bankers in India & abroad for adopting the Book. Some of the noteworthy names are - Shri Samir Kumar - DGM, SIDBI, Kolkatta, Shri SS Nathial,DGM J&K Bank Gurgaon, Sh Arvind Garg, CEO Walnut Financial Service New Delhi, Ex-Senior Banker - Foreign & Indian Banks, Shri Ram Adhar Chopra, Ex-DGM Banker State Bank Of India/Senior Vice President, SBI

(California), San Jose, USA, Shri RK Dubey Ex-General Manager PNB, Head Office New Delhi. (Executive Director Central Bank of India

Various Academicians have been a proactive source of inspiration namely:

Dr Sanjay Sehgal, Dr CP Gupta - FMS South Campus Delhi University,

Dr (Mrs Madhu Vij),Dr Monica Singhania -FMS Delhi University, Dr NK Gupta - Reader Ramjas College Delhi University

Dr Anil Saini -Dean, GGSU IP University, Prof . Mahesh Gandhi -Ex Banker and Adviser Educomp (Raffles Intl)

Dr ML Shrikant SP Jain Institute of Management, Dr Basabi Bhattacharya, Professor- Economics,Jadavpur University, Kolkatta.

Dr Arindam Chaudhry, Prof. Prasoon Prof. Majumdar, Sumanta Sharma and Prof. Joydeep Datta -IIPM New Delhi

Dr(Mrs) Vijayakatti Chairperson,Dr (Mrs) Satinder Bhatia Dr.(Prof) Harkirat Singh -IIFT New Delhi

Dr J.D Singh- Director, Jaipuria Institute of Management Noida, Dr . Vinay Datta - Fore School of Management,Dr Barnali Chaklader, IMT Ghaziabad, Dr Simi Agarwal-Associate Professor and Chair person Finance IMS Noida. Dr S.C. Bihari Prof., IBS Hyderabad, R.K. Uppal,HOD (Economics) DAV College (Malout)

We do extend our sincere thanks to our parents and family members who have showed immense support and interest in our study. We also thank all Faculty members, administrative staff members of DAVV indore, LBSIM and JIMS wherein the authors are currently employed with.

Dr. Deepak Tandon

Dr. Neelam Tandon

Dr. Kanhaiya Ahuja

PREFACE

Indian Banking Industry has translated into a new business paradigm of customer centric solutions, better business processes, improved products and service delivery, improved risk management and control practices. Use of alternate delivery channels and web centric banking. Banks have realized that technology must be used to strengthen internal controls improve the accuracy of records and facilitate promotion of new products and services. Today, banking without information technology is unthinkable, not only in developed countries, but also in many developing, countries. This is transforming brick and mortar banking to electronic banking. Thus electronic banking has liberated the banks and their customers from the traditional constraints of time and place. Customers are no longer forced to deal with banks during limited hours. "24-hour banking" services, "7-days work" services are now buzzwords. The range of services provided by e-banking includes Electronic Fund Transfer, Automated Teller Machine, electronic data in-charge etc. are addons.

Technology has emerged as a key business facilitator for developing new products and services. Banks in India have started to reap the benefits of technology, which commenced in a small way more than a decade ago. Information Technology and technological upgradation has helped in handling large transactional volumes and adapting according to the changing customer expectations, apart from providing almost real time information processing for both the banks and the customer. It is very much evident that technological upgradation has changed the face of banking operations. The wave of technological revolution in banking started after the initiation of banking sector reforms and its multiplier and accelerator effect is visible now. Hence the present study has made an attempt to examine the effect of technological up gradation on banking sector keeping all the pros and cons in mind. It can be said that banks not allocating their resources efficiently would perish unless they could become like their efficient competitors by producing more output with existing inputs. This objective cannot be achieved unless banks have best of the techniques to minimize inputs and maximize returns which is also known as acquiring technical efficiency, profitability, productivity and improving human as well as capital efficiency.

Technology facilitates risk mitigation by identifying, quantifying and managing risks to maximize returns and reducing Net Non Performing Assets of the bank. Technical upgradation promotes scale of operations at a faster and competitive rate promoting higher level of human and capital productivity. It helps to anticipate and meet customer demands through massive Data Warehousing and Customer Relationship Management. Technical upgradation helps banks to hedge in an uncertain global financial world through globalization of its banking / treasury operations through efficient movements of funds across the globe.

The power of information technology by banks should be harnessed for better Customer Relationship Management, Portfolio Management, Risk Management and other Management information needs. Information Technology must be managed as a critical corporate asset for organization to reap its full benefits. Thus the road ahead has immense benefits for the banking sector. The Banks especially public sector banks have to adapt to the changes, innovate and leverage on technology to meet the needs of the customer and compete in the market with new generation private sector techno-savvy banks.

Banks have to adopt new business models which generate more fee based income, increase the float, require less capital and give high risk adjusted returns from fund based activities. Banks who have new and innovative business strategies in place will be geared to meet the challenges and complexities of the business place of the new millennium. These benefits have to be measured not just in terms of traditional financial metrics, but also increasingly in terms of competitive advantage and market leadership i.e.; having an edge over other competitors in the market is the mantra of success.

Banks are now facing difficulties for getting optimum results from increasing complicated sophistication in the banking industry. By the comprehensive training in information technology to the existing employee this problem may be overcome. By use of computers, banks now provide services to each of individual client as per his choice pattern, his needs, and his status by clicking the mouse. The requirements are inquisitiveness of the employees, extensive use of computers and entry of every minor detail of the customers in the machine.

Upgradation of skills at all levels is needed indeed there by to reduce the employee costs by redeploying them for managing functions of marketing, recovery, shift banking, seven day banking etc. This can only be done if there exists hassle-free day-today banking. This can only happen by effective use of information technology. This will help to increase productivity of human and physical capital. By increasing productivity, employee cost may be reduced. In other words, the only way banks can handle the increase in business is by moving routine banking transactions to electronic delivery channels and freeing the employees for more productive value added business and high net worth customers.

The thrust of the book is at analyzing the key differentiating features responsible for difference in the efficiency level of Public and Private Sector Banks operating in India in the new millennium with technology as an important factor. This study makes an empirical investigation of the contribution of technological upgradation to profitability and productivity of the Public and Private Sector Banks. Economic and financial liberalization compelled the Indian commercial banks to desperately explore new avenues of earning enhancements and non-interest income surfaced as a lucrative source for the purpose. Hence non-interest income, diversification and technological upgradation are the factors taken into consideration for research analysis. The study also undertakes an interbank study within each group for comparative evaluation of technical, allocative and operational efficiency of public and private sector banks.

This book consists of four sections. **Section A** explains the relevance of technological upgradation in banking sector. **Chapter one** highlights that diversification has become synonymous with non-interest income also; technological progress facilitates the process of generating non-interest income. **Chapter two** depicts the analytical framework of the present study; the methodological approach of the application of econometric tools and Linear Programming Technique (Data Envelopment Analysis) for empirical investigation on off balance sheet component of Indian commercial banks. **Chapter three** gives a broad overview of the Indian banking sector and technological initiatives taken by public and private sector banks. Also, a comparative analysis further reveals the technological upgradation among two groups.

Chapter four depicts profitability and productivity of public and private sector banks and examines the trend of asset quality, asset management and returns on assets of the bank. The study dwells with each and every bank's trend growth over the research period of 1998-2008. **Chapter five**, deals with empirical analysis of technological upgradation in public and private sector banks by multiple regression analysis. Here an intricate examination of the contribution of non-interest income and also its elements towards bank profitability has been calculated for each bank.

A similar approach is adopted in **Chapter six** to analyze the impact of technological upgradation on technical, allocative and operational efficiency of public and private sector banks by Data Envelopment Analysis. It also tries to analyze time trend efficiency of public and private sector banks by using "Three Window Analyses" for examination of the progress of each bank over the study period. Further correlation analysis has been computed to investigate the exact nature of relationship of the variables of technological progress with respect to technical, allocative and operational efficiency.

Chapter seven summarizes the major findings derived from the research analyses with respect to technological upgradation of public and privates sector banks. It puts forward the most amicable recommendations to strengthen the banking sector by optimum utilization of human and capital resources by harnessing technological development. It also suggests some measures for public sector banks which are lacking behind private sector banks in terms of technological upgradation.

Section B containing chapters highlight the new challenges as perceived by the Indian Banks in the New millenium. This is very relevant to the Current perspectives, Challenges and opportunities in the Indian Banking sector. The challenges ahead, role of marketing of Banking products, Credit proposal, Risk and Management, Non-Performing assets and their approaches in Banks, Forex risks and hedging tools, Riskmetrics have been elucidiated at length. It gives the reader a crystal clear knowlegde of the current happenings in the Banks

The book is relevant for practicing Bankers, M.B.A students, Faculty and research scholars apart from the library resources. Due to the rising demands for Information Technology expenses, bank managements are worried that they have no proper means of measuring the investments or impacts of technological upgradation on their organization. They are increasingly introspecting whether they are making profits. Technology investment decisions rightly and whether such resource commitments will indeed fetch them the envisaged benefits are of importance. Let the benefits be in the form of financial returns, business advantages or enhanced capabilities. Thus, banks are forced to acquire new tools and techniques to evaluate technological upgradation. Knowledge of the nature and extent of contribution of technological upgradation to bank's performance in terms of productivity and profitability has, therefore, come to be considered valuable for a reality check on technological upgradation.It can be concluded that technology enhances choices, creates new markets, improves productivity and has a multiplier effect. In the field of banking, technology is the magic bullet which has the potential to extend in a cost effective manner the penetrative reach of banking services and products to a large section of the excluded society by bringing them into the formal financial system. It promises universal access thereby pushing the frontiers of banking outward. It changes the rules of game for the Banking Industry.

Dr. Deepak Tandon
Dr. Neelam Tandon
Dr. Kanhaiya Ahuja

CONTENTS

SECTION C

BANKING OBJECTIVE QUESTIONS WITH SOLUTIONS

SECTION A

TRANSFORMATION IN BANKS THROUGH TECHNOLOGICAL UPGRADATION

1

New Paradigms in New Millennium of Indian Banking

Indian Banking has changed tremendously in the past few years. The changes are multiple and at a fast pace. The old regime of banking is changing. Banking confined to marketplace has become global, competition from banks has been replaced by competition from brands, limited product line to extensive product breadth,focus on cost has been overtaken by focus on revenue growth by cost minimization, revenues generated through margin has been captured by revenues generated through fees. The major credit for which is attributable to economic liberalization, globalization of the Indian economy, new competitors' in the market, reduced margins and the information processing and communication technology, commonly known as Information Technology (IT).

Today, banks not only help to mobilize financial surpluses of an economy and transfer them to areas of financial deficit but also promote savings by providing a wide variety of financial assets to the general public. Banks have started online share- trading facility through which customers can trade anywhere, anytime even during off-market hours and subscribe to Initial Public Offerings (IPO's), Mutual Funds, debt instruments etc. The role of commercial banks has become very prominent in any economy. Commercial banks improve the allocation of resources by lending money to priority sectors of the economy. These banks act as an intermediary between savers and the investors and have achieved the status of Financial Supermarkets. India's banking system has several outstanding achievements to its credit; the most important is its extensive network in the last thirty years. Indian banks are now spread out in remote areas of the country. The other significant achievement is its contribution in the growth process of the country by financing economic activities in different sectors. It is important for the growth of the country like India to base their growth on leadership in new technology.

In the last one decade the Indian banking sector has shown a very high degree of revolution in business operations, customer service, regulatory compliance and information dissemination and a whole lot. The financial reforms have led to tough competition in the banking industry world over but the competition do enhances quality and efficiency of banks. The Indian banking sector has undergone a tremendous change during the last decade in terms of transformations of technology advancements. It has become completely dependent on technology as the service / product channel.

1.1 PARADIGM SHIFT OF BANKING FUNCTIONS

The functions performed by commercial banks in India relate mainly to acceptance of deposits in various forms and grant of advances through cash credit, overdraft and loan accounts and through purchasing/discounting demand and Usuance Bills. Sec 8(1) (A) of the Banking Regulation Act has set out the other related functions of the Commercial Banks. These functions include granting and issuing of letters of credit, traveler's cheques and circular notes. Commercial banks also perform buying selling and dealing in foreign exchange including foreign back-notes, bonds scripts or other forms of securities on behalf of Constituents or others. Acquiring, holding, and issuing on commission, underwriting and dealing in stocks, funds, shares, debentures stock, bonds, obligations, securities and investment of all kinds are some other functions performed by banks in India.

Many other functions performed by commercial banks include, receiving of all kinds of bonds or valuables, on deposit or for safe custody, providing of safe deposit vaults. Collecting and transmitting of money and securities, borrowing, raising or taking up of money. lending or advancing of money either with or without security. Drawing chaques, accepting, discounting, buying, selling and dealing in bills of exchange, hundies, promissory notes, coupons; drafts bill of lading, railway receipts, warrents, debentures, certificates scripts and other instruments and securities whether transferable or negotiable or note.

The other important ancillary services are: acting as agent for any government or local authority or other person or persons, carrying on of agency business of any description including the clearing and forwarding of goods, giving of receipts and discharges and otherwise acting as on attorncy on behalf of customers but excluding the business of a managing agent or secretary and treasurer of a company. Effecting insuring, guaranteeing, underwriting, participating in managing and carrying out of any issues public or private of state, municipal or other loans or of shares, stock, debentures, or debenture stock of any company, corporate or association and the lending of moneys for the purpose of any such issue.

Further extension in banking operations include carrying on and transacting every kind of guarantee and indemnity business. They also perform acquiring and holding and generally dealing with any title/ property or any right or interest in any such property which may form the security or part of the security for any loans or advances or which may be connected with any such security. Undertaking and executing trusts and undertaking the administration of estates as executor, trustee or otherwise. It can be concluded that while the range of services may vary depending upon the size and type of the bank, commercial banks in India perform for their customers many of the above functions.

Multitasks performed by banking industry are the outcome of requirements of a modern economy concerning settlement of transactions, which are diverse and multifarious. The needs of manufacturing trade and other commercial activated involve large value payments over vast geographic distance. The chief disadvantage with the cheque and the demand draft is that these instruments have to be physically presented often leading to delay in payment. To overcome the delay the telegraphic transfers (i.e) the payment instruction sent in telex mode to an upcountry branch of the same bank or to a correspondent bank to credit the beneficiary's account was started. A cypher code was appended to the text of the message to ensure its integrity and authenticity during transit.

The introduction of the computer supported the business strategies to certain levels. In the beginning the computers only aided one portion of the bank's branch operations like that of the ledger posting operations. Introduction of local area network (LAN) automated the branches in preparation of general ledger and cashbook. The further advancement of the information technology in connecting one branch with another through telephone lines and satellite connection has made the information technology the enabler of the business instead of just a tool. It increases the productivity and efficiency of the business.

The advancement in the communication and digital technology has made revolution in the way of the day to day life and business. As a result business and consumers started increasingly to use computers to create, transmit and store information in the electronic form instead of traditional paper document. Information stored in electronic form had many advantages. The cost of it being cheaper, easier to store, retrieves and speedier to communicate was advantageous to business and other people. The basic difficulty of requiring the documents in writing with signature for legal recognition made many people reluctant to conduct business or conclude any transaction in the electronic form.

Upgradation of technology, innovation and modernization are the key factors of having excellence over others in banking sector. It becomes necessary for a bank to differentiate its products from others. The differentiation can be in terms of specialization, new products and increasing added value by technology convergence. The bank which used the right technology to supply timely information has seen productivity increase and got a competitive edge over others. In other words, banks need greatly enhanced use of technology to the customer friendly, efficient and competitive existing services and business. They also need technology for providing newer products and newer form of services in an increasingly dynamic and globalize environment.

In today's world, technology is identified as the single strongest factor that provides bank with a competitive edge over others. But from an economist view, labour and capital are considered the most important factors in any industry including banking, and information technology in general, is clubbed equally with other factors of production. However, it is believed that information technology sometimes overshadows other factors of production in financial sector.

1.2 TECHNOLOGICAL UPGRADATION AS FACILITATOR IN INDIAN BANKING INDUSTRY

The marriage of technology and banking has changed the face of global banking like never before. New millennium has brought in new technology which will enable new products, better servicing of customer through Customer Relationship Management, better Management of Information System, and better Risk Management and increased Productivity of Banks. It is evident by the level of expenditure incurred on computerization by the public sector banks of India that technology upgradation is must for their survival against competitive threat created by new private sector banks.

Initiatives for technological change have been an integral part of reform process.

Over the years, the imperatives for speeding up the modernization of technology and intensifying the use of technology have become sharper. In response to the compulsions imposed by technological environment, the banking industry has accelerated the pace of computerization of branch operations, controlling offices and head offices. The latest innovation in the arena of technological upgradation is Core Banking Solutions along with ATMs, Internet Banking, Telephone and Mobile Banking, Customer relationship solutions, Risk Management as well as Management Information System and Data warehouse.

Core Banking Solutions is a centralized platform, which creates an environment where the entire bank's operations can be controlled, and run from a centralized hub. This creates a centralized customer database, which makes anytime, anywhere, anyway banking possible. CBS has now become the buzzword for the entire banking sector. The immediate advantages to the banks through core banking applications are: Faster and efficient customer service, offering multiple delivery channels, like ATMs, cards, mobile/ Telephone banking, Internet banking, call centers, etc. Reducing the operational costs, through manpower saving and space saving. Centralizing the back end processes and reporting. Most important, in creating a customer profile database, this is a powerful tool for gaining competitive advantage through cross selling opportunities.

The alternate delivery channels have changed the way in which banks interface with the customers. Till now, customers would have to visit the branch to carry out banking transactions, but now, they have the choice of carrying out their transactions, from the comfort of their home or office or the marketplace through these channels. The main non-branch delivery channels are ATMs, cards, the internet, telephone/ mobile banking, call centers, etc.

Automated Teller Machines (ATMs) have progressed being merely cash dispensers to provide facilities for deposits, balance reporting and inter-account transactions. ATM is a terminal of the bank's computer which can be operated by customer himself to deposit, withdraw cash and to know the balance in the account. The most important feature of ATMs are the twenty-four hour availability, timesaving/ convenience aspects, avoidance of queues and the perception that bank staff have more time to deal with counter customers. The ATMs offer many benefits to the customers include easy access to cash- day and night, weekends or holidays, fast service, convenience of location etc. Benefits to banks include- improved customer service, larger penetration, and alternative to extended hours service, less crowding at the bank counters.

Given the size of Indian population and the low ratio of ATM to branches and ATM to deposits, India has a tremendous potential for growth in the ATM market. Falling costs of machines and connectivity would also be key factors contributing to the growth of ATM network. Banks have also been cutting costs and gaining synergies through ATM sharing agreements amongst themselves, for instance: **Mitr** (Punjab National Bank, Oriental Bank of Commerce, Indian Bank, UTI Bank, Karur Vysya Bank), **Cashnet** (IDBI bank, Citi Bank, Standard Chartered Bank, Dena Bank & Syndicate Bank), **CashTree** (Bank of India, Union Bank Of India, Indian Bank, Dena Bank & Syndicate Bank,SBI, HDFC, UTI Bank, Indian Bank & Andhra Bank and ICICI Bank, Andhra Bank & Federal Bank).

ATMs have now started offering account management and bill payment facilities along with performing cash withdrawal function. Banks are now using ATMs for product promotion as banks market broader financial services to their ATM users. Core Banking Solutions, ATMS and Internet Banking are major contributors in generating fee-based income for banks. However, such facilities always come with attendant problems and risks.

As a business tool, **Internet Banking** is rapidly transforming the world of banking, making banks faster and more efficient and allowing them to provide more personalized services to the customer. The advantage of the internet is that it allows financial institutions to combine content from multiple sources to one computer. This capability is now considered as one of the key enablers for accelerating the use of home banking programme. Moreover, net banking is considered to be the most cost effective channel for the banks. Although this channel is available in India for the past five to six years, it is only in the recent past that internet banking has started picking up. A major impediment in the use of this channel is the concern about the security of internet transactions.

On the retail end, banks have started offering internet banking through a large number of branches. The facilities offered include account enquiry, money transfers, mail alerts, etc. Some banks have also linked it with railway ticketing and bill payments. Many banks also started offering Internet Banking to their corporate customers. The facility of Corporate Internet Banking Service is available to all business enterprises, accessible from anywhere in the globe providing various banking and financial services under single umbrella and giving complete freedom of banking anywhere anytime on 24* 365 basis.

The corporate Internet service offers a huge number of facilities to the corporate clients. These include Online funds transfer facility, Trade Finance Management, Funds Management, Upload features, MIS/ Reconciliation, Straight Through Processing, Account administration and management, Multi level authorization, Requests/Mails/ Alerts, etc.

Call centers combine the use of highly effective and empowered company representatives with a service framework that relies heavily on the state of the art communications and information technologies. **Telephone Banking** has led to the call centre growth in the financial services sector. Many banks –ICICI, HDFC, Standard Chartered Citicorp, American Express to name a few, have deployed call centers for better customer support and care. The Public sector banks are also now following suit, with SBI and PNB taking the lead.

Technological upgradation helps in better Customer Relationship Management. **Customer Relationship Management (CRM) Solution** is the term for the set of methodologies and tools that help banks to manage customer relationships in an organized way. It is a process or methodology used to learn more about customers' needs and behaviors in order to develop stronger relationships with them. There are many technological components to CRM. It is a process that will help bring together lots of pieces of information about customers, sales, marketing effectiveness, and responsiveness and market trends. CRM helps businesses use technology and human resources to gain insight into the behavior of customers and the value of those customers.

Customer relationship management is also defined as finding, getting, and retaining customers. It is the core of any customer-focused business strategy and includes the people, processes, and technology associated with sales, marketing, and service. For a successful CRM, technology provides the base on which processes are built by the people for tracking customer behavior in order to develop marketing and relationship building programs that bond consumers to a brand.

1.3 RISK MITIGATION AND TECHNOLOGICAL UPGRADATION

Risk Management, Management Information System and Data warehouse is effective tool to mitigate risk. Risk management is a fairly new concept to the Indian banking Industry. Presently most of the banks are on a learning curve and the information systems used by the banks for addressing the risks are scattered in separate applications. Good risk management practices require robust, account level and enterprise wide database. Banks should have access to various kinds of data, which will have to be captured by the bank over a period of time. It was with this background that Reserve Bank of India's committee on Technology Upgradation in the banking sector, advised the Indian banks to put in place their strategy for setting up an enterprise wide data warehouse.

Technology has affected Central Banking functions too such as, Banking supervision, Currency Management and Financial and Monetary Stability. Technology has also helped the Central Bank to make its internal processes and functions more effective. RBI has also established a Centralized Database Management System, a Data warehousing and Data mining solution, Off-site Monitoring and Surveillance. RBI introduced a system of Off-site Monitoring and Surveillance, with the primary objective of assessing financial condition of banks in – between on-site examinations. With a view to facilitate banks to submit error-free data in time and with a view to enable the supervisor to make effective use of the data obtained, RBI has developed OSMOS package in an RDBMS environment. RBI has recently expanded the scope of surveillance to include Risk based Supervision and Consolidated Prudential Reporting. Reserve Bank of India monitors the electronic payments made by commercial banks of India.

1.4 ELECTRONIC PAYMENT SYSTEM AND INDIAN BANKING INDUSTRY:

Payments can be made in India in the form of cash, cheque, demand drafts, credit cards, debit cards and also by means of giving electronic instructions to the banker who will make such a payment on behalf of his customers. Electronic payments can be made in the form of Electronic Funds Transfer (EFT), Electronic Clearing Service (ECS) for small value repetitive payments and through Real Time Gross Settlement (RTGS) System for large value payments. A few banks in India have begun to offer certain banking services through Internet that facilitate transfer of funds electronically. India has made significant progress in payment systems by introducing modern payment media viz., smart/credit cards, electronic funds transfer, debit/credit clearing, e banking, etc. RBI has also put in place Real Time Gross settlement System (RTGS) to facilitate efficient funds management and mitigating settlement risks.

Electronic Funds Transfer (EFT) is a system whereby anyone who wants to make payment to another person / company etc. can approach his bank and make cash payment or give instructions / authorization to transfer funds directly from his own account to the bank account of the receiver / beneficiary. Complete details such as the receiver's name, bank account number, account type (savings or current account), bank name, city, branch name etc should be furnished to the bank at the time of requesting for such transfers so that the amount reaches the beneficiaries' account correctly and faster. RBI is the service provider for EFT.

Electronic Clearing Service (ECS) is a retail payment system that can be used to make bulk payments / receipts of a similar nature especially where each individual payment is of a repetitive nature and of relatively smaller amount. This facility is meant for companies and government departments to make/receive large volumes of payments rather than for funds transfers by individuals. The ECS is further divided into two types – ECS (Credit) to make bulk payments to individuals/vendors and ECS (Debit) to receive bulk utility payments from individuals.

ECS Credit, in this method of transaction a series of electronic payment instructions is generated to replace paper instrument. This system works on the basis of one single debit transaction triggering a large number of credit entries. These credits of electronic payment instructions which possess details of the beneficiaries account number, amount and the bank branch are then communicated to the bank branches through their respective service branches for crediting the accounts of the beneficiaries either through magnetic media duly encrypted or through hand copy.

This facility is more adopted by the corporate bodies or government departments, which has to effect payments to a large number of beneficiaries. They submit the details of the payments in magnetic media to the bank managing the clearinghouse, through a sponsor bank. The only requirement is that the beneficiaries have to give mandate to the corporate bodies or to government departments for crediting their accounts under Electronic Clearing System.

ECS Debit is the scheme which facilitates payment of charges to utility services such as electricity, telephone companies, payment of insurance premium and loan installments etc by customers. This scheme facilitates for faster collection of bills by the companies better cash flow management and eliminates the need to go to collection centers/designated banks by the customers. In this scheme, the utility company prepares its bills in three parts. The first part serves as a receipt to the customer. The second part serves as a voucher for the collecting branch. The third part contains a Magnetic Ink Character Recognition (MICR) bond that is sent to the service branch. The first part of the receipt is returned to the customer by the collecting branch duly affixing the paid stamp. In both ECS credit and debit all precaution with regard to the data validation and Integrity are observed in full.

Cheque Truncation is a method of payment processing where under movement of the paper instrument is truncated by substituting with electronic transmission of the cheque details or data. In India the technology with regard to Magnetic Ink Character Recognition (MICR) Processing would need to be upgraded to a full image capture solution. Electronic presentation of images of cheque substitute physical delivery of cheques. This combined with the centralized signature storage and retrieval system will eliminate multiplicity of destination points and reduce clearing time very substantially.

Electronic Fund Transfers (EFT) is the means by which pre- authorized debits and credits are electronically transmitted from a customer's account to the business accounts. It transfers the ongoing inconvenience of banks of accepting, processing and handling monthly payments by cheque, cash or other paper instruments. EFT is designed to effectively improve customer services and reduce the inherent cost of processing paper transactions. The software enables one to utilize electronic fund transfers for one's financial needs without having to become involved in the detailed regulatory or technical aspects of automated clearing house (ACH) item processing. The businesses can use this software to create daily reports of all transactions so that records can be tracked and reconciled quickly and easily.

The **Real Time Gross Settlement System** (RTGS) system is maintained and operated by the RBI and provides a means of efficient and faster funds transfer among banks facilitating their financial operations. As the name suggests, funds transfer between banks takes place on a 'real time' basis. Therefore, money can reach the beneficiary instantaneously and the beneficiary's bank has the responsibility to credit the beneficiary's account within two hours.

1.5 INFORMATION TECHNOLOGY – THE MULTIPLIER EFFECT

It is evident that, technology has brought fundamental shift in the functioning of banks. It not only helps banks in improvement of their internal functions but also enable them to provide better customer service. The efficiency of banks can improve with the help of technology to efficiently deliver products and services to its customers. As well as technology facilitates achieving economies of scale and creates cost efficiencies. The benefits of technological advancement are visible in terms of number of ATMs, that has changed the profile of front offices in bank branches, E-banking and Internet banking have opened new avenues in "Convenience Banking ". Internet banking has also led to reduction in

Transaction costs for banks to about a tenth of branch banking.

The cost efficiency achieved by banks today is the outcome of technology solutions. It has made flow of information much faster, more accurate and enables quicker analysis of data received. In other words, the decision process gets momentum and becomes more efficient. This also enables development of appraisal and monitoring tools which makes credit management much more effective, reducing the transaction costs.

While application of technology would help banks to reduce their operating costs in the long run, the initial investments would be sizeable. According to Banking Statistics expenditure on development of information technology by banking and financial services industry in USA is approximately, seven percent of the revenue as against around one percent in Indian banks. It is expected that IT spending of Indian banking system will increase significantly in coming years.

The banking industry can reduce the *investment costs* in technology applications by sharing of facilities. It is because of this reason; banks are coming together to share ATM networks. Similarly, in the coming years, it is expected that banks will come together to share facilities in the area of payment and settlement, back office processing, data warehousing, etc. This will also help banks to decrease *operational expenses* and increase operational efficiency. The banks meticulously do their homework before adopting or modifying adopted technology but still it is not easy to measure the risk-return tradeoff. It is therefore a need of the hour to assess the impact of technological upgradation on public and private sector banks of India.

Implementation of new technology helps banks to increase their revenue through product innovation, introduction of new services and huge centralized processing. Technology reduces the cost of existing services and improves the spread of new services. It maximizes economies of scale by reducing the percentage of cost incurred on new technology based products introduced in the financial market.

Outcome of technological advancement in banking operations is implementation of core banking solutions. Core banking solutions reduces the transaction cost and improves profitability. It also facilitates creation of new business delivery models which helps in augmenting income levels. It improves communication and dissemination of information among key banking verticals. A wide range of payment instrument like EFT, ECS, e-money, smart card and credit card cater to the needs of different types of economic transaction. At the level of Inter-bank payments and settlements, real-time and online funds transfer plays a major role both in local as well as inter-city transaction. The spread and the reach of the modern system enable equal and convenient access from both small and big centers alike.

It can be summarized as Banking in the new millennium has experienced a shift of customer preferences. They are shifting to debit cards, electronic bill payments and other forms of electronic transfers. These are substituting the traditional cheque usage. Hence the quality of products, services and processes will be highly critical for the success of any bank in the new era. Only business that offer top quality products and services will succeed. With the advancement of technological progress banks face two major risks: Negative Net Present Value Risk and Agency Conflict Risk.

Negative Net Present Value risk arises when the discounted value of excess cash flow generated through implementation of new technology is not sufficient to cover the cost to implement the new technology. This results in reduction in the shareholders value which is a negative feature for any profit making organization. But bank can adopt innovative technology as long as the net present value of increased cash flow is positive. Agency Conflict Risk arises when the management chooses projects which do not increase shareholders value. This can be eliminated by doing proper homework prior to implementing the technological change.

It can be concluded that banks to be successful in techno-savvy environment requires reliable and stable technological initiatives to handle increasing volumes, shrinking margins and changing customer preferences. Banks need to adopt innovative changes to maximize benefits and increase the barriers to entry for competition by redesigning business processes around the technical system so as to eliminate redundant procedures and controls.

2

Technological Progress and Methodological Issues

Information technology is bringing about radical changes in the way in which organizations are being managed, business operations are being performed and state governance is being done. This trend has tremendous implications on the operations and business models of every industry, with financial intermediaries like commercial banks being no exception.

The number of branches providing Core banking Solutions (CBS) in India has increased significantly in recent years. CBS provides a host of benefits such as, anywhere banking, anywhere access and quick fund movement at optimal costs and in an efficient manner. More than 95% of PSB branches were fully or partially computerized at end-March 2006. In 2008 the branches of Bank of Baroda, Canara Bank and Oriental Bank of Commerce, Punjab National Bank and State Bank of India are 100% computerized.

Normal banking transactions such as depositing cash and cheque clearance is going hi-tech as banks opt for sophisticated interactive machines. Rising rentals and staff costs are pushing Indian Banks to go for 'lobby banking'- a bundle of sophisticated automated consoles and next generation software, which enables customers to carry out most of the banking transactions themselves. A customer can deposit or withdraw cash (including coins), or cheques.

which are automatically 'truncated'- electronically processed for clearance. Cash is instantly credited, while cheques are scanned front and back, signatures electronically verified and data transmitted to the Reserve bank of India's electronic cheque clearance system. Electronic Banking can produce real time information for clients at a much lower costs per customer interaction.

In the Indian banking scenario, the pressures of liberalization, privatization and globalization have primarily contributed towards injecting the 'commercial sense', or 'profit orientation' in the banking sector, predominantly the public sector banks. To withstand competition with private sector and foreign banks and also to maintain profitability and market share in increasingly globalised markets, it has become imperative for banks to deliver high quality service at lower cost. Customers have become all the more discerning, and customer–centricity has become one of the vital determinants of business success for players in banking industry.

Technology has played a major role in upgrading the payments and settlement systems, which is the spinal cord of the banking system. Transfer from paper based transactions to electronic means which include Real Time Gross Settlement (RTGS), National Electronic Fund Transfer (NEFT) and other electronic modes have intensified the working of banks. Quicker funds settlement has a direct impact on better management of liquidity by banks. It has provided for better asset-liability management, increasing number of branches all over the country. This has also helped in better fund management, therefore improving profitability for banks.

In the above context, to maintain competitiveness banks have to embrace advanced technology as it can significantly improve operational efficiency by reducing cost and also provide higher order customer service. An attempt is made to identify the factors responsible for varied performance of public and private sector banks in India and examine whether they have any significant influence of technological upgradation on the technical, operational efficiency, profitability and productivity of commercial banks operating in India.

The present study attempts to capture both the time perspective and the cross sectional bank specific and *'Technological Progress'* component specific aspects. The sample for the empirical analysis comprises of ten commercial banks of India. The rationale of selecting five Public and five private sector banks is to have a comparative study between Public Sector and Private Sector Banks in changing banking scenario. Banks considered in the research study are the most representative sample units of the universe (banking Industry).The study period (1998-2008) has been selected keeping financial reforms into consideration. As a matter of fact the commercialization of Banks gained momentum 1998 onwards. The empirical investigation has been carried out separately for different bank-groups, viz., public sector banks and private sector banks. The time series of ten years has been constructed to not only have reliable and authentic information of selected banks but also to evaluate the progress of banks over the period of Economic Liberalization and impact of Technological Advancement in the banking industry. The sampling units considered in the research study are:

Sample Units

S.No.	Public Sector Banks	Private Sector Banks
1	Bank of Baroda	Jammu & Kashmir Bank
2	Canara Bank	IndusInd Bank
3	Oriental Bank of Commerce	ICICI Bank
4	Punjab National Bank	HDFC Bank
5	State Bank of India	Axis Bank

The performance of banks is described in terms of productivity and efficiency. Productivity of a bank can be improved by *reducing the cost of intermediation* (reducing operating cost by effectively deploying Technology, Human Capital and continually refining its work procedures) and by *raising the spread* i.e. deploying capital in most effective way. Productivity is defined as the ratio of output to input for a specific production system. Rising productivity implies either more output is produced for the same amount of input or that less input are required to produce the same amount of output.

The empirical problem and conceptual problems that plague the measurement of physical output in most service industries are particularly acute in banking sector, where there is no clear consensus on an appropriate definition of output. However, most of these measures that are used to study bank's performance can be interpreted more correctly as measuring the bank's efficiency target rather than directly measuring their productivity. Nonetheless, such measures of efficiency are most commonly examined indicators of productivity in banking.

Concept of ***Technical Efficiency*** relate to how well a bank employs its resources relative to the existing production possibilities frontier (or, in other words, relative to current 'best practice') i.e. how an institution simultaneously minimizes costs and maximizes revenue based on an existing level of production technology.

The financial variables selected for all commercial banks for the time period 1998-2008 are Income variables comprising of Interest Income and Non Interest Income. Similarly the expenses of banks comprises of Interest expenses and operating expenses. The performance of the bank can be evaluated from the rise or fall in the absolute figures, but there is a catch here. If the income of the bank rises with no corresponding growth in the assets, it indicates that the bank is able to earn better from the existing assets. However, along with a rise in the income, if there has also been a corresponding growth in the assets, then the growth in the Bank's income may not be the same as indicated by the growth in the absolute figures. For commenting on the Bank's performance, a comparison to the total assets of the bank will give a true picture.

The one important parameter that essentially relates to the bank's ability to sustain the losses due to risk exposures is the Bank's Capital. The intermediation activity exposes the bank to a variety of risks. Cases of big banks collapsing due to their bank's inabilities to sustain the risk exposures are readily available. Considering this, it is highly essential to examine the capital vis-à-vis the risk weighted assets. This is the Capital to Risk Weighted Assets Ratio (CRAR) as given by the Basle Committee. The statutory prescription for CRAR is 9 percent in India, which has been well surpassed by most banks.

Based on the income, expenditure, net interest income, NPAs and capital adequacy one can assess the profitability and the long run sustenance of the bank. The intermediation costs of a bank refer to the operating cost of the bank and include all the administration and operational costs incurred while offering its services. The ratio of the intermediation costs of the bank to the total assets should be kept low to ensure greater profitability. A technology savvy bank will always be in a better position to reduce its operating costs.

The ratio of the net interest income (Spread = Interest earned- Interest expended) to the total assets gives the net interest margin of the bank. This ratio is the actual measure of the bank's performance as an intermediary, as it examines the bank's ability in mobilizing lower cost funds and investing them at a reasonably higher interest. By borrowing short and lending long, banks can earn higher spreads nevertheless by doing so they will be exposed to greater risks. Hence banks need to be cautious and should not accept risks beyond their ability to control/manage them. Product innovation using the right technology is one approach, which can be followed by the banks to mobilize cheaper funds.

For commenting on the Bank's performance, a comparison to the total assets of the bank will give a true picture. Seen in this perspective the realities of the bank's performance will appear in its capacity to withstand challenges; in its profitability; its asset quality; and its sustainability and lowering Non- Performing Assets (NPA) burden. The asset quality of the banks can be examined by considering the NPAs. These NPAs should be considered against not just total assets but also against the advances, because this is where the NPAs primarily arise. When NPAs arise, banks have to make provision for the same as per the regulatory prescriptions. When the provisions are adjusted against the Gross NPAs it gives rise to the Net NPAs. Provisions reduce the risk exposure arising due to the NPAs to a reasonable extent as they ensure that the banks sustain the possible loss arising from these assets.

The deadweight of non-performing assets on the banking industry –which at one time threatened to bring down a few banks - has significantly reduced. The strong momentum in the economy and cleansing of balance sheets through provisioning has brought down bad loans in domestic banks to globally- acceptable level. The expanding asset base along with reductions on the slippage front helped banks maintain lower NPA ratios. The reduction in NPAs was also due to strong recovery of previously written off accounts. Over the years, banks have been aggressively providing for and writing off their NPA portfolios. And over the years, they have been allocating close to 50 percent of operating profits towards provisions. Currently, the provision coverage ranges between 40-80 percent. Provision coverage measures total provisions as a percentage of NPAs.

The financial ratios regarding liquidity, capital adequacy, earnings and liability are widely used measures of organizational performance. However, they have one disadvantage. Each single ratio must be compared with some benchmark ratio one at a time. Financial ratios do provide information on the overall financial performance of an organization, but provide little information about the amount by which performance could be improved or the area where the effort should be focused in order to improve performance. On the other hand, Data Envelopment Analysis (DEA) method not only finds the efficient Decision Making Units (DMUs) but also tells how to make other inefficient DMUs efficient by varying in the input and output parameters by suggested amount.

On the other hand, the regression models are quantitatively robust, they lack the ability to include multiple inputs and outputs because regression models usually restrict the analyst to one dependent variable. Regression models also provide only an estimate of model success, while offering no feedback about improvement possibilities. Additionally, regression models impose a particular functional form on the data, producing a single function that represents a set of hypothetical "average" performers. DEA, on the other hand, produces an efficient frontier consisting of the set of most efficient performers, allowing a direct comparison to the best performers as opposed to average.

While the regression produces an "average line across all DMUs, DEA produces an efficient frontier that encompasses the best performers. While DMUs above the regression line appear to be performing better than the average, they are not performing as well as the best performers or most productive DMUs on the efficient frontier.

DEA MODEL - AN INTERMEDIATION APPROACH

Data envelopment analysis (DEA) is a Linear Programming method of measuring efficiency of a decision making unit (DMU) such as bank/ firm. DEA employs mathematical programming to construct a best practice frontier from the observed data and to measure efficiency relative to the constructed frontier. It is an application of linear programming that has been used to measure the relative efficiency of operating units with the same goals and objectives which are termed as Decision Making Units (DMUs). In these applications, the performance of each institution or organization is measured relative to the performance of all operating units in the same system. This technique aims to measure how efficiently a DMU uses the resources available to generate set of outputs.

The DEA frontier is formed by connecting the set of best practice observations (the piece-wise linear combination). Thus, the DEA efficiency score for a DMU or bank is not defined by an absolute standard but is defined relative to other banks. The best way to explain DEA is by way of ratio form. For each DMU, we would like to obtain a measure of the ratio of all outputs (y) over all inputs (x), such as u'y/v'x, where u is output weight and v is input weight.

Efficiencies estimated using DEA are relative that is relative to the best performing DMU (or DMUs if there is more than one best performing DMUs). The best performing DMU is assigned an efficiency score of unity or 100 per cent, and the performance of other DMUs vary, between 0 and 100 per cent relative to the best performer DMU. Efficiency scores decide the best performing DMU based on the highest ratio of output to input. Remaining DMUs are compared relative to the most efficient Bank. A *fundamental assumption* behind the computation of relative efficiency is that if a given Bank A, is capable of producing Y (A) units of output using X1(A) and X2 (A) units of input, then other banks should also be able to do the same if they were to operate efficiently.

Performance Targets for inefficient banks has to be set to enable them to reach 100 per cent relative efficiency in comparison with Bank A, the most efficient. Bank A has operated in an environment similar to the others and hence using its performance as a benchmark is realistic. Input Target for inefficient or relatively less efficient bank is the amount of inputs that will enable the bank to have the same level of output as most efficient Bank A. For inefficient banks, input target will be less than Actual Input. The difference between actual input and input target is Input Slack.

Inefficient bank can move up to the level of efficien bank in at least three ways:

1. Inefficient bank reduces the input operating expenses, with Interest Expenses and Non Interest Income being unchanged to reach up to the level of most efficient bank.
2. Inefficient bank reduces only its Interest Expenses, keeping Operating Expenses and Non Interest Income unchanged to reach up to the level of most efficient bank.
3. Inefficient Bank reduces both Interest Expenses and Operating Expenses in the same ratio, or increases Non Interest Income (keeping the same ratio of inputs), to move up to the level of most efficient bank.

Economic efficiency estimates drawn through DEA could be decomposed into ***Technical and Allocative efficiency***. Technical efficiency refers to the ability of a bank to obtain maximum output from a given set of inputs, while allocative efficiency refers to ability of the bank to use inputs in optimal proportions, given their respective prices. Relative gains in terms of technical and allocative efficiency provide further insight into the performance of different bank groups.

An attempt has been made to analyze in its time and space dimension the broad structure of the banking system and to place the present structure in the context of historicity of the process in terms of efficiency of the banking industry. There are two approaches to analyze the efficiency in banking system; by production approach and by intermediation approach. In the production approach, a bank is treated as a firm that uses labor and other inputs to produce various outputs like deposits and advances etc. In the intermediation approach, a bank is considered as an inter-mediator of financial services in which inputs are used to produce the spread, the interest margin, non interest income. Following the Intermediation approach deposits, number of employees, interest expenses and operating expenses are taken as inputs. The cost to income ratio indicates how profitably the funds have been deployed by the banks. The ratio reflects the ability of a bank to generate revenue from its expenditure. It captures the impact of off-balance sheet operations and is, thus, a better measure of efficiency than the cost to assets ratio.

Banking, by nature is an information and human capital intensive industry, notwithstanding the increased reliance on technology solutions for improving productivity. Hence, labor cost plays an important role in determining the profitability of banks. Therefore, at a disaggregated level of operating costs, labor cost (expenditure on salaries) per unit of earning assets assumes importance among the components of operating costs.

The productivity of the staff will have a significant bearing on the bank's overall performance. This is the one factor, which can enable the bank to develop a unique competitive advantage. While banks can develop similar products and technology like their competitors, the same may not be possible with the staff performance. Banking being part of the service industry, the staff efficiency becomes an important factor for assessing the bank's performance. Using this, a very strong competitive advantage can be developed by individual banks.

Hence an initial attempt has been made to analyze the ***Technical Efficiency of the bank,*** measured using inputs as *Number of Employees (in thousands) and Deposits (in crores)*; output considered is *Fee-based income (non-interest income)*. Secondly, ***Allocative Efficiency*** has been analyzed using inputs as *Operating Expenses (price of employees)* of the bank and *Interest Expenses (as price of deposits)* of the bank while output considered is same as Fee-based income. The reason responsible for this rational is maximum percentage of operating expenses incurred by the bank accrues to wage-bill expenses and in case of interest expenses most expenses accrue to deposits of the bank. Thirdly, ***Operational Efficiency*** has been analyzed using *Interest Expenses and Operating Expenses* as inputs and *Interest Income* as output. The reason for consideration of interest income as output is based on the fact that deposit mobilization and credit creation is the core of banking business. Hence, the intermediation cost which relates income from credit and cost of deposit would illuminate bank's efficiency in its core function of raising deposits from savers and on lending to user groups. The net interest margin ratio relates how efficiently banks manage their pecuniary risk arising from asset-liability mismatch.

To increase efficiency of the bank, deposits have to be mobilized to generate additional income by the bank. The dramatic increase in non-interest income in banks over the past two decades reflects not only improvement in operational efficiency but also a diversification of banks into non-traditional activities and thus a shift in the way banks earn money from their traditional banking activities. As far as non-fund or fee based activities are concerned, personnel skills and business acumen of bank employees handling the particular desk matters. However, it is difficult to segregate cost incurred by a bank on its personnel staff handling fee-based activities, given the fact that the same set of personnel may be engaged in handling both fund and non-fund based activities.

Net Interest Income is computed by subtracting interest expenses from interest income. Interest Income of the banks comprises of income received from traditional activities like advancing of loans and investment in government and other approved securities. Non Interest Income accounts from off balance sheet items. The inclusion of non interest income enables us to capture the recent changes in the production of services as banks are increasingly engaging in non-traditional banking activities.

It seems that banks will rely less on net interest income and more on non-interest income to improve profitability. The highest earning banks will be those that generate an increasing share of operating revenue from noninterest sources. A related assumption is that all fees are created equal. Some fees are stable and predictable over time, while others are highly volatile because they derive from cyclical activities. The fundamental concern among banks is to determine the appropriate customer mix and business mix to grow profits at high rates, with strong focus on fee based revenues.

Banks differentiate between core deposits and volatile or non-core borrowings. Core deposits are which consists of demand deposits, Negotiable orders of withdrawal and automatic transfers from savings, money market deposit accounts, savings, other savings and time deposits are stable deposits that are typically not withdrawn over short periods of time. The owners are not highly rate sensitive, such that the interest elasticity is low, and do not quickly move their balances to another institution when it pays a higher rate. Core deposits represent a more permanent funding base than large-denomination, volatile (noncore) liabilities. They are also attractive because they are relatively cheap as compared with the interest cost of noncore liabilities. Most banks closely monitor changes in their core deposits as an indicator of liquidity risk and funding cost.

The intermediation costs of a bank refer to the operating cost of the bank and include all the administration and operational costs incurred while offering its services. The ratio of the intermediation costs of the bank to the total assets should be kept low to ensure greater profitability. As mentioned earlier, a technology savvy bank will always be in a better position to reduce its operating costs. Interest expenses comprises of interest paid on deposits, interest paid on borrowings from RBI and other agencies.It is the cost of deposits, borrowings and other long –term debts. Gross interest income minus gross interest expense is net interest income. This figure is important because its variation over time indicates how well management of the bank is controlling interest rate risk.

The book highlights the comparative performance of public and private sector banks operating in India by considering sample of ten banks. It comprises of five public sector banks, namely; Bank of Baroda, Canara Bank, and Oriental Bank of Commerce, Punjab National Bank and State Bank of India and five private sector banks namely; Jammu and Kashmir Bank, HDFC Bank, ICICI Bank, IndusInd Bank and Axis Bank over the period of 1997-98 to 2007-08.

3

Technological Upgradation in Banking Sector

3.1 INTRODUCTION

In India, a small number of industrial houses and a few educational, research and development institutions started using computers in the early 1960s. During the late 1960s and 1970s, service-oriented industries such as airlines, railways and insurance companies introduced computers to improve their efficiency and to expand market size. Banks in India did not, however, introduce computers on a large scale because of the fear that technological advancement will lead to substitution of labor by capital promoting unemployment. Quite a long time Indian banks faced very little competition and operated in a protected environment because of protective financial policies of the country.

Thus no long-term policy or perspective for the banking sector was formulated: it was simply treated as part of the public sector. This conservative approach started changing with financial liberalization in the country. Well-computerized foreign banks and privatized banks begin to challenge nationalized banks. They aim at a profitable and wealthy part of the market and, in contrast to the nationalized banks, do not recognize any social responsibilities to small account holders or to a rural and semi-urban clientele. This promoted change in banking scenario in the country from the past.

Today, Indian banking sector have many strengths some of these are Regulatory Systems Growth Rate, Technological Advancement, Risk Assessment Systems and Credit Quality. The challenges of the Indian banking industry, if overcome can help banks to mark its place on the global banking scene. Some of these challenges are; Diversification of markets beyond big cities, Human Resource Systems, Size of banks, High Transaction Costs, Banking Infrastructure and Labor Inflexibilities. It can be said that technology has given birth to a new era in banking. In other words, technology can be the key differentiator between two banks and a major factor to attain competitive edge. Though slow in the beginning, Indian banks seem to have paced up in adoption of advanced technology, as is evident from FICCI's survey results. Technological systems of Indian banks have rated more advanced than China and Russia; at par with Japan, but less advanced than Singapore, UK and USA.

Figure 3.1

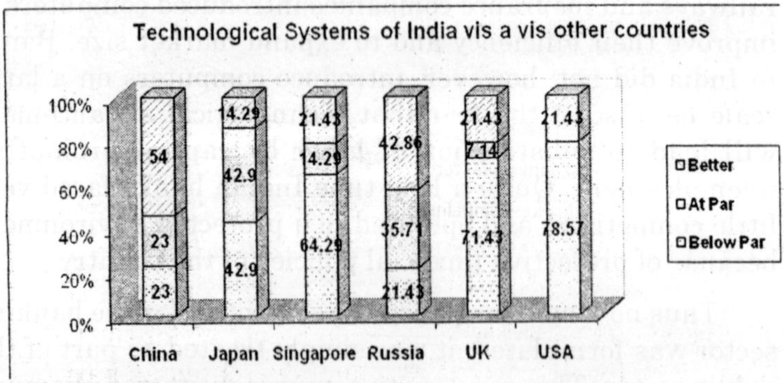

Source: FICCI Report 2006

It is very much evident that technology has moved from being just a business enabler to being a business driver. Be it customer service, reducing operational costs, achieving profitability, developing risk management systems, banks turn to technology for providing necessary solution. It is evident from the above figure that Technological upgradation is clearly one of the most successful strategy in

Customer Acquisition and Retention followed by Expansion of ATM Network, Advertisements and additional sales force.

Customer Retention and Customer Satisfaction are inexorably inter-linked. While consumers may be happy to make payments and interact with their bank through convenient – and cheaper – banking channels, they still expect high standards of service. A consistent service reflects the bank's brand and image across all channels. Superior service pre and post banking has been one of the essential factors rated by the bank's customers. It is believed that Personal touch in the dealings has helped banks in winning customers. The figure below depicts contribution of technological upgradation as the highest contributor on one to eight points scale, for customer acquisition and retention.

Figure 3.2

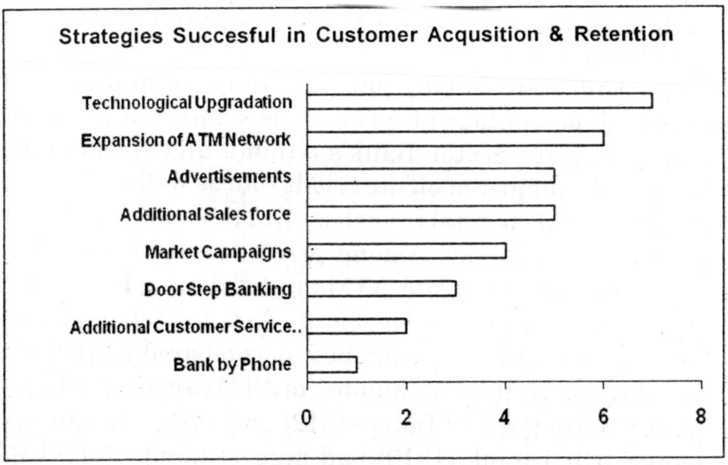

Source: FICCI Report 2006

It is very much evident from the above figure that technological upgradation is first and foremost contributory factor in acquisition and retention of customers by banks followed by expansion of ATM network. This has been realized by private as well as by public sector banks of India.

3.2 BRANCHES AND ATMS OF SCHEDULED COMMERCIAL BANKS

Convenience banking, by means of different delivery channels has become the key word, with new channels like mobile and internet banking coming to the fore. Another channel of banking which has picked up very fast is ATM. The table 3.1 below depicts the spread of rural, semi-urban and urban branches of public and private sector banks. It also depicts number of total ATMS, number of on-site ATMs as well as percentage of offsite ATMs to total branches of respective banks within the financial year 2005.

The table 3.1 depicts that public sector banks have huge network of branches in rural, semi-urban and urban areas. The total number of branches of public sector banks is almost five to four times greater than to private sector banks. Hence, the increase in number of ATMs in public sector banks is not visible at significant level, as compared to their new generation private sector banks operating in India. Private sector banks are having low percentage of branches but a very high percentage of ATMs. It is significant to note that among Private Sector Bank's Jammu and Kashmir Bank has lowest number of offsite ATMs (56) as well as percentage of offsite ATMs to total branches (13.21) as compared to other private sector banks. Among private sector banks highest number (1330) of offsite ATMs to total branches is of Axis Bank. The reason responsible is, Axis bank having almost fifty percent of fewer branches as compared to HDFC and ICICI Bank. In absolute number of ATMs among public sector banks' State Bank of India (3612) and among private sector banks' ICICI Bank (1910) had highest number of ATMs as compared to their competitors in the market. It depicts that banks have realized importance of ATMs and this has promoted rapid increase in installation of ATMs, by not only private sector banks but also public sector banks. It is noteworthy that the commercial banks have made huge progress in ATMs during the year 2007. This is depicted from table 3.2.

Table 3.1

Branches and ATMs of Scheduled Commercial Banks

(As at end - March 2005)

Sr. No:	Name of the Bank	Rural Branches	Semi-Urban Branches	Urban Branches	Metropolitan Branches	Total Branches	On-site ATMs	Off-site ATMs	ATMs Total	Per cent No. of Off-site ATMs to total Branches
1	Bank of Baroda	1,160	558	476	486	2,680	171	1	172	0.04
2	Canara Bank	760	683	551	525	2,519	647	63	710	2.5
3	Oriental Bank of Commerce	253	302	323	260	1,138	306	183	489	16.08
4	Punjab National Bank	1,930	802	752	521	4,005	399	151	550	3.77
5	State Bank of India	4,068	2,475	1,470	1,023	9,036	415	3,197	3.612	35.38
6	HDFC Bank Ltd.	16	90	146	194	446	544	603	1.147	135.2
7	ICICI Bank Ltd.	82	100	168	158	508	569	1.341	1.910	263.98
8	IndusInd Bank Ltd.	–	25	55	36	116	115	80	195	68.97
9	Axis Bank Ltd	5	54	92	96	247	269	1.330	1,599	538.46
10	Jammu and Kashmir Bank Ltd.	232	38	104	50	424	114	56	170	13.21

Table 3.2

Branches and ATMs of Scheduled Commercial Banks

(As at end - March 2007)

Sr. No:	Name of the Bank	Rural Branches	Semi-Urban Branches	Urban Branches	Metropolitan Branches	Total Branches	On-site ATMs	Off-site ATMs	ATMs Total	Percent No. of Off-site ATMs to total Branches
1	Bank of Baroda	1.087	576	479	585	2.727	603	397	1.000	14.55
2	Canara Bank	717	658	596	617	2.588	932	200	1,132	7.73
3	Oriental Bank of Commerce	246	276	370	332	1,224	284	230	514	18.80
4	Punjab National Bank	1.827	806	765	641	4,039	754	255	1,009	6.31
5	State Bank of India	3.825	2,561	1.561	1,323	9.270	2,287	2.120	4.407	22.86
6	HDFC Bank Ltd.	30	136	202	271	639	833	772	1,605	120.81
7	ICICI Bank Ltd.	75	187	203	238	703	1.150	2.185	3,335	310.81
8	IndusInd Bank Ltd.	2	35	83	52	172	144	97	241	56.39
9	Axis Bank Ltd	11	103	196	181	491	586	1.755	2.341	357.43
10	J&K Bank Ltd.	198	79	110	58	445	121	54	175	12.13

Table 3.2 depicts that the public sector banks have made a huge progress in increase in percentage of offsite ATMs to total branches during March 2007, as compared to March 2005. During March 2005, Bank of Baroda had 0.04, Canara Bank 2.5, Oriental Bank of Commerce 16.08, Punjab National Bank 3.77 percent of offsite ATMS as percentage of branches respectively. By the end of March 2007, Bank of Baroda had 14.55, Canara bank 7.73, Oriental Bank of Commerce 18.80, Punjab National Bank to 6.31 percent of offsite ATMS as percentage of branches.

The only public sector bank, State Bank of India depicts decrease in percentage of offsite ATMs as percentage of branches from 35.38 (year 2005) to 22.86 percent in the year 2007. But State Bank of India's onsite ATMs as percentage of branches have increased from 4.59 percent in the year 2005 to 24.6 percent in the year 2007. It is noticeable that all private sector banks, except ICICI bank depict decrease in percentage of offsite ATMs to their branches.

In the year 2007 percentage of offsite ATMs to branches of ICICI Bank has increased to 310.81 percent from 263.98 percent with respect to the year 2005. While among other private sector banks like; HDFC, IndusInd, Axis and Jammu and Kashmir bank there is decrease in percent of offsite ATMs to total branches. It can be observed from the table 3.2 that HDFC bank's, decrease in percent of offsite ATMs as branches is 135.2 to 120.81, IndusInd 68.97 to 56.39, Axis Bank 538.46 to 357.43 and Jammu and Kashmir Bank 13.21 to 12.13, in the financial year 2005 and 2007 respectively.

3.3 TECHNOLOGICAL PROGRESS OF PUBLIC SECTOR BANKS

The reach of the Public Sector Banks is wider in India. Even in the most remote village of India, a public sector bank can be found. However, population-wise the reach of public sector banks is limited. The amount of banks catering vis-à-vis 100 people would be lower than many developed countries. In such a scenario, ATMs come as a boon.

ATM models in India range from simple cash dispensers to scalable ATMs that can be customized according to individual client requirements. Banks also have specialized models that dispense information and non-cash items such as tickets and coupons.

The key idea is to get the customer used to these channels and then shift him to different low cost channels like the Internet. For example, a customer using a Web-enabled ATM would be more likely to go in for, say, a service like Internet banking. Also, from the bank's point of view this would be more cost effective as a transaction over the Internet would only cost the bank approximately Rs 10 - 12 per transaction.

Public sector banks are slowly waking up to the ATM's potential as a serious marketing tool. They are also earning sizeable revenues by using ATMs to advertise products from other companies. A few banks are offering utility bill payment facilities on their machines too. Apart from that, a variety of services ranging from railway card/season tickets and cinema tickets to dispensing of mobile phone smart cards are being thought of as a part of the strategy to attract customers and earn extra revenue.

In rural areas for example, some farmers are extremely rich but do not have access to ATMs. The answer for the question of how do banks reach out to such people, is in the form of intelligent ATMs. Besides, an illiterate person would not be able to use an ATM, whichever language it displays. The answer is an ATM that offers an audio aid which has clear instructions on how to withdraw cash in the language he speaks.

It is believed that the growth in the installed base of ATMs, which was primarily driven by private sector banks, will be intensely followed by Indian Public sector banks in the coming years. The number of ATMs is predicted to reach 30,000 units within seven years, from the current installed base of around 7,165 for the year 2007. The retail - banking scene is getting hotter by the day with banks going all out to increase access points. Ironically, the introduction of ATMs in India was not warmly welcomed by the various labor unions. But now, we can witness ATMs everywhere.

With Public sector banks going all out to tap the retail market through ATMs, the market is ready to explode. India is a boom country for ATMs is corroborated by a report from the 'Global ATM Directory' 2000 edition. Which states that the Indian market for ATMs is expected to grow at an estimated growth rate of 486 percent, while China's growth has been pegged at just over 200 percent. ATM vendors are comparing India as the next China, and are expecting similar growth in India. In China during the years 1982-1993, there were only 2,000 ATMs. But during the years, 1993-2000, it boomed to over 48,000 ATMs. India too is witnessing a similar trend.

It is observed that the Public Sector Banks are installing ATMs to ensure that they do not lose customers, and to cut costs, while private and foreign - owned banks are using it to acquire customers. This does not mean that the cost-factor is not relevant to the latter. Again, of the installed ATM base, nearly 70 percent is accounted for by private and foreign players. ATMs have evolved from only basic cash dispensing solutions to one which can provide value added services. Now Banks have a single window for procuring all their ATM related needs from the vendor.

This includes ATM monitoring, software distribution for ATMs, cash management and network management. Many Indian public sector banks that were hampered because of lack of knowledge of technology are now actively talking to ATM vendors for outsourcing their needs. Now banking is not confined to brick and mortar but has modified to brick and click model of banking. The table 3.3 indicates high level of expenditure incurred by Public Sector Banks on computerization during September 1999 to March 2007.

Table 3.3

Expenditure Incurred on Computerization by Public Sector Banks

			(Amount in Rs. crore)
Sr.	**Name of the Bank**	**Expenditure incurred**	**Expenditure incurred between**
No.		**during half year ended March 2007**	**September 1999 and March 2007**
	Public Sector Banks	1,257.17	12.825.82
1	Bank of Baroda	146.46	750.66
2	Canara Bank	125.25	858.4
3	Oriental Bank of Commerce	42.91	311.46
4	Punjab National Bank	1.66	53.6
5	State Bank of India	263.27	3,306.21

Source: Report on Trend and Progress of Banking in India, 2006-07

The table 3.3 depicts, maximum expenditure on computerization incurred was by State Bank of India during the period of September 1999 to March 2007. Expenditure incurred by State Bank of India was Rs. 3,306.21 crores which was 25.77 percent of total expenditure incurred by Public Sector Banks during the same period. During the same period Punjab National Bank incurred minimum 0.42 of expenditure on computerization as compared to total expenditure incurred by Public Sector Banks. Canara Bank, Bank of Baroda and Oriental Bank of Commerce respectively incurred 6.69 percent, 5.85 percent and 2.42 percent of expenditure on computerization as compared to all other public sector banks. Even during March 2007, State Bank of India incurred maximum percentage of expenditure on computerization.

As it is depicted from the figure 3.3.1 that State Bank of India had maximum number (35.38 percent) of ATMs as percentage of branches. Bank of Baroda had minimum (0.04 percent) and Canara Bank and Punjab National Bank had 2.5 and 3.77 percent of ATMs as percentage of branches respectively.

Figure 3.3.1

ATMs as Percentage of Branches – Public Sector Banks (*Till2005*)

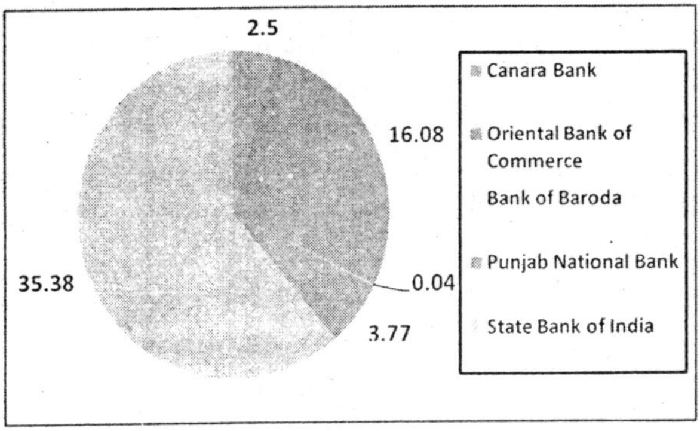

It is clear from the above figure that there is a wide difference between ATMs as percentage of branches between State Bank of India and other public sector banks. The higher level of expenditure incurred by public sector banks is the outcome of increase in customer's expectation and techno-savvy environment created by new private sector banks. Not so long ago, accessing money for customer's was about setting aside a couple of hours, getting to the bank before closing time, standing in one queue to get a token and then in another to collect the cash. Those were the pre-economic reforms days, when the banking was confined to brick and mortar. At the present day the nature of banking has changed beyond recognition. With ATM cards, simple banking transactions like withdrawing and depositing money are easier than ever before. For the tech - savvy, there is the option of banking online.

Even when it comes to products, the changes have been many. Graduating from simple savings accounts and fixed and recurring deposits, banks now offer a host of products like special savings account and sweep - in - account, no frills accounts and easy receive account. Private sector banks may have taken the lead, but public sector banks, with their vast client base and unparalleled treasury of trust, are evolving their own brand of customer -friendliness.

3.4 PROGRESS OF COMPUTERIZATION IN PUBLIC SECTOR BANKS

In recent years the number of branches providing Core Banking Solutions (CBS) in India has increased significantly. CBS provides a host of benefits such as, anywhere banking, anywhere access and quick fund movement at optimal costs and in an efficient manner. While new private sector banks, foreign banks and a few old private sector banks have already put CBS in place, public sector banks are still catching up.

The table 3.4 given below depicts, during March'2005, State Bank of India had maximum 100 percent fully computerized branches and the minimum percentage of fully computerized branches was of Oriental Bank of Commerce at 45.5 percent. Bank of Baroda, Canara Bank and Punjab National Bank had respectively 83.1, 58.5 and 64.2 percent of fully computerized branches.

Table 3.4

Computerization in Public Sector Banks

(As on March 31, 2005)

Sr. No.	*Name of the Bank*	*Branches already fully computerized* #	*Branches under Core Banking* Solution	*Fully computerized branches*	*Partially computerized branches.*
(1)	(2)	(3)	(4)	(3 + 4)	(5)
1	Bank of Baroda	83.1	–	83.1	16.9
2	Canara Bank	58.5	–	58.5	41.5
3	Oriental Bank of Commerce	14.2	31.3	45.5	44.3
4	Punjab National Bank	38	26.1	64.2	33.4
5	State Bank India	87.9	12.1	100	–

Source: Report on Trend and Progress of Banking in India, 2004-05

Note: #: Other than branches under Core Banking Solution.

It is noticeable from the table 3.4 that by the end of financial year 2005, Oriental Bank of Commerce had 31.3 percent of branches under Core Banking Solution, though its total percentage of fully computerized branches was 45.5 percent. During the similar time period State Bank of India had 12.1 percent of branches under Core Banking Solution but indeed State Bank of India incurred maximum expenditure on computerization and development of communication networks. Public sector banks have made huge investment on computerization during March 2005, this is very much evident from the table 3.5.The table depicts that Bank of Baroda had incurred 16.6 percent of total expenditure till end March 2005, 12.9 by Canara Bank, 10.4 percent by Oriental Bank of Commerce, 9.33 percent by Punjab National Bank, and 5.58 percent by State Bank of India had been incurred on computerization and development of communication networks during the same period.

Table 3.5

Expenditure Incurred on Computerization and Development of Communication Networks by Public Sector Banks

(As on March 31, 2005)

Serial. No.	Name of the Bank	Expenditure incurred during half year ended up to March 2005 (Amount in Rs. crore)	Expenditure incurred up to end - March2005 (Amount in Rs. crore)
1	Bank of Baroda	50.34	301.45
2	Canara Bank	80.5	623.12
3	Oriental Bank of Commerce	18.89	181.14
4	Punjab National Bank	62.39	668.28
5	State Bank of India	120.73	2,160.00

The table 3.5 reveals that the level of expenditure on information technology by public sector bank has tremendously increased over a span of six months. It indicates information technology has become an important component of staple diet for growth and progress of (especially) public sector banks in India in a competitive liberalized and technically sound market. Rapid growth of Computerization in Public Sector Banks during March'2008 resulted in 100 percent computerized branches of all selected Public Sector Banks.

Computerization in public sector banks during March 2008 has been depicted by the table 3.6.The table 3.6 depicts that during the March 2008 all branches of Oriental Bank of Commerce and Punjab National Bank were under Core Banking Solution. All selected Banks under study were having 100 computerized branches. It is noteworthy that Bank of Baroda has shown tremendous progress in computerization of its branches and implementing Core Banking Solution to the level of 60.4 percent. Whereas Canara Bank has more number of non Core Banking Solution branches than branches under Core Banking Solution.

Table 3.6

Computerization in Public Sector Banks

(As on March 31, 2008)

(Rs. crore)

Sr. No.	Name of the Bank	Branches Under Core Banking Solution	Branches Already Fully Computerized#	Fully Computerized Branches
	1	2	3	4 =(2+3)
	Public Sector Banks	67.7	26.9	94.6
	Nationalized Bank	56.6	35.7	92.3
1	Bank of Baroda	60.4	39.9	100
2	Canara Bank	21.2	78.3	100
3	Oriental Bank of Commerce	100	-	100
4	Punjab National Bank	100	-	100
5	State Bank of India	92.2	7.8	100

- : Nil/Negligible.

#: Other than branches under Core Banking Solution.

It can be concluded from the table 3.6 that all public sector banks under study are fully computerized but they vary in terms of branches under Core Banking Solution and non Core Banking Branches. State Bank of India has 92.2 percent of branches under Core Banking Solution, it is noteworthy that State Bank of India has largest network of branches spread all over India. Whereas Punjab National Bank and Oriental Bank of Commerce have 100 percent branches under Core Banking Solution. It reduces transaction cost especially for public sector banks which are having huge number of branches and huge workforce. It can be said that Public sector banks to compete with private sector banks, have further increased expenditure on computerization and development of communication networks during March 2008.

Table 3.7

Expenditure Incurred on Computerization and Development of Communication Networks by Public Sector Banks

(As on March 31, 2008)

Sr. No.	Name of the Bank	Expenditure incurred during half year ended March 2008	Expenditure incurred between Sept 1999 and March 2008
	1	2	3
	Public Sector Banks	1,318.35	15,015.84
	Nationalised Banks	853.29	9,591.10
1	Bank of Baroda	34.67	809.85
2	Canara Bank	63.84	952.64
3	Oriental Bank of Commerce	28.45	376.96
4	Punjab National Bank	99.36	1,092.76
5	State Bank of India	279.96	3,777.93

Source: Report on Trend and Progress of Banking in India, 2007-08

Expenditure incurred by Public Sector Banks during September 1999 to March 2008 is depicted in the table 3.7. The table depicts that depicts total expenditure incurred by Public Sector Banks is Rs. 15,015.84 crores between September 1999 to March 2008. Nationalized banks incurred Rs. 9591.10 crores of expenditure on computerization. It is worth to note that maximum percentage of total expenditure incurred on computerization is of State Bank of India at 39.38 percent, followed by 11.39 percent spent by Punjab National Bank. Minimum expenditure on computerization is incurred by Oriental Bank of Commerce at 3.93 percent. It is further justified by the pie chart given below. It depicts the respective level of investment done by public sector banks during September 1999 to March 2008.

Figure 3.4

Expenditure incurred on Computerization – Public Sector Banks

(Sep 1999 – March 2008)

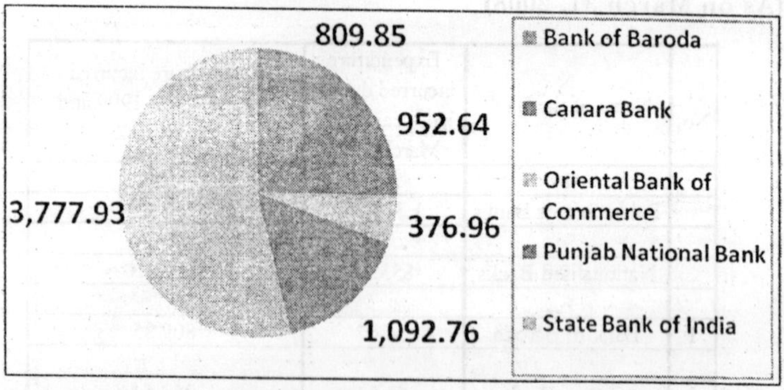

It is evident from the figure above that maximum expenditure of Rs. 3,777.93 crores was incurred by State Bank of India on computerization. Punjab National Bank, Canara Bank, Bank of Baroda and Oriental Bank of Commerce have incurred expenditure on computerization of rupees 1092.76 crores, Rs. 952.64 crores, 809.85 crores and Rs. 376.96 crores respectively. The Public sector banks are marching ahead towards technological advancement. It is very much evident from the figure given below that during half year ended March 2008 Public Sector Banks have further increased expenditure on computerization, to be more productive and competent in the existing market.

Figure 3.5

Expenditure incurred on Computerization – Public banks

(Half year ended March 2008)

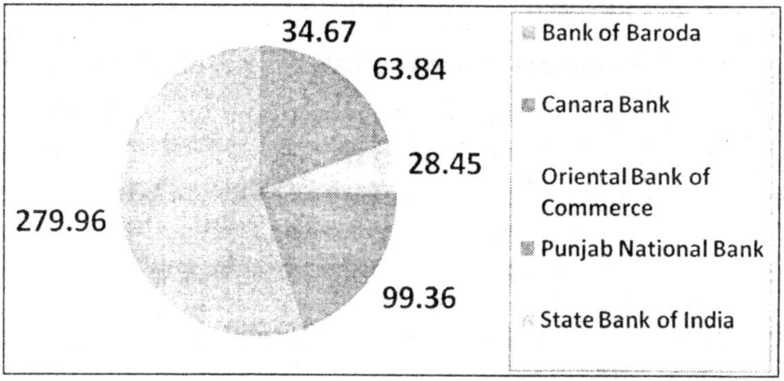

It is well known that the public sector banks are more prominent in terms of number of branches and employees hence incur higher operating cost. To reduce operating expenses public sector banks have tremendously invested in computerization. It is depicted in above figure that State Bank of India had incurred the level of expenditure on computerization which is almost three times of Punjab National Bank, and near about 10 times of Oriental Bank of Commerce. Canara Bank and Bank of Baroda during March 2008 have incurred 63.84 and 34.67 crores respectively on computerization. Till now the overall view of technological progress of public sector has been discussed but it is must to know the technological growth path of each bank considered in research study.

3.5 TECHNOLOGICAL PROGRESS OF PUBLIC SECTOR BANKS

The State Bank of India (SBI) is the oldest and largest bank in the country. Its origins go back to the first decade of the 19th century, when the Bank of Calcutta was established on 2 June 1806. The bank got its present name after an Act of Parliament in May 1955 and the State Bank of India was constituted on 1 July 1955.

At present SBI has a phenomenal 9,559 branches and its ATM network is spread across 5,172 of its own locations, plus 2,328 of those of its associate banks. Its immediately recognizable acronym may not be associated with fancy products, but it is synonymous with simple, no-hassle banking in the remotest parts of the country.

3.5.1 Technological Initiatives Taken by State Bank of India

SBI has successfully kept pace with changing technology. Although, at present, it does not offer facilities like phone and mobile banking, the process of offering these services is in the advanced stages. Its ATMs allows doing a lot more than accessing cash like one can pay the fees for more than 100 education institutions, deposit application fees for competitive exams, and give donations to trusts and temples and also transfer funds.

To widen its ATM network further, SBI has entered into a partnership with 13 banks for bilateral sharing of ATMs. However, this will call for a small fee. SBI has also been actively involved in non-profit activity called Community Services Banking since 1973. All bank branches and administrative offices sponsor and participate in a large number of welfare activities and social causes. The internal evaluation of customer satisfaction is done by the bank's inspection & audit department at the time of their periodic inspection and audit of branches. All branches are audited at a frequency ranging from one year (large and medium branches) to two years (smaller branches). Simple banking solutions at a cheaper cost and its wide reach helped SBI to increase its profitability.

State Bank of India and its IT department

State Bank of India's Corporate Information and Technology Department takes care of System Architecture, Application selection, Software customization and development,

Apex-level support, IT Policies and Training Information System Security. Local head office Information Technology expert's human capital of the bank takes care of Software Implementation Software Support. Zonal Office IT Team is the leader of the IT group, which includes Zonal Team it takes care of ; Software Implementation, Software Support &Training.

The Technological Growth Path of State Bank of India

Transition from Manual Processes (1990s)

↓

Total Branch Automation
Adoption of 'Bankmaster' (1992)

↓

Universal Computerization (2003)
3,700 branches, handling 83% business computerized

↓

CBS implementation launched in parallel (2004)
All branches of the bank fully computerized

Plan launched for 100% CBS Branches (2005)

↓

2710 CBS Branches (2006)

↓

100 percent CBS Branches (2008)

It is noteworthy the benefits which State Bank of India could enjoy because of computerization are superior customer service, improved controls, better management information systems, enhancement of value - added services,electronic funds transfer at large no. of branches, multiple delivery channels, single window and computerized printing of drafts and TDRs reducing transaction cost and increasing overall efficiency.

State Bank of India enjoyed higher returns due to technological upgradation but bank had to face certain challenges.Some of these were branches were not connected, customer was perceived as only a 'Branch' customer but not a 'Bank' customer, multiple applications were performed across the State Bank Group, branches were the main service delivery channels, ATMs were limited in numbers, problem of functionality and unconnected branches, Information technology aimed only at internal efficiency.

To overcome these challenges State Bank of India undertook certain initiatives in the form of networking of enterprise, Core banking solutions (commenced in May 2002 and contract was made with Tata consultancy services for integrated system Hewlett Packard for hardware and software Bancs24-FNS by Australian company was provided for Core banking solution).

Alternate delivery channels (ATMs and internet banking), Treasury & Asset Liability Management (ALM) & Treasury solutions, BPR (Business Process Reengineering) including; orientation of workflows and processes as well as shared operations for back-office functions were promoted. Intranet for corporate communication and knowledge dissemination, Infrastructure Creation (SBI Connect), Core Banking for Foreign Offices, Payment Systems and Information Security was developed.

State Bank of India has diversified resources for retail services through Internet in the form of: customer to self, customer to customer, customer to utility service provider, customer to government and customer to institutions and customer to e-commerce sites service provider. Similarly the bank provides corporate services through internet like; business to self, business to government, business to employees, business to self, business to business services.

Other initiatives undertaken by the bank are video conferencing, the largest facility with 227 locations. The bank introduced SWIFT; as common gateway for the entire State Bank Group. Other initiatives of bank include, Electronic Accounting System in Excise & Service Tax, On-Line Tax Accounting System (OLTAS), and Web payment of Central Excise, Income Tax and Corporate Tax.

3.5.2 Technological Initiatives Taken by Punjab National Bank

Punjab National Bank has initiated lots of value-added services to attract, acquire retain and satisfy its customers. It retained its number one position among nationalized banks in terms of number of branches, asset size, operation and net profit. It has secured 9th place among India's Most Trusted top 50 service brands. It has one of the largest branch networks in India with 4,062 branches and 447 Extension counters spread throughout the country and serving more than 3.5 crore customers. It is ranked as 323rd biggest bank in the world by Bankers Almanac (January 2006), London. It has a banking relationship with more than 217 international banks and more than 50 renowned international banks maintain their Rupee Account with Punjab National Bank.

The aim of the Punjab National Bank is to evolve and position the bank as a world class progressive, cost effective and customer friendly institution providing comprehensive financial and related services, integrating frontier of technology and serving various segments of society.Use latest technology aimed at customer satisfaction and act as an effective catalyst for socioeconomic development.

Technology, Bank and Customer Satisfaction:

All branches of Punjab National Bank have been computerized. It facilitates online banking transaction for its customers. It also helps in quick and accurate data analysis. It makes decision process simple quick and efficient. It makes credit management effective and results in reduction in transaction costs.

The bank launched the concept of "Any Time, Any Where Banking" through the introduction of Centralized Banking Solution. Outcome of it is 1.61 crores of the bank customers are enjoying this facility. It started centralized monitoring critical system by setting up a Network Operation Center. It was the first Public sector bank to begin the networking of its branches. The internet Banking facility of bank offers services like anytime, anywhere access to account, online information of deposits complete details of transactions and statement of account, loan overdraft account etc.

The bank has started Online Payment Facility for railways reservation through IRCTC Payment Gateway Project and Online Utility Bill Payment Services to internet account holders for payment of electricity, telephone, mobile and other bills from anywhere and anytime through Bank's site. The bank has installed 609 ATMs and has also entered into ATM sharing arrangement with other banks, which enabled the customers to access around 13,000 ATMs all over the country. The bank has launched a website for the benefit of farmers, which could provide information related to cultivation practices for food grains and cash crops, prices of agricultural products, medicinal and aromatic plants.

Punjab National Bank with growth in all aspects has passed through certain challenges and certain challenges are ahead like; constant and continual up gradation of technology in the bank, consultation and coordination with best IT companies. To set up Research and Market Intelligence units within the organization to implement market developments and reducing cost by minimizing operational and market risk.

Punjab National Bank has already achieved 100% branch computerization. All the branches using Financle and BancMate software in which the Bank has contributed much in getting the software developed as well as customized. The bank is the first public sector bank to implement Centralized Banking Solution with more than 600 branches in CBS and is set to network 1200 branches by March 2005. With this, the status of the customer changes to 'Customer of the Bank' instead of 'Customer of the Branch'.

Punjab National Bank has installed over 450 ATMs. Besides, the Bank has entered into an agreement with four banks for ATM sharing. Under the arrangement named 'MITR', the customers of all the five banks can access 2050 ATMs nationwide. The Bank has successfully implemented Video Conferencing at more than 30 locations across the country. It is the first Bank in India to implement the image based cheque clearing system in India for providing clearance of Intra-Bank Inter-City cheque within 48 hours after it is presented. PNB's other technology initiatives include: Implementation of Digital Certificates and Digital Signatures, Government Business Computerization, Implementation of payment system including RTGS, PDO-NDS, SFMS, and SEFT etc.

The growth path of technological upgradation of the bank is still in process as Punjab National Bank in the year 2008 had 1094 ATMs, customer base of 3.5 crore customers, 4540 branches and 421 extension counters. It is a member of SWIFT, 150 branches of the bank are connected through computer based terminal at Mumbai. Core Banking Solution (CBS) has been implemented in 2791 Service Outlets (SOLs) at 935 centers, covering 83% of bank's total business, facilitating around 2.23 crores customers with "anytime and anywhere" banking. National Electronic Fund Transfer (NEFT) is operational in 2280 branches. The bank has 2353 RTGS and 1395 SFMS branches.

3.5.3 Technological Initiatives Taken by Bank of Baroda

Bank of Baroda's IT-enabled Business Transfor-mation Programme initiated roll out of Core Banking Solution (CBS). The Banks technology initiatives are clearly focused on the customer. The Business Transformation Programme, encompassing technology, is being implemented by the Bank with a view to providing the customer, convenience banking on 24 X 7 bases. The bank provides its services at major centers in India and abroad, through deployment of Core Banking Solution with integrated delivery channels like ATM, Internet, Phone, Mobile, Kiosk, and Call Centre.

For implementation of Core Banking Solution, which will be a single solution across all the countries where the Bank is operating, the Bank has tied up with a world-class System Integrator – Hewlett Packard (HP). This solution is a comprehensive solution incorporating various applications like Enterprise wide General Ledger, Risk Management, Anti-Money Laundering, Cheque Truncation, Credit Cards, Mutual Funds, On-line Trading, Data Warehousing, Customer Relationship Management, RTGS, NEFT, Global Treasury, Securitization, Human Resources Management System, Employee Pay Roll. Almost 1935 branches of the bank across the country have gone live under CBS.

Bank of Baroda has 1174 ATMs across 270 centers. 513 computerized branches of the bank are connected through cluster approach. The bank has 2800 branches in India, number. of computerized branches are 2176, 450 Number of branches are connected with leased lines, Number of branches operating e-payment product are 340 in 53 centers, 58 Number of branches are serving BOBCASHREACH in 53 centers. For corporate Tele-Banking, PC-Banking and Any Branch Banking services are available at 291 branches in following 7 cities Chennai, Bangalore, Hyderabad, Pune, Mumbai, Ahmadabad, Delhi. 423 branches of the bank provide SMS and WAP based mobile banking services. The bank has 206 branches using interbank electronic transfer funds (ETF). The bank has approximately 3 lakhs number of Debit Cards customers.

Other achievements of the Bank are that it has built and commissioned its own State-of-the-Art Global Data Centre (DC) in Mumbai for running its centralized banking solution and other applications in 1900+ branches across India and 20 other counties where the Bank is operating. The Data Centre will function as a central data hub of the Bank for both its domestic and international operations.

The Data Centre has been designed and implemented by Hewlett Packard (HP), its technology partner. It conforms to critical technology standards and is equipped with full Communication and Network Infrastructure, meeting all the attributes of a Tier III Data Centre and having certification capability for BS 7799. Wide Area Network (WAN) is the Networking of Branches under CBS: more than 1100 branches in India have been networked through Lease Lines, ISDN, and VSATs for running multiple applications under CBS.

Bank has computerized operations in all branches in India. 513 branches have been brought under computerization through cluster approach The Bank's interconnected ATM network in India now stands at 1174 across 270 centers The Bank's plans are to extend this network in stages in future. The Bank also plans to deploy low cost ATMs at Rural centers. Bank's Debit Card holders can use their card at over 15,000 VISA ATMs in India and over 8, 50,000 ATMs around the world. Bank's Debit Cards are also accepted 1, 00,000 Points of Sales (POS) across the country and 13 million POS terminals around the world. Master Card holders and holders of VISA cards issued by other banks can also access their accounts through Bank's ATM network.

The Bank is a member of National Financial Switch (NFS) set up by Institute for Development and Research in Banking Technology (IDRBT). This enables bank customers to use ATMs of other banks who are also members of NFS, at a significantly lower cost. The Bank's ATM cum Debit Card base has now crossed 9 lakhs. Other technological initiatives undertaken by the Bank are: Tele-Banking, PC-Banking, and Any Branch Banking: Centralized Tele banking. PC Banking and Any Branch Banking are available at 294 branches across 7 centers, under the umbrella brand BARODAOMNI.

The bank offers Information based Internet and Mobile Banking (SMS) services to its customers at over 606 branches across 173 centers. The bank also provides SMS and WAP-based Mobile Banking Services to the customers at its branches, using mobile phone. Customers can get a single view of their accounts across various branches; can obtain account view for 2 months as also send request for cheque book. The bank offers many technological services like *BOBCASHREACH - Cash Management Product for Corporate* is available at 58 branches across 53 centers. BOB *Money Express is Bank's exclusive e-Payment Product* is available at 340 branches across 53 centers. *Real Time Gross Settlement System (RTGS)* is operational at the Bank's Treasury Branch, Mumbai. Funds transfer facility for customers is now operational at 544 branches.

Bank provides *Utility Bills Payment (Bill Pay);* this is an internet based service for utility bill payments through BILLDESK.COM. SWIFT facility for worldwide inter-bank financial communication is provided at 105 Authorized Branches (Category 'B') in India as also at all overseas centers. The bank has implemented *On-line Tax Accounting System* (OLTAS) for collection of taxes on behalf of Central Board of Direct Taxes, Govt. of India, at 541 branches.

Bank of Baroda is the first Public Sector Bank in India to implement Integrated Treasury and Risk Management solution at its Treasury Branch, Mumbai.

Disaster Recovery Site (DRS) for Treasury has also been operationalized. *Centralized Fund Management System (CFMS):* NDS-PDO an online negotiated dealing system for Government Securities is operational. Bank of Baroda is the first Public Sector Bank in India to implement a Web-Based Lending Automation System for its Corporate and Retail Lending Operations. The system is now implemented at over 520 branches in India, of which 321 branches are covered under Central Processing Cell cluster. Bank of Baroda has implemented NEFT at 73 branches. The bank runs three MICR centers - at Ahmedabad, Rajkot and Coimbatore.

Bank's Corporate Intranet and e-mail, Web-based Corporate Intranet and e-mail for electronic communication, information sharing and knowledge management is fully operational. Bank's operations at all Banks' overseas branches are 100% computerized. Operations at all Offshore Business Units, Joint Ventures & Subsidiaries are also 100% computerized.

3.5.4 Technological Initiatives Taken by Oriental Bank of Commerce

Oriental Bank of Commerce India was established in the year 1943 on 19th February in Lahore. After partition, Oriental Bank of Commerce shifted its Registered Office from Lahore to Amritsar paying every rupee to its departing customers. Oriental Bank of Commerce was nationalized on 15th April in 1980. Then OBC bank had 307 branches with Rs. 282.61 crores as deposits and as advance Rs. 152.69.

Technology Implementation

Oriental Bank of Commerce has 1320 branches & Extension Counters and 740 onsite / offsite ATMs spread all across India. All the service outlets of OBC are fully computerized with more than 1000 branches connected through Centralized Banking Solution, Internet Banking and Phone Banking. So the customer of an OBC Branch is a CUSTOMER OF ALL CBS BRANCHES since the bank is offering Any Branch Banking (ABB) and Multicity Cheque Book facility to CBS Customers. More than six lac Proton Visa Debit Card holders of the Bank have access to over 8000 MITR and NFS ATMs. It provides host of services like cash deposit / withdrawal, Mobile Top up, Mini Statement, balance enquiries etc.

The bank has in effect card payment for shopping in India and abroad through over 50,000 Point of Sale (POS) locations. The bank provides Phone Banking, Internet Banking, RTGS, ECS, Online Trading, Online Tax collection system (OLTAS), Cash Management System (CMS) and many other services to its customers. The National Institute of Bank Management (NIBM) rated OBC Bank as "Customer Friendly" Bank.

The Bank have been taking major new initiatives in Information Technology from the last few years with the increased focus on customer service and setting up of new delivery channels. As on date the Bank has computerized all the branches & Extension Counters (E/C) and has taken 1353 plus branches on CBS & others are either fully or partially computerized. With this 99% of the total business of the Bank is getting routed through computerized environment. The bank has taken major initiatives such as Centralized Banking Solution (CBS), ATMs etc.

As per the Bank's IT Plan, the Bank has implemented "Centralized Banking Solutions (CBS)" with effect from March 2004. As on 23rd October, 2007 the Bank has taken more than 1353 branches on CBS. The bank has placed entire hardware for the Centralized Banking System, ATM Switch at Vashi, Mumbai where the Data Centre place has been outsourced. Further, bank is also offering various new products and services such as Any Branch Banking, Instant Funds Transfer, Cash Management Services, Flexi Fixed Deposit Scheme, RTGS, Tele Banking, Internet Banking etc through all CBS branches. These value added services offer still better customer service across all the CBS branches.

Any Where Branch Banking (ABB) being implemented more than 1353 plus branches of the bank provides the customer the flexibility to carry out banking activities from any branch of the bank. Facilities like deposit/withdrawal of cash / cheques, multi city cheque books etc. can be availed through CBS branches of the bank.

Bank has launched on 1st November 2006, Flexi Fixed Deposit Scheme, this scheme offers liquidity to customers in shape of saving / current deposit funds as well as higher returns, as available on fixed deposit fund. The scheme was linked with operative saving and current accounts only. OBC Internet Banking Services (iBanking) launched for all CBS

Branches of the Bank with effect from 01.11.2006. iBanking facility is available free of cost to customers of all CBS branches and facilities viz printing of accounts statement, funds transfers. It can be offered to any Saving / Current/ CC/ OD account holders. Only Query based facilities shall be provided to jointly operated Saving / Current / CC / OD / Company Accounts.

The Tele banking System is available for the customers of all the CBS branches of the bank through twenty (20) major cities across the country i.e. at Delhi, Mumbai, Agra, Chandigarh, Ludhiana, Hyderabad, Kolkata, Chennai, Patiala, Amritsar, Jalandhar, Lucknow, Bangalore, Ahmedabad, Jaipur, Karnal, Dehradun, Bareilly, Bhatinda and Bhopal. The Tele banking facility is offered "Free of Cost" to the customers and is available to customers on 24*7*365 basis. Online Tax Accounting System (OLTAS) is a service provided by the bank for acceptance of Income Tax and other direct taxes on behalf of Government. The customers including corporate, Individuals, Proprietorship concerns, Partnership firms, Trusts, Club, Society, etc. can pay their tax liability through bank's OLTAS window available through 145 select branches across the country.

The Bank has introduced the "Cash Management Services for Corporate Clients. It offers IT enabled state-of-the-art solution to the Cash and Receivable Management for large Corporate/ business entities having wide spread areas of business operations. Cash Management Services / Solutions are available both for collections of receivables at more than 250 Direct Deposit Centers (Integrated Collection Centers) and payments (disbursement of salary, mandatory dues, etc.) at any location in India within the shortest possible time. Integrated Collection Centers (locations) for direct deposit of instruments / collection of upcountry instruments are offered by saying "YOU NAME IT, WE HAVE IT".

The Bank has already setup robust, secured and efficient Enterprise Wide Area Network covering approx. 1370 locations. This Network is primarily a Leased Line Based

Network with ISDN as a backup. This network is supporting traffic of major applications such as Mail Messaging, File Transfer, Core Banking Solution, ATMs, Tele Banking, and Internet Banking etc. The network is a three-tier architecture viz. Core, Aggregation and Access layers.

The Bank has also installed 703 ATMS that are operationalized, using which the customers are able to have wider access and avail basic services such as Cash Withdrawal, installments, Cash Deposits, and Balance Enquiry through any of the ATMs round the clock in the networked environment. Further, bank has also become active member of "MITR" and "NFS" for sharing of ATMs with other banks through which the customer of out bank can access about 8000 ATMS deployed by various other participating banks.

The bank has also started Mobile Topup Service through which customer can recharge their mobile of various MSPs (Mobile Topup Service) such as Airtel, Hutch, Reliance, MTNL, BSNL, Tata Indicom etc. by using out bank's ATMs. The bank is also offering Electronic Fund Transfer facility through its 180 computerized branches across 15 Centers. Under this facility, the bank supports any Customer of the bank, at the four Metro Cities to debit his/ her account by a specified amount and transfer the same for the credit into the beneficiary customer's account in any Nationalized Bank at any Metro city, up to the amount of Rs.5lacs.Other facilities provided by the bank include electronic clearing system which can have credit and debit entry.

The Electronic clearing services facilitates single debit and bulk credits or vice-versa. This scheme is useful for giving credits for dividend warrants or for making voluminous debits / credits such as payment of bills, disbursal of salaries etc by the corporate. It eliminates delays due to postal / clearing as the amount gets directly credited to the respective customers account. The bank has established its own MICR Processing Centre at Amritsar, Punjab. More than 200 branches of different banks participate in Clearing Operations through Service / Main branches of respective banks.

3.5.5 Technological Initiatives Taken By Canara Bank

Canara Bank in India has a history of nine decades and is the largest public sector banks in India. Canara Bank of India has a total of 47,843 employees and is spread with 2409 branches throughout the country. Canara Bank India has an exposure to huge number of portfolios ranging from petroleum, engineering, infrastructure, factoring, investment management, venture capital, home finance and securities.

The bank has a network of 2508 branches, spread over 25 States/4 Union Territories of the country and, one overseas branch at London, which are administered through Head Office at Bangalore 13 Circle Offices and 1 International Division 38 Regional Offices. Canara Bank's various initiatives /efforts resulted in an addition of 3 million clients during the year 2007-08. The clientele base of the bank surged to 32.35 million, comprising 28.3 million deposit accounts and 4.05 million borrower accounts.

The bank have been expanded from 500 ATMs in 2003-04 and 1200 ATMS in 2004-05, 2000 ATMs in 2007-08, including branches and, 1000 Delivery channels for closer customer proximity and business potentiality. Number of branches increased to 2678, adding 100 branches during one single year, the highest in the last two decades. Bank has 2700 branches.1351 branches are providing Internet and Mobile Banking services. 2027 branches are offering Anywhere Banking Services. Customer Base of the bank is of 33 million customers. The Bank apart from 111 specialized service branches has 195 Extension Counters.

Enhancing reach and customer convenience, it has significantly expanded its ATM strength to 2006, by adding 874 ATMs during the year, spread across 694 centers. In terms of the number of ATMs, it is on the top with respect to other nationalized banks of India. With ATM sharing agreement with other banks, customers of Canara Bank have access to over 27,000 networked ATMs across the country. The Bank has installed 629 offsite ATMs and 178 ATMs in railway stations. It has also set up 109 e-kiosks for booking railway tickets. The Bank also introduced global Debit Card under VISA and MASTER franchise. The Bank had a Debit-cum-ATM card base of 3.29 million as at March 2008.

Across the borders, the Bank's presence comprised two overseas branches in London and Hong Kong, one representative office in Shanghai, China, slated for conversion into a full-fledged branch and one Offshore Banking Unit at NOIDA, U.P. The Bank has a joint venture, viz., Commercial Bank of India LLC at Moscow. The Bank has already obtained approval from Reserve Bank of India to open five branches in Johannesburg, Frankfurt, Muscat, Manama and QFC – Qatar, out of the 21 international centers identified for global expansion in the medium term.

Introducing technology in the financial inclusion process, the Bank has launched multilingual biometric-voice enabled ATMs during the year 2007. Canara Bank is the first bank in the country to launch mobile Biometric-voice enabled ATM in Bangalore rural.

InfoTech Progress of Canara Bank

In the realm of InfoTech advancements, the Bank made further progress during the year. As of now, the number of Core Banking Solution (CBS) branches moved to 635 branches, 68 Extension Counters, 8 Currency Chests and One Account Section. The Bank also expanded its number of Anywhere Banking (AWB) branches to 1911 and Internet and Mobile Banking (IMB) branches to 1200. Under the payment and settlement system, all branches of the Bank have been covered under RTGS and NEFT facilities. E-payment of excise and service tax, direct tax and custom duty has also been implemented in a number of branches under CBS setup. A Web Based Remittance Solution – REMITMONEY was implemented during the year.

Canara Bank, known for its customer centricity, has been bringing various improvements in the realm of customer service. The Bank has started a Call Centre for providing information on various products/services. The Bank's CBS branches have been enabled so that customers get account related information and place requests for statement of accounts, interest certificates and the like. The Bank also introduced 24X7 ATM cheque deposit facility for the Bank's Debit card holders.

The Bank launched several new products like, Online Trading portal- 'canmoney.in'. Canara Bank became the first major PSB to launch the product in association with its wholly owned subsidiary- M/s Gilt Securities Trading Corporation Ltd. The facility is now available in 24 major centers across the country. SB Gold is a Savings Bank Account, with value added services for High Net worth Individuals (HNWIs). Can Premium Current Account Scheme for a Current Account with added features for HNIs. Canara Super Saving Salary Account Scheme is a zero balance savings account scheme designed for employees/salaried class at the Bank's CBS branches. Canara Guide is a loan scheme for tax return preparers. Canara Jeevan is a reverse mortgage scheme for senior citizens. Krishi Mitra Card and Joint Liability Group Finance Scheme are for tenant farmers. Canara Kisan overdraft is a comprehensive farmer friendly scheme for purposes including repayment of private debt. Smart Card is a pilot project launched for facilitating financial inclusion.

To give a thrust on augmenting non-interest income sources and avenues, the Bank has entered into a Corporate Agency agreement with ECGC for soliciting and procuring export credit insurance business. With as many as nine subsidiaries/sponsored institutions/joint ventures in diverse fields, the Bank operates as a financial supermarket. Another key initiative relates to engaging the services of a world renowned consultant- M/s Boston Consulting Group for a comprehensive study on 'Corporate Business Strategy'. The project aims at taking the Bank on a well-designed transformational journey with a motive to take on emerging global challenges.

The bank has decided to achieve economies of scope by the Bank's target to take the global business well above the

Rs.3,00,000 crore mark, comprising global deposits of Rs.1,75,000 crore and global advances of Rs.125000 crore. The Bank will continue to focus on rebalancing its assets and liabilities portfolio, with the objective of augmenting profits and profitability. The Bank has set a target for CBS coverage of 1000 branches by May 2008 and all branches by March 2009.

The bank has aimed at leveraging the technological up gradation to provide a full range of value-added services to our cross-section clientele. Strengthen overseas presence in accordance with the roadmap already drawn up by the Bank. By implementing the concept of HRMS (Human Resource Management Solution), an efficient centralized global solution, covering all HR activities. After creation of Joint Ventures in insurance and asset management, the Bank is exploring similar options in other financial services.

It is very much evident that Public sector banks have shown keen interest on investment in technological upgradation. Public sector banks are considering technological upgradation the ultimate tool for survival among new private sector banks; as the main competitors in the banking sector. It is a well accepted fact that Private sector banks are marching ahead than public sector banks in technological upgradation but Public sector banks are trying to reduce the gap.

3.6. PRIVATE SECTOR BANKS

3.6.1 Technological Initiatives Taken By ICICI Bank

ICICI Bank is one bank which has seen a massive surge in volumes, since the introduction of ATMs. The number of ATMs, which numbered around 90 in December 1999, has now swelled to 2250 ATMs, 624 branches and extension counters. Currently, the total volume of ATM transactions is pegged at an astronomical 2, 00,000 transactions a day. The large volume of transactions results in the less cost per transaction. Also, the convenience of anytime money has attracted a lot of customers, and the bank has seen its customer base swell three-fold from 6.5 lakh in March 2000 to 20 lakh in March 2001. In 2006 the bank has gained a base of 15 million customers.

ICICI has also shown how technology can translate into reduced costs. Typically, a transaction through a bank branch costs approximately Rs 45. The identical transaction done telephonically, costs Rs 30, through an ATM costs about Rs 18, and through the Internet in huge volumes, costs only Rs 4. Just a look at the volumes of transactions done at the ICICI, ATMs indicates the high level of success the project has seen. The Bank offers a complete range of commercial banking products and services to customers in all its target segments.

The Bank's branches have increased by 13% in 2006 from 2005 ATMs have increased by 43% in 2006 from 2005, internet banking has increased by 18%, mobile banking by 11% in 2006 from March 2005.The bank had over 4 lakh NRI customers on March 2006. In 2006 the bank had a pool of 15 million customers which has increased tremendously over the years. All branches of the bank are linked through Very Small Aperture Terminals (VSAT) technology, giving the Bank a powerful technology edge over its nearest competitors in terms of the service levels it can provide its customers. The Bank proposes to rapidly broaden the reach of its branch network and aggressively maintain the service differentiation derived by its high technology focus.

The expansion of the Bank's retail network is crucial in developing a stable resource base on which to build the Bank's future business plans. The Bank also offers its retail customers significant technology driven products, primary among them being access at all branches to Automated Teller Machines (ATMs) over and above the normal range of products offered by other commercial banks. The Bank's electronic funds transfer facility is an added attraction to all customers, individuals and corporate alike.

The Bank has established a reputation for its skills in corporate advances, advisory services and treasury management. The Bank is an Authorized Dealer in foreign exchange and is one of the first banks ('designated bank') allowed to maintain the accounts of Foreign Institutional Investors in India. The Bank is also a registered underwriter and can act as bankers to primary market issuances. The Bank is a member of the Society for Worldwide Interbank Financial Telecommunication (SWIFT) and consequently can provide trade related services to all its customers with unmatched speed and efficiency.

ICICI Bank prides itself on having developed its current scale of business with an adherence to a strong system of institutional values, ethics and customer friendliness. ICICI bank has spent two years identifying the market needs and conceptualizing the Financial Information Network and Operations Pvt. Ltd. (FINO).It is India's first company focused on providing innovative technology solutions-systems, services and networks – to enable financial providers to reach millions of underserved and un-served throughout the world. In 2007-08 ICICI bank had 1,400 branches and 4530 ATMs. The Bank's technology-agnostic approach allowed the bank to operate on a per transaction cost basis that is 10% of the cost incurred by a global bank. It is ICICI Bank's belief that its commitment to technology will help it maintain edge it currently enjoys.

3.6.2 Technological Initiatives Taken By Jammu And Kashmir Bank

Jammu and Kashmir Bank Limited was incorporated on 1st October, 1938 and commenced its business from 4th July, 1939 at in Kashmir (India). The Bank was the first in the country as a State owned bank. According to the extended Central laws of the state, Jammu & Kashmir Bank was defined as a govt. Company as per the provision of Indian Company's Act 1956. In the year 1971, the Bank received the status of scheduled bank. It was declared as "A" Class Bank by Reserve Bank of India in 1976.Today, J&K Bank is one of the fastest growing banks in the country with more than 500 branches/offices. Is the Main Bank Service Provider of the State and its branches are all over the state.

The Bank has a far reaching and widespread network of ATM which literally reach all nooks and corner of the Valley and is even present at Tourist Resorts like Pehalgam, Gulmarg and etc. The Bank has tie up with MAESTRO for ATM and MASTERCARD for Credit Card services so it's preferred for visitors to have a MAESTRO, CIRRUS or MASTERCARD branded Card for their own convenience.

The Bank also provides other Value added services like Anywhere Banking, Foreign Currency Exchange, and Western Union Money Transfer service. Depository Services Scheme of J&K Bank, Dematerialization (Demat),Stock Broking through INVESTMART an initiative of ILFS, Depository Participant, Market transaction, Off-market transactions,Pledge of securities, Rematerialization (remat). The Bank offers insurance in association with Bajaj Allianz General Insurance Co. Ltd are: Motor insurance, Hospital cash, and Burglary and Shop keepers. It is only possible because of technological advancement to reach maximum number of customers. The bank is also working in association with MetLife.

The Bank is offering many Life Insurance Policies to its customers like; Met Bhavishya is a flexible money-back plan, Met Junior- Par Endowment,Met Mortgage Protector SP - Single Premium Mortgage Protection Plan,Met 100-Limited Pay Whole Life Insurance, Met 100 Gold - Par Whole Life, Met Platinum (Endowment) - Participating endowment assurance for face amounts above Rs. 3 lakh. Met Riders is the Customization tools for these policies. The bank also offers Credit Card of Jammu and Kashmir Bank. Initially there were three types of Credit Cards issued by Jammu and Kashmir Bank. They are as Gold Card, Silver Card and Blue Card. All the cards are also available with photo along with a family/add on Cards. The Card is accepted by all those Merchant Establishments who honor MASTER cards. ATMs linked with MASTER cards accept Jammu and Kashmir Bank Credit Card.

It can be concluded that Jammu and Kashmir bank has to go a long way to be at par competent in technological implementation with new generation private sector banks as well as public sector banks operating in India.

3.6.3 Technological Initiatives Taken By HDFC BANK

The Housing Development Finance Corporation (HDFC) was among the first to receive an 'in principle' approval from the RBI to set up a bank in the private sector as part of the liberalization of the Indian banking industry in 1994. The bank was incorporated in August 1994. As on 30 June 2007, the bank has 753 branches and an ATM network spread across 1,716 locations. HDFC Bank is one of the first banks in India to offer its customers the bill pay facility. HDFC Bank is also a leader in online purchase (using the HDFC Bank Direct Pay product). The bank also offers its customers a free personalized payable-at-par cheque book and services like real time gross settlement and national electronic fund transfer.

The HDFC bank offers microfinance directly to self-help groups - mainly those involving economically backward women - and indirectly to other poor groups through microfinance institutions. The bank has assisted 1.3 million poor families in this manner, and has disbursed close to Rs 650 crore (Rs 6.5 billion) to these weaker sections, and has enjoyed a 100 per cent repayment. ATMs are a part of the VISA International plus ATM Network and the Master Card International Cirrus ATM Network, and can be accessed by all domestic and international MasterCard, Cirrus or Maestro and VISA Electron card holders for cash withdrawals and balance inquiries.

Bank has partnered with American Express to offer their domestic and international cardholders the benefits of cash advances from any of their ATMs. Credit Card Payment is the service which makes payment of customer's credit card bill using the ATM. The primary account of customer's Debit / ATM card will be debited. Cheque Status Enquiry helps

HDFC customer's to get information about status of a cheque issued to his/her account. Regenerate Internet PIN is the facility to request for re-generation of Internet PIN (IPIN) for the customer. Customer ID of the customer is same as that of the Card being used. The bank also provides 24-hour access to cash - Withdraw up to Rs.10, 000/- per day on customer's ATM Card and up to Rs. 15,000 on customer's Debit Card. The fast cash option saves time by providing the cash in denominations of Rs.500.View Account Balances & Mini-statements helps to get details of the last nine transactions on customer's account with the mini-statement, along with his/her balance.

The customer through Transfer Funds between accounts can also transfer money from one of his/her accounts to another. Both accounts must be linked to the ATM Card and Customer ID. A maximum of 5 saving and 5 Current Accounts can be linked. Pay your utility bills is used to pay cellular, telephone and electricity bills through the ATM using Bill Pay, a comprehensive bill payments solution. Deposit cash or cheques can help the bank customer to deposit cash or cheques into his/her account and the ATM will immediately print a receipt for the same.

3.6.4 Technological Initiatives Taken By IndusInd Bank

IndusInd Bank started its business in India in 1994-95 and with a successful and profitable year of operations, it pioneered by launching Internet Banking. In 2001-02, the Bank's business volume touched Rs. 14,000 crores and became the highest productive bank in the Indian banking sector. The Bank became one of the first banks to implement the Reserve Bank of India's Electron Funds Transfer Scheme. IndusInd Bank, the new generation bank with its cutting edge technology and service-oriented staff, brings in new-age banking to suit the financial requirement of its customers.

IndusInd Bank provides multi-channel facilities including ATMs, Internet banking, mobile banking, phone banking, multi-city banking, and international debit and credit cards. It was one of the first few banks to become a part of Reserve Bank of India's Real Time Gross Settlement System (RTGS). The Bank is implementing an enterprise-wide risk management system encompassing global best practices in the area of Risk Management, with help from KPMG. This has enabled the Bank to remain in the forefront in complying with the requirements of Basel II.

The merger with the Bank in June 2004 of Ashok Leyland Finance Ltd., among the largest leasing finance and hire purchase companies in India, set in motion a process of consolidation through the combined customer base of the merged entity and its increased geographical penetration. IndusInd Bank has become one of the fastest-growing banks in the Indian banking sector today with its branch network expanding from 61 as on March 31, 2004 to 137 as on March 31, 2006 – reflecting an increase in excess of 125% in 24 months. The Bank had approximately 150 ATMs of its own in 2006 and in the year 2007 it has ATMs to 316. The number of Branches of the bank increased to 172.

The bank has concluded multilateral arrangements with other banks with a total network of 16,000 ATM outlets. All the outlets of the Bank, including its branches and ATMs, are connected via satellite to its central database that operates on the latest version of IBM's AS400-720 series hardware and Midas Kapiti (now, Misys) software. IndusInd Bank's broad lines of business include Corporate Banking, Retail Banking, Treasury and Foreign Exchange, Investment Banking, Capital Markets, Non-Resident Indian (NRI) / High Net worth Individual (HNWI) Banking, and (through a subsidiary) Information Technology.

IndusInd Bank provides multi-channel facilities including ATMs, Net Banking, Mobile Banking, Phone Banking, Multi-city Banking and International Debit Cards. It was one of the first banks to become a part of RBI's Real Time Gross Settlement (RTGS) system. It has implemented an enterprise-wide risk management system encompassing global best practices in the area of Risk Management, with help from KPMG. This has enabled the Bank to remain in the forefront in complying with the requirements of Basel II. It is the first bank in India to receive ISO 9001:2000 certification for its Corporate Office and its entire network of branches.

The Bank posted a total business turnover of Rs.29, 714 crores (as on September 30, 2007) and is poised for greater growth in the years ahead. Its network expansion received a fillip with the Bank securing 40 authorizations from Reserve Bank of India for new branches and 100 offsite ATMs in the last calendar year. The Bank currently has a network of 172 branches, spread over 141 geographical locations in 27 states and union territories across the country. The remaining 8 authorization will be used shortly and the total number of branches would reach 180. In addition, IndusInd Bank also has a representative office each in Dubai and London.

IndusInd Bank has been a pioneer in the introduction of technologically innovative products and services. Since its inception in 1994, it has established a low-cost branch network of 41 outlets. These consist of a combination of branches, ATMs, and offsite or convenience outlets as an important part of its service-channel strategy.

The bank has increased its branches to 90 by the end of 2002. As a technologically innovative financial institution, the platform selected would have to be an open system using open standards, which would allow the bank to integrate any additional banking channel software or Bank World's own channel specific software in the future as required.

Driven by technology, IndusInd constantly upgrades its support systems for the introduction of retail banking products and alternative delivery channels. The Bank continues to display its commitment to global benchmarks in technology, as testified by its winning the prestigious IBA Award for the year 2006 (Runner Up) for the Overall Implementation of Straight - Through - Processing between various systems. It is one of the first banks to go live on the

Real Time Gross Settlement (RTGS) initiative of RBI. It enjoys clearing bank status for both major stock exchanges - BSE and NSE and three major commodity exchanges in the country – MCX, NCDEX, and NMCE. It also offers DP facilities for stock and commodity segments.

IndusInd bank aims to blend technology with good service and innovative products, to continue to thrive in the competitive environment, to implement a channel banking infrastructure and create operational efficiency. To improve information network of customers, increasing database. To introduce cost effective new services across additional touch points. To emerge as an international bank with traditional roots.To acquire global capabilities.To provide world-class services.To maintain the highest standards of professionalism and integrity

The bank offers their customers the following online services, Funds Transfer Bill Payment Credit Card Payment Cheque Book Request Standing Order Request Notification of Lost or Stolen Cards Foreign Currency Remittance Multiple Authorization Secure Email with Personal Banking.

3.6.5 Technological Initiatives Taken By AXIS Bank

Axis Bank formerly known as UTI Bank Ltd. was promoted by Unit Trust of India, Life Insurance Corporation of India, General Insurance Corporation of India and its four subsidiaries. The bank was the first private sector bank to get a license under the new guidelines issued by the RBI.

In 1997 the Bank obtained license to act as Depository Participant with NSDL and applied for registration with SEBI to act as 'Trustee to Debenture Holders'. Rupees 100 crores was contributed by UTI, the rest from LIC Rs 7.5 crores, GIC and its four subsidiaries Rs 1.5 crores each. In 1998 the Bank had 28 branches in urban and semi urban areas as on 31st July. All the branches were fully computerized and networked through VSAT. ATM services were available in 27 branches. In 1999 AXIS Bank and Citibank had launched an international co-branded credit card.

AXIS Bank and Citibank had come together to launch an international co-branded credit card under the MasterCard umbrella. In 2001 AXIS Bank had opened two offsite ATMs and one extension counter with an ATM in Mangalore, taking its total number of ATMs across the country to 355. In 2005 Bank entered into a banc-assurance partnership with Bajaj Allianz General for selling general insurance products through its branch network.

Today AXIS Bank is one of the top retail Indian Bank with its reach to 352 cities, and townships across India through 594 Branches & Extension Counters and 2500 ATMs. The Bank offers internet banking including retail and corporate services, trading and investment banking etc. Their deposit base currently stands at over INR 64,000 Crores (USD 16 Billion) with over 7.1 million user accounts. About 3.5 million customers access bank's website for their banking activities. Bank has undertaken Core Banking Solution to derive benefits of CBS as increased performance by 20% to 25% of all bank's servers. Increased availability of greater products and reduced maintenance cost also simplified bank's operational and maintenance processes, resulting in increase in Return on Investments and reduced total cost of ownership for the product.

From the start, the Bank placed great significance on technology, having acquired IBM's AS 400 hardware and Midas Kapiti (now, Mysis) software for its core banking operations. Its superior connectivity through VSAT and lease lines made it possible for the Bank to extend "Anywhere Banking" facilities to its customers from its early days, almost eleven years ago. Its commitment to technology further saw the Bank launch Internet Banking in 1996 and Mobile Banking in 1997, well in advance of other Indian banks.

In September 2002, the Bank introduced a new paradigm in Internet Banking the online access to personal bankers – in partnership with the Dublin based CR2, a global provider of channel banking and card payment solutions. World-class Treasury software, enhancing the Bank's capability to offer new and innovative products in the areas of Treasury and Investment Banking, is in the final stages of being installed.

The Bank has a sharp focus on servicing customers and leverage cutting edge technologies to enable high service quality. It offers a complete range of retail and corporate services. The Bank is using Finacle universal Banking solution from Infosys.

Bank's Belief is that effective IT solutions are a combination of knowledgeable people and right skills, backed by an aggressive business transformation plan and focus on the latest technological trends. The bank constantly improvises its IT systems to meet challenges and enable smooth migration to new versions of applications. Axis Bank in 2007-08 had 729 branch offices and 3082 ATMs.

Technological initiatives are always coupled with certain challenges, which a bank needs to overcome. These Challenges are of scaling up of the Core Banking Solutions to handle the expected growth in business volumes, customer accounts, and transaction load. The bank undertakes over two million transactions per day with more than 4000 concurrent users. The introduction of performance governance and increase in performance awareness within the internet user customers and improvement in response time especially in case of critical transactions are other major challenges which bank has to overcome.

It has been realized by Public sector as well as by Private sector banks that with technological progress and by collaboration with each other, the most optimum decision to increase market share can be achieved.

3.7 COLLABORATION BETWEEN PUBLIC AND PRIVATE SECTOR BANKS FOR TECHNOLOGICAL ENHANCEMENT

Three big banks namely; State Bank of India, ICICI Bank and HDFC bank took the initiative of mutual cooperation by signing the agreement in November 2007.

SBI, along with its associate banks has the largest network of over 2,000 ATMs in the country. All the ATMs of SBI and its associate banks are interconnected through a single switch. ICICI Bank has around 1,700 ATMs while HDFC Bank has 830 ATMs. It is beneficial for both public as well as private sector banks. An SBI customer will now be able to use more than 4,500 ATMs across the country, which is larger than any multi-bank network.

The country now has four multilateral ATM networks - IDBI Bank's Cashnet, Bank of India's Cashtree, PNB's Mitr and Canara Bank's Cash On line. Both HDFC Bank and ICICI Bank are likely to charge their customers for the use of SBI ATMs. However these charges would be lower than what is charged by MasterCard and Visa for debit card usage at ATMs of other banks.

It can be summarized that individual technological progress of banks with this mutual collaboration has delivered many benefits for public and private sector banks. The advantage for the private sector banks by this collaboration is definitely much greater coverage. It is because HDFC Bank and ICICI Bank have ATMs in more than 100 cities, while SBI has the machines in 500 cities and towns. On the other hand SBI's customers will benefit as both HDFC Bank and ICICI Bank have a larger ratio of off-site ATMs. ICICI Bank has a debit card base of around 4 million, while HDFC Bank has a debit card base of 2 million. For the bigger banks with larger ATMs, multilateral and bilateral networks help in increasing the card acceptance. Banks with a larger card base need to tie up with banks having more ATMs as this would help their customer base use more ATMs.

It can be concluded that Indian banks especially Public Sector Banks need to focus on stepping up fee-based income, as this would be the optimum solution to improving their quality of earnings and maintaining profitability. In other words, it can be concluded that, with the collapse of geographical distances, banks need to treat the customer as a customer of the whole bank and not a customer of a particular branch. This is now possible due to technological upgradation of banking sector whereby large scale centralized data bases are possible in a bank with decentralized access. Banks need to constantly look for innovative services which offer customers the convenience of transacting from anywhere, at any time and using delivery channels more suitable for them. These are frontiers which would add value to the services offered to customers and at the same time act as a means for increasing the profits for banks and reducing transaction costs.

4

Profitability and Productivity of Public and Private Sector Banks

Today, we have a vibrant banking sector, powered by both improved efficient public sector banks and growth hungry private ones. The number of instruments available; the number of services banks provides to retail and corporate customers; and the levels of technology involved would have been considered pure science fiction even ten years ago. As India Inc has gained confidence and eyed more and more global deals, Indian banking has kept pace, with its advisory services, financial structuring expertise, negotiating skills; indeed, they have partnered India Inc in its global journey without missing a beat.

Now the banking sector has been working in a more open and globalized environment for almost two decades. The liberalization process of Indian economy has made the entry of new private banks possible and allowed foreign banks to increase their branches in the banking sector. The increased presence of the private and foreign banks during the past decade has made the market structure of banking sector oligopolistic in nature. The presence of this market system can be seen in terms of competitive pricing of services, squeezing spreads, and improvement in quality of services by using better technique and innovations in products.

The flurry of reforms witnessed over the last one and a half decade has brought about significant changes in the banking arena in the country and technology has been a major facilitator of this transformation. ATMs, Internet banking, credit cards, and now mobile banking have helped revolutionize the banking market in the country. So in banking sector also, as elsewhere in business, competitive environment is inducing efficiency and innovation. Leveraging on their new found tech savvy and increased thrust on product/service innovation, the banks in the country witnessed a phenomenal growth in the last few years as the economic growth moved into top gear to be amongst the best in the world.

Financial sector reforms initiated by Reserve Bank of India, the regulatory norms with respect to capital adequacy, income recognition, asset classification and provisioning have progressively moved towards convergence with the international best practices. These measures have enhanced transparency of the balance sheet of the banks and infused accountability in their functioning. Besides sub-standard assets, provisioning has also been introduced for the standard assets. Measures to reduce the levels of NPAs concentrated on improved risk management practices and greater recovery efforts facilitated by the enactment of Securitization and Reconstruction of Financial Assets and Enforcement of Security Interest (SARFAESI) Act, 2002. Several other channels of NPA management have also been instituted, including Debt Recovery Tribunals, Lok Adalats (People's court) and corporate debt restructuring mechanism with separate schemes for small and medium industries.

The minimum capital to risk assets ratio (CRAR), which was earlier stipulated at eight per cent was revised to 9 per cent in 1999, which is one percentage point above the international norm. As some banks in the public sector were not able to comply with the CRAR stipulations, there was a need to recapitalize them to augment their capital base. Banks were allowed to raise capital from the market. In line with the amendment to incorporate market risk in Basel I, separate capital charge for market risk was also introduced in 2004.

Accounting standards and disclosure norms were strengthened with a view to improving governance and bringing them in alignment with the international norms. The disclosure requirements broadly covered capital adequacy, asset quality, and maturity distribution of select items of assets and liabilities, profitability, country risk exposure, risk exposures in derivatives, segment reporting, and related party disclosures. In April 2005, commercial banks were advised to put in place business continuity measures, including a robust information risk management system within a fixed time frame.

In view of the increasing degree of deregulation and exposure of banks to various types of risks, the Reserve Bank initiated measures for further strengthening and fine-tuning risk management systems in banks. The guidelines on asset-liability management and risk management systems in banks were issued in 1999 and Guidance Notes on Credit Risk Management and Market Risk Management in October 2002 and the Guidance Note on Operational Risk Management in 2005.

As part of the reform programme, due consideration has been given to diversification of ownership of banking institutions for greater market accountability and improved efficiency. The public sector banks expanded their capital base by accessing the capital market, which diluted the Government ownership. To provide banks with additional options for raising capital funds with a view to enabling smooth transition to the Basel II, the Reserve Bank in January 2006, allowed banks to augment their capital funds by issue of additional instruments.

With a view to enhancing efficiency and productivity through competition, guidelines were laid down for establishment of new banks in the private sector and the foreign banks have been allowed more liberal entry. Since the year 1993, 12 new private sector banks have been set up. As a major step towards enhancing competition in the banking sector, foreign direct investment in the private sector banks is now allowed up to 74 per cent, subject to conformity with the guidelines issued from time to time. The regulatory framework in India, in addition to prescribing prudential guidelines and encouraging market discipline, is increasingly focusing on ensuring good governance through 'fit and proper' owners, directors and senior managers of the banks. Transfer of shareholding of five per cent and above requires acknowledgement from the Reserve Bank and such significant shareholders are required to meet rigorous 'fit and proper' requirements. Banks have also been asked to ensure that the nominated and elected directors are screened by a nomination committee to satisfy 'fit and proper' criteria. Directors are also required to sign a covenant indicating their roles and responsibilities.

The positives of banking industry, high Capital Adequacy Ratio with minimum total risk weighted assets, continuous decline in Net Non performing Assets and high Return on Assets are the three prime parameters to measure the profitability, efficiency and management of the bank.

Return on Assets (ROA) is net profit expressed as a percentage of total assets, is widely accepted as an indicator of profitability of a bank, providing a measure of the efficiency of profit generation of the assets of the bank. Since profitability reflects quality of assets of a bank, we may construe that ROA is a qualitative measure of the business of a bank. Net profit is the outcome of two factors; size of assets and return on assets.ROA of a Bank denotes how much net profit is generated by every hundred rupees of assets of the bank. It is the rate at which the assets generate profit. It is an indicator of assets management efficiency of an organization. The net profit is obtained when Provisions and contingencies are deducted from operating profit. The five contributing factors for the net profit of a bank are: Interest income from advances and investments, Interest expenses on deposits and other borrowings, Net interest income (Interest income – Interest expenses), Non- interest income, Operating expenses and Operating profit (net interest income + non-interest income – operating expenses).

4.1 RETURN ON ASSETS AND PUBLIC SECTOR BANKS

The deregulation of lending rates from the year 1991 has given public sector banks the flexibility to price loan products on the basis of their own business strategies and the risk profile of the borrower but now below Base Rate since July 1st 2010. It has also lent a competitive advantage to banks with lower cost of funds. This is very much reflected from higher returns on assets of public sector banks depicted in the table 4.1 given below:

Table: 4.1

Public Sector Bank Group-Wise Return on Assets

	BOB		Canara Bank		OBC		PNB		SBI	
Years	R.O.A.	GR	R.O.A.	GR	R.O.A.	GR	R.O.A.	GR	R.O.A.	GR
1997-98	1	0	0.47	0	1.4	0	1.2	0	1.04	0
1998-99	0.81	-19	0.47	0	1.2	-14.28	0.8	-33.33	0.46	-55.76
1999-2000	0.9	11.1	0.43	-8.51	1.1	-8.33	0.75	-6.25	0.78	69.56
2000-01	0.45	-50	0.43	0	0.75	-31.81	0.73	-2.66	0.51	-34.61
2001-02	0.77	71.1	1.03	139.53	0.99	32	0.77	5.47	0.7	37.25

Note: GR stands for growth rate.

Source: Calculated

Figure 4.1.1

Average Growth Rate of Return of Assets of Public Sector Banks in India

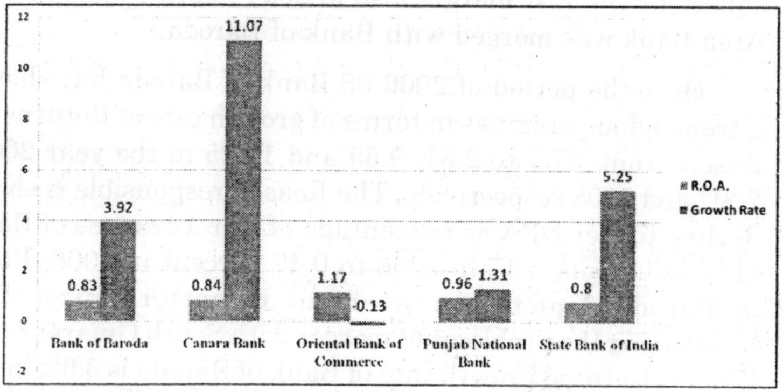

The figure 5.1 depicts that average growth rate of Returns on Assets over the study period is maximum of Oriental Bank of Commerce but at the same time the bank depicts overall negative growth rate of 0.13 percent because of merger with Global Trust Bank. All public sector banks considered under the research study reflects overall higher rate of returns on assets. But there are variations from the average over the study period, which is evident from the table 4.1.

4.1.1 Returns on Assets: Bank of Baroda

For the year 1997-98, Bank of Baroda recorded return on Assets of 1% but growth rate declined in 1998-99 to -19%. This decline in growth rate is because of decline in interest income as well as non-interest income of the bank. In the year 1999 Bareilly Corporation Bank was merged with Bank of Baroda. In the year 2000-01, Bank of Baroda recorded negative growth rate of 50%. Decrease in non-interest income as percentage to assets, merger of Banaras State Bank with Bank of Baroda and consolidation of bank as per prudential norms led down by Reserve Bank of India were the reasons responsible for 50% negative growth rate of Bank of Baroda. During 2002 to 2004 Bank of Baroda recorded a positive growth rate of 71.1%, 31.16% and 12.87% respectively. The reasons responsible for declining trend in positive growth rate of the bank is decrease in non-interest income as well as squeezing interest margin also in 2004 South Gujarat Local Area Bank was merged with Bank of Baroda.

Over the period of 2006-08 Bank of Baroda has shown a tremendous progress in terms of growth rate of Returns on Assets from -37.7 to 2.81, 9.59 and 11.25 in the year 2006, 2007 and 2008 respectively. The Reason responsible is sharp decline in Net NPA as percentage of Net Advances of Bank of Baroda from 1.45 in 2006 to 0.47 percent in 2008. Bank of Baroda depicts improvement in performance after overcoming the problems of merger with South Gujarat Local Bank. The trend growth rate of Bank of Baroda is 3.92, lower than Canara Bank and State Bank of India but definitely higher than Punjab National Bank and Oriental Bank of Commerce.

4.1.2 Returns on Assets: Canara Bank

Canara Bank depicts stability in efficiency management of the organization to great extent with fewer variations as compared to Bank of Baroda. The trend growth rate of Bank of Baroda is 3.92 % while Canara Bank reflects 11.07% growth rate trend, reason being tremendous growth rate of Canara Bank in 2001-02 from 2000-2001of 139.53%. The table 4.1 depicts no change in growth rate of Canara Bank from 1997 -1999 but 1999-2000 reflected negative growth of 8.51% because of decrease in interest income and non-interest income as percentage to assets as well as consolidation of banks. Year 2000 was the year of consolidation by banks as well as of investment in new technology.

During the years 2007 and 2008 Canara Bank reflects negative growth rate of Returns on Assets but is still higher than that of Bank of Baroda over the same time period. It depicts better performance of Canara Bank than Bank of Baroda. It may be because of increase in operating expenses of Canara Bank from Rs 2347 crores in 2006 to 2791 crores in 2008.

4.1.3 Returns on Assets: Oriental Bank of Commerce

The above table 4.1 depicts that Oriental Bank of Commerce recorded highest Return on Assets 1.45% in 1997-98 as compared to Punjab National bank (1.2%), State bank of India (1.04%), Bank of Baroda (1.00%) and Canara Bank (0.47%). But from 1998-2001 Oriental bank of Commerce recorded negative growth rate of 14.28% in 1998-99, 8.33% in 1999-2000 and 31.81% in 2001, indicating the bank invested heavily in assets formation in general, and particularly on new technology. The other reason responsible was consolidation of bank.2001 to 2004 indicates positive growth rate of Oriental bank of commerce reflecting its success story, increasing returns of investment in technology, increase in interest and non interest income as percentage of assets and increase in assets. But in 2004 Global Trust Bank was merged with Oriental Bank of Commerce. At the time of merger Global trust Bank was at the verge of collapse, merger with oriental Bank of commerce resulted in negative growth rate of Oriental Bank of Commerce 19.76 in 2004-05 and 29.10 in 2005-06 and 15.7 in 2008.

4.1.4 Returns on Assets: Punjab National Bank

Decrease in interest income, rapid increase in investment in general and consolidation of bank (prudential norms) resulted in negative growth rate of Punjab National Bank over three consecutive years. In the year 1998-99 growth rate of the bank declined by 33.3%. During 1999-2000 the growth rate further decreased to 6.25% and in the year 2001 it fell to 2.66%.The fruits of technology upgradation and minimization of risk strategy helped Punjab National Bank to enjoy positive growth rate over four consecutive years. In the year 2002 growth rate increased to 5.47%, it further accelerated to 27.27% in 2003; in 2004 the bank achieved the growth rate of 10.20%. The Non-interest income of the bank decreased and net NPA as percentage of net advances increased over 2005-06. This resulted in negative growth rate of Punjab National Bank to 11.60%. Heavy investment in technology by converting its branches into CBS, consolidation of Bank and decrease in interest income as percentage to assets are few reasons which have resulted in negative trend growth rate of Punjab national Bank.

4.1.5 Returns on Assets: State Bank of India

The State Bank of India had recorded negative growth rate of 55.76% in 1998 as reflected from the table 4.1. In the year 1998 investment of the bank increased by 29.6% as compared to 1997 and interest income as well as non interest income as percentage to net assets decreased. But net NPA to net advances increased resulting in negative growth rate of 55.76%. In the year 1999 State Bank of India recorded a tremendous growth rate of 69.56%. Similarly in the year 2000 State bank of India recorded negative growth rate of 34.61%

the prominent reason was implementation of prudential norms. The bank has a strategy to strengthen their market risk management capacity that has helped the bank to achieve positive growth rate of 37.25% in 2001-02, 18.57% in 2002-03 and 8.43% in 2003-04 also 4.44% in the year 2004-05.

SBI has registered significant improvements in its operating margins since year 2003. Technology upgradation has enabled the bank to reduce inconsistencies. SBI had the highest net income (US$1.2 billion in 2005) among the peer group due to increased focus on retail operations which resulted in an increase in deposits by 12.2%. SBI depicts trend growth rate of 5.25% depicting its strong asset management efficiency.

During 2006-07 the return on assets of State Bank of India declined to 0.84 from 0.89 though Net NPA as percentage of Net Advances of the bank had declined from 2.65% in 2005 06 to 1.9% in 2006-07.The probable reason of decrease in returns of assets of the bank could be interest income to interest expenses ratio from 1.77 in 2005-06 to 1.67 in 2006-07 and 1.53 in 2007-08. During the year 2007-08 the growth rate of State Bank of India's Return on Assets increased to 20.2%. It is because of decrease in Net NPA as percentage of Net Advances and increase in operating ratio of interest income to operating expenses of the bank from 3.14 in 2006-07 to 3.88 in 2007-08.

It can be concluded that overall public sector banks have shown efficient management of assets and hence have achieved trend positive growth rate of returns on assets. State Bank of India and Bank of Baroda have efficiently managed their assets and the outcome of it is in the form of higher trend growth rate of Return on Assets over the study period. But on the other hand, Punjab National Bank and Oriental Bank of Commerce are lacking behind in terms of significant trend growth rate, because of mergers and higher level of non-performing assets of the bank. The efficient management of resources results in generating higher returns. On the other hand, private sector banks' have diversified their operations. This has helped the bank to generate higher returns on assets.

4.2 RETURNS ON ASSETS OF PRIVATE SECTOR BANKS

Returns on assets of private sector banks are at higher level than public sector banks because of a more diversified income portfolio as compared with Public Sector Banks. To overcome the potential for higher provisions arising from its strategy of lending to riskier assets, a private bank may charge a higher rate of interest to its borrowers (with a consequently higher Net Interest Margin) than Public Sector Banks.This is very much evident from the table 4.2.

The table 5.2 depicts that among private sector banks Axis Bank has made a progress in terms of Returns on Assets or in other words, the net profit of the bank has increased over the years. This has generated better returns on assets for the bank. On the other hand, IndusInd Bank depicts negative trend in terms of growth of returns on assets. This reflects decreasing net profit of the bank and deteriorating asset quality.

Table 4.2

Private Sector Banking Group-Wise Return on Assets in India

Banks	J & K		HDFC		ICICI		INDUSIND		AXIS	
Years	ROA	GR	ROA	GR	ROA	GR	ROA	GR	ROA	GR
1997-98	1.16	0	2.23	0	1.53	0	1.81	0	0.51	0
1998-99	1.14	-1.72	1.89	-15.2	0.91	-40.5	0.6	-66.85	0.79	54.9
1999-2000	1.13	-0.87	1.84	-2.64	0.87	-13	0.7	16.66	0.77	-2.53
2000-01	1.32	16.8	1.35	-26.63	0.82	-5.7	0.47	-32.85	0.8	3.89
2001-02	1.77	34	1.25	-7.4	0.25	-69.51	0.5	6.38	0.93	16.25
2002-03	2.01	13.55	1.52	21.6	1.13	352	0.91	82	1.17	25.8
2003-04	1.92	-4.47	1.45	-4.6	1.31	15.92	1.74	91.2	1.42	21.36
2004-05	0.47	-75.5	1.47	1.37	1.48	12.97	1.5	-13.79	1.21	-14.78
2005-06	0.67	42.5	1.38	-6.12	1.3	-12.16	0.22	-85.33	1.18	-2.47
2006-07	0.96	43.28	1.33	-3.62	1.09	-16.15	0.34	54.55	1.1	-6.78
2007-08	1.09	13.54	1.32	-0.75	1.12	2.75	0.34	0	1.24	12.73
Trend GR	1.24	7.36	1.54	3.99	1.07	20.54	0.83	4.73	1.01	9.85

Note: GR stands for growth rate.

Source: Calculated

Figure 4.2

Average Growth Rate of Returns of Assets of Private Sector Banks

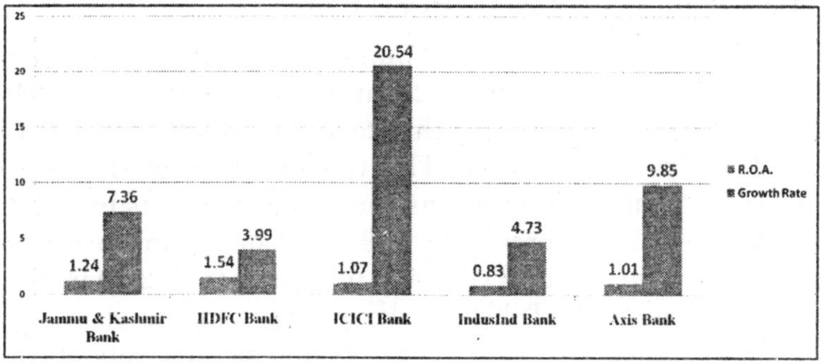

The figure 5.2 depicts that average rate of Returns on Assets over the study period is maximum of HDFC Bank at 1.54% and minimum is of IndusInd Bank at 0.83 %. But growth rate of returns on assets is maximum of ICICI Bank at 20.54 % depicting higher level of fluctuations in Returns on Assets of the bank. It is evident from the table 4.2 that all Private Sector Banks considered under the research study reflects overall higher rate of returns on assets but with greater level of fluctuations than Public Sector Banks.

4.2.1 Returns on Assets: Jammu and Kashmir Bank

The table 4.2 depicts that during 2000-03 Jammu & Kashmir Bank had a positive growth rate in terms of return on assets by 16.8%, 34.0% and 13.55% respectively. The positive growth trend was due to increase in interest income as percentage to assets from 8.38% to 8.46% and further to 9.21%. But the lower rate of returns on assets during 2004 and 2005 was due to decline in interest income as well as non interest income as percentage to assets. In the year 2005 there was a tremendous decrease in non-interest income of the bank, from 302 crores to 96 crores. This resulted in 75.5% decline in growth rate as compared to previous years. It can be concluded that Jammu & Kashmir Bank indicates overall a positive trend in the growth path of returns on assets over the period of 1998-2006.In the year 2007 the Return on

Assets of Jammu and Kashmir Bank increased to.96 and 1.09 in the year 2008.

4.2.2 Returns on Assets: HDFC Bank

The table 4.2 depicts declining trend of return on assets of HDFC Bank till year 2002.But during 2003 and 2005 the bank depicts positive growth rate of return on assets of 21.6 and 1.37% respectively. The reasons responsible were increase in interest income as percentage to assets from 1.40 in 2002 to 1.56 percent in 2003 and operating profit as percentage to assets of the bank increased from 2.29 in 2002 to 2.34% in 2003. Table 5.2 depicts that in the year 2006 indicates negative growth rate of returns on assets of 6.12 percent It could be due to huge increase in investment expenditure by the bank to 28394 crores from 19350 crores. The declining growth rate of HDFC Bank over.the period of 2006 to 2008 from 1.38 to 1.32 is responsible because of increase in Net NPA as percentage of Net Advances from 0.44 percentage in 2006 to 0.47 percent in 2008, Interest Expenses of the bank increased from 1930 crores 4887 crores and Operating expenses increased from 1691 crores to 3746 crores in 2006 and 2008 respectively.

4.2.3 Returns on Assets: ICICI Bank

ICICI Bank in the table 4.2 depicts negative growth rate of return on assets over the years 1999-2002. The reasons responsible could be increase in interest expended from 426 to 15,559 crores from 1999 to 2002. Similarly establishment expenses of the bank increased by almost 100% from 18 to 147 crores over the period of 1999 to 2002.During the study period of 2003-05 ICICI Bank depicts 12.97% increase in return on assets. This tremendous upward swing in the growth rate of return on assets was due to increase in operating profit as percentage of assets. Other factors responsible were increase in spread and decline in Net NPA to Net Advances in percentage. The growth rate of Return on Assets of the bank decreased in the year 2007 to 16.15 percent. It is because of decrease in Return on Assets from 1.3 percent to 1.09 percent. Interest expenses of the bank increased from 9597 to 16358 and 23484 crores in 2006, 2007 and 2008 respectively also operating expenses of the bank increased from 5001 to 6691 to 8154 crores in respective years.Net NPA as Percentage of Net Advances of the bank increased from 0.72 to 1.55 in the year 2008. This resulted in decrease in growth rate of Return on Assets of ICICI Bank to 12.16 in 2006 and 16.15 in 2007. In the year 2008 the return on assets of the bank increased to 1.12 percent with a growth rate of 2.75 percent. It can be concluded that ICICI Bank reflects the highest trend growth rate of 20.54 percent. The growth rate of returns on assets of the bank was minimum at -69.51 in the year 2002 and maximum in the year 2003 at the level of 352 percent

4.2.4 Returns on Assets: IndusInd Bank

IndusInd Bank in thc table 4.2 indicates positive growth rate of return on assets. But during 1999, 2001 and 2004 the bank recorded negative growth rate of 66.85, 32.85, 13.79 and 85.33 percent respectively. Possible reasons responsible for negative growth trend of return on assets the bank may be due to decrease in interest income as percentage to assets, decline in operating profit as percentage to working funds and decline in non-interest income as percentage to working funds. The positive growth rate of return on assets of the bank was possible because of increase in interest spread, decrease in net NPA to Net Advances, increase in operating profit as percentage to average working funds of the bank. IndusInd Bank had the lowest Return on assets with respect to other banks till 2003 because of relatively less number of branches as compared to other banks and less spread that lowers net profit as compared to HDFC, ICICI, J& K and Axis Bank. After 2004 onwards IndusInd Bank's Return on Assets declined continuously from 1.5 to 0.22 and finally to 0.34 till 2008. The reason responsible is increase in interest expenses as percentage of interest income as well as increase in operating expenses as percentage of interest income coupled with higher level of Net NPA as percentage of Net Advances.

4.2.5 Returns on Assets : Axis Bank

Axis Bank indicates low rate of return on assets till 2002 though there was a gradual increase in rate of return on assets of the bank over the years 1998 (.51%), 1999 (.79%), 2000(.77%), 2000-01 (0.8%) and 2002 (.93%). The reason responsible for low rate of return on assets of Axis Bank was low operating profit as percentage to average working funds at the average level of 2.14 percent and low level of interest spread over the following years. The table 5.2 depicts that in the year 2003 Axis Bank had a positive growth rate of 25.80 percent and 21.36 percent in the year 2004. The reason responsible was decline in Net NPA as percentage to Net Advances from 2.74 to 2.26 percent and further to 1.29 percent in the years 2002, 2003 and 2004 respectively but in the year 2004 interest income as percentage to assets of the bank declined from 8.92 to 8.08 percent.

This resulted in negative growth rate of return on assets of the Bank to 14.78 percent and further to 2.47 percent. In the year 2007 the Return on Assets of Axis Bank was 1.1 with declined in growth rate of 6.78 percent. The decline in growth rate of the bank is because of increase in net interest margin as percentage of assets. In other words, increase in interest expenses as percentage of interest income is the cause of decline in growth rate of the bank. Increase in interest income to interest expenses and increase in non-interest income with low level of Net NPA as Percentage of Net Advances resulted increase in growth rate of the Axis Bank by 12.73 percent in the year 2008.

It can be concluded that private sector banks have higher trend growth rate than public sector banks. At the same time it is worth to note that HDFC Bank though depicts lowest level of growth rate among five selected private sector banks but is the most consistent performer in terms of management of asset quality. On the other hand, ICICI Bank has the highest growth rate of returns on assets at 20.54 percent but the bank depicts huge variation in its growth rate.

It can be summarized as Return on Assets is one of the important indicators of the overall efficiency of banks. Private sector banks depict higher level of variation in terms of growth rate of Returns on Assets. It reflects lack of efficient management of funds by private sector banks. At the same time higher level of volatility among private sector banks is because of lower level of risk mitigation strategy and higher level of exposure. On the other hand, Public Sector Banks play safe in the market. The decrease in growth rate of returns on assets can be overcome by bringing down non-performing assets and reducing high intermediation costs due to overstaffing, etc. It can be said that lower level of Net NPA as percentage of Net Advances can increase the level of net profit of banks and hence can enhance Returns on Assets of banks.

4.3 NET NPA AS PERCENTAGE TO NET ADVANCES

Net Non Performing Assets (NPAs) are net of provisions on NPAs and suspense account. Net NPA is obtained by deducting items like interest due but not recovered, part payment received and kept in suspense account etc., from Gross NPA. *Net NPAs are measured as a percentage of Net Advances.* Percentage change in Net NPAs measure gives the movement in Net NPAs in relation to Net NPAs in the previous year. The lower the percentage change, better the quality of assets.

TREND ANALYSIS OF NET NPA AS PERCENTAGE TO NET ADVANCES OF PUBLIC SECTOR BANKS

Over the years the percentage of non-performing assets (NPAs) to total advances /total assets has been declining. The trend is a positive indication of having a sound health of Public sector and Private sector Banks in India.

During 1999-2000, there was an overall decline in the share of NPAs to total advances as well as total assets reflecting the impact of the revised guidelines/directives regarding the prudential norms for banks resulting in the reduction in doubtful and loss assets. Public sector banks show lower level of variations in terms of Net Non – Performing Assets though they have higher level of priority lending. It is because of Public Sector Banks are operating at lower market risk as compared to their competitors. The table 5.3 illustrates the trend of Net NPA as percentage of Net Advances of Public Sector Banks during 1998-2008

Table 4.3

Net NPA as Percentage to Net Advances of Public Sector Banks

	BOB		Canara Bank		OBC		PNB		SBI	
Years	**Net NPA**	**GR**	**Net NPA**	**GR**	**Net NPA**	**GR**	**Net NPA**	**GR**	**Net NPA**	**GR**
1997-98	6.6	-	7.52	-	4.5	-	9.57	-	6.07	-
1998-99	7.7	16.6	7.09	-5.71	4.5	0	8.96	-6.37	7.18	18.28
1999-2000	6.95	-9.7	5.28	-25.52	3.8	-15.55	8.52	-4.91	6.41	-10.72
2000-01	6.77	-2.5	4.84	-8.33	3.6	-5.26	6.74	-20.89	6.03	-5.92
2001-02	5.06	-25.25	3.89	-19.62	3.2	-11.11	5.32	-21.06	5.63	-6.63
2002-03	3.72	-26.48	3.59	-7.71	1.4	-56.25	3.86	-27.44	4.12	-26.82
2003-04	2.99	-19.62	2.89	-19.49	Nil	-100	0.98	-74.61	3.48	-15.53
2004-05	1.45	-51.5	1.88	-34.94	1.29	100	0.2	-79.59	2.65	-23.85
2005-06	0.87	-40	1.1	-41.48	0.5	-61.24	0.3	33.33	1.9	-28.3
2006-07	0.6	-31.03	0.94	-17.02	0.49	-2.04	0.76	60.53	1.56	-17.89
2007-08	0.47	-21.67	0.84	-11.90	0.99	50.51	0.64	-18.75	1.78	14.10
Trend GR	3.92	-19.2	3.62	-17.43	2.42	-9.18	4.16	-14.52	4.25	-9.39

Note: GR stands for growth rate.

Source: Calculated

It is a healthy indication that Public Sector Banks depicts nine plus level of negative growth rate of Net NPA as Percentage of Net Advances. Table 4.3 depicts the level of variation in level of growth rate of Net NPA as Percentage of Net Advances of Public Sector Banks over the study period.

Figure 4.3.1

Public Sector Banking Group-Wise Net NPA as Percentage to Net Advances in India

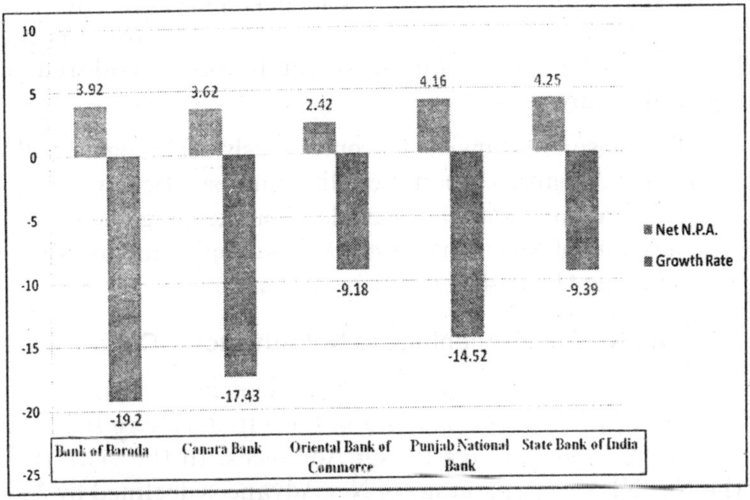

The figure 4.3.1 depicts that Oriental Bank of Commerce has the lowest average level of Net NPA as Percentage of Net Advances at 2.42 percent and State Bank of India has the highest average level of Net NPA as Percentage of Net Advances at 4.25percent.

4.3.1 Net NPA as Percentage to Net Advances: Bank of Baroda

Bank of Baroda indicates a positive trend in terms of Net NPA as percentage to Net Advances except in the year1999 at 16.6% growth rate as compared to 1998. After 1999 the rate of Net NPA as percentage of Net Advances of Bank of Baroda has continuously declined. In the year 2000 it was 9.7%, in 2001 it further declined by 2.5%. In the year 2002 the percentage of reduction in Net NPA as percentage to Net Advances was 25.5% depicting better credit efficiency of the bank. In the year 2003 the Net NPA as percentage to Net Advances further declined to 26.48%. During 2004 the bank was further able to reduce the Net NPA as percentage to Net Advances by 19.62%. The bank was able to reduce its Net NPA as percentage of Net Advances in 2005 to 51.5%

and in the year 2006 it declined by 40%. During 2007 and 2008 the trend continued and Net NPA as percentage of Net Advances of the bank declined to 0.47 percent. The 0.47 percent of Net NPA as Percentage of Net Advances is the lowest among all the public sector banks considered in research analysis.

The reason responsible for continuously declining net NPA as % to net Advances is better credit administration, as well as technological up gradation has made record keeping and regular feedback data of Non - Performing Assets simplified, time saving and reducing the cost of updating accounts.

4.3.2 Net NPA as Percentage to Net Advances: Canara Bank

The table 4.3 depicts that over the period of nine years from 1998 to 2006, Canara Bank has efficiently reduced its Net NPA as percentage to Net Advances. In the year 1999 the Net NPA as percentage of Net Advances declined by 5.71 percentage. During 2000 the Net NPA as percentage of Net Advances of the bank decreased by 25.52% and further by 8.33%. The trend of decrease in the rate of Net NPA as percentage of Net Advances continued from 19.62% in 2002, 7.71% in 2003, 19.49% in 2004, 34.9% in 2005 and 41.4% in 2006. Possible reasons responsible for this positive trend over years are upgradation of credit appraisal skills and systems, strengthening the follow-up of advances including loan review mechanism for large loans as well as effective follow-up of suit filed / decreed debts. Cash recovery of the bank has gone up from Rs. 6060 mn in FY 04 to Rs. 8690 mn in FY 05.

Better cash recovery and lower slippages has resulted in gross NPA coming down and huge NPA provision of Rs. 5499 mn in Q4 FY 05 has resulted in net NPAs coming down from 2.93% as on Q3 FY 05 to 1.88% as on Q4 FY 05. Canara Bank has also followed the trend of lowering down Net NPA as percentage of Net Advances to.94 and.84 percent in 2007 and 2008 but at a lower rate than Bank of Baroda. The overall growth rate trend of Canara Bank is 17.43 percent.

4.3.3 Net NPA as Percentage to Net Advances: Oriental Bank of Commerce

Oriental Bank of Commerce has shown a positive trend in declining growth rate of Net NPA as percentage to Net Advances from 1999 to 2004. The Net NPA as percentage to Net Advances of the bank was constant during 1998 and 1999 at 4.5%. But it continuously declined to 15.55%, 5.26%, 11.11 % in the year 2000, 2001, and 2002 respectively. The rate of Net NPA as Percentage of Net Advances of the bank further declined to 56.25% in 2003 and it was zero in 2004. The bank has utilized bond gains arising from falling interest rates to make loan loss provisions.

Bond gains as a percentage of loan loss provisions have been increased from 37% in FY01 to 96% in FY02 and to 87% in FY03.The higher loan loss provisioning has been supported in part by higher operating profitability. Accumulation of loan-loss reserves has also been driven by bank booking gains on their bonds and effectively transferring these to loan loss reserves, rather than showing them as profits. In the year 2005 the Net NPA as percentage to Net Advances increased to 1.29% which is 100% negative growth rate with respect to 2004. The main reason responsible was merger of Oriental Bank of Commerce with Global Trust Bank in 2004. Drive for recovery of NPAs, upgradation of skills, revamping of credit administration and risk management systems and entertaining only high quality proposals helped the bank to recover the loss in 2006. During 2007 and 2008 the Net NPA as percentage of Net Advances of Oriental Bank of Commerce declined by 2 percent but increased by 50.51% percent respectively.

4.3.4 Net NPA as Percentage to Net Advances: Punjab National Bank

The table 4.3 depicts that Punjab National Bank's Net NPA as percentage of Net Advances has decreased continuously from 1998 to 2006. In the year 1998 Net NPA as percentage to Net Advances was at 9.57 %. But the growth rate has continuously declined over the years from 6.37% (1999) to 4.91 % (2000). In the year 2002 the Net NPA as percentage of Net Advances of the bank further declined to 21.06%. During 2002-03 the Net NPA as percentage to Net Advances declined by 27.44%. In the year 2004 the bank's asset quality in terms of management of NPA increased to that extent that decreasing rate raised to 74.61% hence in 2005 the positive trend continued to 79.59%. In the year 2006 the Net NPA as percentage to Net Advances increased by 33.33%. Strengthening follow-up of advances including loan review mechanism for large loans and technological upgradation by keeping track on bad debt has helped bank to reduce Net NPA as percentage to Net Advances over the years. It is evident that PNB's asset quality is at the higher end.

The management of Punjab National Bank is taking efforts by implementing the Securitization Act. Recently, the Act has been challenged in the Supreme Court on the grounds that it's harsh on the borrowers and is giving more powers to lenders. However, it is believed that the decision would be in favor of lenders. In an attempt to lower non-performing assets (NPAs), PNB has decided to act against defaulters. The bank has recovered Rs. 41mn from 67 units. During 2007 and 2008 the table 5.3 depict decrease in Net NPA as percentage of Net Advances of Punjab National Bank to.76 and.64 percent respectively. It can be concluded that efforts undertaken by Punjab National Bank are still inefficient to curtail Net NPA as percentage of Net Advances of the bank.

4.3.5 Net NPA as Percentage to Net Advances : State Bank of India

The State Bank of India has shown a positive trend at decreasing rate of Net NPA as percentage to Net Advances from 2000 to 2006. In the year 1998 Net NPA as percentage to Net Advances of the bank was 6.07 %. But the growth rate indicates increase in Net NPA as percentage to Net

Advances to 18.28% in the 1999. The growth rate started declining from the year 2000 by 10.72%, 5.92%, in 2001 and 6.63% in 2002. In the year 2003 the growth of Net NPA as percentage of Net Advances declined to 26.82%. During 2004, 2005 and 2006 the decline percentage was 15.53%, 23.85% 28.30% respectively. The State Bank of India has made significantly high provision for NPAs in 2004 quarter and has brought down net NPAs to 2.65 % from 2.88% on third quarter of the financial year 2004 and 2.96% as on second quarter of the financial year 2005. But still due to high net interest income growth and higher treasury income has resulted in net profit growth to increase by 20% to Rs. 10994 million.Net NPA as percentage of Net Advances of State Bank of India has declined over the years but it is still at higher level from its competitors considered in the research analysis. The possible reason responsible could be its huge network of branches and provisions and contingencies are at the level of 5000 crores to 6000 crores whereas of other banks it is just 500 to 1000 crores.

It can be concluded that Public sector banks despite huge priority sector lending and higher number of branches are able to decrease the level of Net NPA as percentage of Net Advances over the years. It was possible because of better credit risk management strategy adopted by Public Sector Banks but still there is a long way to go. It is because Net NPA as percentage of Net Advances adversely affects the entire positive financial indicators of the bank. On the other hand, Private Sector Banks have huge level of disparity in terms of Net NPA as percentage of Net Advances.

TREND ANALYSIS OF NET NPA AS PERCENTAGE TO NET ADVANCES OF PRIVATE SECTOR BANKS

Private Sector Banks depicts higher level of Net NPA as percentage to Net Advances with respect to Public Sector Banks. The Private Sector Banks need to vigilantly monitor Standard assets to arrest any account slippage into the non-performing category. The figure 5.4 depicts very high level of growth rate of Net NPA as percentage to Net Advances of ICICI Bank. Hence ICICI Bank need to churn its credit portfolio so as to maximize returns while keeping the risks pegged at acceptable levels.

The variations in Net NPA as Percentage of Net Advances depicts lack of implementation of credit and market risk strategy by private sector banks. The table 5.4 given below depicts the overall growth trend of Net NPA As percentage of Net Advances of Private sector banks over the period of 1998-2008.

Table 4.4

Net NPA as Percentage to Net Advances of Private Sector Banks

	J & K		HDFC		ICICI		INDUSIND		Axis	
Years	Net NPA	GR	Net NPA	GR	Net NPA	GR	Net NPA	GR	Net NPA	GR
1997-98	4.57	0	1.18	0	1.14	0	3.96	0	5.63	0
1998-99	3.79	-17.06	0.73	-38.13	2.88	152.63	7.2	81.81	6.32	12.25
1999-2000	3.22	-15.03	1.09	49.31	1.53	-46.87	5.98	-16.94	4.54	-28.16
2000-01	2.45	-23.91	0.45	-58.71	2.19	43.13	5.25	-12.2	3.43	-24.44
2001-02	1.88	-23.26	0.5	11.11	5.48	150.22	6.59	25.52	2.74	-20.11
2002-03	1.59	-15.42	0.37	-63	5.21	-4.92	4.25	-35.5	2.26	-17.51
2003-04	1.48	-6.91	0.16	-56.75	2.21	-57.58	2.72	-36	1.29	-44.24
2004-05	1.41	-4.72	0.24	50	1.65	-25.33	2.71	-0.36	1.39	7.75
2005-06	0.92	-34.75	0.44	83.33	0.72	-56.36	2.09	-22.87	0.98	-29.49
2006-07	1.13	22.82	0.43	-2.27	1.02	41.7	2.47	18.18	0.72	-26.53
2007-08	1.07	-5.3	0.47	9.3	1.55	51.9	2.27	-8.1	0.42	-41.67
Trend GR	2.13	-11.23	0.55	-1.437	2.32	22.593	4.13	-0.587	2.70	-19.29

Note: *In case of Net NPA as % to Net Advances negative value is an indication of positive growth rate.*

Figure 4.4.1

NPA as Percentage to Net Advances of Private Sector Banks

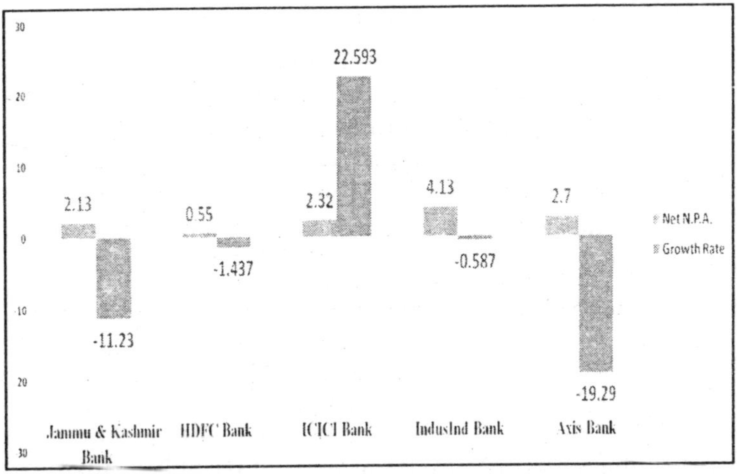

The above figure 4.4.1 depicts that growth rate of Net NPA as percentage of Net Advances of Axis Bank has decreased to the level of 19.29. This indicates better asset management of the bank. But still the Net NPA as percentage of Net Advances of the bank is higher than the HDFC Bank. HDFC Bank depicts lowest rate of Net NPA as percentage of Net Advances at 0.55. It is because of HDFC Bank's safe strategy of lending loans and minimizing credit risk.

4.4.1 Net NPA as Percentage to Net Advances : Jammu and Kashmir Bank Ltd

Jammu and Kashmir Bank depicts a positive trend with continuous decrease in Net NPA as percentage to Net Assets over the period of 1998 to 2006. The net profit of the Bank increased from 51 crores to 85 crores from 1998 to 1999 decreasing Net NPA as percentage to Net Advances by 17.06%. During 1999-2000 net profit of the Bank increased to 120 Crores from 85 crores resulting in decline in Net NPA as percentage to Net Advances by 15.03 %.The percentage decline in Net NPA as Percentage to Net Advances was due to decline in percentage of Interest spread from 30.19% in

1999 to 8.74% in 2000. In the year 2001 the decline in Net NPA as percentage to Net Advances of the bank was by 23.91%. In the year 2002 it further declined to 23.26%. The reason responsible was increase in net profit of the bank from 120 to 168 crores. As well as there was increase in spread of 24.82% and 22.68% in respective years. During 2003-05 the Net NPA as percentage to Net Advances declined from 15.42% to 4.72%. The rate of decrease in Net NPA as percentage to Net Advances is because of decrease in spread percentage over the years and increase in interest risk. In the year 2006 the decrease in rate of Net NPA as percentage to Net Advances reached to 34.75%. This is an indication of better risk management capacity of the bank. The overall decline in percentage of growth rate of Net NPA to Net Advances of Jammu and Kashmir Bank is -11.23% which is better than HDFC, ICICI and IndusInd Banks. The bank indicates increase in Net NPA as percentage of Net Advances during 2007 and 2008 at 1.13 and 1.07 percent respectively depicting poor asset quality of the bank.

4.4.2 Net NPA as Percentage to Net Advances: HDFC Bank

The table 4.4 depicts decline in growth rate of Net NPA as percentage to Net Advances of HDFC Bank in the year 1999 by 38.13% but in 2000 it increased by 49.31%. In 2001 the growth rate of Net NPA as percentage of Net Advances was negative by 58.71%.The reason responsible is increase in operating profit as percentage to assets from 2.21% in 2000 to 2.44% in 2001. Again the operating profit as percentage to assets declined from 2.44% to 2.29% in 2002. However, HDFC Bank has improved the credit management over the years by decreasing the Net NPA as percentage to Net Advances from 1.18% in 1998 to 0.44% in 2006.The growth rate depicts a negative trend of -1.45% over the period of nine years indicating a positive impact of One Time Settlement Schemes launched by the Bank. HDFC Bank indicates lowest Net NPA as percentage to Net Advances as compared to Jammu and Kashmir Bank Ltd, ICICI Bank, IndusInd Bank and Axis Bank, depicting efficient credit management system of the Bank. HDFC Bank has maintained low level of Net NPA as percentage of Net Advances over the period of 1998 to 2008 though the declining growth rate is not high but it reflects consistent performance of the bank with fewer deviations in Net NPA as percentage of Net Advances.

4.4.3 Net NPA as Percentage to Net Advances : ICICI Bank

The table 4.4 depicts that ICICI Bank has relatively low Net NPA as percentage to Net Advances with respect to Jammu and Kashmir Bank, IndusInd and Axis Bank till 2001. In the year 1998 the Net NPA as percentage to Net Advances of ICICI Bank was 1.14%. It increased to 2.88% in 1999.This further declined in 2000 to 1.53%. But during 2001 the bank depicts increase in Net NPA as percentage to Net Advances to 2.19%. In the year 2001 the interest income as percentage to average working funds declined from 10.59 %. In the year 2001 Bank of Madura was merged with ICICI Bank resulting in 150.22% increase in Net NPA as percentage to Net Advances. It took two years for the bank to bring down the Net NPA as percentage to Net Advances from 5.48 to 2.21% and further decline from 2.21% to 1.65% in 2005. In the year 2006 the Net NPA as percentage to Net Advances of ICICI Bank reached to 0.72% depicting efficient recovery management system of the Bank. ICICI Bank indicates increase in Net NPA as percentage of Net Advances in 2007 and 2008 from 0.72 to 1.02 and 1.55 percent respectively. The reason responsible could be increase in advances from 146163 crores to 225616 crores and increase in provisions from 1348 crores to 3803 crores in 2006 and 2008. ICICI Bank has to adopt cautious strategy for secured loans respectively.

4.4.4 Net NPA as Percentage to Net Advances: IndusInd Bank

IndusInd Bank indicates highest Net NPA as percentage to Net Advances as compared to Jammu and Kashmir Bank, HDFC, ICICI and Axis Bank over the period of nine years. In the 1998 the Net NPA as percentage to Net Advances was 3.96% which increased to 7.2% in 1999. In the year

2000 the Net NPA as percentage to Net Advances declined from 7.2 to 5.98 % and further declined to 5.25%. But in the year 2002 the Net NPA as percentage to Net Advances reached to 6.59%. This is a clear indication of poor asset quality of IndusInd Bank which necessitates infusion of additional capital for stabilization of asset quality of the Bank. IndusInd Bank has improved its credit risk assessment strategy over the years which have resulted in decline in Net NPA as percentage to Net Advances to 2.09% in 2006 but still better asset quality is the prime requisite of the Bank. IndusInd Bank reflects highest Net NPA as percentage of Net Advances with respect to other private sector banks considered in research analysis. During 2007 and 2008 IndusInd Bank recorded Net NPA as percentage of Net Advances at 2.47 and 2.27 respectively. High level of Net NPA as percentage of Net Advances is because of decline in net profit from 210 crores in 2005 to just 75 crores in 2008 as well as decrease in spread as percentage of assets from 2.10 in 2004 to 1.46 in 2008.It reflects poor management of credit system in IndusInd Bank.

4.4.5 Net NPA as Percentage to Net Advances: Axis Bank

Axis Bank had maximum rate of Net NPA as percentage to Net Advances in1997-98 at 5.63% as compared to 4.57% of Jammu & Kashmir Bank, 1.18% of HDFC Bank and 1.14% of ICICI Bank. The Net NPA as % to Net advances increased by 12.25% in 1998-99 as compared to 1997-98 at 5.63%. Years 1999-2000, 2000-01, 2001-02 and 2002-03 resulted in decline in Net NPA as % to Net Advances from 4.54 to 3.43, 3.43 to 2.27, from 2.74 to 2.26 and 2.26 to 1.29%. This reflects better recovery management and efficient credit management of the bank. The outcome of strategic decisions was decline in Net NPA as % to Net Advances from 1.39 % to 0.98 % in 2005-06 and increase in Net Profit of the Bank to 485 crores in 2005-06 from 335 crores in 2004-05.Axis Bank has shown a great progress over the years. In 2005-06 the Net NPA as percentage of Net Advances of the bank was 0.98 percent which has declined to 0.42 percent in 2007-08. Increase in credit deposit ratio and increase in spread as percentage of assets has resulted in lower level of Net NPA as percentage of Net Advances for Axis bank.

It can be concluded that private sector banks have to cautiously plan their "market- to- market" investment portfolios and strengthen their credit and market risk management systems, thus enabling them bring down their NPA generation rate and improve asset liability management. At the same time recycling of capital is essential for ensuring growth and sustained liquidity.

Hence Public and Private Sector Banks have to minimize NPAs, if not to be brought to zero level. A bank is considered healthy in case its NPA level is maintained at minimum level and regarded best if zero level is achieved. Over the years the Public Sector Banks have made significant strides in bringing down the level of Non Performing Assets in their books in the post economic reform era. At the same time Private Sector Banks especially IndusInd Bank has to frame a strategy to multifaceted attacks on NPAs by the bank and the perseverance. The emerging trend in the field of NPA reduction also indicates that the banks are seriously pursuing all avenues in the recovery front, despite the bottlenecks faced in certain modes of recovery.

4.5 CAPITAL ADEQUACY RATIO

Capital adequacy is an indicator of the financial health of the banking system. It is measured by the Capital to Risk-weighted Asset Ratio (CRAR), defined as the ratio of a bank's capital to its total risk-weighted assets. Financial regulators generally impose a capital adequacy norm on their banking and financial systems in order to provide for a buffer to absorb unforeseen losses due to risky investments. A well adhered to capital adequacy regime does play an important role in minimizing the cascading effects of banking and financial sector crises.

In pursuance of the Narasimhan Committee recommendations, India adopted Basel I norms for commercial banks in 1992, the market risk amendment of Basel I in 1996 has committed to implement the revised norms, the Basel II, from March 2008. Basel I: Basel I is a framework for calculating 'Capital to Risk-weighted Asset Ratio' (CRAR). It defines a bank's capital as two types: core (or tier I) capital comprising equity capital and disclosed reserves; and supplementary (or tier II) capital comprising items such as undisclosed reserves, revaluation reserves, general provisions/general loan-loss reserves, hybrid debt capital instruments and subordinated term debt. Under Basel I, at least 50 per cent of a bank's capital base should consist of core capital. In order to calculate CRAR, the bank's assets should be weighted by five categories of credit risk – 0%, 10%, 20%, 50% and 100 %. For example, if an asset is in the form of cash or claims on central governments, it will get a risk weight of zero, if it is in the form of a claim on domestic public sector entities, then it will get a risk weight of 10, 20 or 50 per cent at the discretion of the National Supervisory Authority. Claims on the private sector will get a risk weight of 100 per cent.

Market risk amendment: In 1996, an amendment was made to Basel I to incorporate market risk in addition to credit risk, in the calculation of CRAR. To measure market risk, banks were given the choice of two options: A standardized approach using a building block methodology and an 'in-house' approach allowing banks to develop their own proprietary models to calculate capital charge for market risk by using the notion of Value-at-Risk (VaR). These approaches, however, calculated the capital charges for market risk and not the risk-weighted asset.

Therefore, this measure of capital charges would have to be multiplied by a factor 12.5 (reciprocal of 8 per cent, the minimum regulatory capital adequacy ratio) and then added to the risk-weighted assets computed for credit risk. In the calculation of CRAR, the numerator will be the sum of the bank's tier I and tier II capital (tier II capital should be limited to a maximum of 100 per cent of tier I capital), plus a tier III capital introduced in the 1996 amendment to support market risk.

Basel II is a much more comprehensive framework of banking supervision. It not only deals with CRAR calculation, but has also got provisions for supervisory review and market discipline.

Basel II stands on three pillars:

1. *Minimum regulatory capital (Pillar 1)*: This is a revised and extensive framework for capital adequacy standards, where CRAR is calculated by incorporating credit, market and operational risks.
2. *Supervisory review (Pillar 2):* This provides key principles for supervisory review, risk management guidance and supervisory transparency and accountability.
3. *Market discipline (Pillar 3):* This pillar encourages market discipline by developing a set of disclosure requirements that will allow market participants to assess key pieces of information on risk exposure, risk assessment process and capital adequacy of a bank.

Under Basel II, CRAR is calculated by taking into account three types of risks; credit risk, market risk and operational risk.

The credit risk is measured in the same manner as in Basel I, but in a more risk sensitive manner, i.e. by linking credit ratings of credit rating agencies to risk of the assets of the bank. The responsibility of providing the risk-weights corresponding to various assets, under SA, lies with the supervisory authority of a country. Basel II has introduced a new kind of risk, called the 'operational risk' in calculating CRAR. It is defined as "the risk of direct or indirect loss resulting from inadequate or failed internal processes, people and systems or from external events." In order to calculate the capital charges for operational risk, three approaches have been suggested:

- Basic Indicator Approach (BIA),
- Standardized Approach (SA) and
- Advanced Measurement Approaches (AMA)

In the BIA, an estimate of the capital charge for operational risk is provided by averaging over a fixed percentage of positive annual gross income of the bank over the previous three years. In this estimate, negative incomes are excluded. Under SA, at first the bank's business activities are divided into eight business lines. For each business line, a capital charge is calculated by multiplying the gross income of the business line by a factor. A capital charge for each business line is thus calculated for three consecutive years. The overall capital charge is calculated as the three-year average of the simple summation of the charges across business lines in each year. Under AMA, a bank can, subject to supervisory approval, use its own mechanism for determining capital requirement for operational risk.

India adopted Basel I norms for scheduled commercial banks in April 1992, and its implementation was spread over the next three years. It was stipulated that foreign banks operating in India should achieve a CRAR of 8 per cent by March 1993 while Indian banks with branches abroad should achieve the 8 per cent norm by March 1995. All other banks were to achieve a capital adequacy norm of 4 per cent by March 1993 and the 8 % norm by March 1996.

In its mid-term review of Monetary and Credit Policy in October 1998, the Reserve Bank of India (RBI) raised the minimum regulatory CRAR requirement to 9 per cent, and banks were advised to achieve this 9 per cent CRAR level by March 31, 2000. Thus, the capital adequacy norm for India's commercial banks is higher than the internationally accepted level of 8 per cent.

India has gone a step ahead of Basel I in that the banks in India are required to maintain capital charges for market risk on their 'available for sale' portfolios as well as on their 'held for trading portfolios' from March 2006 while Basel I requires market risk charges for trading portfolios only. The RBI has announced the implementation of Basel II norms in India for internationally active banks from March 2008 and for the domestic commercial banks from March 2009.

4.5 TREND ANALYSIS OF CAPITAL ADEQUACY RATIO OF PUBLIC SECTOR BANKS

Public Sector Banks are facing tough competition from private sector banks. It is because of greater flexibility in expanding their business operations. At the same time Public Sector Banks are accessing the capital market to raise funds. This has increased the level of risk banks are exposed to; hence higher capital adequacy ratio is necessary for Public sector banks as well as Private Sector Banks. This is very much evident from the table 5.5.The public sector banks are able to manage market risk to great extent but it is necessary for public sector banks to make appropriate strategy for operational risk management. This will help public sector banks to acquire sustenance of asset quality.

Table 4.5

Capital Adequacy Ratio Public Sector Banking Group in India

	BOB		Canara Bank		OBC		PNB		SBI	
Years	CRAR	GR	CRAR	GR	CRAR	GR	CRAR	GR	CRAR	GR
1997-98	12.05	-	9.54	-	15.28	-	8.81	-	14.58	-
1998-99	13.3	10.37	10.96	14.88	14.1	-7.72	10.79	22.4	12.51	-14.19
1999-2000	12.1	-9.7	9.64	-12.04	12.72	-9.78	10.31	-4.48	11.49	-8.15
2000-01	12.8	5.78	9.84	2.03	11.81	-7.15	10.24	-0.67	12.79	11.31
2001-02	11.32	-11.56	11.88	20.73	10.99	-6.94	10.7	4.49	13.35	4.37
2002-03	12.65	11.74	12.5	4.96	14.04	27.75	10.43	-2.52	13.5	1.12
2003-04	13.91	9.96	12.66	1.28	14.47	3.34	13.1	25.5	13.53	0.22
2004-05	12.61	-9.34	12.78	0.94	9.21	-36.35	14.78	12.82	12.45	-7.98
2005-06	13.65	8.24	11.22	-12.2	12.46	35.28	11.95	-19.14	11.88	-4.57
2006-07	11.8	-13.55	13.5	20.32	12.51	0.4	12.29	2.84	12.34	3.87
2007-08	12.91	9.4	13.25	-1.85	12.12	-3.11	12.96	5.45	13.47	9.15
Trend GR	12.46	0.10778	11.5	3.905	12.56	-0.428	11.48	4.669	12.90	-0.485

Note: GR stands for growth rate

Source: Calculated

Figure 4.5.1

Capital Adequacy Ratio of Public Sector Banks

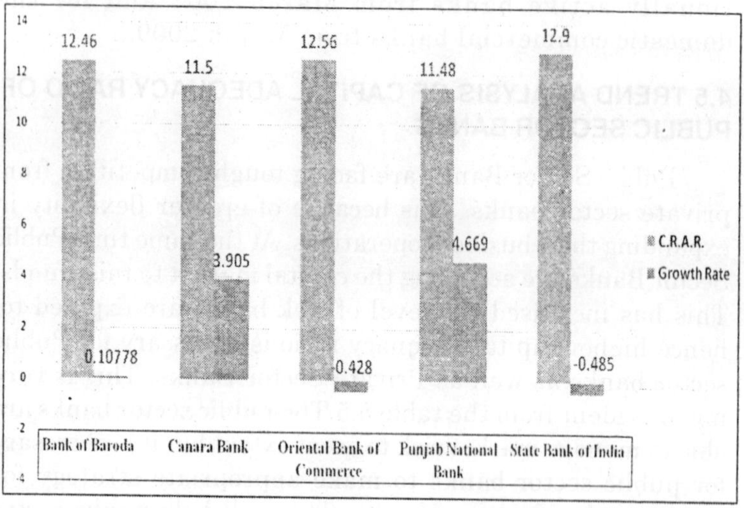

The figure 4.5.1 depicts that average Capital to Risk-weighted Asset Ratio of Public Sector Banks is at higher level than 9 percent.The growth rate of CRAR is highest of Punjab National Bank at 4.669 percent but is negative of State Bank of India at 0.48 5 percent and Oriental Bank of Commerce at 0.428 percent. The reason responsible for the negative growth rate of CRAR of State Bank of India is its huge size and higher market risk. The variation in CRAR of Public Sector Banks is depicted in table 5.5.

4.5.1 Capital Adequacy Ratio: Bank of Baroda

Bank of Baroda indicates increase in CRAR in the year 1999 from 1998 by 10.37% but year 2000 depicts decline in growth rate by 9.7% as compared to 1999.The reason responsible may be increase in credit and market risk weights.Year 2001 indicated increase in CRAR by 5.78 percent but it declined by 11.56% in 2002 reason being increase in risk weighted assets without concomitant increase in capital. In the year 2003 and 2004 CRAR increased by 11.74% and 9.96% from 11.32 to 12.65 and from 12.65 to 13.91% in respective years. Market fluctuations and volatile market resulted in decrease in CRAR by 9.34% in 2005 as compared to 2004. The CRAR rate is increased by 8.24% in 2006 indicating increase in assets and decrease in concomitant cost of risk weighted assets. The overall growth trend of Bank of Baroda indicates a positive trend of 1.72 percent growth rate till 2006 depicting increase in assets and well management of risk weighted assets by Bank of Baroda till 2006 but in 2007 and 2008 the CRAR of the bank is reduced to 11.8 and 12.91 percent respectively from 13.65 percent.

4.5.2 Capital Adequacy Ratio :Canara Bank

Canara Bank indicates a positive trend in CRAR percentage growth rate except in 2000 at 12.04% and 2006 as 12.20 % as compared to 1999 and 2005 respectively. The table depicts marginal increase in CRAR percentage in 2001, 2004 and 2005 by 2.03%, 1.28 % and 0.94 % respectively. The overall growth trend is positive over nine years period from 1998 to 2006.This is a clear indication of value added risk weights and portfolio risk weights resulted in negative growth rate with decrease in quality of assets but overall bank could manage the risk weight and increase assets to certain extent resulting in overall positive growth rate of 3.905 percent which is though less than a Punjab National Bank but definitely higher than Oriental Bank of Commerce, State Bank of India and Bank of Baroda. Canara Bank has shown a positive trend in growth rate of CRAR from 11.22 percent in 2005-06 to 13.5 percent in 2006-07, the growth rate has declined in 2007-08 by 1.85 percent.

4.5.3 Capital Adequacy Ratio: Oriental Bank of Commerce

Oriental Bank of Commerce indicates negative growth rate from 1999 to 2002 depicting decrease in CRAR; 7.72 percent, 9.78%, 7.15% and 6.94% during 1999, 2000, 2001 and 2002 respectively. Decrease in returns on assets and decrease in assets with technological advancement were main reasons of negative growth rate of CRAR over 1998-2002. Returns on Assets increased in 2002 and 2003 resulted in positive growth rate of CRAR. But merger with

Global trust Bank in 2004 resulted in negative growth rate of CRAR of the bank by 36.35% as compared to 2004.The bank could overcome its portfolio risk assets, market, credit and operational risk and increased the CRAR from 9.21 in 2005 to 12.46 in 2006 resulting in increase in growth rate of 35.28% which is big achievement for a bank. The overall growth trend is marginally negative because of sharp decline in CRAR in 2005 to 9.21 from 14.47 in 2004. During 2007and 2008 Oriental Bank of Commerce maintained the CRAR rate at 12.51 and 12.12 percent respectively but the overall negative growth rate of Oriental Bank of Commerce is because of 36.35 percent negative growth rate in 2005.

4.5.4 Capital Adequacy Ratio: Punjab National Bank

Punjab National Bank indicates a strong positive growth trend over nine years period from 1998-2008 of 4.66%. It increased by 22.4% in 1999 from 8.81 (1998) and 10.79 during 2000. Year 2000 was a year of decline in growth rate of CRAR for majority of banks due to decrease in bank's share capital, the CRAR declined from 10.79 to 10.31. In the year 2001 it further declined to 10.24 indicating a marginal decrease in growth rate of CRAR of Punjab National Bank. The possible reason may be increase in expenditure on information technology infrastructure and not increase in assets of the banks to same proportion. Increase in operation risk and market risk promotes bank to increase capital base. Except 2003 and 2006 there was a positive trend in the growth rate of CRAR of Punjab National Bank depicting a strong capital base of the bank and adequate risk provisions are being made by the bank. In 2007 and 2008 the growth rate of CRAR of Punjab National Bank increased to the level of 2.84 and 5.45 percent respectively.

4.5.5 Capital Adequacy Ratio: State Bank of India

The State Bank of India depicts negative growth rate 14.19 % in 1999 from 1998 followed by 8.1% decrease in growth rate of CRAR in 2000. In the year 2001 the growth rate of State Bank of India increased to 11.31 % indicating a positive trend in bank's asset profile. High risk weighted assets or higher share price of the bank may lead to higher CRAR. The CRAR of the bank increased to 4.37 percent in the year 2002. During 2002-2004 State Bank of India's CRAR increased continuously within the range of 13.35 to 13.53.Year 2005 and 2006 depicts negative growth rate of CRAR of the bank.

The reason responsible for negative growth rate of CRAR of SBI in due to increase in expenditure with no concomitant in cost. State Bank of India overall depicts a positive growth trend indicating strong foundation of State Bank of India. State Bank of India in the year 1999 depicts decrease in CRAR by 14.19 percent reflecting consolidation of bank for better performance in future. In the year 2007 and 2008 the growth rate of CRAR of the bank increased to 3.87 and 9.15 respectively. State Bank of India has the highest level of CRAR in 2008 at 13.47 percent with respect to other public sector banks considered in the research analysis, though the overall growth rate of State Bank of India is -0.487 percent but with minimum level of deviations.

It can be concluded that increase in higher operation risk of Public Sector Banks promotes bank to increase capital base. But Public Sector Banks are less prone to Market risk. Credit Risk Management among public sector banks has improved but still has a long way to go. It is because Public Sector Banks are working on a larger scale and hence risk mitigation is a difficult process. These banks keep themselves safe by acquiring higher CRAR.

4.6 TREND ANALYSIS OF CAPITAL ADEQUACY OF PRIVATE SECTOR BANKS

Private Sector Banks are more prone to market risk and hence show higher level of variations in CRAR. The trend CRAR maintained by private sector banks over the period of 1998-2008 is 11 percent to 12 percent as depicted in Table 4.5.

Table No: 4.5

Capital Adequacy Ratio of Private Sector Banks

Banks	J & K		HDFC		ICICI		INDUSIND		Axis	
Years	CRAR	GR	CRAR	GR	CRAR	GR	CRAR	GR	CRAR	GR
1997-98	20.48	0	13.92	0	13.48	0	17.91	0	9.72	0
1998-99	24.48	19.5	11.86	-14.79	11.06	-17.95	15.16	-15.35	11.64	19.75
1999-2000	18.82	-23.12	12.19	2.78	19.64	77.57	13.24	-12.66	11.37	-2.31
2000-01	17.44	-7.33	11.09	-9.02	11.57	-41.08	15	13.29	9	-20.84
2001-02	15.46	-11.35	13.93	25.6	11.44	-1.12	12.51	-16.6	10.65	18.33
2002-03	16.48	6.59	11.12	-20.17	11.1	-2.97	12.13	-3.03	10.9	2.34
2003-04	12.98	-21.23	11.66	4.85	10.36	-6.66	12.75	5.11	11.21	2.84
2004-05	15.15	16.71	12.16	4.28	11.78	13.7	11.62	-8.86	12.66	12.93
2005-06	12.14	-19.86	11.41	-6.16	13.35	13.32	10.54	-9.29	11.08	-12.48
2006-07	13.24	9.061	13.08	14.636	11.69	-12.43	12.54	18.975	11.57	4.4224
2007-08	12.8	-3.323	13.6	3.9755	14.92	27.63	11.91	-5.024	13.73	18.669
Trend GR	16.31	-3.123	12.36	0.5438	12.76	4.546	11.26	-3.04	11.23	3.9683

Note: GR stands for growth rate;

Source: Calculated

Figure 4.6

Capital Adequacy Ratio of Private Sector Banks

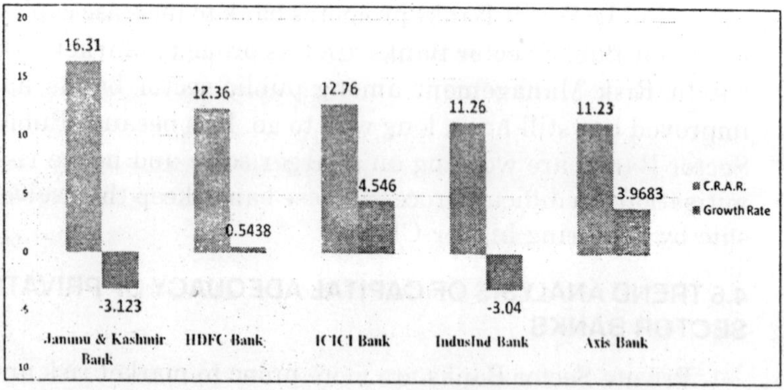

The above figure 4.6 depicts that capital adequacy ratio of Private Sector Banks is higher than Public Sector Banks. It is because the risk weight assigned to assets results in higher level of CRAR. It is a cushion against risk for the lending and operational risk associated with banking operations. IndusInd Bank has higher level of Net NPA as percentage of Net Advances, depicting negative growth rate of CRAR of the bank. Jammu and Kashmir Bank depicts highest CRAR but still the growth rate of CRAR for the bank has negative value of 3.1233. The growth rate presents the overall image of the performance of the bank but true variations can be depicted by considering each year of the research period depicted in the table 4.5.

4.6.1 Capital Adequacy Ratio: Jammu and Kashmir Bank Ltd

In the year 1998 the Tier I capital of J&K Bank was 14.28 percent and Tier II capital was 6.20 percent but in 1999, paid up equity capital and capital reserve of the bank increased to 19.46 percent and Tier II capital decreased to 5.02 percent resulting in increase in growth rate by 19.5 percent. In the year 2000, 2001 and 2002 the growth rate of the bank decreased to 23.12 percent, 7.33 percent and finally to 11.35 percent. The capital of the J& K Bank remained constant at 48 crores from 1999 to 2002. But advances of the bank increased from 2951 crores to 6424 crores and at the same time investment of the bank also increased resulting in decline in capital adequacy ratio of the bank.

This decline in growth rate was because of decline in paid up equity capital and capital reserves in respective years and increase in equity investment resulting in higher weights assigned to market risk investments and decrease in core capital of the bank. Increase in risk weighted assets has declined the overall rate of Capital Adequacy Ratio over the period of nine years from 20.48 percent in 1997-98 to 12.14 percent in 2005-06. In the 2007 Jammu and Kashmir bank recorded 13.24 percent with growth rate of 9.061 percent and in 2008 the bank recorded CRAR of 12.38 percent which is 3.23 percent less than 2007.Bank indicates decline in CRAR from 1998 at 20.48 percent to 12.38 percent in 2008. It records maximum negative growth rate of -3.123 percent with respect to all other private sector banks considered in the empirical analysis.

4.6.2 Capital Adequacy Ratio : HDFC Bank

The table 5.5 depicts that HDFC Bank's growth rate of Capital Adequacy has declined by 14.79 percent in 1999. It increased by 2.78 percent in 2000 but further declined by 9.02 percent in 2001. The capital of the bank remained constant at 200 crores in 1998 and 1999 but advances, fixed assets and investments of the bank increased at a rapid rate resulting in decline in bank's capital adequacy growth rate. In the year 2000 bank's paid up equity capital and capital reserves increased resulting in increase in Tier I capital from 8.34 percent in 1999 to 9.56 percent in 2000. In the year 2001 decline in growth rate of capital adequacy ratio was 9.02 percent which increased in 2002 by 25.60 percent indicating better asset quality of the bank. But in the year 2003 CRAR of the HDFC Bank further declined to 20.17 percent. This fluctuation in growth rate of CRAR of the bank is because of volatile market and market risk weight assigned to such investments done by the bank. HDFC Bank in 2007 achieved increase in growth rate of CRAR by 14.63 percent and has continued in 2008 depicting sound financial position of HDFC Bank.

4.6.3 Capital Adequacy Ratio : ICICI Bank

The capital adequacy ratio of ICICI Bank in 1998 was 13.48 percent but it declined to 11.06 percent in 1999 and increased to 19.64 percent in 2000. Capital of the bank remained constant at Rs.165 crores in 1998 and 1999 but it increased to 197 and 220 crores in 2000. Reserves and surplus of the bank increased from 102 in 1998 to 143 in 1999 and 953 crores in 2000. During 2000-2004 the declining trend of CRAR continued by 41.08 percent to 6.66 percent. The reason responsible is marginal increase in capital of 963 crores 2003, and 966 crores in 2004.The bank recorded decline in Tier I capital from 7.47 percent in 2002 to 7.05 percent in 2003 and 6.09 percent in 2004. Advances of the bank increased from 64948 crores in 2004 to 91405 in 2005 and 146163 in 2006. Investment of the bank increased from 46267 crores in 2004 to 50487 and 71547 crores in 2005 and 2006. Assets of the bank increased from 130748 crores in 2004 to 167659 in 2005 and 251389 in 2006.The increase in CRAR of ICICI bank in 2005 and 2006 was of 13.70 percent and 13.32 percent respectively. In the year 2007 ICICI Bank's CRAR growth rate decreased by 12.43 percent and in 2008 the Capital adequacy ratio of the bank reached to 14.92 from 11.69 with the growth rate of 27.63 percent. The overall growth trend of ICICI Bank is 4.54 percent but with huge variations over the period of 1998 to 2008. Growth rate reached to 77.57 in 2000 but decreased by 41.08 in 2001.

4.6.4 Capital Adequacy Ratio : IndusInd Bank

IndusInd Bank had a CRAR of 17.91 percent in 1998 because of high percentage of equity capital, reserves and surplus but decline in Tier I capital from 17.91 percent to 15.11 percent in 1999 and 12.09 percent in 2000. This resulted in negative trend of growth rate of 15.35 percent and 12.66 percent during the period of 2000. In the year 2001 the growth rate increased by 13.29 percent because of increase in Tier I capital to 12.56 percent in 2001 from 12.09 percent in 2000. At the same time Tier II capital increased from 1.15 percent to 2.44 percent in respective years. Tier I capital of IndusInd Bank declined from 12.56 percent in 2001 to 10.45 percent in 2002 and 10.06 percent in 2003.

Tier II capital of the bank declined from 2.44 percent to2.06 and 2.07 percent during 2002 and 2003, resulting in decline in growth rate of CRAR by 16.6 percent and 3.03 percent respectively. Assets of the bank increased (3.55percent) from 15086 crores in 2004 to 15622 crores in 2005 and (12.8 percent)17623 crores in 2006 and advances increased from (23.2 percent) 7301 crores to 9000 crores and (3.44 percent) 9310 crores in respective years. The growth rate of CRAR declined to 8.86 percent in 2005 and 9.29 percent in 2006. IndusInd Bank depicts negative growth rate over a longer period of time but in 2007 the capital adequacy ratio of the bank increased to 18.97 percent. In the year 2008 the CRAR growth rate of the bank declined again to 5.02 percent. The trend growth rate of the bank is -3.04 depicting poor asset quality management of the bank.

4.6.5 Capital Adequacy Ratio :Axis Bank

The growth rate of capital adequacy ratio of Axis Bank increased to 19.75% in 1999 but declined in 2000 and 2001 by 2.31% and 20.84% respectively. Tier I capital of the bank increased 9.63% in 1998 to 11.60% in 1999 but it declined in 2000 and 2001 to 7.99% and 5.84% respectively. Advances of the bank increased to 33.8% in 1999, 61.61% in 2000 and 37.46% in 2001.From year 2002 to 2006 the growth rate of capital adequacy ratio of Axis Bank has increased by 18.33%, 2.34%, 2.84% and 12.93% over the years. Tier I capital of the bank has increased from 5.85% in 2001 to 6.42% in 2002 and 6.44% in 2003.Assets of the bank increased to (23.13%) 24150 crores in 2004, (56.28%) 37744 crores in 2005 and (31.75%) 49731 crores in 2006. Advances of the bank increased (30.40%) to 9363 crores in 2004, (66.64%) 15603 crores in 2005 and (43%) 22314 crores in 2006. In the year 2007 the growth rate of capital adequacy ratio of Axis Bank has increased by 4.42 percent. In the year 2008 it increased to 13.73 depicting growth rate of 18.66 percent. Axis Bank reflects positive trend in maintaining capital adequacy ratio last seven years except 2006 at 11.08 percent capital adequacy ratio. Increase in risk weighted assets results in lower capital adequacy ratio. The increase in risk-weighted assets is due to a higher growth in the loan portfolio of banks and higher risk weights made applicable for housing loans, the most rapidly increasing component of retail loans for banks.

4.7 CHAPTER SUMMARY

It can be concluded that Capital to Risk-weighted Assets Ratio is one of the significant indicators of the financial soundness of banks. CRAR normally comes down either due to unrestricted growth in assets, especially risk-weighted assets without concomitant increase in capital or inadequate internal generation because of low earnings or high expenditure or poor asset quality resulting in heavy provisioning requirement. Such banks will have little cushion to absorb any shocks, triggered by credit / market risk or other external developments.

Strong capital base is very essential for absorbing unexpected losses which will help the bank to reduce Net Non Performing Assets as Percentage of Net Advances and increase Return on Assets. In public sector banks considered in research analysis Canara Bank has really managed well all its portfolios better than other competitors. In private sector banks HDFC Bank has performed better than other banks considered in research study. IndusInd Bank reflects poor asset quality management depicting low level of return on assets, higher Net Non Performing Assets as Percentage of Assets as well as low capital adequacy ratio. In Public sector banks Oriental Bank of Commerce depicts poor credit asset quality resulting in lower level of Capital Adequacy Ratio.

It can be summarized that in the era of increasing competition due to technological upgradation and globalization of the banking sector it is more important to maintain quality of assets financed, as the large bad loans will not only reduce yield on advances but will also have serious implications on profitability of bank. The State Bank of India indicates higher level of Non- Performing Assets because of high proportion of lending to priority sector. In private sector banks like ICICI Bank and IndusInd Bank, Non-Performing Assets are increasingly occurring on borrowable accounts of the industrial sector and real estate industry.

IndusInd Bank indicates maximum Net Non-Performing Assets as Percentage of Net Advances and low rate of Capital Adequacy Ratio. IndusInd Bank needs to have better follow up, recovery writ-offs, compromise proposals and vigilant credit lending to reduce net non performing assets of the bank. It can be summarized as public sector banks have lower market risk but have to take of operational risk factor to reduce NPA. Whereas private sector banks have to take care of market risk and credit risk lending to the customers. Public Sector Banks due to less volatile operations have lower level of CRAR than Private Sector Banks. Better asset quality, vigilant lending strategy and monitoring of assets will definitely help public and private sector banks to achieve higher level of returns on assets.

With upgradation of technology and increasing use of internet banking operational risk need to be taken care by Public as well as Private sector banks. The "Know Your Customer" norms led down by RBI has helped banks to mitigate credit risk to a great extent. Similarly "Know Your Employees" can also help banks to mitigate their operational risk.

5

Diversification of Banking Operations with Special Reference to Non-Interest Income

In the de-regulated environment in which banks have to function now, Bank's operations are more and more buffeted by the increasing pace of dynamics, the movements of interest rates, the mismatches between maturities of assets and liabilities, market risks such as those emerging from movement of prices, exchange rates etc; operational/ transactional risks, the risk arising from change in rules and regulations, etc. Banks have to therefore, be adapt at recognizing, measuring and guarding against such myriad risks by improved management. Deregulation has given rise to numerous growth opportunities. On the other hand, new threats and challenges have emerged as a result, of intensifying competition, globalization and stricter prudential norms. The Public Sector Banks have taken their own time to come to terms with the changes sweeping the banking industry.

Deregulated interest rate regime, coupled with the imperatives for soft interest rates is here to stay. Therefore, that stark reality is that "spread" of banks will be continually squeezed. Secondly, the pressure on the Indian banks to remain safe and sound is immense, both from internal and international financial institutions/communities, and rightly so. Therefore, they have to adhere to certain benchmarks pertaining to the CRAR, NPAs, etc, which are continuously being pegged to the international standards.

It can be concluded that, banks have started looking into minimizing the "Burden" (non-interest income minus non-interest expenditure). This is being attempted by a) augmenting non-interest income, b) reducing operating expenses and c) both.

The multiple regression analysis has been performed to analyze the prominent factors contributing in non-interest income of public and private sector banks. In the following pages, an attempt is made to evaluate as to how non-interest income, a parameter of technological upgradation in banks, gets influenced by various factors such as Net NPA per branch, business per branch, ATMs per branch, employees per branch and operating expenses per branch.

The model used is specified as:

$Y_i = \beta_0 + \beta_1 X_{1i} + \beta_2 X_{2i} + \beta_3 X_{3i} + \beta_4 X_{4i} + \beta_5 X_{5i} + \mu_i$ where;

Dependent variable:

Y_i = *Non-Interest-Income per branch*

The dependency of *Non Interest Income per branch* is assessed on following 5 different variables

Independent variables:

X_1 = *Net NPA per branch*

X_2 = *Business per branch*

X_3 = *ATMs per branch*

X_4 = *Employees per branch*

X_5 = *Operating expenses per branch*

i = *Number of banks for respective models*

The above five independent factors are taken into consideration to study their relative impact on non interest-income per branch of the bank. With technological advancement it becomes easy for commercial Banks to not only reduce their transaction cost but also to get higher level of non interest income per branch. Various independent factors assessed represent three broad categories. Independent factors such as Net NPA per branch, business per branch are considered to assess the impact of quality of assets on non-interest income per branch of the bank. ATMs per branch and employees per branch have been taken to reflect the impact of technological progress and diversification on non-interest income per branch of the bank. Finally, operating expenses per branch has been taken to reflect the impact of intermediation cost in terms of operating expenses of banks on per branch of the bank in terms of non-interest income generated by the bank.

The analyses of results are presented in two parts:

Part A: It deals with the results of regression estimates on factors affecting in generating non-interest income at *branch* level. The results are also analyzed with respect to the following five public sector banks selected:

Bank of Baroda

Canara Bank

Oriental Bank of Commerce

Punjab National Bank

State Bank of India

Part B: It deals with the results on generation of non-interest income by private sector banks and the factors affecting it. The regression estimates are analyzed with respect to following five private sector banks:

Jammu and Kashmir Bank

HDFC Bank

ICICI Bank

IndusInd Bank

Axis Bank

PART-A

5.1 EMPIRICAL TESTS AND RESULTS: PUBLIC SECTOR BANKS

The results of regression at each public sector bank level are analyzed separately and are arranged in Table: 5.1 to Table: 5.5 respectively. The results of regression estimate for Public Sector Banks are as follows:

Table: 5.1

Regression Estimates for Bank of Baroda

Variables	Standardized Coefficients	Std. Error	T value
Net NPA/Branch	-0.37	0.07	4.012*
Operating Exp/Branch	0.31	2.48	3.830*
Emp/Branch	0.23	2.24	3.052*
Business/Branch	0.50	1.41	6.251*
ATM/Branch	0.45	0.98	5.812*

Dependent Variable:

NII/Branch R Square=0.78

Durbin Watson=2.2*

significant at 5% level of significance

The R square value reflects that 78.38 percent variance in the criterion variable can be made from the predictor variables selected in the model A. The Durbin Watson value is 2.202 which is little exceeding 2 indicating independent errors is tenable in the model to great extent. The beta value depicts low negative relationship between Net NPA per Branch of the Bank of Baroda to Non Interest Income per Branch. Per unit change in standard deviation in Net NPA per Branch decreases Non Interest Income per Branch of Bank of Baroda by.367018 standard deviations. Per unit change in standard deviation of operating expenses per branch results in 0.31255 increase in standard deviations of Non Interest Income per Branch of the bank.

The value of beta for operating expenses contributing in non- interest income per branch is low because public sector banks have incurred higher expenses on employee's salaries and other heads but less on technological progress.

Table: 5.2

Regression Estimates for Canara Bank

Variables	Standardized Coefficients	Std. Error	T value
Net NPA/Branch	-0.39	0.09	5.032*
Operating Exp/Branch	0.33	1.91	4.130*
Emp/Branch	0.21	2.6	4.752*
Business/Branch	0.57	1.31	7.410*
ATM/Branch	0.47	1.23	4.902*

Dependent Variable:

Non Interest Income /Branch

R Square=0.77

Durbin Watson=2.06*

significant at 5% level of significance

The R square value reflects that 76.84 percent variance in the criterion variable can be made from the predictor variables selected in the model. The Durbin Watson value is 2.05901613 which exceed 2 to little extent indicating independent errors are tenable in the model to a great extent. The beta value depicts negative relationship between Net NPA per Branch of the Canara Bank to Non Interest Income per Branch. Per unit change in standard deviation in Net NPA per Branch decreases Non Interest Income per Branch of Canara Bank by 0.394039766 standard deviations. Per unit change in standard deviation of ATMs per branch results in increase in Non Interest Income per Branch by.469017 standard deviations of Canara Bank. Per unit change in standard deviation of Business per Branch results in 0.567 increases in standard deviations of Non Interest Income per

Branch of the bank. Canara Bank needs to provide training to human resources of the bank for higher level of returns.

Table: 5.3

Regression Estimates for Oriental Bank of Commerce

Variables	Standardized Coefficients	Std. Error	T value
Net NPA/Branch	-0.40	0.26	5.236*
Operating Exp/Branch	0.26	2.94	3.248*
Emp/Branch	0.21	2.28	2.962*
Business/Branch	0.49	0.86	8.324*
ATM/Branch	0.38	1.42	5.002*

Dependent Variable:

Non Interest Income /Branch

R Square=0.68

Durbin Watson=1.93*

significant at 5% level of significance

The R square value reflects that 68.36 percent variance in the criterion variable can be made from the predictor variables selected in the model A. The Durbin Watson value is 1.93489479 which is quite closer to 2 indicating independent errors is tenable in the model. The beta value depicts negative relationship between Net NPA per of the Oriental Bank of Commerce Bank to Non Interest Income per Branch. Per unit change in standard deviation in Operating Expense per branch increases Non Interest Income per Branch of Oriental Bank of Commerce Bank by.2602128 standard deviations. It is very evident that Oriental Bank of Commerce needs to increase investment in technology so that higher level of operating expenses can contribute in increase in higher level of non interest income. Per unit change in standard deviation of ATMs per Branch results in 0.38325increase in standard deviations of Non Interest Income per Branch of the bank. Employees of the bank are positive contributors but if they can diversify their job profile which is a very rare feature among public sector banks of India.

Table: 5.4

Regression Estimates for Punjab National Bank

Variables	Standardized Coefficients	Std. Error	T value
Net NPA/Branch	-0.39	0.16	4.142*
Operating Exp/Branch	0.28	1.06	3.020*
Emp/Branch	0.31	2.32	3.902*
Business/Branch	0.51	0.68	5.650*
ATM/Branch	0.48	1.06	4.961*

Dependent Variable:

Non Interest Income /Branch

R Square=0.75

Durbin Watson=1.83

*significant at 5% level of significance

The R square value reflects that 75.4264 percent variance in the criterion variable can be made from the predictor variables selected in the model. The Durbin Watson value is 1.8330443 which is quite closer to 2 indicating independent errors is tenable in the model. The beta value depicts low negative relationship between Net NPA per branch of the Punjab National Bank to Non Interest Income per branch. Per unit change in standard deviation in Net NPA per branch decreases Non Interest Income per branch of Punjab National Bank by.38662 standard deviations. Per unit change in standard deviation of ATMs per Branch results in increase in Non Interest Income per branch by.482251 standard deviations of Punjab National Bank. The unit change in standard deviation of employees per branch results in 0.31416 increases in standard deviations of Non Interest Income per branch. The lower level of beta value for employees per branch and their contribution in non-interest income is due to huge number of branches and employees of Punjab national bank.

Table: 5.5

Regression Estimates for State Bank of India

Variables	Standardized Coefficients	Std. Error	T value
Net NPA/Branch	-0.41	0.02	4.661*
Operating Exp/Branch	0.34	1.36	3.249*
Emp/Branch	0.26	1.18	2.752*
Business/Branch	0.58	0.46	6.240*
ATM/Branch	0.52	1.03	5.052*

Dependent Variable:

Non Interest Income /Branch

R Square=0.71

Durbin Watson=2.03

*significant at 5% level of significance

The R square value reflects that 71.27 percent variance in the criterion variable can be made from the predictor variables selected in the model. The Durbin Watson value is 2.02540 which is quite closer to 2 indicating independent errors is tenable in the model. The beta value depicts strong negative relationship between Net NPA per Branch of the State Bank of India to Non Interest Income per branch. The unit change in standard deviation in Net NPA per branch decreases Non Interest Income per branch of the State Bank of India by 0.41014 of standard deviation.

Per unit change in standard deviation of ATMs per Branch results in increase in Non Interest Income per branch of State Bank of India by.52453 standard deviations. Per unit change in standard deviation of Operating expenses per branch results in.34329 increases in standard deviations of Net Interest Margin of the bank. Number of ATMs is a positive indicator for the growth of the Non Interest Income. The prime concern of State Bank of India to increase the contribution of operating expenses incurred on computerization to generate higher level of Non Interest Income per branch.

It can be concluded that public sector banks have lower level of negative elasticity coefficient of Net NPA per branch on Non interest Income per branch. But at the same time public sector banks contributes at lower level in terms of employees per branch as significant regression parameter and its contribution to non -interest income per branch of the bank. Hence Public sector banks need huge investment on training and promotion of technically sound manpower to contribute at higher level for Non Interest Income.

PART – B

5.2 EMPIRICAL TESTS AND RESULTS: PRIVATE SECTOR BANKS

In this part, an attempt has been made to analyze from the aspect of private sector banks, the factors affecting non-interest income of private sector banks. The results are analyzed in the same format and the result-tables are presented for five respective private sector banks. However, as the model used is same as before, the description of variables used has already been dealt with. In this section (Table: 6.6 to Table: 6.10), the regression results describe the significance of each independent variable in generating fee based income by taking care of assets quality, human resource productivity, branch productivity and intermediation cost of the bank.

The R square value reflects that 69.20 percent variance in the criterion variable can be made from the predictor variables selected in the model. The Durbin Watson value is 2.03062744 which are almost 2; hence the assumption of independent errors is tenable. The beta value depicts strong negative relationship between Net NPA ratios of the Jammu and Kashmir Bank to Non Interest Income/ Branch.

Table 5.6

Regression Estimates for Jammu and Kashmir Bank Ltd

Variables	Standardized Coefficients	Std. Error	T value
Net NPA/Branch	-0.51	0.36	4.035*
Operating Exp/Branch	0.39	1.29	2.439*
Emp/Branch	0.58	3.79	4.256*
Business/Branch	0.76	0.34	9.680*
ATM/Branch	0.66	0.47	5.402*

Dependent Variable:

NII/Branch

R Square=0.69

Durbin Watson=2.03

*significant at 5% level of significance

Per unit change in standard deviation in Net NPA per branch decreases Non Interest Income/ Branch of by 0.486411 standard deviations.

Per unit change in standard deviation of Operating Expense per branch results in increase in Non Interest Income/ Branch by 0.29283331 standard deviations of J & K Bank. Per unit change in standard deviation of ATM per branch results in increase in Non Interest Income/ Branch by 0.36289954 standard deviations of J & K Bank.

Jammu and Kashmir Bank depicts great degree of negative impact of Net NPA per branch and contribution of ATM per branch in increasing Non- Interest Income per branch is quite less than negative impact of Net

NPA per branch. Hence Jammu and Kashmir Bank needs to keep an eye on its Net NPA by risk mitigation approach and invest more in higher level of technological upgradation.

Table 5.7

Regression Estimates for HDFC Bank

Variables	Standardized Coefficients	Std. Error	T value
Net NPA/Branch	-0.51	0.36	4.035*
Operating Exp/Branch	0.39	1.29	2.439*
Emp/Branch	0.58	3.79	4.256*
Business/Branch	0.76	0.34	9.680*
ATM/Branch	0.66	0.47	5.402*

Dependent Variable:

NII/Branch

R Square=0.78

Durbin Watson=2.08

*significant at 5% level of significance

The R square value reflects that 77.79 percent variance in the criterion variable can be made from the predictor variables selected in the model. The Durbin Watson value is 2.076852 which is almost 2; hence the assumption of independent errors is tenable. The beta value depicts strong negative relationship between Net NPA / Branch of the HDFC bank to Non Interest Income/ Branch. Per unit change in standard deviation in Net NPA per Branch decreases Non Interest Income/ Branch of HDFC Bank by.5066495 standard deviations. Per unit change in standard deviation of Operating expense per branch results in increase in Non Interest Income/ Branch by.394398213 standard deviations of HDFC Bank. Per unit change in standard deviation of ATMs per branch results increase in Non Interest Income/ Branch by 0.6614851 of standard deviation. We can conclude that Net NPA/Branch has a great extent of negative impact on Non Interest Income/ Branch of the bank's productivity hence the bank has to decrease its Net NPA by better asset management. HDFC Bank can increase its Non Interest

Income/ Branch to great extent by decreasing Net NPA The negative impact of net NPA is greater than the positive impact of operating expense per branch.

Table 5.8

Regression Estimates for ICICI Bank

Variables	Standardized Coefficients	Std. Error	T value
Net NPA/Branch	-0.61	0.17	7.042*
Operating Exp/Branch	0.35	2.93	3.050*
Emp/Branch	0.46	1.28	5.021*
Business/Branch	0.81	0.45	12.402*
ATM/Branch	0.72	0.38	8.112*

Dependent Variable:

Non Interest Income/Branch

R Square=0.67

Durbin Watson=2.06

*significant at 5% level of significance

The R square value reflects that 67.2446 percent variance in the criterion variable can be made from the predictor variables selected in the model. The Durbin Watson value is 2.06352 which is almost 2, hence the assumption of independent errors is tenable. The beta value depicts strong negative relationship between Net NPA/Branch of ICICI Bank to Non Interest Income/Branch. Per unit change in standard deviation in Net NPA /branch decreases Non Interest Income/Branch of ICICI Bank by.61034 standard deviations. Per unit change in standard deviation of ATM/ branch results in increase in Non Interest Income/Branch by 0.7241 standard deviations of ICICI Bank. Per unit change in standard deviation of Business/Branch results in 0.8104 increase in standard deviations of Non Interest Income/Branch of the bank. The main factor responsible for negative impact on Non Interest Income/Branch of ICICI Bank is Net NPA per branch. Hence ICICI Bank needs to adopt cautious approach in its credit lending strategy.

Table 5.9

Regression Estimates for IndusInd Bank Ltd

Variables	Standardized Coefficients	Std. Error	T value
Net NPA/Branch	-0.48	1.6	5.032*
Operating Exp/Branch	0.26	0.09	4.130*
Emp/Branch	0.33	1.15	4.752*
Business/Branch	0.64	1.02	7.410*
ATM/Branch	0.42	0.76	4.902*

Dependent Variable:

Non Interest Income /Branch

R Square=0.75

Durbin Watson=1.97

*significant at 5% level of significance

The R square value reflects that 74.5476 percent variance in the criterion variable can be made from the predictor variables selected in the model. The Durbin Watson value is 1.967270616 which is almost 2; hence the assumption of independent errors is tenable. The beta value depicts strong negative relationship between Net NPA per Branch of the IndusInd Bank to Non Interest Income/ Branch.

Per unit change in standard deviation in Net NPA/ Branch decreases Non Interest Income/ Branch of IndusInd Bank by.482597489 standard deviations. Per unit change in standard deviation of Operating Expense per branch results in decrease in Non Interest Income/ Branch by.263112443 standard deviations of IndusInd Bank. Per unit change in standard deviation of ATM per branch results in increase in Non Interest Income/ Branch by 0.42185954 standard deviations of IndusInd Bank. IndusInd Bank's Non Interest Income/ Branch is adversely affected by Net NPA hence first priority of the bank should be to decrease the level of Net NPA.

Table: 5.10

Regression Estimates for Axis Bank

Variables	Standardized Coefficients	Std. Error	T value
Net NPA/Branch	-0.56	0.17	4.062*
Operating Exp/Branch	0.33	1.66	3.160*
Emp/Branch	0.54	0.39	4.186*
Business/Branch	0.78	0.45	10.680*
ATM/Branch	0.59	0.38	5.162*

Dependent Variable:

Non Interest Income/Branch

R Square=0.7667

Durbin Watson=1.99

*Significant a 5% level of Significance

The R square value reflects that 76.67 percent variance in the criterion variable can be made from the predictor variables selected in the model. The Durbin Watson value is 1.9937 which is quite closer to 2 indicating independent errors is tenable in the model. The beta value depicts negative relationship between Net NPA per Branch of the Axis bank to Non Interest Income per Branch. Per unit change in standard deviation in Net NPA per branch decreases Non Interest Income per Branch of Axis Bank by 0.56 standard deviations. Per unit change in standard deviation of Operating expenses per branch results in increase in Non Interest Income per branch by.33 standard deviations of Axis Bank. Per unit change in standard deviation of Employee per branch results 0.59 increases in standard deviation of Non Interest Income per branch.The main factor making negative impact on Non Interest Income per branch of Axis Bank is net NPA per Branch. Positive impact of ATM per Branch is less than negative impact of Net NPA/Branch. Hence Axis Bank has to decrease Net NPA/Branch to increase efficiency of the bank.

It can be summarized as old Private Sector Bank like Jammu and Kashmir Bank needs higher level of training of employees to increase its contribution in Non Interest Income. But techno-savvy banks like ICICI, IndusInd Bank need to adopt precautionary step in going for higher level of non-interest income because there is a significant positive relation between higher level of non-interest income and increase in NPA of the bank.

It can be concluded that Net NPA per branch is a significant but negative parameter for all public and private sector banks. With increase in net NPA per branch the non-interest income of the bank decreases. Business per branch, ATMs per branch have positive and significant impact on non-interest income of banks. With increase in business per branch the non-interest income of the bank increases. Same is true for number of ATMs per branch, higher number of ATMs per branch results in higher level of non-interest income for the bank. Employees per branch make positive and significant contribution to increase in non-interest income of the bank. This is true only when banks can provide their employees proper training and increase their efficiency to generate higher non-interest income. Operating expenses per branch has positive and significant impact on increase in non-interest income of the bank.

CHAPTER SUMMARY

It is evident that a public sector banks have lower beta coefficient value for Net NPA per branch as compared to private sector banks. It is because private sector banks are operating in a volatile market with higher risk and higher returns but public sector banks play safe.Similarly there is significant coefficient value of ATMs per Branch of private sector banks than public sector banks. On the other hand, Banks investing in technology with proper training to employees' results in increase in contribution of employees to non- interest income. It depicts technological advancement helps in generation of higher level of fee based income. Hence, banks should make increasing use of advanced software tools and techniques for evaluation of disclosure controls and measures. Frequency of audit and inspection should be increased as it will facilitate checking of majority of transactions, thereby minimizing chances of default in retail lending (home loans, credit cards, etc).

As well as in banking, risk cannot be eliminated altogether but can be minimized by recognizing the changing business environment and taking appropriate proactive measures. In this day and age, the onus of responsibility needs to reside within the organization, where selected bank staff can manage risk in their own area of control and come together to create an accurate, comprehensive risk profile in real time and can facilitate the process of higher income generation at minimum risk.

6

Technical and Allocative Efficiency Analysis of Public and Private Sector Banks

DEA AN INTERMEDIATION APPROACH

6.1 INTRODUCTION

Technological advancements can give most efficient output if human resources are efficient. Changes in manpower requirements of a bank are influenced by its business. There are several factors which can claim to represent the business of the bank. They are total deposits, total credit, total number of branches, total number of deposit accounts, and total number of advances accounts, total investments, and net profit and so on. The manpower planner will have to make a careful selection of one or a group of these factors in such a way that the total business is adequately represented.

Although all the factors listed above pass through an essential test of availability in the form of time series, only total amount of deposits and total amount of credit pass through the other essential test of predictability with maximum accuracy. However, interdependence of these two factors is very high. This implies that only one of the two is systematic variable and the other one is constant conditional on the value of variable factor. In a study conducted by the

National Institute of Bank Management (NIBM), it is found that the correlation between total deposits and total staff is 0.9940. This establishes the fact that the manpower demand is greatly influenced by the quantum of deposits. As the bank gets more deposits, its capacity to lend increases and then there is an expansion in other banking activities which calls for extra manpower.

But technological advancement may turn the coin upside down with less number of employees and more efficient employees' bank can increase its business. With declining interest income and interest margins of banks in India there is urgent need to generate more fee based income to fill the gap created by declining net interest margin. Thus non interest fee based income is becoming a significant source of revenue for the banks.

Private sector banks have highly skilled techno savvy staff to offer fee based services, which provide better margins and leads to higher capital productivity. Public sector banks have also inculcated the culture of increasing proportion of non interest income in total income by diversification of services and products. Hence the empirical study considered deposits and employees as inputs and non interest income as output.

Less deposits and less number of employees with higher level of non interest income is definitely an indicator of technological advancement and increase in capital productivity of the bank. If interest margin of the bank increases simultaneously with increase in non-interest income the bank will have benchmark as compared to its competitors in terms of achieving higher level of productivity and profitability with click and mortar banking. Of late, fee-based products, or products that generate noninterest income, are attracting the attention of more and more banks, including the private ones as well as the state-owned monoliths. For three very good reasons: One, they don't require much capital; two, they carry little risk; and, three, for good measure, they can also boost profitability.

6.2 EFFICIENCY MEASUREMENT

The performance of the productive units is typically described in terms of productivity or efficiency. Productivity refers to the output produced per unit of input while efficiency implies a comparison of actual output/input to optimal output/ input. In fact both can serve as good indicators for evaluating a performance of the productive units. In respect of the productive units, efficiency is measured with reference to the cost/revenue/production function. If the objective is output maximization then productive efficiency can be measured by the ratio of observed output to maximum output. The Productive efficiency has two components: Technical and Allocative efficiency. The purely technical component refers to the ability to avoid waste by producing as much output as input can be use optimally. The allocative efficiency has price component and it refers to the ability to combine inputs and outputs in optimal proportions with respect to the prevailing prices.

In the research study, an attempt has been made to measure Technical, Allocative and Operational efficiency of ten banks, comprising of five public and five private sector banks. The technique used for the measurement of technical, allocative and operational efficiency is linear programming technique by Data Envelopment Analysis (DEA). For the purpose of efficiency measurement, two output indicators have been used; Non-Interest Income and Interest Income and inputs used are employees, deposits, operating expenses and interest expenses.

6.2.1 TECHNICAL EFFICIENCY

Technical efficiency is defined as minimizing inputs to maximize output with a given set of inputs and in given time. The empirical study considered deposits and employees as inputs and non interest income as output. It is because less deposits and less number of employees with higher level of non-interest income is considered as an indicator of technological advancement and increase in capital productivity of the bank. The table given below depicts the technical efficiency of ten banks computed by using DEA technique.

Table 6.1

Technical Efficiency of Banks

Years	1998	1999	2000	2001	2002	2003	2004	2005	2006	2007	2008
Banks											
Bank of Baroda	20.13	36.98	32.63	42.19	29.29	20.59	35.76	32.35	32.58	26.91	31.34
Canara Bank	23.29	43.94	41.98	50.38	39.56	21.75	29.68	31.90	30.76	28.61	31.21
Oriental Bank of Commerce	15.66	30.28	25.29	36.88	32.06	21.05	34.28	24.57	32.97	29.82	20.61
Punjab National Bank	26.05	36.49	36.60	43.99	26.32	16.83	30.64	31.32	27.68	19.59	24.88
State Bank of India	30.98	53.70	43.64	53.24	27.19	20.23	34.71	37.48	49.98	34.49	33.64
Jammu and Kashmir Bank	17.23	19.20	28.11	24.46	37.91	22.62	27.44	10.17	14.26	18.93	19.37
IndusInd	100.00	100.00	100.00	100.00	83.62	76.10	79.47	59.85	49.12	53.12	39.56
ICICI Bank	60.53	72.61	69.92	52.02	42.03	100.00	100.00	100.00	100.00	100.00	100.00
HDFC Bank	49.61	83.26	44.52	64.24	46.41	33.57	36.32	45.19	62.70	62.98	45.36
Axis Bank	47.55	71.07	57.69	88.21	100.00	49.87	63.41	42.22	69.74	61.84	56.53

The table 6.1 depicts technical efficiency of selected banks during the research period from 1998 to 2008. During 1998 to 2001 IndusInd bank has acquired the position of most technically efficient bank but in the year 2002 Axis Bank secured the position of the best bank. During 2003-2008, ICICI Bank secured the position of most technically efficient bank. All other banks have been measured with respect to the most technically efficient bank.It is evident from the table 7.1 that the under the category of least technically efficient banks over the period of 1998-2008 are Jammu and Kashmir Bank and Oriental Bank of Commerce.

The performance of each bank is measured relative to the performance of all banks operating in the same system. This helps to measure how efficiently a bank (DMU) uses the (employees and deposits) resources available to generate set of outputs (non-interest income). The parameters used are employees and deposits because employees are the main resources of the bank. They represent the competence, operating skill and scale of the bank. At the same time, core deposits of the bank increases lending capacity of the bank. The inclusion of non interest income enables us to capture the recent changes in the production of services as banks are increasingly engaging in non-traditional banking activities.

Inefficient banks are those banks which are scoring score of less than 100 percent. Input Target for inefficient or relatively less efficient bank is the amount of inputs that will enable the bank to have the same level of output as most efficient Bank. Input target will be less than Actual Input. The difference between actual input and input target is Input Slack. It can be expressed in terms of input slack percentage. Inefficient bank for example Jammu and Kashmir Bank can move up to the level of IndusInd bank, the most efficient bank in the year 1998 by two ways. The one possible option could be that the Jammu and Kashmir bank reduces the inputs; employees and deposits and Non Interest Income being unchanged to reach up to the level of most efficient bank, the IndusInd bank.

Table 6.2 Input Slack Percentage of Public Sector Banks

	Efficiency Type	1998	1999	2000	2001	2002	2003	2004	2005	2006	2007	2008
1	2	3	4	5	6	7	8	9	10	11	12	13
Bank of Baroda	Technical (Non Interest Income	79.87	68.40	67.37	59.75	75.95	80.28	64.24	76.10	67.42	73.09	68.66
	Allocative (Non Interest Income)	67.46	47.71	33.94	47.43	55.50	48.32	23.39	31.38	51.14	45.74	39.87
	Operational (w.r.t. Interest Income)	31.42	27.49	32.10	29.58	28.70	26.14	26.35	26.55	30.38	21.34	32.10
Canara Bank	Technical (Non Interest Income	76.71	62.45	58.02	51.93	61.05	79.17	70.32	68.10	69.24	71.39	68.79
	Allocative (Non Interest Income)	63.13	39.23	30.92	31.44	40.69	44.54	21.32	31.06	50.55	51.96	41.10
	Operational (w.r.t. Interest Income)	34.41	28.84	36.73	31.19	29.37	25.54	25.91	26.18	25.84	15.69	27.67
Oriental Bank of Commerce	Technical (Non Interest Income	84.34	74.12	74.71	64.82	68.43	79.84	65.72	75.43	67.03	70.18	79.39
	Allocative (Non Interest Income)	73.25	55.42	34.29	53.83	50.67	51.70	26.80	45.65	55.39	52.60	60.77
	Operational (w.r.t. Interest Income)	23.51	21.27	22.62	20.82	15.53	8.94	8.15	16.16	21.54	10.15	17.96
Punjab National Bank	Technical (Non Interest Income	73.95	68.81	63.40	58.03	74.09	83.89	69.36	68.68	72.32	80.41	75.12
	Allocative (Non Interest Income)	60.65	48.70	35.37	44.82	60.01	55.11	31.62	39.11	60.21	44.76	49.29
	Operational (w.r.t. Interest Income)	33.57	29.44	37.17	31.98	27.38	21.11	23.90	32.72	25.91	17.37	28.59
State Bank of India	Technical (Non Interest Income	69.02	54.11	56.36	49.21	73.22	80.63	65.29	62.52	50.02	87.53	66.36
	Allocative (Non Interest Income)	56.25	31.61	29.23	37.74	61.88	54.07	35.77	28.82	40.22	40.40	38.94
	Operational (w.r.t. Interest Income)	33.70	33.24	31.81	33.67	27.29	26.02	30.71	29.16	30.84	24.58	32.32

Second possibility is that Jammu and Kashmir bank reduces both number of employees and deposits in the same ratio, or increases non-interest income (keeping the same ratio of employees and deposits), to move up to the level of most efficient bank the IndusInd bank. The table 7.2 shown below depicts the level of input slack percentage with respect to the most efficient bank.

Table 6.3

Table 6.2 Input Slack Percentage of Public Sector Banks

Bank Group	Input Slack Percentage										
	Efficiency Levels										
	Efficiency Type	1998	1999	2000	2001	2002	2003	2004	2005	2006	2007
1	2	3	4	5	6	7	8	9	10	11	12
Jammu and Kashmir Bank	Technical (Non Interest Income	82.77	83.59	71.89	76.66	62.67	78.34	72.56	89.83	85.74	81.07
	Allocative (Non Interest Income)	67.07	68.24	29.87	59.15	39.59	40.31	35.07	75.92	71.70	64.38
	Operational (w.r.t. Interest Income)	16.91	15.56	22.08	9.10	15.03	10.28	9.91	15.43	14.72	5.75
Indus Ind Bank	Technical (Non Interest Income	0.00	14.55	0.00	4.60	17.65	27.12	20.53	40.15	50.88	46.88
	Allocative (Non Interest Income)	10.68	26.34	0.07	15.89	11.68	0.00	0.00	20.77	45.68	44.90
	Operational (w.r.t. Interest Income)	13.23	15.56	17.41	20.06	9.07	11.21	21.23	21.85	32.69	25.14
ICICI Bank	Technical (Non Interest Income	39.47	37.95	41.29	50.37	58.61	4.23	0.00	0.00	0.00	0.00
	Allocative (Non Interest Income)	13.92	14.82	10.71	24.01	33.56	21.09	20.10	0.00	5.43	5.60
	Operational (w.r.t. Interest Income)	29.27	16.31	27.32	29.43	33.57	28.67	35.78	39.84	37.91	32.20
HDFC Bank	Technical (Non Interest Income	50.39	28.85	55.48	38.72	54.30	67.85	63.68	54.81	37.30	37.02
	Allocative (Non Interest Income)	27.30	14.37	27.45	29.28	43.66	39.26	42.89	23.41	20.13	19.76
	Operational (w.r.t. Interest Income)	23.97	21.12	23.40	21.31	23.03	23.06	19.68	20.31	23.23	17.43
Axis Bank	Technical (Non Interest Income	52.45	39.27	-1305.12	15.85	1.52	52.25	36.59	57.78	30.26	38.16
	Allocative (Non Interest Income)	33.20	30.74	6.71	10.75	0.00	32.15	29.29	11.59	25.12	24.46
	Operational (w.r.t. Interest Income)	23.43	12.26	16.20	17.57	24.36	26.61	11.02	42.86	29.70	24.57

The above table 6.2 depicts input slack percentage of public sector banks with respect to Technical, Allocative and Operational Efficiency over the study period. The table 6.3 depicts input slack percentage of private sector banks with respect to technical, allocative and operational efficiency.

The most efficient bank is the one which uses minimum inputs to produce maximum output. Most efficient bank is calculated for each year to have time series analysis and find the impact of technological advancement. The figure 6.1 depicts technical efficiency of ten banks over the period of 1998.

Figure 6.1

Technical Efficiency of Banks during 1997-98

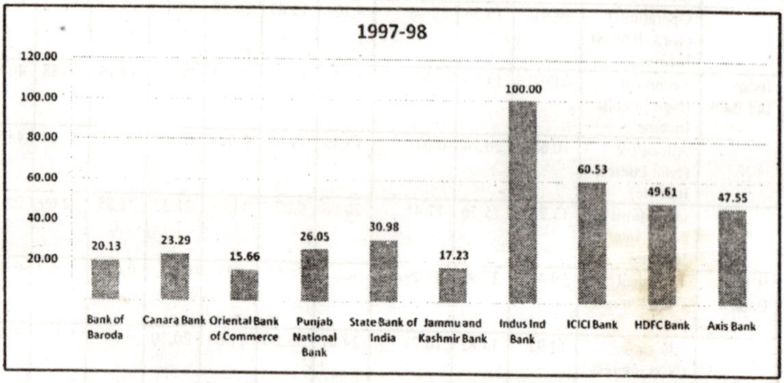

It is evident from the figure 6.1 that IndusInd Bank was the most efficient bank in the year 1998, by generating maximum non-interest income with minimum inputs of employees in thousands, deposits in crores. Second most efficient bank was ICICI Bank with least input slack 39.47 percent (table 6.3). It means ICICI Bank has used 39.47 percent of surplus inputs to produce the same level of non interest income as IndusInd Bank. The least efficient banks are Oriental Bank of Commerce and Jammu and Kashmir Bank with input slack percentage of 84.33 and 82.77 percent and efficiency score of 15.66 and 17.23 percent. All public sector banks are in the efficiency range of 15 to 31 percent because of surplus employees resulting in higher establishment expenses. Private sector Banks were at higher efficiency level than public sector banks because of less reliability on deposits for income generation accompanied by less number of employees and higher level of technological advancement.

Figure 6.2

Technical Efficiency of Banks during 1998-99

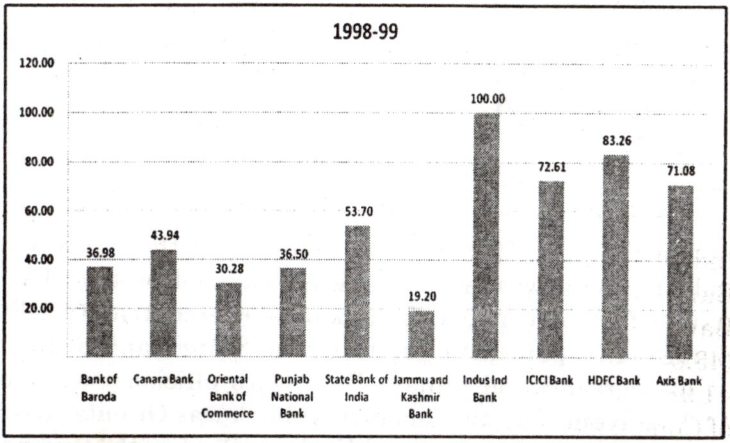

The figure 6.2 depicts that in the financial year 1998-99 IndusInd Bank maintained its score of 100 percent efficiency with minimum input and maximum output followed by HDFC Bank at 83.26 percent, ICICI Bank at 72.61 percent and Axis Bank 71.07 percent.

The input slack percentage of HDFC Bank was 28.85 percent, ICICI Bank was 37.95 percent and Axis Bank had 39.6 percent (Table 6.2). Among public sector banks efficiency scores of all banks had increased with State Bank of India leading the show at score of 53.7 percent and input slack of 54.11 percent followed by Canara Bank with efficiency score of 43.94 percent.

The most inefficient bank was Jammu and Kashmir Bank with efficiency score of 19.20 percent and maximum input slack of 85.59 percent and second most inefficient bank was Oriental Bank of Commerce at efficiency level of 30.28 percent.

Figure 6.3

Technical Efficiency of Banks during 1999-2000

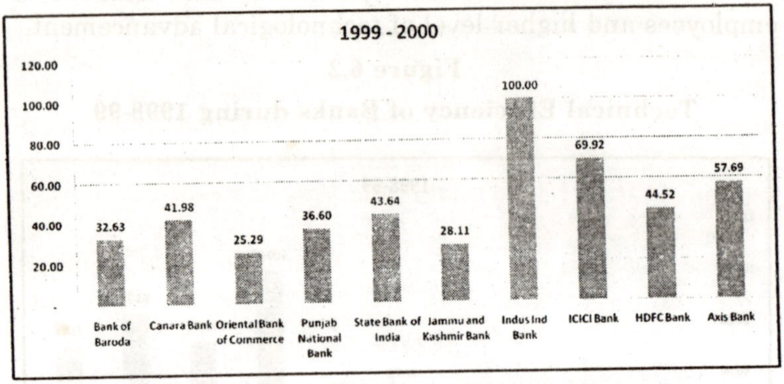

In the year 1999-2000 as depicted in the figure 6.3, IndusInd Bank was the most efficient bank followed by ICICI Bank (69.92 percent), Axis Bank (57.69 percent) and HDFC Bank (44.52 percent) close to it was State Bank of India (43.64 percent) and Canara Bank with efficiency score of 41.98 percent. The most inefficient bank was Oriental Bank of Commerce and Jammu and Kashmir Bank with efficiency score of 25.29 and 28.11 percent. The input slack percentage of Oriental Bank of Commerce was 74.70 and 71.88.

Figure 6.4

Technical Efficiency of Banks during 2000-01

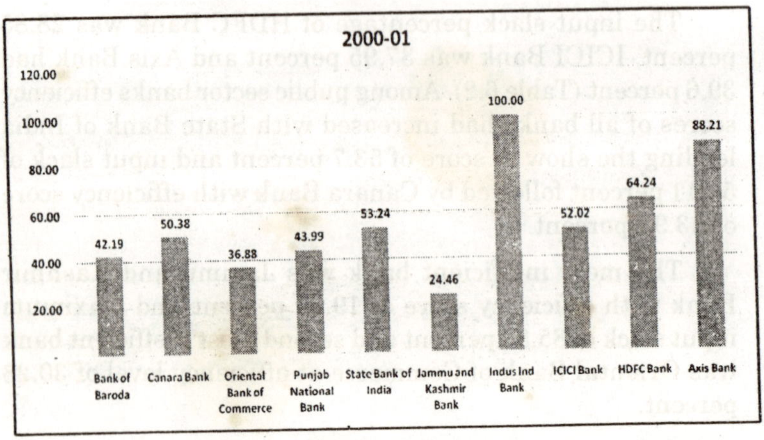

Hence Oriental Bank of Commerce and Jammu and Kashmir Bank generated low level of non interest income by using more than 70 percent surplus inputs.

The figure 6.4 depicts that during 2000-2001 IndusInd Bank secured highest technical score followed by Axis Bank (88.21), HDFC Bank (64.24), but ICICI Bank slipped at lower level of efficiency at 52.02 percent. It happened because of Increase in input slack of ICICI Bank from 41.29 to 50.37 percent. Whereas HDFC Bank's input slack percentage declined from 55.48 to 38.7. Least efficient banks were Jammu and Kashmir Bank and Oriental Bank of Commerce with minimum efficiency score of 24.46 and 36.88 percent.

Figure 6.5

Technical Efficiency of Banks during 2001-02

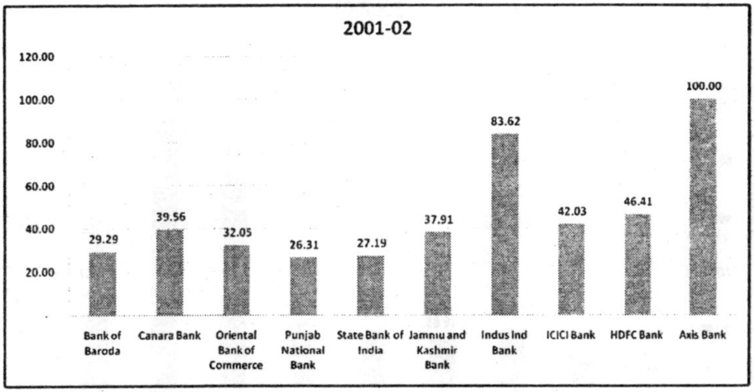

The figure 6.5 depicts in the year 2001-02 Axis Bank acquired the position of the most efficient bank while all other banks slipped on the level of efficiency because in year 2001-02 banking industry was in a transition phase. On the one hand, the Public sector banks, which are the mainstay of the Indian Banking system, were in the process of shedding their flab in terms of excessive manpower, excessive non Performing Assets (NPAs) and excessive governmental equity, while on the other hand the private sector banks were consolidating themselves through mergers and acquisitions. For example HDFC Bank was merged with

Times Bank, ICICI Bank had acquired ITC Classic, Anagram Finance and Bank of Madura. The UTI bank- Global Trust Bank merger however opened a Pandora's box and brought about the realization that all was not well in the functioning of many of the private sector banks too.

In financial 2001 the economic slowdown resulted in a Gross Domestic Product (GDP) growth of only 6.0 percent as against the previous year's 6.4 percent. The Wholesale Price Index (a measure of inflation) increased by 7.1 percent as against 3.3 percent in financial year 2000. The industrial slowdown also affected the earnings of banks.

Figure 6.6

Technical Efficiency of Banks during 2002-03

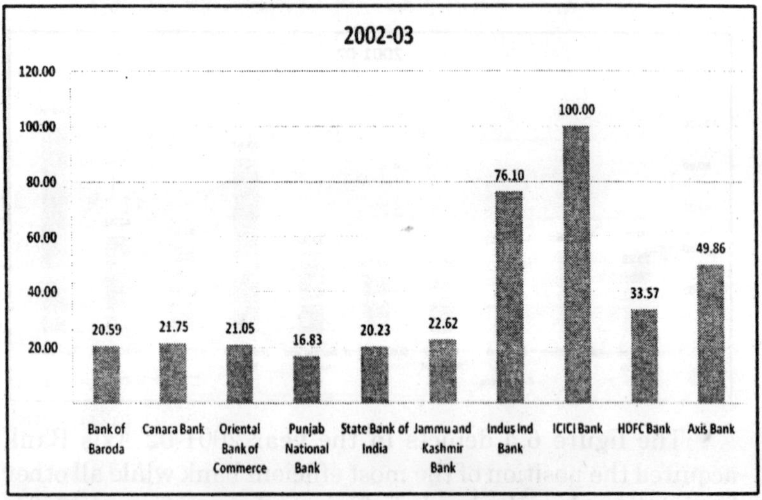

The impact of economic slowdown was also visible in the year 2002-03.The figure 7.5 depicts that the State Bank of India had efficiency score of 20.23 and Bank of Baroda with efficiency score of 20.59.

ICICI Bank adopted technological advancement and lead the show by securing position of most efficient bank followed by IndusInd Bank and Axis Bank at efficiency score of 76.1 and 49.87 respectively.

Figure 6.7

Technical Efficiency of Banks during 2003-04

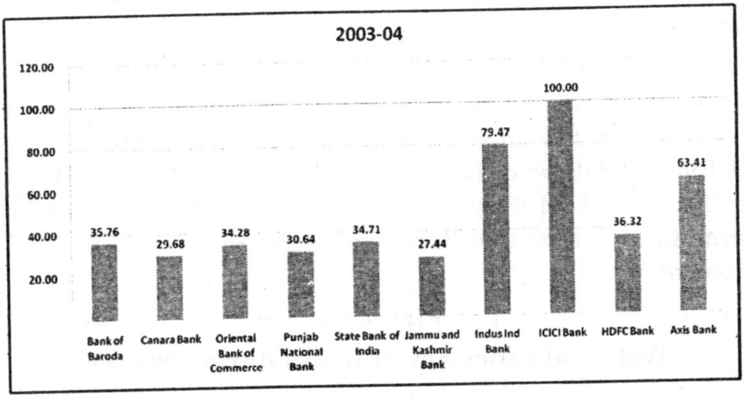

Financial year 2003-04 reflected positive results of consolidation in banking industry in terms of climbing ladder up to efficiency score of thirties from twenties of public sector banks as compared to 2002-03. Bank of Baroda scored maximum efficiency score of 35.76 among other public sector banks considered in research. State Bank of India ranked second among public sector banks with efficiency score of 34.71.IndusInd Bank had efficiency score of 76.10 and Axis Bank 49.87 percent. Low level of efficiency score of public sector banks is because of low level of investment in technology.

Figure 6.8

Technical Efficiency of Banks during 2004-05

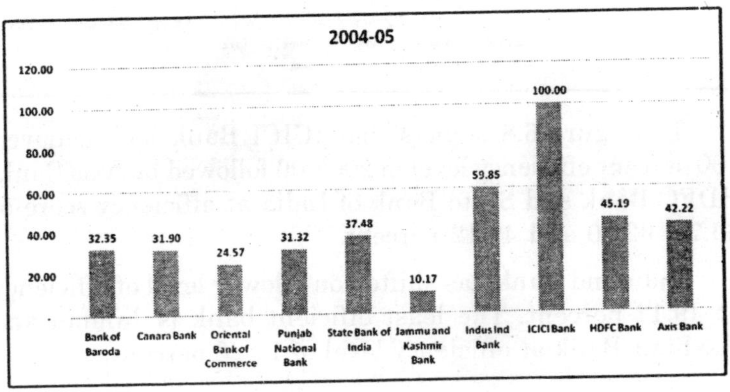

The figure 6.8 depicts that in financial year 2004-05 ICICI Bank secured 100 percent efficiency level followed by IndusInd Bank at 59.85, HDFC Bank at 45.19 and Axis Bank at 42.22 percent.

The most efficient bank among public sector banks is State Bank of India at efficiency score of 37.48 with reference decision making unit IndusInd Bank. State Bank of India is followed by Bank of Baroda and Canara Bank at 32.35 and 31.90 percent. The least efficient bank is Jammu and Kashmir Bank with efficiency score of 10.17 percent.

Figure 6.9
Technical Efficiency of Banks during 2005-06

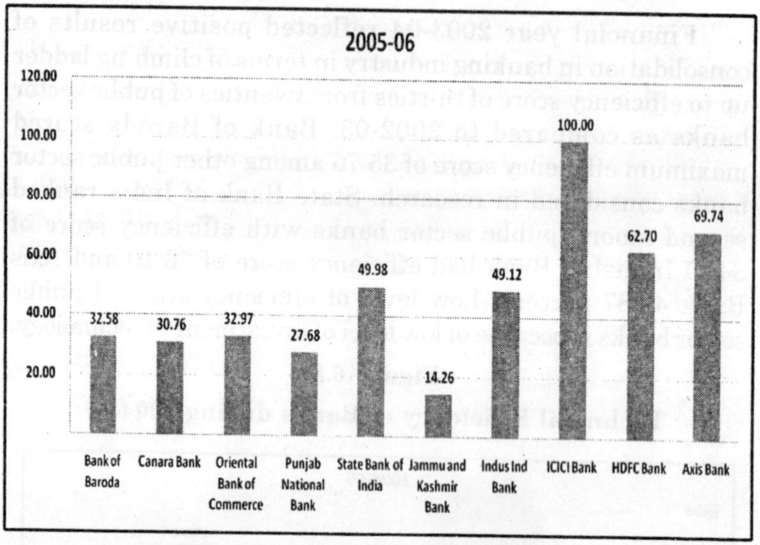

The figure 6.8 depicts that ICICI Bank had achieved 100 percent efficiency level in 2005-06 followed by Axis Bank, HDFC Bank and State Bank of India at efficiency score of 69.74, 62.70 and 49.12 percent.

IndusInd Bank has shifted on a lower level of efficiency at 49.12 percent. The least efficient bank is Jammu and Kashmir Bank at efficiency level of 14.26 percent.

Figure 6.10

Technical Efficiency of Banks during 2006-07

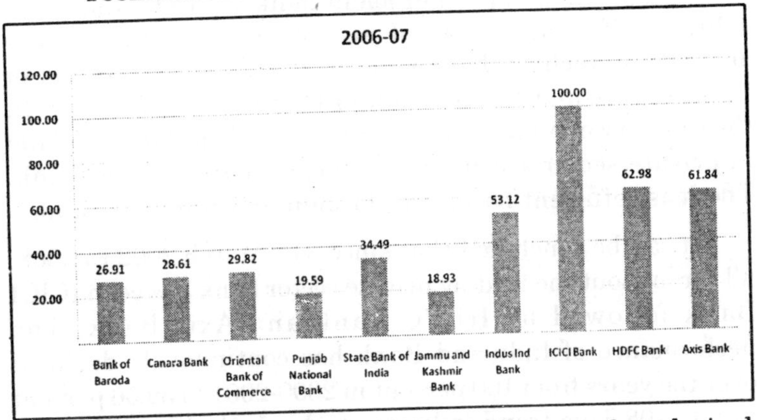

Even during 2006-07 ICICI Bank scored technical efficiency rating of 100 percent and Jammu and Kashmir Bank as least efficient bank at the score of 18.93 percent. Jammu and Kashmir Bank is followed by Punjab National Bank because of input slack percentage of number of employees in thousands of 89.78 percent as compared to the most efficient bank, ICICI Bank. The deposits of the bank are in surplus to the extent of 71.03% but non-interest income generated of Punjab National Bank was 1.042 crores and ICICI Bank's non interest income was 5.929 crores.

Figure 6.11

Technical Efficiency of Banks during 2007-08

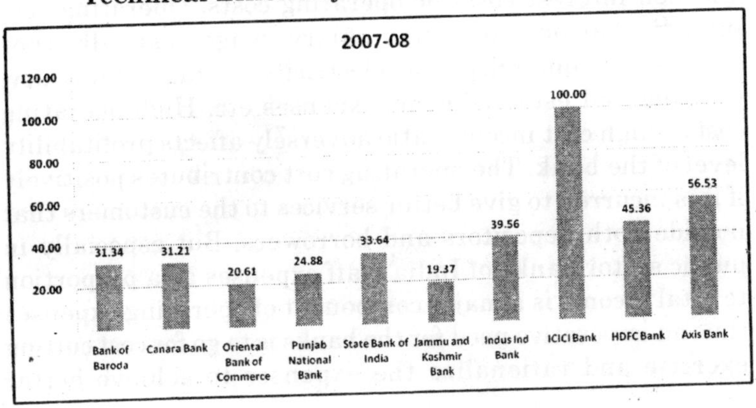

In 2007-08 ICICI Bank maintained the lead by securing position of most efficient bank but IndusInd Bank achieved efficiency score of just 39.56 percent depicting decrease in technical efficiency of the bank. State Bank of India still scored the position of best bank and second in the category of public sector banks is Bank of Baroda. While in private sector second most efficient bank is Axis Bank. The least efficient bank was Jammu and Kashmir Bank.

It can be concluded that since 31st March 2002 to 2008, all throughout the leading private sector bank has been ICICI Bank followed by HDFC Bank and Axis Bank. The performance of IndusInd Bank has continuously declined over the years from 100 percent in 2000-2001 to 39.56 percent in 2007-08.This trend indicates technological up gradation is an ongoing process, to get higher returns from the given set of inputs technological up gradation acts as a facilitator but not as the end product. Over the years, ICICI Bank has acquired higher level of technological upgradation in its operations which has resulted in higher returns. IndusInd Bank started with a bang but could not maintain the same level of technological progress as compared to its competitors in banking Industry.

6.2.2 ALLOCATIVE EFFICIENCY

Banks' cost structure normally includes interest costs and non interest costs or operating costs. Operating cost includes various costs like salary, wage cost, all other expenses as rent, telephone, electricity, postage, stationary, printing and establishment expenses etc. High operating cost or high cost income ratio adversely affects profitability level of the bank. The operating cost contributes positively if it is incurred to give better services to the customers that include both depositors and borrowers. But especially in public sector banks of India staff expenses as a proportion to total income is a major component of operating expenses thus an imperative need for the banks is to go for cost cutting exercise and rationalize the expenses to achieve better efficiency levels in operation to withstand declining interest rate regime. Price of employees and deposits is operating expenses and interest expenses respectively; the degree of efficiency with which banks combine theses inputs to produce a given level of output at minimum expenses depicts a higher level of technical efficiency of the bank. Technical inefficiency implies that too many inputs are required to produce a unit of output; this is usually the result of weak competitive forces.

The overall economic efficiency is a function of:

- Technical Efficiency: Producing higher output per unit of given input.
- Allocative Efficiency: Getting the mix of output right, given relative prices of inputs.

Most efficient bank will be the one which incurs minimum expenses on employees and deposits but generates higher level of non interest income as output. Non -interest income is an important parameter to measure allocative and technical efficiency of Banks in India because increased competition in the Indian Banking industry has driven the interest yields and consequently, the Net Interest Margins has decreased. Hence, banks are increasingly concentrating on non interest income to shore up profits.

On the other hand the operating expense ratio reveals how expensive it is for a bank to maintain its fixed assets and human capital that are used to generate that income streams. Another important factor of shrinking net interest margin is increasing interest expenses ratio, hence lowering interest expense ratio and operating expense ratio at higher level of non interest income will definitely improve the level of productivity, technical efficiency, allocative efficiency and hence economic efficiency of the banking industry.

Table 6.4

Allocative Efficiecny of Banks

Years	1997-98	1998-99	1999-2000	2000-01	2001-02	2002-03	2003-04	2004-05	2005-06	2006-07	2007-08
Banks											
Bank of Baroda	36.43	61.07	48.67	58.91	44.50	51.68	76.61	68.62	51.66	56.06	66.69
Canara Bank	43.26	70.97	59.86	76.82	59.31	55.46	78.68	68.94	52.29	50.89	65.33
Oriental Bank	29.95	52.06	37.48	51.74	49.33	48.30	73.20	54.35	47.17	50.21	43.51
Punjab National Bank	44.05	59.91	48.88	61.83	39.99	44.89	68.38	60.89	42.08	58.52	56.24
State Bank of India	48.99	79.86	59.89	69.76	38.12	45.93	64.23	71.18	63.22	63.14	67.72
Jammu and Kashmir	36.86	37.09	49.98	45.77	60.41	59.69	64.93	24.08	29.93	37.73	49.07
Indus Ind	100.00	86.03	100.00	94.25	88.32	100.00	100.00	79.23	57.44	58.37	52.32
ICICI Bank	96.37	99.48	88.82	85.14	66.44	78.91	79.90	100.00	100.00	100.00	100.00
HDFC Bank	81.40	100.00	77.77	79.25	56.34	60.74	57.11	76.59	84.46	85.00	86.75
Axis Bank	74.79	80.89	83.70	100.00	100.00	67.85	70.71	88.41	79.18	80.02	90.99

The table 6.4 depicts that there is not much difference between technical efficiency score of banks and allocative efficiency. The most efficient bank in the year 1998 is IndusInd bank and the second most efficient bank is ICICI bank. The least efficient bank is Jammu and Kashmir bank at the score of 36.86. All banks are better performer in terms of allocative efficiency score than technical efficiency score. The possible reason could be resources are utilized better in terms of pricing of inputs but not in terms of quantity of inputs. It is noteworthy that IndusInd bank's allocative efficiency score is not 100 percent as was in case of technical efficiency. It could be due to higher level of non-performing assets of the bank.

It can be concluded that there is less difference in terms of allocative efficiency between public and private sector banks. This is because one of the components of operating expenses is wage bill expenses along with other expenses. Since public sector banks have huge number of employee force and they spend more on wage bill expenses and less on technological upgradation. On the other hand, private sector banks have less number of employees and they spend more on technological upgradation. The year wise allocative analysis of banks is covered below.

Figure 6.12

Allocative Efficiency of Banks during 1997-98

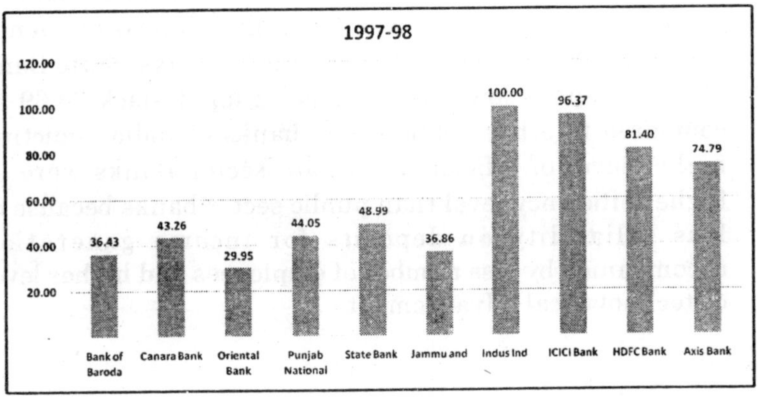

In 1997-98 IndusInd Bank was the most efficient bank by generating maximum non- interest income with minimum inputs of operating expenses and interest expenses. The input slack percentage of operating expenses of IndusInd Bank is zero but for Interest income to the ratio of interest expenses ICICI Bank is a better performer. Technical efficiency of IndusInd Bank is higher than ICICI Bank because output slack of IndusInd Bank is zero but of ICICI Bank is 29.64 percent.

That is, with given inputs ICICI Bank should generate more non- interest income than IndusInd Bank. Hence second most efficient bank is ICICI Bank with least input slack percent of 13.92 percent. It means ICICI Bank has used 13.92 percent of surplus inputs to produce the same level of non interest income as IndusInd Bank. The least efficient banks are Oriental Bank of Commerce and Jammu and Kashmir Bank with input slack percentage of 73.24 (table 6.2) and 67.07 (table 6.3) percent and efficiency score of 29.95 and 36.86 percent.

All private sector banks are in the efficiency range of 75 to 100 percent except Jammu and Kashmir Bank. The input slack percentage of HDFC Bank is 27.29 and of Axis Bank 33.20 percent whereas public sector banks have input slack percentage of more than 55 percent but less than 68 percent depicting the lower level of technical efficiency among public sector than private sector banks. State Bank of India depicts lower percentage of input slack 33.69 as compared to other public sector banks of India depicting higher level of efficiency. Private sector Banks were at higher efficiency level than public sector banks because of less reliability on deposits for income generation accompanied by less number of employees and higher level of technological advancement.

Figure 6.13

Allocative Efficiency of Banks during 1998-99

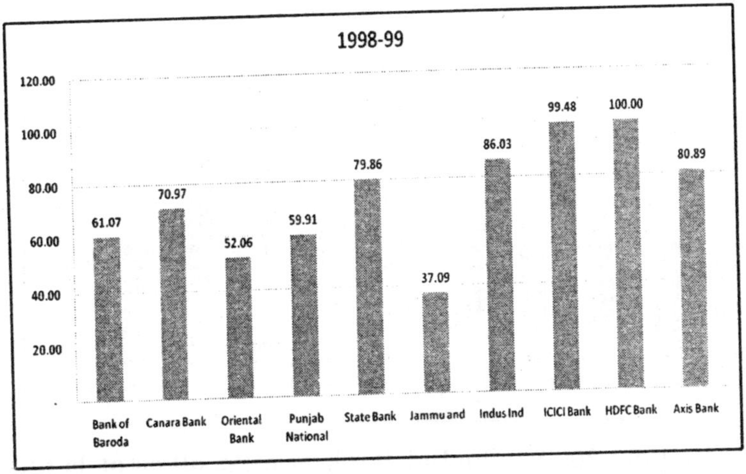

The figure 6.13 depicts that in the year 1998-99, HDFC secured allocative score of 100 percent efficiency with minimum input and maximum output followed by ICICI Bank at 99.48 percent, IndusInd Bank at 86.03 percent and Axis Bank 80.89 percent. The input slack percentage of HDFC Bank was 14.37 percent because of high operating expenses to non interest income but bank incurred low interest expenses to non interest income. ICICI Bank has input surplus of 14.82 percent because of higher interest expenses to non interest income. Among public sector banks efficiency scores of all banks had increased with State Bank of India leading the allocative efficiency score of 79.86 percent and input slack of 31.6 (table 6.3) percent followed by Canara Bank with efficiency score of 70.97 percent. The most inefficient bank was Jammu and Kashmir Bank with efficiency score of 37.09 percent and maximum input slack of 68.23 percent and second most inefficient bank was Oriental Bank of Commerce at efficiency level of 52.06 percent and input slack of 55.41 percent.

Figure 6.14

Allocative Efficiency of Banks during 1999-2000

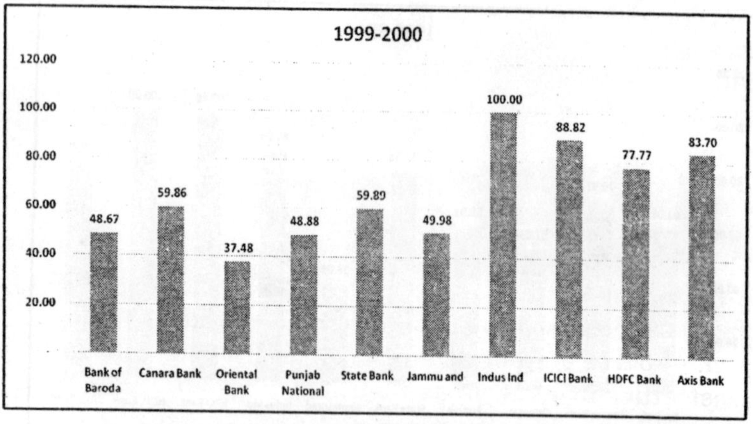

In 1999-2000 IndusInd Bank is most efficient bank followed by ICICI Bank (88.82 percent), Axis Bank (83.70 percent) and HDFC Bank (77.77 percent). Among public sector banks most efficient bank is State Bank of India (59.89 percent) and very close to it is Canara Bank with efficiency score of 59.86 percent.

Figure 6.15

Allocative Efficiency of Banks during 2000-01

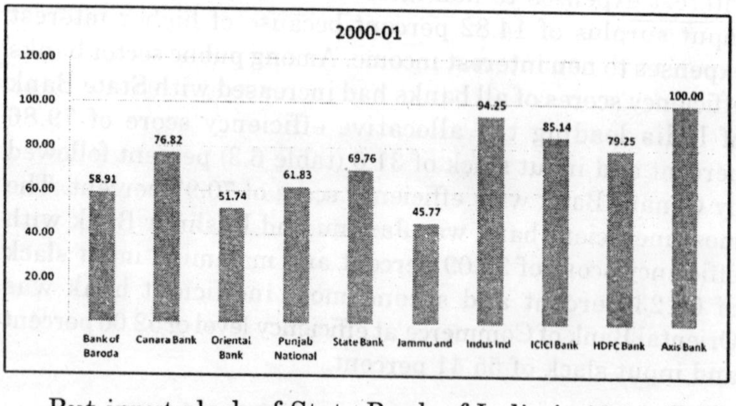

But input slack of State Bank of India is 29.23 (Table 6.2) percent and of Canara Bank is 30.91 percent. The most inefficient bank is Oriental Bank of Commerce and Jammu and Kashmir Bank with efficiency score of 37.48 and 49.98 percent. The input slack percentage of Oriental Bank of Commerce was 34.28 and 29.87 percent. Hence Oriental Bank of Commerce and Jammu and Kashmir Bank generated low level of non interest income by using more than 34.28 and 29.87 percent surplus inputs respectively.

In 2000-2001 Axis Bank secured highest score followed by IndusInd (94.25), ICICI Bank (85.14), and HDFC Bank (79.25). Among public sector banks most efficient bank is Canara Bank at efficiency level of 76.82 percent. Input slack of Canara Bank is 31.43 and State Bank of India with input slack of 37.74 percent at efficiency level of 69.76 percent. Least efficient bank is Jammu and Kashmir Bank and Oriental Bank of Commerce at efficiency level of 45.77 and 51.74 percent. Input slack percentage of least efficient banks with respect to most efficient bank is 59.14 and 53.82 percent respectively depicting more than 50 percent surplus inputs are used by Jammu and Kashmir Bank and Oriental Bank of Commerce to produce the same level of non interest income as generated by Axis Bank.

Figure 6.16

Allocative Efficiency of Banks during 2001-02

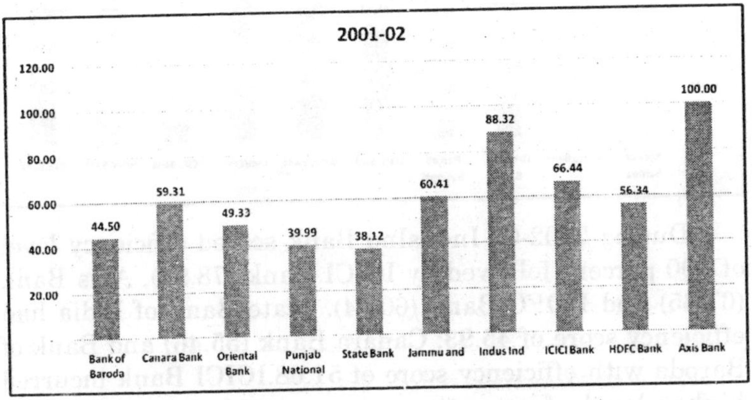

In 2001-02 Axis Bank acquired the position of most efficient bank while all other banks slipped on the level of efficiency because in year 2001-02 banking industry was in a transition phase. IndusInd Bank achieved efficiency score of 88.32 percent but ICICI Bank, HDFC Bank, State Bank of India and Canara Bank scored 66.44, 56.34, 38.12 and 59.31 percent respectively. In 2001-02 State Bank of India scored minimum because of Increase in interest expenses to 20729 crores from 21109 crores but resulted in marginal increase in non- interest income from 4018 crore to 4174 crore. Amongst public sector banks Canara Bank scored highest at 59.31 percent. Jammu and Kashmir Bank was the only bank which depicted decrease in interest expenses from 915 to 901 crores. Majority of banks have scored low level of efficiency because of high interest expenses incurred by these banks.

Figure 6.17

Allocative Efficiency of Banks during 2002-03

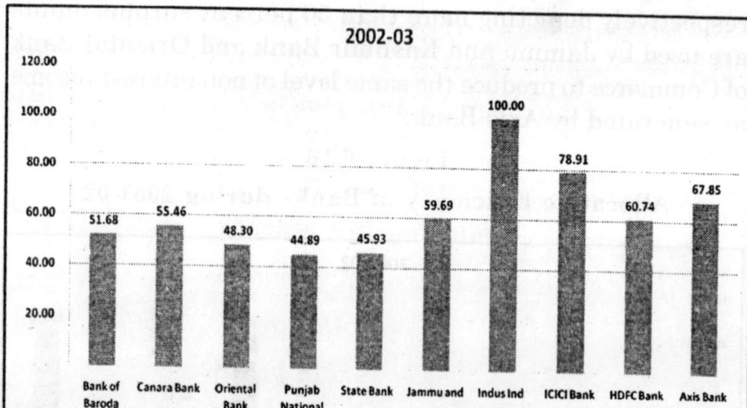

During 2002-03 IndusInd Bank scored efficiency level of 100 percent followed by ICICI Bank (78.91), Axis Bank (67.85) and HDFC Bank (60.74). State Bank of India had efficiency score of 45.93; Canara Bank (55.46) and Bank of Baroda with efficiency score of 51.68.ICICI Bank incurred higher level of operating expenses (2012) and interest expenses (7944) but still generated higher level of non interest income of 3159 crores. Similarly among public sector banks Canara Banks' operating expenses accounted for 1748 crores, interest expenses to 4425 crores and non interest income generated of 1478 crores, which is higher than all public sector banks except State Bank of India.

Figure 6.18

Allocative Efficiency of Banks during 2003-04

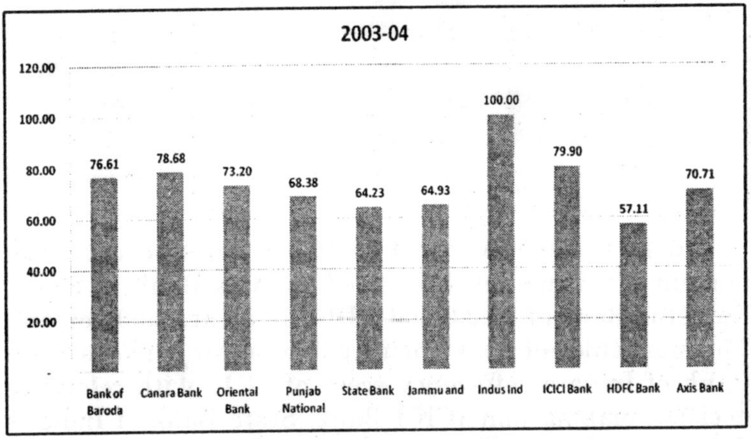

Financial year 2003-04 reflected positive trend in efficiency scores of public sector banks as IndusInd Bank acquired efficiency score of 100 percent followed by ICICI Bank at efficiency score of 79.90. Canara Bank scored 78.68 on efficiency scale followed by Bank of Baroda at 76.61. HDFC Bank scored 57.11 percent which makes it least efficient bank in 2003-04 because of high operating and interest expenses but low non interest income, the ratio of non interest income to operating expenses is minimum at 0.59 and input slack percentage of 42.89.

Jammu and Kashmir Bank and State Bank of India are other least efficient banks because of high Input slack percentage of 35.07 and 36.76 percent. Canara Bank is the most efficient bank among all other public sector banks with input slack percentage at 21.31 percent which is 1.22 percent higher than the second most efficient ICICI Bank.

Figure 6.19

Allocative Efficiency of Banks during 2004-05

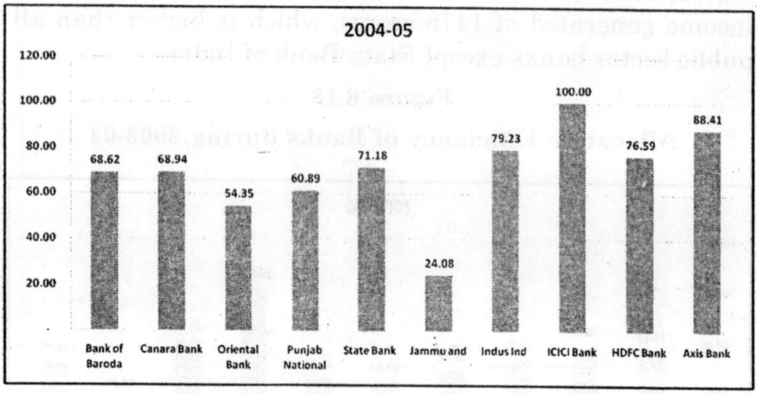

In financial year 2004-05 ICICI Bank secured 100 percent efficiency level followed by Axis Bank at 88.41, IndusInd Bank at 79.23, and HDFC Bank at 76.59 percent. The most efficient bank among public sector banks is State Bank of India at efficiency score of 71.18 with reference decision making unit ICICI Bank. State Bank of India is followed by Canara Bank and Bank of Baroda at 68.94 and 68.62 percent. The least efficient bank is Jammu and Kashmir Bank with efficiency score of 24.08 percent. The input slack percentage of Jammu and Kashmir Bank is 75.91 because of high ratio of operating expenses to non interest income as much as 71.23 percent and interest expenses to non interest income ratio 80.59 percent more than ICICI Bank for the same level of output.

The figure 6.18 depicts that the ICICI Bank has achieved 100 percent efficiency level in 2005-06 followed by HDFC Bank, Axis Bank and State Bank of India at efficiency score of 84.46, 79.18 and 63.22 percent. IndusInd Bank has shifted on a lower level of efficiency from 79.23 in 2004-05 to 57.44 percent in 2005-06. The least efficient bank is Jammu and Kashmir Bank at efficiency level of 29.93 percent. The input slack percentage of Jammu and Kashmir Bank is still high at 71.69 percent.

Figure 6.20

Allocative Efficiency of Banks during 2005-06

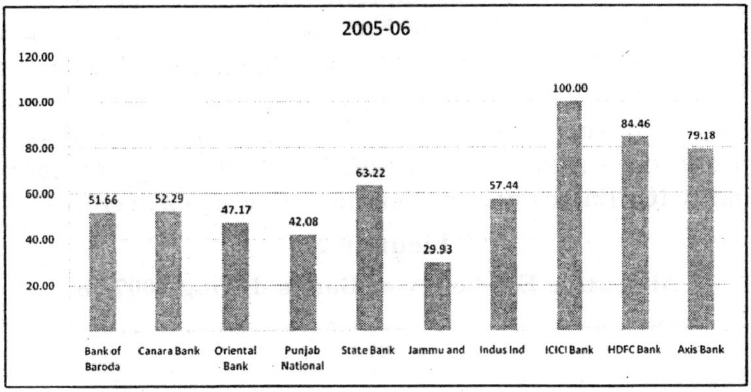

Second inefficient Bank in the order is Punjab National Bank at 60.20 percent input slack percentage and efficiency score of 42.08 percent because of decline in non- interest income of the bank from 1676 to 1231 crorc but increase in interest expenses of the bank from 4453 to 4917 crores in 2004-05 and 2005-06 respectively.

Figure 6.21

Allocative Efficiency of Banks during 2006-07

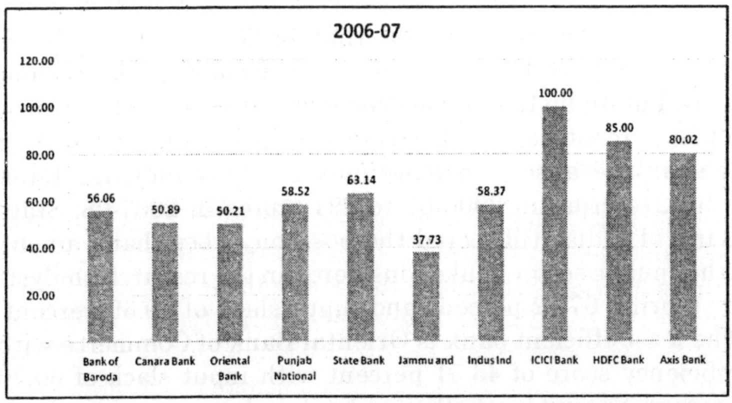

The figure 6.21 depicts that in 2006-07 also ICICI Bank scored efficiency rating of 100 percent followed by HDFC

Bank, Axis Bank and State Bank of India with efficiency score of 85, 80.02 and 63.14 percent respectively. Jammu and Kashmir Bank is least efficient bank at the score of 37.73 percent followed by Punjab National Bank because of high input slack percentage of number of employees (in thousands) of 89.78 percent as compared to ICICI Bank and deposits of the bank in surplus to 71.03 but non- interest income generated of Punjab National Bank was 1.042 crores and ICICI Bank's non interest income was 5.929 crores.

Figure 6.22

Allocative Efficiency of Banks during 2007-08

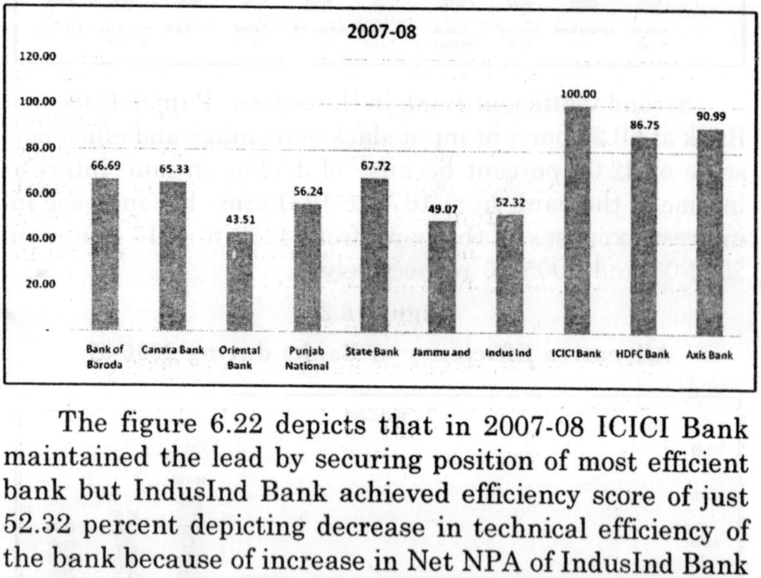

The figure 6.22 depicts that in 2007-08 ICICI Bank maintained the lead by securing position of most efficient bank but IndusInd Bank achieved efficiency score of just 52.32 percent depicting decrease in technical efficiency of the bank because of increase in Net NPA of IndusInd Bank from 274 crore in 2006-07 to 291 crores in 2007-08. State Bank of India still scored the position of best bank among other public sector banks considered in the research analysis by scoring 67.72 percent and input slack of 40.39 percent. The least efficient bank is Oriental Bank of Commerce with efficiency score of 43.51 percent with input slack of 60.76 percent. Second least efficient bank is Jammu and Kashmir Bank with efficiency score of 49.07 percent and input slack of 55.76 percent.

It can be concluded that during financial year 2004-05 till 2007-08 among all the banks considered in research analysis ICICI Bank has scored efficiency score of most efficient bank but prior to 2004-05 ICICI Bank secured second or third position in terms of efficiently utilizing inputs as interest expenses and operating expenses to produce output as non interest income. IndusInd performed better than ICICI Bank from 1997-98 to 2003-04 but gradually its performance has declined to the allocative efficiency score of 52.3the year 2 percent in 2007-08. However in the year 1998-99 HDFC Bank scored 100 percent but in 2001 and 2002 Axis Bank scored allocative efficiency score of 100 percent and IndusInd bank scored second position. Among public sector banks most efficient bank is the State Bank of India except in 2001, 2002, 2003 and 2004 during these years Canara Bank performed better than State Bank of India. The most inefficient public sector bank is Oriental Bank of Commerce and Private sector bank is Jammu and Kashmir Bank.

The change in ICICI Bank's technology strategy over the years has indeed brought a paradigm shift from what initially evolved as a purely computer support system to the today's technology executive as an essential cog in the wheels of business. This executive support system has resulted in better performance of ICICI Bank as compared to other competitors in the field of Banking Industry. On the other hand IndusInd Bank because of higher level of Net NPA, low level of growth of net profit at 10.02 percent, low level of Return on Assets at 0.22 in 2006, 0.34 percent in 2007 and 2008. These are few factors responsible for decline in allocative efficiency score of IndusInd Bank from most efficient bank to the efficiency score of 52.2 percent in the year 2008. State Bank of India with low level of Net NPA, higher level of investment in technology, higher Return on Assets and higher level of Net Profit are few factors responsible for improvement in performance of State Bank of India. Axis Bank and HDFC Bank are investing in technology and bringing innovation in products of the Bank promoting non-interest income for the bank. HDFC Bank has focused on retail deposits besides working with mutual funds, stock exchanges and also on tax collection for the government to ensure access to low cost funds.

6.2.3 OPERATIONAL EFFICIENCY

A salient aspect of the reforms process initiated in 1991 was the deregulation of the financial sector, which aimed at lowering intermediation costs and raise efficiency levels of the banking system, is still promoted because of globalization and introduction of technology in the banking arena. A crucial aspect of the intermediation process is the net interest margin which serves as a key factor of the efficiency of resource intermediation. The techno savvy market has resulted in increase in competition within banking sector. The emergence of disintermediation pressures from liberalized financial marketplace, the advent of 'Virtual' banking and the increasing product sophistication demanded by customers are responsible for both the decline in margins as well as their progressive convergence. Hence operational efficiency of banks is analyzed by using interest income as output variable with operating expenses and interest expenses as input variables. The table 7.23 depicts operational efficiency of ten banks considered in the research analysis during 1998 to 2008.

The table 6.5 depicts that the best performer is Jammu and Kashmir Bank with average efficiency score of 90 percent and above over the period of 1998 to 2008 and second in the order is Oriental Bank of Commerce at average efficiency score of more than 80 percent. The higher level of efficiency of Jammu and Kashmir Bank and Oriental Bank of Commerce is because of low operating expenses and marginal increase in interest expenses. Third bank in the efficiency score is IndusInd Bank. It is because of low operating expenses of Jammu and Kashmir Bank and IndusInd Bank. Because these two banks have a low level of wage bill as there is less number of employees and expenditure incurred

Table 6.5

Operational Efficiency of Banks

Banks	1998	1999	2000	2001	2002	2003	2004	2005	2006	2007	2008
Bank of Baroda	79.04	82.64	81.03	77.47	78.41	81.12	80.19	86.86	81.63	82.62	81
Canara Bank	75.59	81.1	75.5	75.69	77.67	81.77	80.66	87.3	86.96	89.29	86.29
Oriental Bank of Commerce	88.16	89.73	92.34	87.1	92.89	100	100	99.14	92	95.7	97.87
Punjab National Bank	76.56	80.42	74.98	74.83	79.86	85.64	82.85	79.56	86.88	86.4	85.19
State Bank of India	76.41	76.1	81.37	72.97	99.74	81.25	75.44	83.77	81.1	78.94	80.74
Jammu and Kashmir Bank	95.75	96.24	92.98	100	93.44	98.53	98.09	100	100	100	100
Indus Ind Bank	100	96.24	98.56	97.21	100	97.51	85.75	92.41	78.92	79.78	79.99
ICICI Bank	81.52	95.39	86.74	77.63	73.06	78.33	69.92	71.14	72.81	71.49	73.34
HDFC Bank	87.63	89.91	91.41	86.57	84.65	84.5	87.45	94.24	90.03	85.6	85.08
Axis Bank	88.25	100	100	90.68	83.18	80.6	96.87	67.56	82.43	79.56	76.29

on computerization is also very low as compared to other peer units. But after March end' 2005 IndusInd Bank has fallen on efficiency scale because of increase in non-performing assets of the bank.

HDFC Bank has maintained consistency in efficiency score over the empirical study period. State Bank of India is on lower level of efficiency because of higher operating expenses as State Bank of India has incurred huge expenditure on computerization and development of communication network as well as its huge employee force increases operating expenses of the bank. ICICI Bank is on lower level of efficiency because of greater reliance on non-interest income and higher level of operating expenses and interest expenses. Canara Bank's operating expenses is less than Punjab National Bank, State Bank of India, and Bank of Baroda so it secures higher level of efficiency ranking among other public sector banks but it has been ranked at lower level than Oriental Bank of Commerce because of higher input slack percentage with respect to the reference unit.

It can be concluded that interest spreads tend to be affected by the amount of non-interest income being earned by a bank. It is because of this ICICI Bank scores the efficiency score of 100 percent in terms of non- interest income as output but it gets least efficient score when interest income is considered as output. On the other hand Jammu and Kashmir Bank has secured last position in terms of technical efficiency with output Non Interest Income and best bank score in terms of Interest Income as output. State Bank of India despite its huge elephant size has maintained creditable position in terms of Interest Income and Non Interest Income as output among other public sector banks considered in empirical analysis.

6.3 PUBLIC SECTOR BANKS: EFFICIENCY LEVEL

It can be concluded that Public Sector Banks have scored least for technical efficiency. It may be because of public sector banks are having surplus of employees and higher level of deposits as compared to private sector banks but generate lower level of non-interest income. Allocative efficiency score of public sector banks is better than technical efficiency score and operational efficiency score of public sector banks is better than private sector banks. The table 6.6 depicts group wise efficiency score of each bank during the period of 1998-2008.

Table 6.6

Group Wise Efficiency Levels - Public Sector Banks

Public Sector Bank - Group Wise Efficiency Levels												
Bank Group	**Efficiency Levels**											
	Efficiency Type	1998	1999	2000	2001	2002	2003	2004	2005	2006	2007	2008
1	2	3	4	5	6	7	8	9	10	11	12	13
Bank of Baroda	Technical (Non Interest Income	20.13	36.98	32.63	42.19	29.29	20.59	35.76	32.35	32.58	26.91	31.34
	Allocative (Non Interest Income)	36.43	61.07	48.67	58.91	44.50	51.68	76.61	68.62	51.66	56.06	66.69
	Operational (w.r.t. Interest Income)	79.04	82.64	81.03	77.47	78.41	81.12	80.19	86.86	81.63	82.62	81.00
Canara Bank	Technical (Non Interest Income	23.29	43.94	41.98	50.38	39.56	21.75	29.68	31.90	30.76	28.61	31.21
	Allocative (Non Interest Income)	43.26	70.97	59.86	76.82	59.31	55.46	78.68	68.94	52.29	50.89	65.33
	Operational (w.r.t. Interest Income)	75.59	81.10	75.50	75.69	77.67	81.77	80.66	87.30	86.96	89.29	86.29
Oriental Bank of Commerce	Technical (Non Interest Income	15.66	30.28	25.29	36.88	32.06	21.05	34.28	24.57	32.97	29.82	20.61
	Allocative (Non Interest Income)	29.95	52.06	37.48	51.74	49.33	48.30	73.20	54.35	47.17	50.21	43.51
	Operational (w.r.t. Interest Income)	88.16	89.73	92.34	87.10	92.89	100.00	100.00	99.14	92.00	95.70	97.87
Punjab National Bank	Technical (Non Interest Income	26.05	36.49	36.60	43.99	26.32	16.83	30.64	31.32	27.68	19.59	24.88
	Allocative (Non Interest Income)	44.05	59.91	48.88	61.83	39.99	44.89	68.38	60.89	42.08	58.52	56.24
	Operational (w.r.t. Interest Income)	76.56	80.42	74.98	74.83	79.86	86.64	82.85	79.56	86.88	86.40	85.19
State Bank of India	Technical (Non Interest Income	30.98	53.70	43.64	53.24	27.19	20.23	34.71	37.48	49.98	34.49	33.64
	Allocative (Non Interest Income)	48.99	79.86	59.89	69.76	38.12	45.93	64.23	71.18	63.22	63.14	67.72
	Operational (w.r.t. Interest Income)	76.41	76.10	81.37	72.97	99.74	81.25	75.44	83.77	81.10	78.94	80.74

The above table 6.6 depicts that all public sector banks are scoring technical efficiency score within range of 20-40 but only State Bank of India is scoring technical efficiency score of more than 40.The most technically efficient bank over the research period among five public sector banks is State Bank of India and technically least efficient bank is Oriental Bank of Commerce.

In terms of allocative efficiency score public sector banks are scoring efficiency score within range of 30-80. Allocative efficiency score of Oriental Bank of Commerce has improved over the years. Bank of Baroda and State Bank of India are better performers in terms of allocative efficiency. Operational efficiency score of five public sector banks is within the range of 70 to 100 percent. It depicts public sector banks still has a greater reliance on interest income as compared to non-interest income. It is noteworthy that Oriental Bank of Commerce has the highest score among all other public sector banks considered in research analysis.

6.4 PRIVATE SECTOR BANKS: EFFICIENCY LEVEL

It can be concluded that Private Sector Banks have scored least for operational efficiency. It may be because of private sector banks are relying more on fee based income and less on interest income.

It depicts higher level of diversification in private sector banks than public sector banks. At the same time private sector banks have higher level of techno-savvy employees and technological progress. This helps banks to generate higher level of non-interest income.The most technically efficient private sector banks are IndusInd Bank and ICICI Bank during the research period. Allocative efficiency score of private sector banks is within the range of 36 to 100 percent.

The least efficient bank in terms of allocative efficiency among private sector banks is Jammu and Kashmir Bank Ltd. The table 6.25 given below depicts group wise efficiency score of each bank during the period of 1998-2008.

Table 6.7: Group Wise Efficiency Levels - Private Sector Banks

Public Sector Bank - Group Wise Efficiency Levels												
Bank Group	Efficiency Levels											
	Efficiency Type	1998	1999	2000	2001	2002	2003	2004	2005	2006	2007	2008
1	2	3	4	5	6	7	8	9	10	11	12	13
Bank of Baroda	Technical (Non Interest Income	20.13	36.98	32.63	42.19	29.29	20.59	35.76	32.35	32.58	26.91	31.34
	Allocative (Non Interest Income)	36.43	61.07	48.67	58.91	44.50	51.68	76.61	68.62	51.66	56.06	66.69
	Operational (w.r.t. Interest Income)	79.04	82.64	81.03	77.47	78.41	81.12	80.19	86.86	81.63	82.62	81.00
Canara Bank	Technical (Non Interest Income	23.29	43.94	41.98	50.38	39.56	21.75	29.68	31.90	30.76	28.61	31.21
	Allocative (Non Interest Income)	43.26	70.97	59.86	76.82	59.31	55.46	78.68	68.94	52.29	50.89	65.33
	Operational (w.r.t. Interest Income)	75.59	81.10	75.50	75.69	77.67	81.77	80.66	87.30	86.96	89.29	86.29
Oriental Bank of Commerce	Technical (Non Interest Income	15.66	30.28	25.29	36.88	32.06	21.05	34.28	24.57	32.97	29.82	20.61
	Allocative (Non Interest Income)	29.95	52.06	37.48	51.74	49.33	48.30	73.20	54.35	47.17	50.21	43.51
	Operational (w.r.t. Interest Income)	88.16	89.73	92.34	87.10	92.89	100.00	100.00	99.14	92.00	95.70	97.87
Punjab National Bank	Technical (Non Interest Income	26.05	36.49	36.60	43.99	26.32	16.83	30.64	31.32	27.68	19.59	24.88
	Allocative (Non Interest Income)	44.05	59.91	48.88	61.83	39.99	44.89	68.38	60.89	42.08	58.52	56.24
	Operational (w.r.t. Interest Income)	76.56	80.42	74.98	74.83	79.36	86.64	82.85	79.56	86.88	86.40	85.19
State Bank of India	Technical (Non Interest Income	30.98	53.70	43.64	53.24	27.19	20.23	34.71	37.48	49.98	34.49	33.64
	Allocative (Non Interest Income)	48.99	79.86	59.89	69.76	38.12	45.93	64.23	71.18	63.22	63.14	67.72
	Operational (w.r.t. Interest Income)	76.41	76.10	81.37	72.97	99.74	81.25	75.44	83.77	81.10	78.94	80.74

6.5 DEA EFFICIENCIES OF PUBLIC AND PRIVATE SECTOR BANKS USING A THREE YEAR WINDOW ANALYSIS

The technical, allocative and operational efficiency has been compared by data envelopment analysis, of each bank in a particular period of time. Further attempt has been made to compare performance of banks over time, is referred to as a Time Series Analysis. The variations of efficiency of banks over time can help in making important conclusions. The statistical technique used is Window Analysis. Three window analyses is a moving average pattern of analysis. A bank in each period is treated as if it is a different decision making unit. The performance of a decision making unit (bank) is compared with its performance in other periods, in addition comparing it with the performance of other banks in the same time period.

The performance of ten banks, Bank of Baroda, Canara Bank, Oriental Bank of Commerce, Punjab National Bank and State Bank of India and five private sector banks Jammu and Kashmir Bank, HDFC Bank, ICICI Bank, IndusInd Bank and Axis Bank over a period of 1997-98 to 2007-08 is compared using a three- year 'Window' (the analog of 'moving average' in traditional time series econometric analysis). *Three Window Analysis* presentations facilitate an easy comparison of the performance of a bank over time as well as comparison with its competitors at particular point in time. The bank-wise technical and allocative efficiency of banks selected is analyzed.

6.5.1 Technical Efficiency of Banks using Three Window Analyses

Bank of Baroda

The performance of Bank of Baroda is reflected in the graph based on technical efficiency parameters. It is clear that over year's efficiency score of Bank of Baroda has improved from 20.13 percent in 1998 to 30.28 percent in 2008.

Figure 6.23: Technical Efficiency

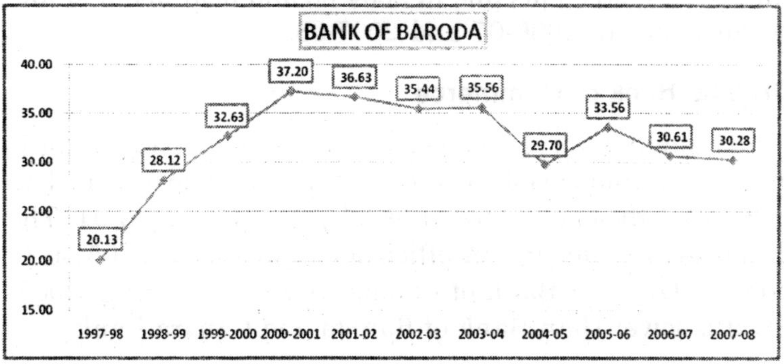

The graph 6.23 depicts that Bank of Baroda has achieved a relatively higher level of technical efficiency from 1997-98 to 2003-04 but in 2004-05 it slipped to 29.70 percent. A financial year 2006-07 and 2007-08 depicts almost steady performance of the bank.

Canara Bank

In terms of Technical efficiency Canara Bank has performed better than Bank of Baroda till 2003-04 but scored relatively less than than Bank of Baroda in 2004-05 and 2005-06. Both public sector banks were at marginal difference in 2006-07 and 2007-08.

Graph 6.24: Technical Efficiency

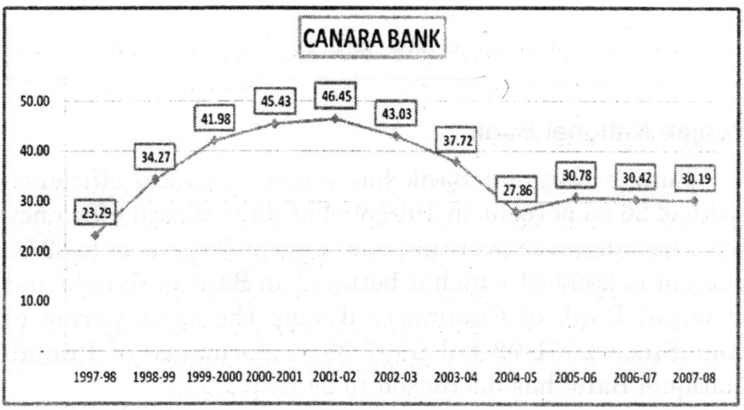

Common trend visible is increase in technical efficienct till 2003-04, steep decline in 2004-05 and near about stable performance in 2006-07 and 2007-08.

Oriental Bank of Commerce

Oriental Bank of Commerce scored 15.66 percent in 1997-98 but has improved over the years and had reached to technical efficiency score of 36.27 percent in 2003-04. The graph depicts decline in efficiency scores from 2005-06 to 2007-08.Oriental Bank of Commerce scored 27.80 in 2007-08, it is lower than Bank of Baroda and Canara Bank.

Graph 6.25
Technical Efficiency

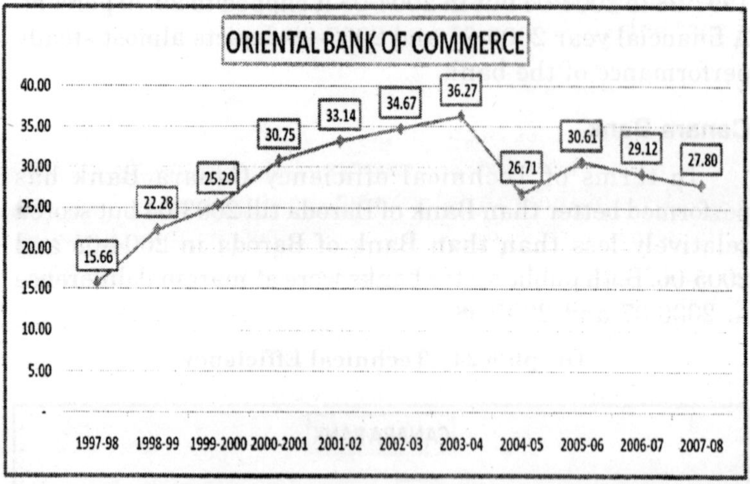

Punjab National Bank

Punjab National Bank has scored technical efficiency score of 26.05 percent in 1997-98 but its technical efficiency score has improved over the years from 26.05 percent to 39.08 percent in 2000-01 which is better than Bank of Baroda and Oriental Bank of Commerce during the same period of time.Since 2001-02 till 2007-08 performance of Punjab National Bank has decreased to 24.05 percent.

Graph 6.26

Technical Efficiency

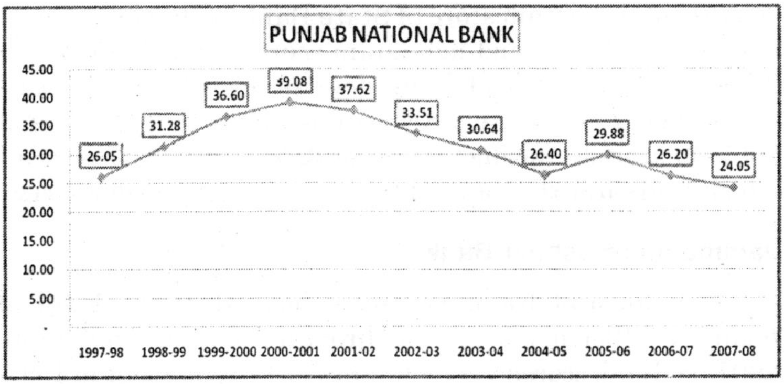

Punjab National Bank was the leat efficienct bank during 2006-07 and 2007-08 as comapred to its competitior public sector banks.

State Bank of India

Performance of State Bank of India is better than all other public sector banks considered in empirical anlysis. State Bank of India in 1997-98 achieved efficiecny score of 30.98 percent while Bank of Baroda scored 20.13, Canara Bank scored 23.29,Oriental Bank of Commerce 15.66 and Punjab Natioanl Bank scroed 26.05 percent.

Graph 6.27

Technical Efficiency

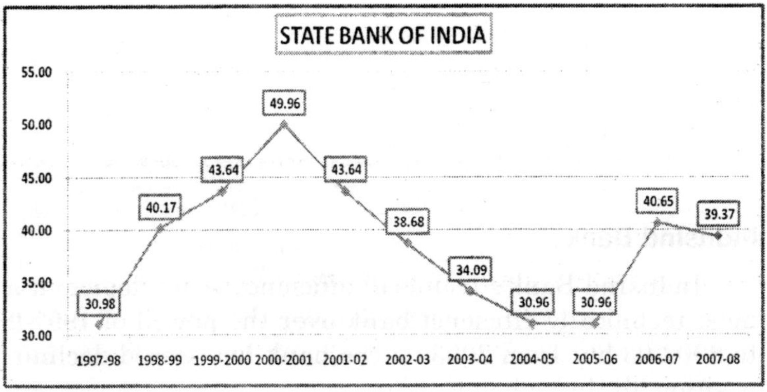

Not only this over the period of eleven years from 1997-98 to 2007-08 State Bank of India always scored more than 30 percent, minimum score of State Bank of India was 34.09 percent in 2003-04 and maximum score of 49.96 percent in 2000-01. State Bank of India depicts decline in efficiency score from 2001 -02 to 2004-05 but again in 2006-07 and 2007-08 scored efficiency score of 40.65 and 39.37 percent which is greater than all public sector banks of sample size.

Jammu and Kashmir Bank

Jammu and Kashmir Bank depicts lower level of technical efficiency score all through out from 1997-98 to 2007-08. Bank scored very low score of 17.23 percent in 1997-98 and similarly lowest score over maximum time period depciting least technically efficient bank.Highest technical efficiency score of Jammu and Kashmir Bank is 36.45 percent.Jammu and Kashmir Bank has shown downward trend in technical efficiency score not only in absolute term but also in relative term over the study period.

Graph 6.28: Technical Efficiency

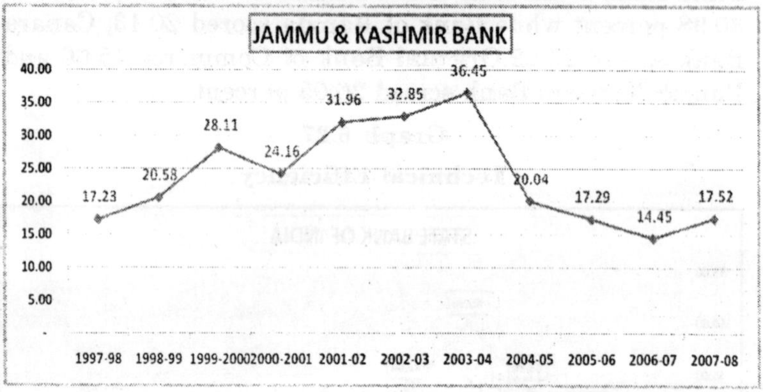

IndusInd Bank

IndusInd Bank's technical efficiency score depicts it as most technically efficienct bank over the period of 1997-98 to 2002-03 but from 2003-04 the bank has scored declining position all through out.

Figure 6.29: Technical Efficiency

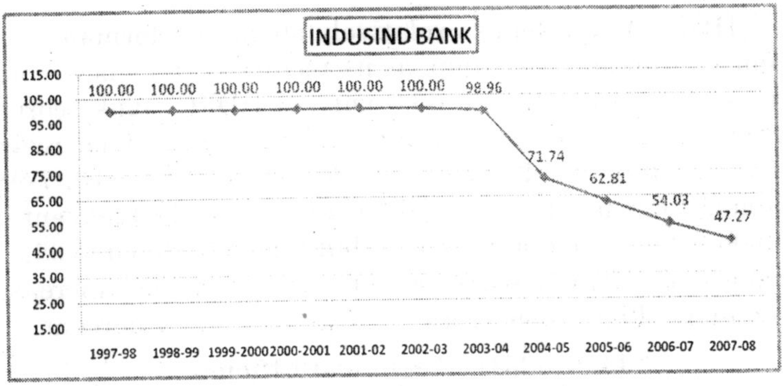

The Bank shows huge deviation in its technical efficiecny score from 100 percent to 47.27 percent in 2007-08 depicting highly inconsistent performance of Indus Ind Bank.

ICICI Bank

ICICI Bank's technical efficiency score is just opposite of its competitior Indus Ind Bank. ICICI Bank scored 60.53 percent in 1997-98 and has scored higher level of technical efficiency score of 64.16 in 1998-99, 69.92 in 1999-2000, 64.66 in 2001. During fianancial year 2001-02 ICICI Bank recorded technical efficiency score of 57.94 percent. From 2003-04 till 2007-08 ICICI Bank has scored the position of the best techncially efficient bank amongst all its peer group considered in empirical analysis.

Figure 6.30: Technical Efficiency

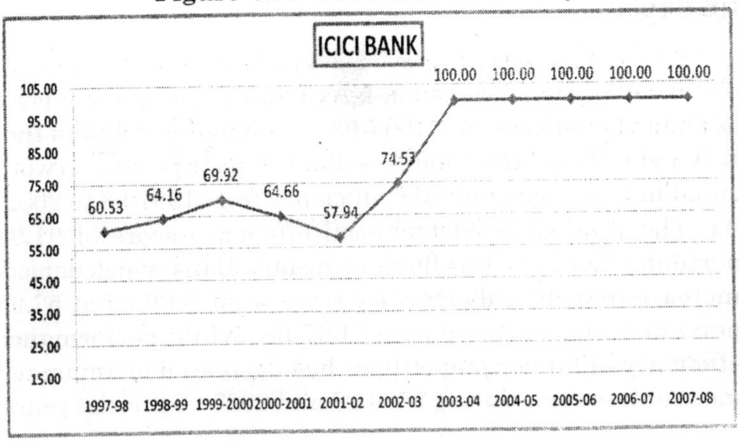

HDFC Bank

HDFC Bank depicts relatively steady performance as compared to its peer group, as its technical efficiency score ranges between 44.52 to 63.0 percent.HDFC Bank scored maximum techncially efficient score in 2000-01 at 63 percent and minimum in 2004-05 at 38.43 percent.In 1997-98 technical efficiency score of HDFC Bank was 49.61 percent,it reached to 63 percent in 2000-01 but finally declined to 38.43 percent in 2004-05. Since 2005-06 the bank depicts increase in technical efficiency score from 48.07 to 57.01 percent.

Figure 6.31 : Technical Efficiency

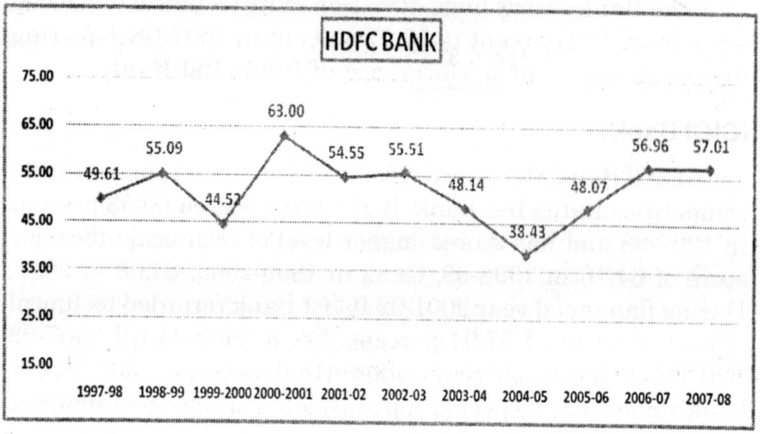

AXIS Bank

Axis Bank has improved over the years in terms of technical efficieny of the bank.Axis Bank had a lower level of technical efficiency in 1997-98 as compared to Indus Ind, ICICI and HDFC Bank but Axis Bank depicts positive grwoth trend in terms of technically efficiency from 1997-98 to 2002-03. The Banks scored technical efficiency score of 91.92 percent in 2002-03.Axis Bank is the only Bank which depicts increase in technical efficiency score from 2006-07 at 57.93 percent to 62.70 percent in 2007-08, while performance efficiency of all its competitiors has decreased or remained more or less same during 2006-07 and 2007-08 finacial years.

On a a comparative analysis of technical efficiency growth path between 1997-98 and 2007-08 of ten banks selected in the research study.It can be concluded through three window analyses that among public sector banks Bank of Baroda, Canara Bank, Oriental Bank of Commerce and State Bank of India has made progress over the time period though marginally but still there is increase in efficiency score. Punjab National Bank reflects marginal decrease in technical efficiency growth. Among private sector banks Indus bank reflects a huge decline in technical efficiency score from 100 percent in 1997-98 to 47.27 percent in 2007-08.ICICI Bank reveals progress in technical efficiency score from 60.53 in 1997-98 to 100 percent in 2007-08.

Figure 6.32: Technical Efficiency

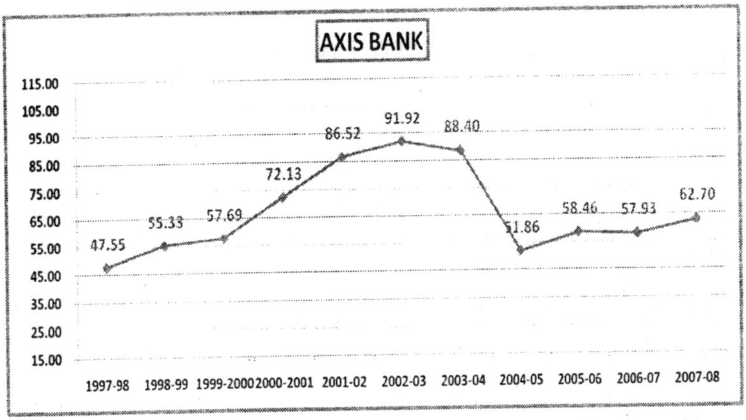

In the graph 6.32 HDFC Bank and Axis Bank reflects increase in technical efficiency score from 1997-98 to 2007-08 by 14.9 percent and 31.86 percent respectively it is note worthy that. Jammu and Kashmir bank has maintained a lowest level of relative technical efficiency and its absolute technical efficiency has decreased from 17.23 to 17.52 percent.

6.3 ALLOCATIVE EFFICIENCY: THREE WINDOW ANALYSES

Bank of Baroda

Bank of Baroda reflects 36.43 percent allocative efficiency in financial year 1997-98. The Bank depicts increasing allocative efficiency score over the period of 1998 to 2000-01 at 60.17 percent but is less than Canara Bank, State Bank of India and Punjab National Bank over the same time period. Again from 2001-02 allocative efficiency score of Bank of Baroda depicts growth in absolute terms from 53.61 percent to 70.52 percent in 2004-05 but in relative terms it is less than Canara Bank at72.73 percent.In 2006-07 and 2007-08 Bank of Baroda scored allocative efficiency score of 58.78 and 58.14 Percent, is higher than Canara Bank, Punjab National Bank and Oriental Bank of Commerce.

Figure 6.33
Allocative Efficiency

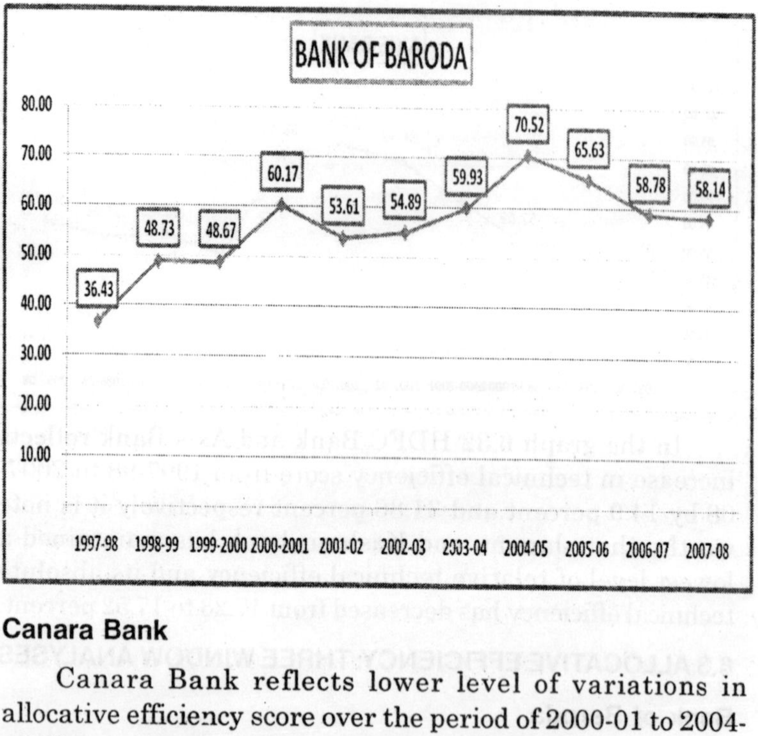

Canara Bank

Canara Bank reflects lower level of variations in allocative efficiency score over the period of 2000-01 to 2004-05. Canara Bank performed better during 2000-01 to 2004-05 than Bank of Baroda, Punjab National Bank, Oriental

Bank of Commerce and State Bank of India.In financial year 2005-06 State Bank of India and Canara Bank were almost at par in terms of allocative efficiency but in 2006-07 and 2007-08 allocative efficiency score of the bank slipped to 57.37 and 56.17 percent respectively. Hence Canara Bank's allocative efficiency score was less than Bank of Baroda and State Bank of India in financial year 2007 and 2008.

Figure 6.34

Allocative Efficiency

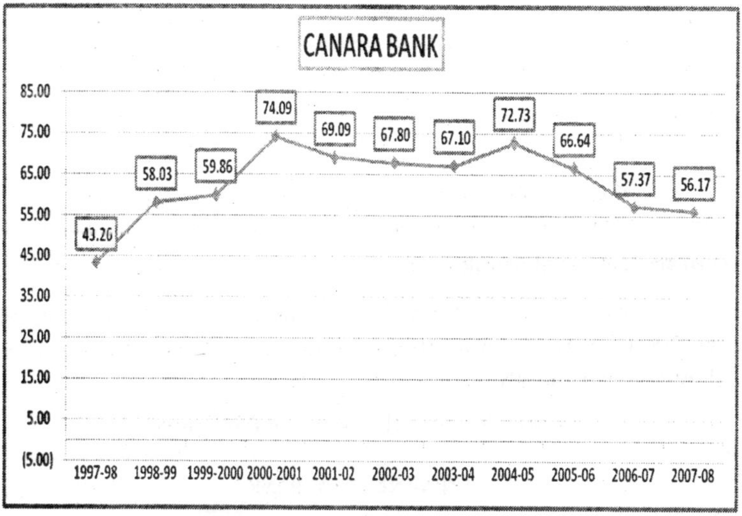

Oreintal Bank of Commerce

Oriental Bank of Commerce scored minimum allocative efficiency score of 29.95 percent in 1997-98 and has shown almost continuous growth in allocative efficiency score till 2004-05. The bank reached to allocative efficiency score of 62.98 percentin financial year 2005 but still less than Bank of Baroda, Canara Bank, State Bank of India though marginally greater than Punjab National Bank over the same time period.The Oriental Bank of Commerce performed at the lower level of allocative efficiency in absolute terms and at least efficienct level among all other selected public sector banks at50.58 and 46.97 percent in 2006-07 and 2007-08 respectively.

Figure 6.35: Allocative Efficiency

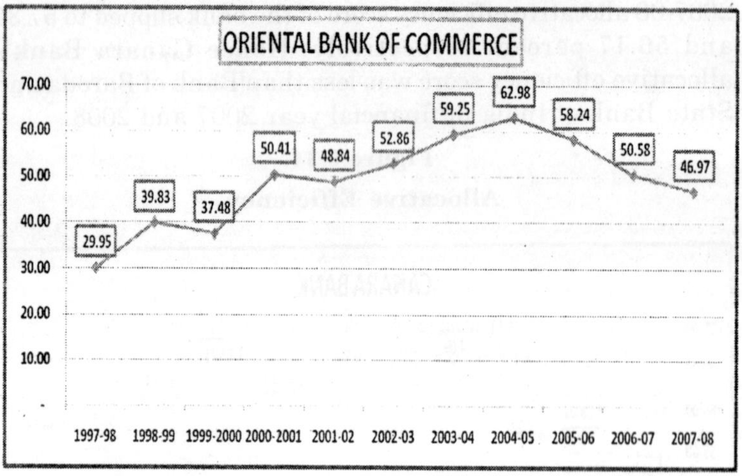

Punjab National Bank

Punjab National Bank performed at peak in 2000-01 and 2004-05 at 60.88 and 62.37 percent in absolute terms of allocative efficiency.

Figure 6.36: Allocative Efficiency

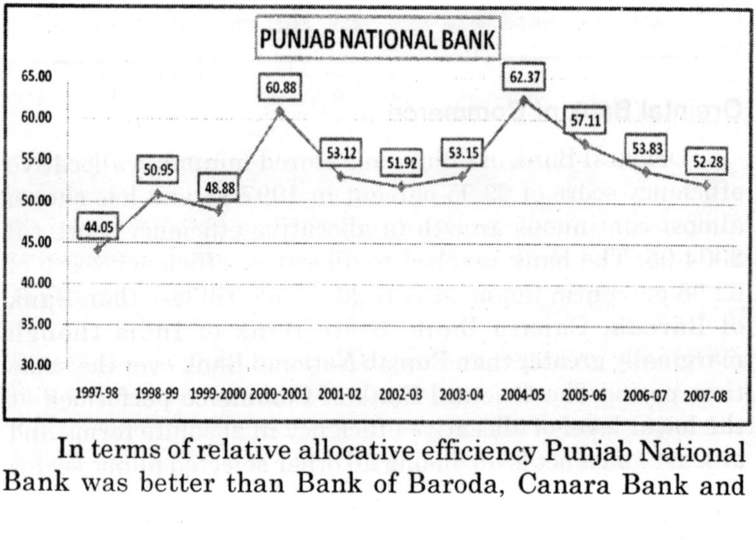

In terms of relative allocative efficiency Punjab National Bank was better than Bank of Baroda, Canara Bank and

Oriental Bank of Commerce in 1997-98 but gradually performance of other banks have increased at a higher rate than Punjab National Bank except Oriental Bank of Commerce. The graph reflects a trough in allocative efficiency score of Punjab National Bank during 2001-02, 2002-03 and 2003-04. The bank scored less than Bank of Baroda, Canara Bank, State Bank of India but greater than Oriental Bank of Commerce in 2007-08 at 52.28 percent.

State Bank of India

State Bank of India is the best bank among all other public sector banks included in sample. In 1997-98 allocative efficiency score of State Bank of India was 48.99 percent,in terms of relative allocative efficency State Bank of India achieved highest scroe with respect to its competitors Bank of Baroda, Canara Bank, Oriental Bank of Commerce and Punjab National Bank.State Bank of India reflects a trough in its performance during 2001-02 to 2003-04 and has scored less than Canara Bank during a particular period of time.Bank depicts higher level of allocative efficiency score during 2004-05 to 2007-08 in absolute terms as well as in relative terms to other public sector banks at 64.94, 66.21, 65.84 and 64.69 percent respectively.

Figure 6.37 : Allocative Efficiency

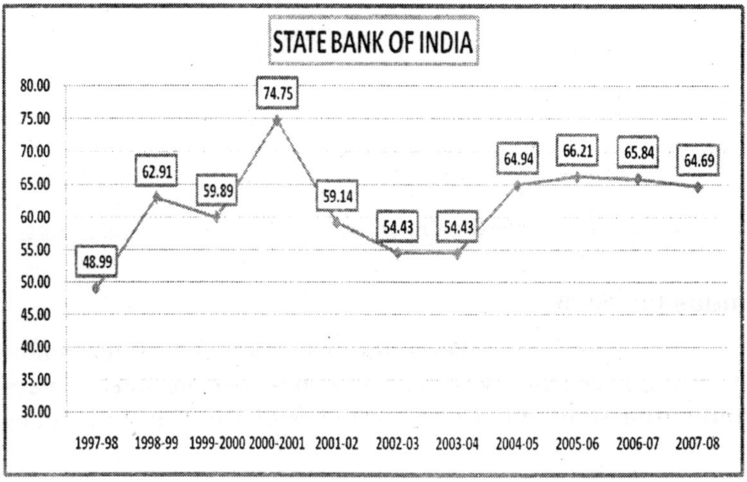

Jammu and Kashmir Bank

Jammu and Kashmir Bank depicts huge fluctuations in its allocative efficeicny score from 36.86 percent in 1997-98 to 64.17 percent in 2003-04 and form 64.17 percent to sudden decrease in efficeicny score to almost 50 percent less at 39.65 percentin financial year 2004-05 as well as in 2005-06. Jammu and Kashmir Bank shows further decline in efficiency score to 30.58 and 38.91 in 2006-07 and 2007-08 respectively. The bank reflects abnormal trend of increase in allocative efficiency score during 2001 to 2004 because almost all banks during this period reflects decreasing trend in efficeicny score but Jammu and Kashmir Bank reflcets positive trend in this particular period.Indus Ind and Jammu and Kashmir Bank have both scored same lowest ranking in 2006-07 and 2007-08.

Figure 6.38

Allocative Efficiency

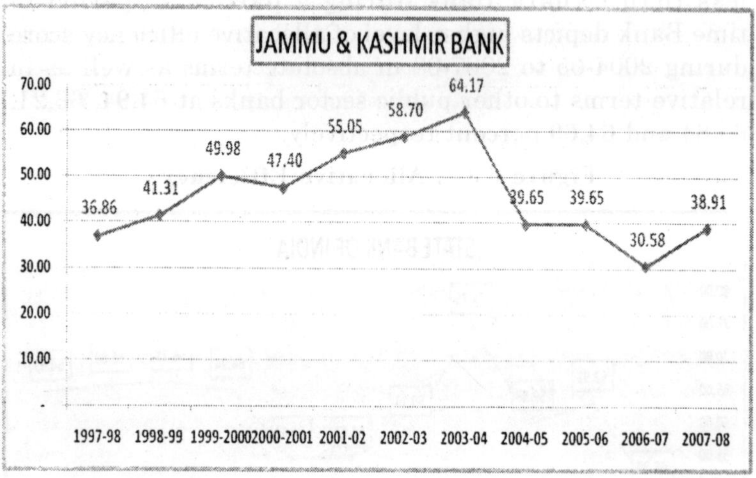

Indus Ind Bank

Indus Ind Bank reflects huge variation in its performance over the study period of eleven years. During initial years Indus Ind Bank dominated in terms of allocative efficiency score by scoring 100 percent consecutively over the period of 1997-98, 1998-99 and 1999-2000. But the bank depicts decrease in efficiency score over 2000-01 and 2001-02 and 2002-03 by scoring 97.42, 99.60 and 94.1 percent respectively.During finacial year 2000-01 and 2001-02 ICICI Bank scored 100 percent.As well as during 2002-03 Axis Bank scored 100 percent allocative efficiency score. The Bank depicts complete downfall from 100 percent in 2003-04 to 38.91 percent in 2007-08 which is at par with Jammu and Kashmir Bank and secured least efficient position amongst its peer group.

Figure 6.39

Allocative Efficiency

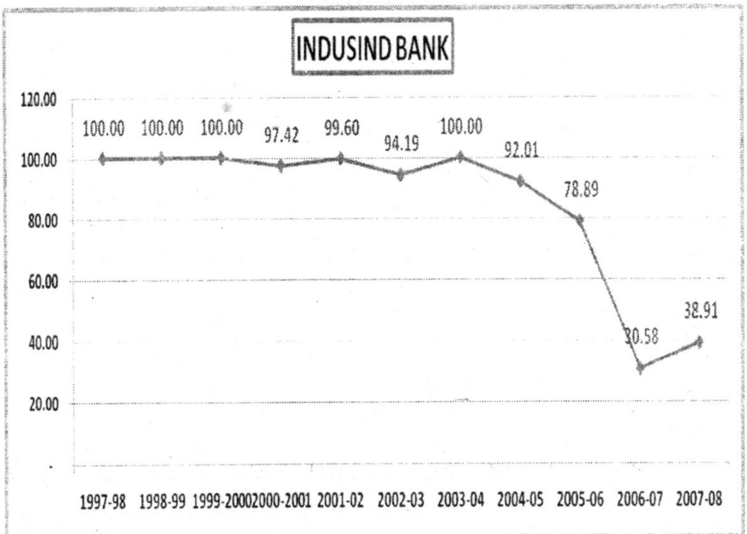

ICICI Bank

ICICI Bank has performed the best over the period of 2003-04 to 2007-08 in terms of allocative efficiency than its peer group. In 1997-98 ICICI Bank scored allocative efficiency score of 96.37 percent and secured second position to Indus Ind Bank.

The same trend continued in 1998-99 and 1999-2000 as ICICI Bank scored 94.89 percent and 88.82 percent respectively while Indus Ind Bank scored efficiency score of 100 percent in both the years.During 2001-02 and 2002-03 ICICI Bank scored 84.74 and 78.13 percent at a lower allocative efficiency score than Axis Bank and Indus Ind Bank.During 2003-04 to 2007-08 ICICI Bank has maintained a position of most efficient bank by scoring 100 percent all through out.

Figure 6.40

Allocative Efficiency

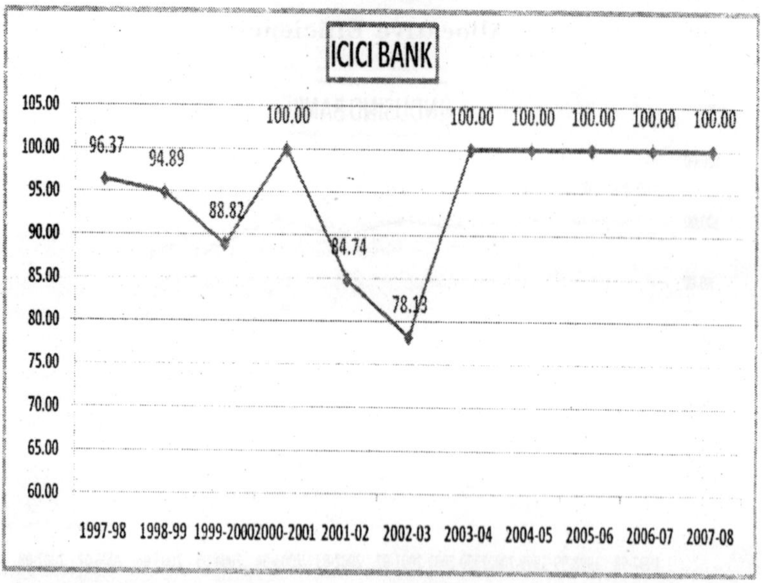

HDFC Bank

HDFC Bank scored allocative efficiency score of 81.40, 86.39 percent in 1997-98 and 1998-99 respectively, is greater than Axis Bank and Jammu and Kashmir Bank over the same time period. HDFC Bank scored third position in 2000-2001 by scoring efficiency score of 91.70 percent and ICICI Bank scored 100 percent while Indus Ind Bank scored 97.42 percent. During the period of 2001-02, 2002-03 and 2003-

04 HDFC Bank depicts decreasing trend in efficiency from 75.20, 69.48 to finally 60.42 percent respectively. The Bank has shown continuous increase in allocative efficiency score over the time period 2003-04 to 2007-08. HDFC Bank 's allocative efficiency score reflects its progress path over the period of 2003-04 to 2007-08. The HDFC Bank secured higher position than Axis Bank over the period of 2007-08. The Bank reflects peak in 1998-99, 2000-01 and 2007-08 and trough in 1999-2000 and 2003-04.

Figure 6.41

Allocative Efficiency

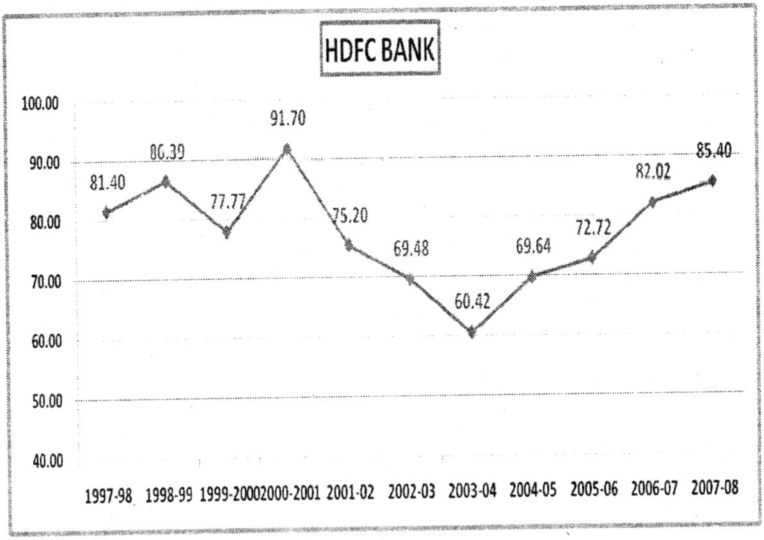

Axis Bank

Axis Bank scored allocative efficiency score of 74.79, 79.79 percent in 1997-98 and 1998-99 but at a lower level than Indus Ind Bank, ICICI Bank and HDFC Bank though greater than Jammu and Kashmir Bank. Axis Bank could achieve the position of most efficient bank in 2001-02 and 2002-03 but has shown continuous decline in allocative efficiency score over the period of 2003-04, 2004-05 and 2005-06 at 82.74, 81.28 and 79.43 percent respectively.The bank has improved over the period of 2006-07 and 2007-08 by scoring allocative efficiency score of 82.53 and 83.40 percent respectively.

On a a comparative analysis of allocative efficiency growth path between 1997-98 and 2007-08 of ten banks selected in the research study.It can be concluded through three window analyses that that all public sector banks have made progress in allocative efficiency score from 1997-98 to 2007-08. It is evident from the figure 7.43 that there is increase in absolute allocative efficiency score of Bank of Baroda in 2007-08 is 37.34, Canara Bank is 29.84, 56.82 of Oriental Bank of Commerce, and 18.68 of Punjab National Bank also of State Bank of India by 32.04 percent.

Figure 6.42: Allocative Efficiency

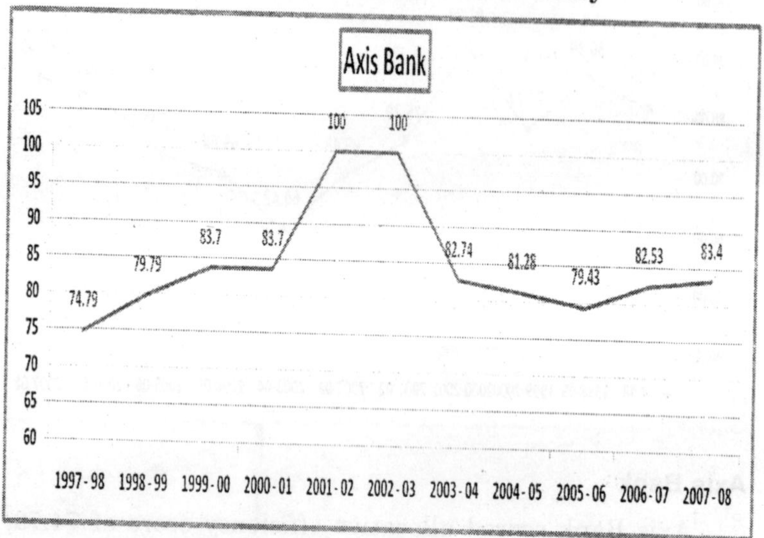

Among private sector banks Indus bank reflects a huge decline in allocative efficiency score from 100 percent in 1997-98 to 56.04 percent in 2007-08.ICICI Bank reveals progress in allocative efficiency score from 96.37 in 1997-98 to 100 percent in 2007-08.HDFC Bank and Axis Bank reflects increase in allocative efficiency score by 4.93 percent and 11.51 percent respectively.

Figure 6.43 : A Trend of Tehnical Efficiency : Three Window Analysis

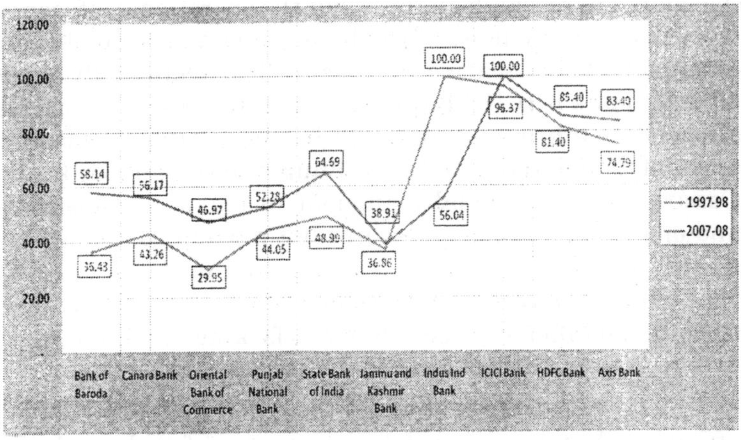

Jammu and Kashmir bank has maintained a lowest level of relative allocative efficiency but its absolute allocative efficiency has increased marginally from 36.86 to 38.91 percent.

6.4 OVERALL PERFORMANCE OF BANKS

Overall Performance of ten banks in terms of technical (model1), allocative (model 2) and operational (model3) efficiency is depicted in the figure 6.44.

Figure 6. 43: Trend Efficiency Growth of Banks during 1998-2008

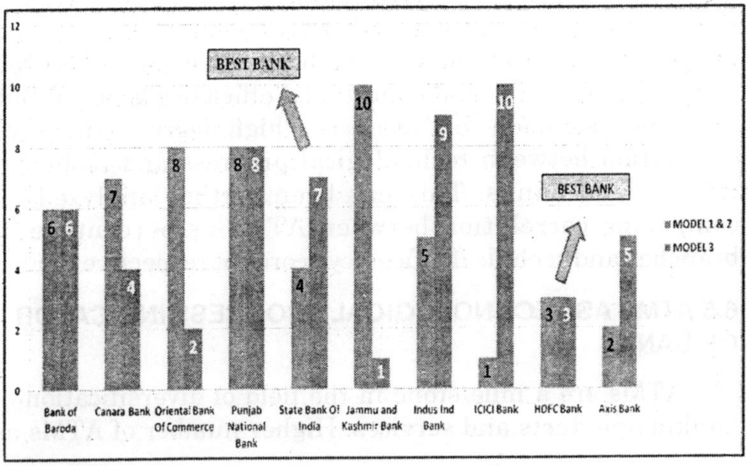

It can be concluded that there is a high degree of consistency in technical and allocative efficiency of ten banks considered in research analyses but the operational efficiency score achieved by most of the banks is just reverse of their technical and allocative efficiency. The technically most efficient bank is ICICI Bank as well as in terms of allocative efficiency bank has scored well but operational efficiency score of ICICI Bank is least. Punjab National Bank and Canara Bank are equally efficient in technical, allocative and operational efficiency scores but have to go a long way ahead to be the best bank. It is depicted in the figure 7.44 that Oriental Bank of Commerce has higher level of operational efficiency score but it is lacking behind to great extent in terms of technical and allocative efficiency score.

Canara Bank is a better performer in terms of operational efficiency but has scored low in terms of technical and allocative efficiency. State Bank of India is a better performer in terms of operational efficiency and a still better performer in terms of technical and allocative efficiency with respect to other public sector banks. It can be concluded that among public sector banks State Bank of India is the best bank but has to perform better in terms of technical and allocative efficiency. Among private sector banks Axis Bank is a better performer in terms of allocative, technical and operational efficiency. But the best bank among all banks considered under research study is HDFC Bank. It is because HDFC Bank is maintaining balance between technical, allocative and operational efficiency. No bank excels in all three technical, allocative and operational efficiency aspects. But it can be concluded that there is a high degree of positive correlation between technological progress and technical efficiency of banks. This has been further analyzed by computing correlation between ATMs as percentage of branches and technical efficiency scores of respective banks.

6.5 ATMS AS TECHNOLOGICAL PROGRESS INDICATOR OF BANKS

ATMs are a mile stone in the field of diversification of banking products and services. Higher number of ATMs as percentage of branches of each decision making unit depicts higher level of technological infrastructure and more customer base with easy accessibility of banking services. Computer related investment contributes greater percent increase in productivity, whereas non Information technology capital contributes minor percent increase in productivity. Information Technology is more of strategic necessity to stay within competition but definitely increase in Information Technology investment in information system labor results in higher returns. This is the area where public sector banks are lacking behind with respect to their private sector competitors. The figure 6.44 depicts correlation between ATMs as percentage of branches and technical efficiency (reference appendix 1).

Figure 6.45: ATMs as percentage of Branches and Technical Efficiency

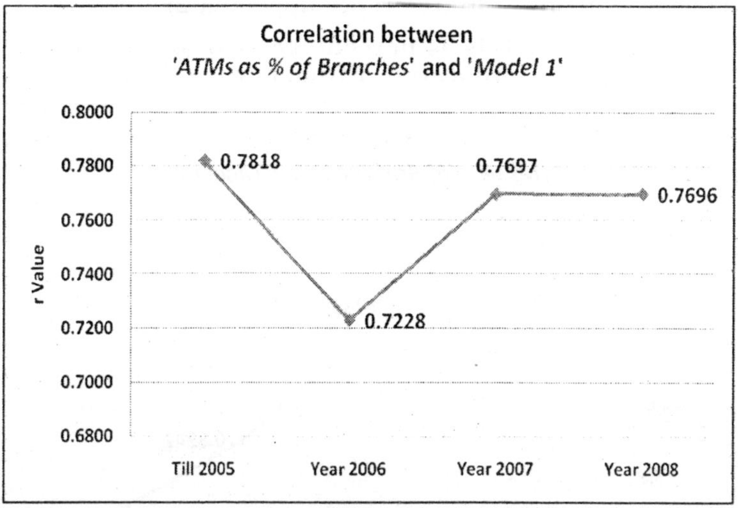

The figure 6.45 depicts high degree of positive correlation between efficiency of ten decision making units based on model 1considering number of employees, deposits as intermediaries which generate non- interest income as output. Correlation coefficient values of 0.7818, 0.7228, 0.7697 and 0.7696 degree of positive correlation is established between the efficiency score and ATMs as percentage of branches till 2005, 2006, 2007 and 2008 respectively. It is significant to note that higher technological upgradation is positively associated to higher non-interest income of the bank. To find relation between allocative efficiency and ATMs as percentage of branches correlation analyses has been conducted.

6.6 ATMS AND ALLOCATIVE EFFICIENCY OF BANKS

Allocative efficiency of banks is cost efficiency of banks in terms of price paid to factor inputs and returns generated. Factor inputs used in the research analysis are employees and deposits. The price paid to these factor inputs are measured under operating expenses and interest expenses. The technological progress is another component of operating expenses. Hence ATMS as percentage of branches and allocative efficiency of banks has been correlated and is depicted in figure 7.46 (reference appendix 2).

Figure 6.46: ATMs as percentage of Branches and Allocative Efficiency

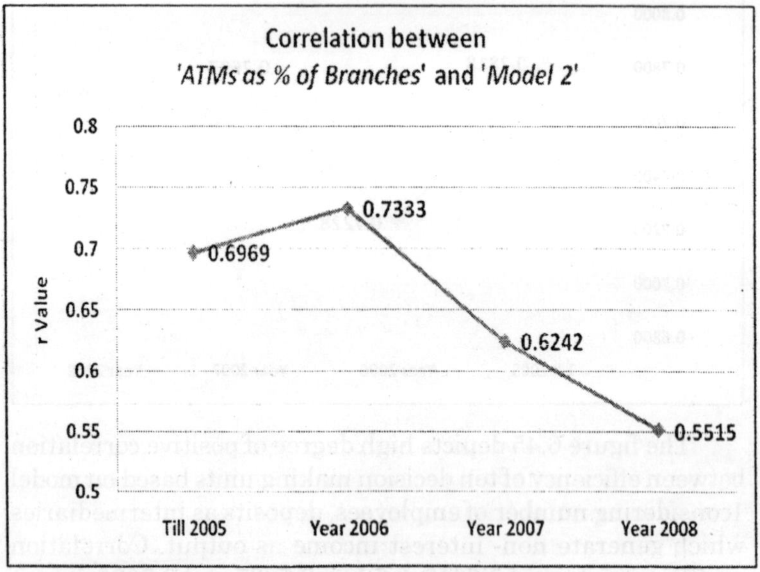

The figure 6.46 depicts declining degree of positive correlation between efficiency of ten decision making units based on model 2 considering employees and deposits as inputs and non interest income as output. Correlation coefficient values of 0.6969, 0.7333, 0.6242 and 0.5515 degree of positive correlation is established between the efficiency score and ATMs as percentage of branches till 2005, 2006, 2007 and 2008 respectively. The declining trend may be due to increasing operating expenses due to higher wage expenses especially among public sector banks and rising emoluments paid by private sector banks to their employees also increase in number of employees, has not contributed to same extent increase in non-interest-income. The positive correlation between ATMs as percentage of branches and non interest income as output is significant factor responsible for diversification of products and services in banking industry. The most important component of operating expenses is wage bill. The labor cost of public sector banks has declined mainly on account of vigorous implementation of voluntary retirement scheme in 2000-01. But the labor cost for new private sector banks is still lower than public sector banks, essentially as they rely more on technology for routine work than labor force, apart from outsourcing most of the routine marketing jobs. However, their labor costs are on the rise, mostly due to expansion in their branch network and recruitment of staff. In the following section relationship has been established between interest income as output and ATMs as percentage of branches.

6.7 ATMS AND OPERATIONAL EFFICIENCY OF BANKS

ATMs are the contributing factor of technological advancement of the bank and interest income as output is the core source of income of the bank. Hence correlation analysis has been established between the two variables. The correlation between ATMs as percentage of branches and operational efficiency of banks are depicted below in the figure 6.47 (reference appendix 3).

The significant factor depicted in the figure 6.47 is that over the years from 2005 to 2008 there is a trend of negative correlation between efficiencies of the banks by taking interest expenses and operating expenses as input but interest income as output and ATMs as percentage of branches. Higher level of technological upgradation is associated with lower level of interest income for the bank. Over the years banks have improved in terms of technological upgradation but the interest income has squeezed. The figure 6.47 depicts that there is a negative relationship between ATMs as percentage of branches and interest income earned by the bank.

Figure 6.47: ATMs as Percentage of Branches and Operational Efficiency

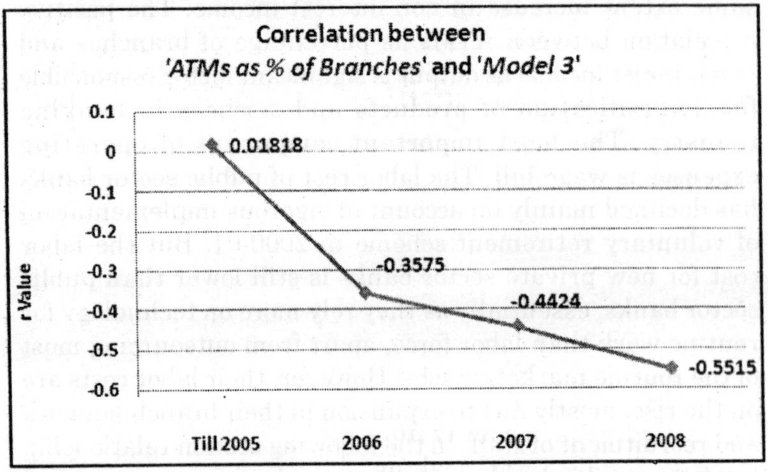

It can be concluded that there is increasing negative relationship between ATMs as percentage of branches and operational efficiency of banks over the years. Hence if bank is achieving higher level of operational efficiency it is not because of non-interest income but because of core banking services that generates interest income for the bank. On the other hand, if the bank is achieving higher level of technical efficiency and allocative efficiency it is because of higher level of non-interest income as output. At the same time ATMs as percentage of branches and non-interest income as output of the bank establishes positive correlation. Hence we can conclude that bank with increasing competition, decreasing interest margin and wider banking operations are all factors that are compelling banks to enhance their fee-based income with cautious approach by adopting appropriate risk mitigation strategy.

7

Conclusions and Recommendations

7.0 INDIAN BANKING SCENARIO AT A GLANCE:

Indian Banking is at threshold of a paradigm shift. The applications of technology and product innovations are bringing about structural changes in the Indian banking system. Off-site ATMs, on-line debit cards and core banking solutions, electronic payments and anywhere banking are transforming the traditional concept of branch banking. While banks are striving to strengthen customer relationship and move towards 'relationship banking', customers are increasingly moving away from the boundaries of traditional branch banking and seeking the convenience of remote electronic banking.

Information Technology and the communication networking systems have brought revolution in the working of banks in India. While advances in technology have dramatically increased the efficiency of banks providing services, they have also simultaneously increased competition. The internet makes obtaining information on marginal business customers less costly and easier to process the formalities. It increases competition for the bank's primary business of lending to small and medium size businesses. Technology also makes it less costly to offer banking services and expands a company's market geographically with little cost. This also leads to increased competition for banking services but at the same time technological advances allow firms to compete for customers electronically without branch facilities on every street and corner.

There can be no end to the variety of services that can be provided through the electronic channel by banks. Every bank is trying constantly to innovate and offer new products to impress the customer. The benefit to the customer on account of electronic communication is that he is able to know at a time the types of facilities being provided by different banks and he is able to make the best choice suited for his needs.

Technology is a big drawer for customer acquisition these days. Many customer-friendly banking services require a high level of technology which banks are fast developing. There is a sense of urgency in the way the banks are implementing their information technology platforms. Most public sector banks are setting up Core Banking Solutions (CBS) as they want to take the fight to the turf of the new private banks and foreign banks which have been wooing away their customers, due to better services and latest technology.

It is very much evident that technology has emerged as a key business facilitator for developing new products and services. Banks in India have started to reap the benefits of technology, which commenced in a small way more than a decade ago. Information Technology and technological upgradation has helped in handling large transactional volumes and adapting according to the changing customer expectations, apart from providing almost real time information processing for both the banks and the customers.

7.1 DIVERSIFICATION AND TECHNOLOGICAL UPGRADATION IN INDIAN

Banking Sector:

The second phase of financial reforms has resulted in the increasing competition within the banking sector, and the emergence of disintermediation pressures from a liberalized financial marketplace. The advent of 'virtual' banking and the product sophistication demanded by customers, have been, in all likelihood, responsible, for both the decline in Net Interest Margin (NIM) as well as their progressive convergence. NIM measures the core earning capacity of the bank and is an indicator of the overall portfolio management of the bank.

Disintermediation in commercial banking combined with new capital adequacy rules and squeezing interest margins has led to an increased pressure on the bank's profitability. This challenge to some extent is being overcome by diversification in the Indian banking sector. In other words increasing competition has compelled banks to diversify their resources and increase non-interest income. It helps bank to eliminate the geographical limitations, enhance product – process innovation, achieve economies of scale and scope, reap benefits of technological advancement, and diversify risk with mobilization of additional capital.

Diversification has opened the door for commercial banks to earn non-interest income from investment banking, merchant banking, insurance agency, securities brokerage and other non-traditional financial services. Non- Interest-Income is becoming increasingly important because of pricing pressure on net interest income. In other words, it has been realized by banks that the expected returns from lending are not as attractive as they once were, given the associated risks. Fortunately many customers are demanding additional products and services such as brokerage accounts and insurance which generate non-interest income.

While all banks are increasing their non-interest-income, the private banks rely much more on non-interest income as the source of revenue than majority of public sector banks. Public sector banks still rely more heavily on net interest income. One of the probable reasons could be lack of technological advancement and techno-savvy employee force. Private Banks not only have greater amount of non interest income, they also rely on a wider variety of sources of non interest income. It could be due to the fact that computer related investment contributes to a great extent in increase in output. But the non information technology related investment contributes marginal increase in the output. It can be concluded that Information technology is more of strategic necessity to stay within the competition.

7.2 Rationale of the Study:

Introducing technological initiative has been the second most important milestone in the banking industry after nationalization of major banks in 1969. Reserve Bank of India has taken persistent efforts to establish an enabling regulatory framework with prompt and effective supervision, and development of legal, technological and institutional infrastructure and adoption of international benchmarks, as appropriate to Indian conditions. The Reserve Bank had instituted a state of-the-art Off-site Monitoring and Surveillance system (OSMOS) for banks in the year 1995 as part of crisis management framework for Early Warning System (EWS) and as a trigger for on-site inspections of vulnerable institutions. The scope and coverage of off-site surveillance has since been widened to capture various facets of efficiency and risk management of banks.

Banks today are moving towards web-based banking as it is cost efficient and more convenient for the customers. But still there exist wide disparities within the banking sector as far as computerization is concerned. Computerization requires higher level of technically sound employees and huge investment on technological upgradation. According to Reserve Bank of India, only about 20 percent of the total staff of public sector banks was computer literate in the year 2002. Whereas new private sector banks had 100 percent computer literate staff. It is noteworthy that the level of computerization in public sector banks has increased to great extent over the financial years 2005 to 2008. Reason being sound technological systems can ensure higher level of efficiency, economies of scope and better customer relationship management.

Banks are transforming to universal banking, adding new channels with lucrative pricing offer. Natural fall out of this, new products new players and height have led to a series of innovative product offerings catering to various customer segments, specifically retail credit. This in turn has made it necessary to look for efficiencies in the business. Banks need to access low cost funds and simultaneously improve the economic efficiency. The banks are facing pricing pressure, squeeze on spread and have to give thrust on retail assets. It will definitely impact Customer preferences, as they are bound to react to the value added offerings. Customers have become demanding and the brand patronage has become a biggest challenge for banks. There are multiple choices; the wallet share is reduced per bank with demand on flexibility and customization. It is therefore necessary to the review the current status of Indian banking industry on various parameters of technical, operational and allocative efficiency of public and private sector banks promoting customer centric technological upgradation.

The research study aims at analyzing the key differentiating factors responsible for difference in the level of efficiency of public and private sector banks operating in India. Efficiency is a function of input efficiency (minimize input) and output efficiency (maximize output). Both input and output efficiencies are function of many factors that are allocative and technical in nature. The most prominent differentiating factor responsible for higher level of efficiency is technological upgradation in banking sector. The range of services provided by banks now include Automated Teller Machine, Electronic Clearing System(ECS), Electronic Fund Transfer (EFT), Real Time Gross Settlement(RTGS), Tele-banking, Internet Banking, Mobile Banking etc. Technology can help banks in ensuring efficient management, lower operating costs, greater geographic diversification, improved and sustained competitive position, new revenue opportunities and higher level of customer satisfaction. The research also aims at analyzing the prominent factors to contribute for improving performance of public sector banks which are operating in a most competitive computer savvy environment.

7.3 Objectives:

With a view to developing a sound analytical framework for the research analysis of impact of technological upgradation on Public and Private sector banks operating in India, a review of literature on performance of banks in India with technological advancement has been done. The present study has focused on how public sector banks and private sector banks can improve productivity profitability, technical efficiency by managing some of the important elements relating to Technology, Process, Organizational issues, Labor in a better way. The prime objectives of the study are to do the comparative assessment of the technological upgradation in Public and Private sector banks in India and to evaluate its effectiveness. An attempt has been made to assess the extent to which technological upgradation has helped banks in enhancing their productivity and profitability. The research study has also tried to explore the technological spread in banking sector in terms of inter-branch connectivity and networking. An attempt has also been made to analyze the problems faced by banks, especially public sector banks in adoption of new technologies.

7.4 Methodology:

The sample for the empirical analysis comprises of ten commercial banks of India. Among these ten commercial banks, five banks are Public sector banks and five are Private sector banks. The five public sector banks are Bank of Baroda, Canara Bank, and Oriental Bank of Commerce, Punjab National Bank and State Bank of India. On the other hand, the five private sector banks are Jammu and Kashmir Bank (old Private sector bank) and new generation private sector banks are HDFC Bank, ICICI Bank, IndusInd Bank and Axis Bank.

The research is based on secondary research and the empirical analysis has been done to analyze heterogeneity in performance of public and private sector banks with a key differentiating factor as technological upgradation. The data collected is from secondary sources for the period of ten years from year 1997-98 to year 2007-08 to assess the trend in technological upgradation as well as to increase the reliability of the findings. The study period is selected keeping financial reforms into consideration. To have comparative evaluation, the empirical investigation has been carried out separately for different bank-groups, viz., public sector banks and private sector banks.

The time series of ten years has been constructed to not only have reliable and authentic information of selected banks but also to evaluate the progress of banks over the period of economic liberalization and impact of technological advancement in the banking industry. To undertake comparative assessment of the technological upgradation in Public and Private sector banks in India and to evaluate profitability, productivity, technical efficiency and allocative efficiency of selected banks, statistical tools used are ratio analysis, multiple regression analysis, data envelopment analysis (DEA) and three window analysis. Finally in the research analysis efficiencies of banks are calculated in terms of Technical, Allocative and Operational Efficiency. All banks are ranked in terms of Technical, Allocative and Operational Efficiency and ten decision making units are correlated with ATMs as percentage of Branches.

7.5 MAJOR FINDINGS:

7.5.1 Technological Upgradation in Banking Sector

Technology has given birth to a new era in banking. Technology can be the key differentiator between two banks and a major factor to attain competitive edge. Most of the new generation private banks and few public sector banks have succeeded in shifting counter transaction to self service mode through new delivery channels like ATMs, cash dispensing machine, terminals for balance enquiry, self operated pass book updates, Tele-banking and internet banking.

At present the nature of banking has changed beyond recognition. With ATM cards, simple banking transactions like withdrawing and depositing money are easier than ever before. For the tech-savvy, there is the option of banking online. The next medium is just a mobile phone. Even when it comes to products, the changes have been many. Graduating from simple savings accounts and fixed and recurring deposits, banks now offer a host of products like special savings account and sweep-in-account, no frills accounts and easy receive account.

ATMs have evolved from only basic cash dispensing solutions to one which can provide value added services. Now Banks have a single window for procuring all their ATM related needs from the vendor. This includes ATM monitoring, software distribution for ATMs and cash management and network management. Many Indian banks that were hampered because of lack of knowledge of technology are now actively talking to ATM vendors for outsourcing their needs. Banks have implemented Core Banking Solutions along with public private collaboration for centralizing back-office operations. Other measures taken are implementing single window services, optimizing the human resources at branch level. This will ultimately result in reduction in the operational cost of the bank branches.

Public Sector Banks are slowly waking up to the ATMs potential as a serious marketing tool. They are also earning sizeable revenue by using ATMs to advertise products from other companies. A few banks are offering utility bill payment facilities on their machine too. Apart from that, a variety of services ranging from railway card/season tickets and cinema tickets to dispensing of mobile phone, smart cards are being thought of as a part of the strategy to attract customers and earn extra revenue. It is heartening that the growth in the installed base of ATMs, which was primarily driven by private sector banks, is intensely followed by public sector banks. The Retail-banking scene is getting hotter by the day with banks going all out to increase access points.

It is well known that the public sector banks are more prominent in terms of number of branches and employees hence incur higher operating cost. To reduce operating expenses public sector banks have tremendously invested in computerization. It is observed that State Bank of India had incurred the level of expenditure on computerization which is almost three times of Punjab National Bank, and near about 10 times of Oriental Bank of Commerce. Canara Bank and Bank of Baroda during March 2008 have incurred 63.84 and 34.67 crores respectively on computerization.

It can be concluded that, with the collapse of geographical distances, banks need to treat the customer as a customer of the whole bank and not a customer of a particular branch. This is now possible due to technological upgradation of banking sector whereby large scale centralized data bases are possible in a bank with decentralized access. Banks need to constantly look for innovative services which offer customers the convenience of transacting from anywhere, at any time and using delivery channels more suitable for them. These are frontiers which would add value to the services offered to customers and at the same time act as a means for increasing the profits for banks and reducing transaction costs.

The following analysis focuses on the growth and the existing structure of technological progress of public and private sector banks selected in research study.

7.5.2 Technological progress of Public Sector Banks

The Public Sector Banks of India have incurred huge expenditure on computerization during March'2005 to March'2008. The number of ATMs as percentage of branches during March'2005 of Bank of Baroda was 6.34 percent, Canara Bank 24.21 percent, Oriental Bank of Commerce 42.97 percent, Punjab National Bank 13.73 percent and State Bank of India 39.97 percent. The numbers of fully computerized branches of Bank of Baroda were 83.1 percent, Canara Bank 58.5percent, Oriental Bank of Commerce 45.5

percent, Punjab National Bank 64.2 percent and State Bank of India 100 percent. The level of expenditure incurred on computerization and development of communication Networks of Bank of Baroda was 301.45 crores, Canara Bank 623.12 crores, Oriental Bank of Commerce 181.14 crores, 668.28 crores by Punjab National Bank and 2,160 crores by State Bank of India.

The number of ATMs as percentage of branches during March'2008 has increased to 23.09 percent of Bank of Baroda, 31.94 percent of Canara Bank, 45.13 percent of Oriental Bank of Commerce, 17.37 percent of Punjab National Bank and 46.28 percent of State Bank of India. Public sector banks analyzed in this study have 100 percent fully computerized branches.

7.5.3 Private Sector Banks and Technological Progress

Among the Private sector banks; Jammu and Kashmir Bank has tie up with MASTERO for ATM and MASTERCARD for credit card services but the bank has to go a long way to compete with not only private sector banks like ICICI, HDFC, IndusInd and Axis Bank but also with fast upcoming technologically sound Public Sector Banks like SBI, Canara Bank, Bank of Baroda, Punjab National Bank and Oriental Bank of Commerce.

HDFC Bank is the leader in online purchase (using the HDFC Bank Direct Pay Product). IndusInd Bank provided multi-channel facilities including ATMs, Internet Banking, mobile banking, multi-city banking, and international debit and credit cards. It is one of the first banks to go live on the Real Time Gross Settlement (RTGS), an initiative of Reserve Bank of India. Axis Bank has a sharp focus on servicing customers and leverage cutting edge technologies to enable high service quality. The bank has placed great significance on technology and has acquired IBM's Midas Kapiti (now Mysis) software for its Core Banking Solutions, in year 2007-08. All private sector are ahead of public sector banks in terms of technological progress but public sector banks are catching them at a very fast pace.

7.5.4 Profitability and Productivity in Banking Sector:

The flurry of reforms witnessed over almost two decades has brought about significant changes in the banking arena in the country and technology has been a major facilitator of this transformation. ATMs, Internet banking, credit cards, and now mobile banking have helped revolutionize the banking market in the country. Leveraging on their new found tech savvy and increased thrust on product/service innovation, the banks in the country witnessed a phenomenal growth in the last few years as the economic growth moved into top gear to be amongst the best in the world.

Bank's profitability performance is measured in terms of growth rate of Return on Assets. If return on assets measures is higher than peers, the bank enjoys the status of "high performance bank". The percentage of reduction in Net NPA as percentage to Net Advances depicts better efficiency of a bank. Capital adequacy is an indicator of the financial health of the banking system. It is measured by the Capital to Risk-weighted Asset Ratio (CRAR), defined as the ratio of a bank's capital to its total risk-weighted assets.

A well adhered to capital adequacy regime does play an important role in minimizing the cascading effects of banking and financial sector crises. For a bank to report higher returns, the bank must either take on more risk, price assets and liabilities better, or realize cost advantages compared with peers. It is a known fact that all these obstacles can be overcome by higher level of investment in technology.

In the following pages an attempt is made to assess the effectiveness of technical upgradation on profitability and productivity of public and privates sector banks separately

7.5.5 Productivity and Profitability of Public Sector Banks:

The Return on Assets of public sector banks of India since year 1998, till year 2008 has been much stable, Net NPA as percentage of Net Advances since year 1998 has continuously declined. **Bank of Baroda** recorded trend growth rate of 3.92 percent with average Return on Assets of 0.83. Decrease in Non Interest Income as Percentage to Assets, merger of Banaras State Bank with Bank of Baroda (2002) and consolidation of bank as per prudential norms led down by Reserve Bank of India were the reasons responsible for lower growth rate of return on assets of Bank of Baroda. The overall growth trend of Capital to risk weighted asset ratio of Bank of Baroda indicates a positive trend of 1.72 percent growth rate till year 2006 depicting increase in assets and management of risk weighted assets by the Bank.

Canara Bank depicts stability in efficiency management of the organization to great extent with fewer variations as compared to Bank of Baroda. The trend growth rate of Bank of Baroda is 3.92 percent.There is no change in growth rate of Canara Bank from year 1997 –1999 but year 1999-2000 reflected negative growth of 8.51 percent because of decrease in interest income and Non Interest Income as Percentage to Assets as well as consolidation of banks. The overall decline in Net NPA as percentage to Net Advances is highest of Canara Bank at 17.43 percent growth rate. Reasons responsible for this positive trend over years are upgradation of credit appraisal skills and systems, strengthening the follow-up of advances including loan review mechanism for large loans as well as effective follow-up of suit filed / decreed debts.

Oriental Bank of Commerce recorded average Return on Assets of 1.17 percent but overall trend growth rate of Oriental Bank of Commerce is negative because of merger of Global Trust Bank of India with oriental Bank of Commerce in the year 2004. At the time of merger Global trust Bank was at the verge of collapse. Drive for recovery of NPAs, Upgradation of skills, revamping of credit administration and risk management systems and entertaining only high quality proposals helped the bank to recover the loss in the year 2006.

The minimization of risk strategy helped **Punjab National Bank** to enjoy positive growth rate of Return on Assets over the years but decrease in non interest income and increase in Net NPA as percentage of Net Advances resulted in negative growth rate of Punjab National Bank in the year 2006 at 11.60 percent. Except year 2003 and 2006 there was a positive trend in the growth rate of CRAR of Punjab National Bank depicting a strong capital base of the bank. In year 2007 and 2008 the growth rate of CRAR of Punjab National Bank increased to the level of 2.84 and 5.45 percent.

State Bank of India had a strategy to strengthen their market risk management capacity. SBI has registered significant improvements in its operating margins since 2003. State Bank of India overall depicts a positive growth trend of CRAR indicating strong foundation of State Bank of India but the negative growth trend of 1.9 percent is mainly because of decrease in CRAR of State Bank of India in the year 1999 by 14.19 percent reflecting consolidation of bank for better performance in future.

Therefore, the overall productivity and profitability of Public sector banks indicates increase in growth percentage due to better risk management, continuous decline in Net NPA as percentage of Net Advances and improvement in asset quality by assigning risk weight. The reason responsible for continuously declining Net NPA as percentage to Net Advances of public sector banks are better credit administration.

7.5.6 Productivity and Profitability of Private Sector Banks

Private sector banks are techno-savvy banks, with greater level of reliance on technology for banking operations. Higher level of reliance on technology has made it possible for private sector banks to achieve economies of scope and economies of scale. The average return on assets of Private sector banks is greater than Public sector banks, considered in research analysis. But Net NPA as percentage of Net Advances is higher of Private Sector Banks as compared to Public Sector Banks.

The least techno savvy bank among private sector banks considered in sample is **Jammu and Kashmir Bank**. The bank has 22.06 percent of ATMs to total branches. The bank is relying more on interest income and less on non-interest income. Jammu and Kashmir Bank depicts a positive trend with continuous decrease in Net NPA as percentage to Net Assets. Jammu and Kashmir Bank indicates increase in Net NPA as percentage of Net Advances in the year 2007 and 2008 depicting poor asset quality of the bank. Increase in risk weighted assets has declined the overall rate of Capital Adequacy Ratio over the period of nine years from 20.48 percent in year 1998 to 12.14 percent in the year 2006. It records maximum negative growth rate of 3.123 percent with respect to all other private sector banks considered in the empirical analysis.

Highest average Return on Assets among private sector banks is of **HDFC Bank** but the growth trend shows continuous decline in Return on Assets from 1.52 in the year 2003 to 1.32 in year 2008. But in relative terms, HDFC Bank has the highest percentage of Return on Assets. HDFC Bank has maintained low level of Net NPA as percentage of Net Advances over the period of year 1998 to 2008 though the declining growth rate is not high but it reflects consistent performance of the bank with fewer deviations in Net NPA as percentage of Net Advances.

ICICI Bank incurred almost hundred percent increase in establishment expenses to the amount of 147 crores over the period of 1999 to 2005 resulted in 12.97 percent increase in return on assets of ICICI Bank. This tremendous upward swing in the growth rate of return on assets was due to increase in operating profit as percentage of assets, increase in non-interest income as percentage of assets. The other factors responsible were increase in spread and decline in Net NPA to Net Advances in percentage over these years.

Return on Assets of **IndusInd Bank** depicts a negative trend over majority of the research time period. The reasons responsible are decrease in interest income of the bank as percentage to assets, decline in operating profit as percentage to working funds and decline in non-interest income as percentage to working funds and higher level of Net NPA as percentage of Net Advances. IndusInd Bank reflects highest Net NPA as percentage of Net Advances with respect to other private sector banks considered in the research study. It reflects poor management of credit system by IndusInd Bank.

Axis Bank has very well overcome its asset quality by continuously bringing down the rate of Net NPA as percentage of Net Advances. Axis Bank reflects positive trend in maintaining capital adequacy ratio during last seven years except in the year 2006 which was 11.08 percent capital adequacy ratio. Increase in risk weighted assets results in lower capital adequacy ratio. The increase in risk-weighted assets is due to a higher growth in the loan portfolio of banks and higher risk weights made applicable for housing loans, the most rapidly increasing component of retail loans for banks.

The overall productivity and profitability of Private sector banks indicates high variance among various private sector banks in increase in growth percentage due to huge difference in risk management strategy, Net NPA as percentage of Net Advances and improvement in asset quality by assigning risk weight, operational portfolios and technological advancement. The outcome of strategic decisions was decline in Net NPA as percentage to Net Advances increase in Net Profit of the Bank. This reflects better recovery management and efficient credit management of the bank. Better risk management strategy, higher level of investment in technology, Increase in credit deposit ratio and increase in spread as percentage of assets has resulted in lower level of Net NPA as percentage of Net Advances.

7.6 Comparative analysis of Public and Private sector banks

Thus the study depicts that the Private Banks have higher level of risk exposure. This is because of the fact, that their operational portfolio is more inclined towards retail banking with higher level of risk attached. On the other hand, Public sector banks have relatively lower level of Net NPA as percentage of Net Advances. The reason responsible is lending by public sector banks is more conventional and hence there is at lower level of risk of conversion of standard assets to sub- standard assets. The technological upgradation has also made record keeping and regular feedback data of Non-Performing Assets simplified time saving and reducing the cost of updating accounts. Strengthening follow-up of advances including loan review mechanism for large loans and technological Upgradation by keeping track on bad debt has helped bank to reduce Net NPA as percentage to Net Advances over years. Private sector banks have to maintain higher level of CRAR because of higher level of reliance on non-interest income. Higher level of dependence on non-interest income is always associated with higher level of risk and hence higher provisioning has to be mad e. Higher level of Net NPA adversely affects profitability and productivity of the bank. Hence it needs to be checked.

The current scenario of volatile interest rate and securities prices and continuous strain on spread and burden of the Private Banks cannot be overlooked. It emphasizes continuous monitoring of movement of Return on Assets and it requires revision of the benchmark Return on Assets. Strong capital base is very essential for absorbing unexpected losses which will help private banks like IndusInd and ICICI Bank to reduce Net Non Performing Assets as percentage of Net Advances and increase Return on Assets

It can be summarized that in the era of increasing competition due to globalization of the banking sector it is more important to maintain quality of assets financed, as the large bad loans will not only reduce yield on advances but will also have serious implications on profitability and productivity of banks. In private sector banks non-performing assets are increasingly occurring on borrowable accounts of the industrial sector and real estate industry. IndusInd Bank indicates maximum net non performing assets as percentage of net advances and low rate of capital adequacy ratio. IndusInd Bank needs to have better follow up, recovery writ-offs, compromise proposals and vigilant credit lending to reduce net non performing assets of the bank.

Private Sector Banks as well as Public Sector Banks has made huge investment on technological upgradation. The outcome of it is therefore visible in terms of better credit risk management, monitoring of standard and sub standard assets, diversification of products, increase in non- interest income, and improvement in asset quality, continuous decrease in Net NPA as percentage of Net Advances, better customer relationship management and higher level of accessibility by installing ATMs.

7.7 Empirical Analysis of Technological Upgradation in Banking Sector

The multiple regression analysis has been performed to analyze the prominent factors contributing in non-interest income of public and private sector banks. In the following pages, an attempt is made to evaluate as to how non-interest income, a parameter of technological upgradation in banks, gets influenced by various factors such as Net NPA per branch, business per branch, ATMs per branch, employees per branch and operating expenses per branch.

The regression results highlights that Net NPA per Branch is negatively related to Non Interest Income per Branch such that an increase in Net NPA per Branch will lead to decrease in Non Interest Income per Branch of the bank. The regression parameter is statistically significant at 5 percent level of significance. It also explains the elasticity coefficient in this case is (-) 0.56. One percent change in Net NPA per branch results in decrease in non- interest income per branch by.56 percent. Hence for commercial banks first and most important concern is decreasing the level of Net NPA per branch.

The second most significant independent variable making positive and significant impact on criterion variable i.e non- interest income per branch is business per branch. The regression parameter is statistically significant at 5 percent level of significance. The elasticity coefficient value of business per branch is 0.751. It means one percentage increase in business per branch leads to 0.75 percent increase in Non Interest income per branch. Higher level of business depends on higher level of deposits and advances. Higher level of business requires better customer relationship management and better level of credit risk management and better asset management.

The third significant independent variable is ATMs per branch making positive and significant impact on non interest income per branch. The regression parameter is significant at 5 percent level of significance.The elasticity coefficient value of ATMs per branch is.052. It means one percentage increase in ATMs per branch leads to 0.52 percent increase in Non Interest income per branch. ATM reduces operating expenses of the bank as well as generates higher level of fee based (non-interest income) income. It is very much evident from continuous increase in ATMs by each bank also increase in partnership among banks for sharing ATMs.

The next independent variable is Employees per branch. The regression equation highlights that employee per branch is positively related to non interest income per branch, such that an increase in employees per branch will increase non interest income.But this will only be true if the employee force is techno savvy. The regression parameter is significant at 5 percent level of significance, indicating employee per branch is a significant factor in contributing non- interest income per branch. The regression coefficient value is.41. It is evident that employee per branch contributes marginally in increase in non-interest income per branch. Especially in public sector banks where there is surplus of employees their contribution can be increased by providing training to them for the software they are using and increasing their incentives.

The independent variable operational expense per branch depicts positive relation with non interest income. The regression parameter is significant at 5 percent level of significance. It means with increase in operating expenses per branch, non-interest income per branch of the bank will increase. The regression coefficient is 0.39; it indicates the responsiveness of non interest income per branch to change in operating expenses per branch The operating expenses per branch contributes in non-interest income of the bank because operating expenses apart from salary of employees also includes expenses incurred on computerization and technical upgradation of the bank. But in public sector banks major part of operating expenses is incurred on salary of employees rather than on computerization and technological upgradation.

The above explained regression analysis thus depicts that for private as well as public sector banks that net NPA per branch is negative and significant.Hence banks need to decrease the level of net NPA for higher level of non interest income. All other independent variables such as ATM per branch, employee per branch and operating expenses per branch contributes positively to increase in non-interest-income of the bank. But employees can contribute positively in non-interest income only if they are technically efficient. At the same time operating expenses can contribute positively for increase in non-interest income if operating expenses increases on technological advancement of the bank.

Regression Model B analyses private sector banks by taking same set of variables to know the level of variance among different banks. Not only it depicts difference between Public and Private Sector banks but also it reflects the level of variance between different public sector banks as well as between private sector banks considered in the research study.

Findings of regression analysis for each bank can be summarized as the net NPA per branch is a significant but negative parameter for all public and private sector banks. With increase in net NPA per branch the non-interest income of the bank decreases. Business per branch, ATMs per branch have positive and significant impact on non-interest income of banks. With increase in business per branch the non-interest income of the bank increases. Same is true for number of ATMs per branch, higher number of ATMs per branch results in higher level of non-interest income for the bank. Employees per branch make positive and significant contribution to increase in non-interest income of the bank. This is true only when banks can provide their employees proper training and increase their efficiency to generate higher non-interest income. Operating expenses per branch has positive and significant impact on increase in non-interest income of the bank.

It can be concluded that public sector banks have lower level of negative elasticity coefficient of Net NPA per branch on Non interest Income per branch. But at the same time public sector banks contributes at lower level in terms of employees per branch as significant regression parameter and its contribution to non -interest income per branch of the bank. Hence Public sector banks need huge investment on training and promotion of technically sound manpower to contribute at higher level for Non Interest Income.

As a matter of fact, old Private Sector Bank like Jammu and Kashmir Bank needs higher level of training of employees to increase its contribution in Non Interest Income. But techno-savvy banks need to adopt precautionary step in going for higher level of non-interest income.It is because of a positive relation between higher level of non-interest income and increase in NPA of the bank. On the other hand, Banks investing in technology with proper training to employees' results in increase in contribution of employees to non-interest income.

7.8 TECHNICAL AND ALLOCATIVE EFFICIENCY IN BANKING SECTOR: DEA

Analysis

With declining interest income and interest margins of banks in India there is urgent need to generate more fee based income to fill the gap created by declining net interest margin. Thus non interest fee based income is becoming a significant source of revenue for the banks. Private sector banks have highly skilled techno savvy staff to offer fee based services, which provide better margins and leads to higher capital productivity. Public sector banks have also inculcated the culture of increasing proportion of non interest income in total income by diversification of services and products.

Hence the empirical study considered deposits and employees as inputs and non interest income as output. Less deposits and less number of employees with higher level of non interest income is definitely an indicator of technological advancement and increase in capital productivity of the bank. If interest margin of the bank increases simultaneously with increase in non-interest income the bank will have benchmark as compared to its competitors in terms of achieving higher level of productivity and profitability with click and mortar banking. Of late, fee-based products, or products that generate noninterest income, are attracting the attention of more and more banks, including the private ones as well as the state-owned monoliths. For three very good reasons: One, they don't require much capital; two, they carry little risk; and, three, for good measure, they can also boost profitability.

The pages below depict Technical, Allocative and Operational efficiency of five public and five private sector banks considered in research study.

7.8.1 Technical efficiency of Public and Private Sector Banks:

The most efficient bank is the one which uses minimum inputs to produce maximum output. Most efficient bank is calculated for each year to have time series analysis and find the impact of technological advancement. The analysis of Technical efficiency by **Data Envelopment Analysis (DEA)** taking employees in thousands and deposits in crores as inputs and non interest income in crores as output reveals that:

All public sector banks are in the technical efficiency range of 15 to 50 percent because of surplus employees resulting in higher establishment expenses. Private sector

Banks were at higher technical efficiency level between 17 to 100 percent. Private sector banks are at higher level of technical efficiency score than public sector banks because of less reliability on deposits for income generation accompanied by less number of employees and higher level of technological advancement.

IndusInd Bank was the most technical efficient bank by generating maximum non- interest income with minimum inputs of employees in thousands, deposits in crores till financial year 2001. The least technical efficient banks are Oriental Bank of Commerce and Jammu and Kashmir Bank with input slack percentage of 84.33 and 82.77 percent and minimum technical efficiency score of 15.66 of Oriental Bank of Commerce and minimum technical efficiency score of 17.23 percent of Jammu and Kashmir Bank.

During financial year 2002, technical efficiency of all banks slipped. It is because of the fact that, the PSBs were in the process of shedding their flab in terms of excessive manpower, excessive non Performing Assets (NPAs) and excessive governmental equity, while on the other hand, the private sector banks were consolidating themselves through mergers and acquisitions. For example HDFC Bank got merged with Times Bank, ICICI Bank had acquired ITC Classic, Anagram Finance and Bank of Madura. The UTI bank- Global Trust Bank merger however opened a Pandora's box and brought about the realization that all was not well in the functioning of many of the private sector banks too.

The impact of economic slowdown was also visible in the year 2003. ICICI Bank adopted technological advancement and secured the position of most efficient bank. IndusInd Bank and Axis Bank were second and third in technical efficiency. Financial year 2004 reflected positive results of consolidation in banking industry in terms of climbing ladder up to efficiency score of thirties from twenties of public sector banks. Low level of efficiency score of public sector banks is because of low level of investment in technology. During financial year 2005, ICICI Bank secured 100 percent technical efficiency level. Among public sector banks most efficient public sector bank is State Bank of India at efficiency score of 37.48, with reference decision making unit IndusInd Bank. The least efficient bank is Jammu and Kashmir Bank with efficiency score of 10.17 percent.

Even in the year 2007 and 2008, ICICI Bank scored efficiency rating of 100 percent and Jammu and Kashmir Bank as least efficient bank at the score of 18.93 percent followed by Punjab National Bank. In the year 2008, IndusInd Bank achieved efficiency score of just 39.56 percent depicting decrease in technical efficiency of the bank. State Bank of India still scored the position of best bank and second in the category of public sector banks is Bank of Baroda. While in private sector second most efficient bank is Axis Bank. The least efficient bank is Jammu and Kashmir Bank.

It can be summarized that over the years, ICICI Bank has acquired higher level of technological upgradation in its operations which has resulted in higher returns. IndusInd Bank could not maintain the same level of technological progress as compared to its competitors in banking Industry. Among Public sector banks, State Bank of India is technically most sound and is followed by Canara Bank and Bank of Baroda. On the other hand, Oriental Bank of Commerce is the least technical efficient but definitely better than Jammu and Kashmir Bank (old private sector bank).

7.8.2 Allocative Efficiency of Public and Private Sector Banks:

The Most allocative efficient bank will be the one which incurs minimum expenses on employees and deposits but generates higher level of non interest income as output. Non-interest income is an important parameter to measure allocative and technical efficiency of Banks in India because increased competition in the Indian Banking industry has driven the interest yields and consequently, the Net Interest Margins has decreased. Hence, banks are increasingly concentrating on non interest income to shore up profits. On the other hand, the operating expense ratio reveals how expensive it is for a bank to maintain its fixed assets and human capital that are used to generate that income streams. Hence it is need of the hour for the banks to allocate its resources in most efficient manner to generate higher level of productivity, profitability and human efficiency.

Allocative efficiency score of public sector banks is better than their technical efficiency score. It is very much evident from the allocative efficiency score of Public Sector Banks; in the range of 30 percent to 78 percent. Among Public sector banks the most allocative efficient bank is State Bank of India with allocative efficiency score of 38 percent to 68 percent. The minimum allocative efficiency score of State Bank of India 38.12 percent was in financial year 2003 due to economic slowdown and consolidation in banking industry.

Allocative efficiency score of Private sector banks is in the range of 37 percent to 100 percent. The most allocative efficient bank among private sector banks is ICICI Bank with allocative efficiency score ranging from 44 percent to 100 percent. But financial year 2008 reflects lowest allocative efficiency score of 44 percent of ICICI Bank.Decline in non-interest income due to global financial crunch was the main contributory factor responsible for the lowest allocative efficiency score of ICICI Bank.

The least efficient banks among public sector banks is Oriental Bank of Commerce with allocative efficiency score of 29.95 percent to 73.20 percent and among private sector banks is Jammu and Kashmir Bank with allocative efficiency score of 24.08 percent to 66.69 percent. It is significant to notice that Oriental Bank of Commerce is relatively better performer than Jammu and Kashmir Bank, though public sector banks have higher percentage of employees and to great extent higher operating expenses in terms of higher level of input but still better output than the one using fewer inputs.

All private sector banks are in the allocative efficiency range of 56.24 to 100 percent except Jammu and Kashmir Bank at the lowest level of 29.93 percent. The input slack percentage of HDFC Bank is at lower level than of Axis Bank depicting better allocative efficiency of HDFC Bank than Axis Bank. Among Public Sector Banks State Bank of India depicts lower percentage of input slack 33.69 as compared to other public sector banks of India depicting higher level of allocative efficiency.

The allocative efficiency results depicts that Private sector Banks were at higher allocative efficiency level than public sector banks because of less reliability on deposits for income generation accompanied by less number of employees and higher level of technological advancement as well as higher reliance on non interest income with squeezing level of spread.

7.8.3 Operational Efficiency of Public and Private Sector Banks:

Model three depicts Operational efficiency of Public Sector Banks by taking inputs as operating expenses and interest expenses in crores and interest income as output. Interest income has been taken as output in Model three to highlight the level of variance in efficiency of Public and Private Sector Banks.Interest income is the core income of banking industry but decreasing gap between interest income and interest expended has promoted Para-Banking activities and higher level of reliance on non interest income. But banks performing at lower level in terms of technical efficiency and allocative efficiency are better performers in terms of interest income as output.

Among private sector banks, the best performer is Jammu and Kashmir Bank with average efficiency score of 90 percent and above over the period of 1998 to 2008 and among public sector banks, the best performer is Oriental Bank of Commerce.Second in the order of operational efficiency is Oriental Bank of Commerce at average efficiency score of more than 80 percent.

The higher level of efficiency of Jammu and Kashmir Bank and Oriental Bank of Commerce is because of low operating expenses and marginal increase in interest expenses. Third bank in the operational efficiency score is IndusInd Bank. It is because of the reason of low operating expenses of Jammu and Kashmir Bank, IndusInd Bank due to lower level of wage bill.The other possible reason could be less number of employees and low level of expenditure incurred on computerization as compared to other peer bankers considered in the research study. But after March end' 2005, IndusInd Bank has fallen on operational efficiency score because of increase in non- performing assets of the bank.

HDFC Bank has maintained consistency in operational efficiency score over the empirical study period. State Bank of India is on lower level of operational efficiency because of higher operating expenses. State Bank of India has incurred huge expenditure on computerization and development of communication network as well as its huge employee force increases operating expenses of the bank.

ICICI Bank is on lower level of operational efficiency because of greater reliance on non interest income and higher level of operating expenses and interest expenses. Canara Bank's operating expenses is less than Punjab National Bank, State Bank of India, and Bank of Baroda. Hence it secures higher level of operational efficiency ranking among other public sector banks but it has been ranked at lower level than Oriental Bank of Commerce because of higher input slack percentage with respect to the reference unit.

It is evident that interest spread tends to be affected by the amount of non-interest income being earned by a bank. It is significant to note that ICICI Bank scores the efficiency score of 100 percent in terms of non interest income as output but it gets least efficient score when interest income is considered as output. On the other hand Jammu and Kashmir Bank has secured last position in terms of technical efficiency with output Non Interest Income but best bank score in terms of Interest Income as output. State Bank of India despite its huge elephant size has maintained creditable position in terms of interest income and non-interest income as output among other public sector banks considered in empirical analysis. It is equally true to great extent for consistent performance of HDFC Bank.

7.9 Efficiency of Public and Private Sector Banks: Three Window Analysis

On the basis of technical efficiency, allocative efficiency and operational efficiency of all public sector and private sector banks has been analyzed using three window moving average analysis then ranks are assigned according to efficiency score scored by them.

The most inefficient bank is Jammu and Kashmir Bank; second in order of inefficiency is Punjab National Bank. The most efficient Public Sector Bank is State Bank of India and second in order is Canara Bank followed by Bank of Baroda. The most efficient bank is ICICI Bank with 100 percent efficiency score. It is really a creditable performance of ICICI bank in terms of technical efficiency. Axis Bank is better performer than IndusInd Bank and HDFC Bank. The most consistent performer is Axis Bank getting score always from first rank to fourth rank with reference unit during the study period. The second in order is HDFC Bank by getting higher score over the competitors.

7.10 Conclusions:

The research analysis based on different parameters reveals that the growth rate of Return on Assets (ROA) of private sector banks show huge variation but have higher value of ROA with respect to public sector banks. At the same time Net NPA as percentage of Net advances is higher of private sector banks then public sector banks. It is evident that private sector banks have adopted less efficient credit risk management strategy as compared to Public sector banks. Public sector banks have shown remarkable progress in terms of decrease in Net NPA as percentage of Net Advances. CRAR of private sector banks is higher than public sector banks because they have to cushion themselves from the risk of credit portfolio.

Multiple Regression analysis reveals that Private sector banks have higher degree of significant but negative level of elasticity coefficient of the Net NPA per branch revealing negative contribution to Non Interest Income per branch. The most prominent reason responsible is higher level of reliance of private sector banks on Para- banking activities than public sector banks. Public sector banks have lower level of significant and positive value for contribution of employee per branch to non-interest income. The probable reason could be higher level of work force public sector banks than private sector banks but lack of training and relatively less technical knowledge. This results in lower contribution of employees in generating non- interest income for the bank. The analyses reveals lower level of contribution of operating expenses in generating non -interest income for public sector banks. It is because operating expenses incurred by public sector banks is more on salaries and allowances of employees and very less on technological progress of the banks. The main reason responsible is huge size of employees in public sector banks than private sector banks. ATMs per branch are an important contributory factor for generating non-interest income among private sector banks than public sector banks. It is because private sector banks are techno savvy from quite before than public sector banks. Private sector banks have higher number of ATMs than public sector banks.

According to the DEA estimates, it can be concluded that Public Sector Banks have improved in terms of technical and allocative efficiency during the study period. The higher level of operational efficiency of public sector banks reflects higher dependence on interest income. Lower level of technical efficiency of public sector banks can be attributed to lack of sufficient alternative non –interest, fee based sources of earnings. Public sector banks performance is the best in term of operational efficiency. The probable reason could be excessive dependence on interest income of public sector banks as compared to their peers in the private sector and therefore their fee based earnings coming from services remain quite low.

Still, despite the large gains by private bank groups, public sector banks, particularly the State Bank group, continued to be the market leader in so far as absolute efficiency levels were concerned along with HDFC Bank. The higher level of efficiency of State Bank of India could be accounted due to adoption of a strategy by bank to motivate employees by giving them incentives, better training in new techno –savvy areas, foreign postings and specialized jobs. Bank is also recruiting laterally consultants and contractual employees and the outcome is launch of mobile banking by the bank itself not as a separate subsidiary. On the other hand, the success mantra of ICICI bank is its technology driven employee team with entrepreneurial mindset. The bank has business specific technology groups and budgets embedded within the business verticals; this has empowered the technology team to facilitate initiatives that the market place is still evaluating.

Technological upgradation to achieve higher level of productivity, profitability and efficiency needs measures relating to customer orientation, market focus, greater use of multiple channels like ATMs, Internet and Mobile Banking, efficient credit dispensation and monitoring, sharing of ATMs, swapping of branches, co-branding of products, besides building up sound financials. Public sector banks for sustenance of profits requires attention on declining spread, high operating cost, stiff competition, transformed economic environment and new prudential regulations.

It is essential that public sector banks' along with technological upgradation do associate strong, skilled, competent, passionate and professional human resource force. The research reveals that during the study period, the leading private sector bank in terms of technical efficiency has been ICICI Bank followed by HDFC Bank and Axis Bank. The technical efficiency performance of IndusInd Bank has continuously declined over the years. The main cause of continuous decline in technical efficiency of banks is increase in non-performing assets of the bank. This trend indicates that the technological upgradation is an ongoing process, to get higher returns from the given set of inputs technological upgradation thus acts as a facilitator but not as the end product. It is further analyzed that Private sector Banks were at higher allocative efficiency level than public sector banks because of less reliability on deposits for income generation accompanied by less number of employees and higher level of technological advancement as well as higher reliance on non interest income with squeezing level of spread.

It is evident from both the models that Jammu and Kashmir Bank is least efficient bank in terms of technical efficiency as it is evident in terms of technical progress of the bank is lacking behind with respect to their competitors in the financial market. The most efficient Bank is ICICI Bank. It depicts technological advancement and benefit to the bank in terms of generation of fee income and mobilization of deposits. In Public Sector banks most efficient bank is State Bank of India with maximum score with respect to the reference unit, depicting higher level of efficiency of State Bank of India.

It can be concluded that as regards bank groups, the State Bank group and nationalized banks adopted technology long after new private sector banks. Hence, while private sector banks were mostly defining the grand technological frontier of the Indian banking system, public sector banks closely pursued the frontier to stay competitive. Many public sector banks also computerized their branches and introduced core banking solutions. Although in the initial years, it pushed up the cost, it however, appeared to have resulted in cutting operating cost and improving efficiency in the subsequent years. As a matter of fact, private and public sector banks are excelling in one of the portfolios. Public sector banks are better than private sector banks in terms of generating core interest income and hence have higher operational efficiency but are far behind private sector banks, especially new private sector banks in generating non-interest income. Similarly private sector banks are techno-efficient and hence have higher level of technical and allocative efficiency than public sector banks but are more risk prone and are lacking in generation of interest income.

It can be summarised that in an era of globalisation and consequent demolition of protectionist barriers, banks with the help of technology must adopt appropriate business and delivery models enabling acquisition of new customers and expansion into hitherto unchartered territory.There should not be a disjuncture between information and technology; both together will enable banks to meet the expectations of demanding and tech-savvy customers.

Banks and financial institutions do recognise the potential of Information Technology as an enabler of sophisticated product development, better market infrastructure and implementation of reliable techniques for control of risks. With adaption to a continuous and rapid advance in technology, banking will experience transformational growth. Technology will further open up existing markets and create new markets, new products and services and efficient delivery channels for the banking industry. Information Technology will provide banking industry with the wherewithal to deal with the challenges of the new economy. Technology must be implemented with the customer in focus. Technology must enable customer facilitation in terms of cost, time and convenience. It should be dovetailed to customer needs and expectations. In sharp contrast, technology implementation in our public sector banks appears to be more for regulatory and policy compliance. This has oriented the banking technology to be more employees friendly rather than customer-friendly.

7.11 RECOMMENDATIONS:

Need to Reduce Intermediation Cost

The intermediation cost of the banking sector in India has come down significantly, reflecting the growing competitive pressures. However, the intermediation cost for public sector banks, in general, is still high as compared with private banks. High intermediation cost can affect the level of investment and hurt growth. Banks, therefore, need to make concerted efforts to bring down the intermediation cost further by increasing investment in technological upgradation.

Need to bring down the Operating Cost

One of the major reasons of high intermediation cost is the high operating cost. Although banks have been able to bring down the operating cost, the operating cost to income ratio for all bank groups is still not in sync with the international best practice. Technology can play a major role not only in reducing operating cost but also improving productivity. As public sector banks complete the computerization of remaining branches and implement core banking solutions, non-labor costs are expected to move up initially. However, in the long run, it should help bring down the operating costs.

Need to Improve Labor Productivity in Public Sector Banks

A major reason for high operating cost for public sector banks is the low labor productivity. Although the labor productivity of public sector banks has improved, it continues to be far below that of new private sector banks. Public sector banks, therefore, need to look into various aspects of labor productivity and take necessary measures to improve it further. Thus, the development of human resource skills assumes significance and public sector banks need to pay greater attention to the training requirements of their staff.

Need to Increase Non-Interest Sources of Income

Banks' main source of income is net interest income, which provides stability to earnings. However, non-interest sources of income can help in sustaining the earnings. This is particularly the case when activity of non-interest source of income and the main activity are negatively co-related. At present, banks' non-interest sources of income constitute very small portion of their total income. This is particularly so in the case of public sector banks as their non-interest income ratio in the year 2006-07 was more or less at the same level as in the year 1991-92, although there were periods (between 2001-02 to 2003-04) when non-interest income ratio improved significantly mainly due to trading profits on Government securities. As net interest income margins are expected to come further under pressure in future, banks need to seek newer non-interest sources of income to sustain their profitability.

Need to Improve Technical Efficiency and Allocative Efficiency Further

There is also evidence that banks in the public and private sectors are gradually catching up with their more efficient peers. Inefficient banks are present in both public and private sectors but technologically sound banks have higher level of technical and allocative efficiency and lower level of operational efficiency. Inefficient bank Jammu and Kashmir and Oriental Bank of Commerce need to diversify their income earning by promoting techno-savvy products and services to modern day ever demanding customers and reduce cost to minimum. Punjab National Bank and IndusInd Bank need to adopt risk mitigation credit strategy. ICICI needs to improve the traditional source of income by expanding in rural areas and investing in minimum risk international market. State Bank of India needs to sustain its manpower and all public sector banks need to enhance technology driven products and services. The need is to bring improvement in the efficiency of all those banks which are far away from the efficiency frontier by identifying the underlying causes of their low efficiency.

Need to Adopt Efficient Risk Management Strategy

The risk weights and provisioning requirements has to be enhanced to moderate the credit flow to certain sectors and protect the asset quality of banks. The banks with better risk management skills would not only have competitive advantage in the marketplace but would also be better positioned to capitalize on the opportunities for organic and inorganic growth. Risk management is critically important for banks and in the emerging economic scenario; there is a greater need for banks to implement risk-based practices.

Need to Retain and Train Manpower

With uniform implementation of technology for delivery of products in more efficient and effective manner to customers across major banks in the country, the quality of manpower interacting with customers will ultimately become the deciding driver of business growth for commercial banks. It is in this context that the manpower planning assumes importance for public sector banks of India. Besides meeting the manpower demand by the supply in terms of numbers, the more important aspect is the manpower planning exercise to take steps to improve the quality of available manpower resources from within organization by identifying individual strengths and weaknesses and providing proper training to be comfortable with technological innovative products and services of the bank.

Need to Adopt Information Technology Governance

With the high rate of technological obsolescence, the need for proper IT governance, particularly in the case of banks, is must. Adoption of Information Technology Governance in banks would result in effective control and derive better value on the huge IT infrastructure created by banks. This would ultimately result in enabling better alignment between IT and Business, create efficiencies, enhance conformity to internationally accepted best practices and improve overall IT performance of banks.

It can be concluded that Public sector banks to great extent and private sector banks need to integrate technology with business to significantly raise productivity bar. Foster innovation and strategic differentiation leading to higher value-added products and services. It needs to create a competitive advantage by enhancing organizational effectiveness through management of deregulated interest, judicious asset-liability management (ALM) and realistic market segmentation. Product differentiation, technology upgradation, corporate governance, reduced transaction cost is needed for higher yield of assets. It has been realized that Public Sector Banks incur higher expenses on employee salaries and other heads but less on technological progress.

It can be concluded that ATMs contributes in increase in non -interest income of banks. Public sector banks need to provide training to human resources of the bank for higher level of returns. Banks are increasingly beginning to recognize Human resources as a possible area of core competence, and seek to pursue and retain the best talent in the industry. There is a realization that skill development is extremely important for staff retention as well as the quality of manpower.There is, at the same time, an urgent need for Indian banks (especially public sector banks) to move beyond retail banking, and further grow and expand their fee- based operations, which has globally remained one of the key drivers of growth and profitability. Indian banks are fast realizing that fee-based sources of income have to be actively looked at as a basis for future growth, if the industry is to become a global force to reckon with.Most profitable non interest income opportunities for Indian Banks facilitated by information technology are Foeign exchange management, derivatives trading, bancassurance, wealth management, selling of mutual funds and credit and debit cards.Hence, banks have realized that Information Technology holds the way forward for a more cost effective and yet, inclusive banking system.

SECTION B

CHALLENGES AND OPPORTUNITIES IN BANKING

8

"INDIAN BANKING" - THE CHALLENGES AHEAD

The enhanced role of the banking sector in the Indian economy, the increasing levels of deregulation and the increasing levels of competition have placed numerous demands on banks. Operating in this demanding environment has exposed banks to various challenges:

1. CUSTOMER SERVICE: It is no longer adequate for banks to provide only traditional banking services. Apart from providing the conventional banking services, banks have begun offering a bouquet of financial services to their clients, including cross selling of financial products. The ultimate aim is to offer a one-stop-shop for meeting varied customers' financial needs. Some banks have begun employing customer relationship management systems to not only retain the existing customers but also to attract new customers.

The establishment of new private sector banks and foreign banks has rapidly changed the competitive landscape in the Indian consumer banking industry and placed greater demands on banks to gear themselves up to meet the increasing needs of customers. For the discerning current day bank customers, it is not only relevant to offer a wide menu of services but also provide these in an increasingly efficient manner in terms of cost, time and convenience.

While banks are focusing on the methodologies of meeting the increasing demands placed on them, there are legitimate concerns in regard to the banking practices that tend to exclude rather than attract vast sections of population, in particular pensioners, self-employed and those employed in unorganised sector. While commercial considerations are no doubt important, banks have been bestowed with several privileges, especially of seeking public deposits on a highly leveraged basis, and consequently they should be obliged to provide banking services to all segments of the population, on equitable basis. Further, experience has shown that consumers' interests are at times not accorded full protection and their grievances are not properly attended to. Feedback received reveals recent trends of levying unreasonably high service/user charges and enhancement of user charges without proper and prior intimation. It is in this context that the Governor, Reserve Bank of India had mentioned in the Annual Policy Statement 2005-06 that RBI will take initiatives to encourage:

- The enhanced role of the banking sector in the Indian economygreater degree of financial inclusion in the country;
- Setting up of a mechanism for ensuring fair treatment of consumers; and
- Effective redressal of customer grievances.

It would, therefore, be reasonable to expect banks to focus on the above aspects while designing their products for customers.

2. **BRANCH BANKING:** Traditionally banks have been looking to expansion of their branch network to increase their business. Against this background it is interesting to observe that the new private sector banks as well as the foreign banks have been able to achieve business expansion through other means. It has been realized that it might not be necessary to establish a wider brick and mortar network to reach a wider population. Banks are, therefore, examining the potential benefits that may

accrue by tapping the agency arrangement route and the outsourcing route. While proceeding in this direction banks ought not to lose sight of the new risks that they might be assuming and hence put in place appropriate strategies and systems for managing these new risks.

3. **COMPETITION:** With the ever increasing pace and extent of globalisation of the Indian economy and the systematic opening up of the Indian banking system to global competition, banks need to equip themselves to operate in the increasingly competitive environment. This will make it imperative for banks to enhance their systems and procedures to international standards and also simultaneously fortify their financial positions.

4. **TECHNOLOGY:** A few banks which have impressive branch networks have not been able to meet their customers' expectations due to inefficiencies arising out of inadequate investment in technology and consequently faced an erosion of their market shares. The beneficiaries are those banks which have invested in technology. Another distinct advantage of use of technology is the ability to effectively use quantitative techniques and models which can enhance the quality of their risk management systems. Recognising the benefits of modernising their technology infrastructure banks are taking the right initiatives. The challenge in this regard will be for banks to ensure that they derive maximum advantage out of their investments in technology and to avoid wasteful expenditure which might arise on account of

   a. Uncoordinated and piecemeal adoption of technology;

   b. Adoption of inappropriate/ inconsistent technology and

   c. Adoption of obsolete technology.

A case in point is the implementation of core banking solutions by some banks without assessing its scalability or adaptability to meet Basel II requirements.

5. **BASEL II IMPLEMENTATION:** As you are aware, Basel II is the revised framework for capital adequacy for banks. Implementation of Basel II is seen as one of the significant challenges facing the banking sector in many jurisdictions. With the introduction of capital charge for market risks with effect from the year ended March 31, 2005 banks in India are compliant with all elements of Basel I. I will now outline the approach to Basel II implementation in India. Commercial banks in India will start implementing Basel II with effect from March 31, 2007. They will initially adopt the Standardised Approach for credit risk and the Basic Indicator Approach for operational risk. After adequate skills are developed, both by the banks and also by the supervisors, some banks may be allowed to migrate to the Internal Rating Based (IRB) Approach. Implementation of Basel II will require more capital for banks in India due to the fact that operational risk is not captured under Basel I, and the capital charge for market risk was not prescribed until recently. Though in has not been a very good year for banks, they are exploring all avenues for meeting the capital requirements under Basel II. The cushion available in the system, which has a CRAR of over 12 per cent now, is, however, comforting.

With a view to ensuring migration to Basel II in a non-disruptive manner, a consultative and participative approach has been adopted for both designing and implementing Basel II in India. A Steering Committee comprising senior officials from 14 banks (public, private and foreign) has been constituted wherein representation from the Indian Banks' Association and the RBI has also been ensured. The Steering Committee had formed sub-groups to address specific issues. On the basis of recommendations of the Steering Committee, draft guidelines to the banks on implementation of the New Capital Adequacy Framework have been issued. Though Basel II implementation is considered as a challenge generally, the above approach has lightened the burden on banks in India.

Notwithstanding the above, capacity building, both in banks and the regulatory bodies is a serious challenge, especially with regard to adoption of the advanced approaches. RBI initiated supervisory capacity-building measures to identify the gaps and to assess as well as quantify the extent of additional capital which may be required to be maintained by such banks. The magnitude of this task appears daunting since we have as many as 90 scheduled commercial banks in India.

6. **IMPROVING RISK MANAGEMENT SYSTEMS:** With the increasing degree of deregulation and exposure of banks to various types of risks, efficient risk management systems have become essential. As you are aware, as a step towards further enhancing and fine-tuning risk management systems in banks, Reserve Bank has issued guidelines on asset-liability management and risk management systems in banks in 1999 and Guidance Notes on Credit Risk Management and Market Risk Management in October 2002 and the Guidance Note on Operational risk management in 2005. Though Basel II focuses significantly on risks its implementation should not be seen as an end in itself. It should be seen as a medium whereby the risk management systems in banks are constantly upgraded to address the changing environment.

At the initial stages of development of the risk management systems, banks were managing each risk in isolation. The current business environment demands a more integrated approach to risk management. It is no longer sufficient to manage each risk independently or in functional silos. Enterprises worldwide are, therefore, now putting in place an integrated framework for risk management which is proactive, systematic and spans across the entire organisation. Banks in India are also moving from the individual silo system to an enterprise wide risk management system. This is placing greater demands on the risk management skills in banks and has brought to the forefront the need for capacity building. While the first milestone would be risk integration across the entity, banks are also aware of the desirability of risk aggregation across the group both in the specific risk areas as also across the risks. Banks would be required to allocate significant resources towards this objective over the next few years.

In the Reserve Bank, we have adopted the risk based approach to supervision since 2003 and have brought about 23 banks under the fold of risk based supervision (RBS) on a pilot basis. On the basis of the feedback received from the pilot project, the RBS framework has now been reviewed. The risk based approach to supervision is also serving as a catalyst to banks' migration to the integrated risk management systems. In view of the relevance of improved risk management systems under the changing circumstances and the larger emphasis placed on risk management systems in banks under Basel II, it is essential that the RBS stabilizes at an early date and serves as an important feedback not only to bank managements but also to RBI. However, taking into account the diversity in the Indian banking system, stabilizing the RBS as an effective supervisory mechanism will be a challenge to the RBI.

7. **IMPLEMENTATION OF NEW ACCOUNTING STANDARDS:** Derivative activity in banks has been increasing at a brisk pace. While the risk management framework for derivative trading, which is a relatively new area for Indian banks (particularly in the more structured products), is an essential pre-requisite, the absence of clear accounting guidelines in this area is matter of significant concern. It is widely accepted that as the volume of transactions increases, which is happening in the Indian banking system, the need to upgrade the accounting framework needs no emphasis. The World Bank's ROSC on Accounting and Auditing in India has commented on the absence of an accounting standard which deals with recognition, measurement and disclosures pertaining to financial instruments. The Accounting Standards Board of the Institute of Chartered

Accountants of India (ICAI) is considering issue of Accounting Standards on the above aspects pertaining to financial Instruments. These will be the Indian parallel to International Accounting Standards 32 and 39. The proposed Accounting Standards will be of considerable significance for financial entities and could therefore have implications for the financial sector. The formal introduction of these Accounting Standards by the ICAI is likely to take some time in view of the processes involved. RBI is considering the need for banks and financial entities adopting the broad underlying principles of IAS 39. Since this is likely to give rise to some regulatory / prudential issues all relevant aspects are being comprehensively examined. The proposals in this regard would, as is normal, be discussed with the market participants before introduction. Adoption and implementation of these principles are likely to pose a great challenge to both the banks and the Reserve Bank.

8. **TRANSPARENCY AND DISCLOSURES (BASLE III):** In pursuance of the Financial Sector Reforms introduced since 1991 and in order to bring about meaningful disclosure of the true financial position of banks to enable the users of financial statements to study and have a meaningful comparison of their positions, a series of measures were initiated. The disclosure requirements broadly covered the following aspects:

- Capital adequacy
- Asset quality
- Maturity distribution of select items of assets and liabilities
- Profitability
- Country risk exposure
- Risk exposures in derivatives
- Segment reporting
- Related Party disclosures

With a view to moving closer towards international best practices including International Accounting Standards (IAS) and the disclosure requirements under Pillar 3 of Basel II, Reserve Bank has proposed enhanced disclosures which lay a greater emphasis on disclosure of certain qualitative aspects. Transparency and disclosure standards are also recognised as important constituents of a sound corporate governance mechanism. Banks are required to formulate a formal disclosure policy approved by the Board of directors that addresses the bank's approach for determining what disclosures it will make and the internal controls over the disclosure process. In addition, banks should implement a process for assessing the appropriateness of their disclosures, including validation and frequency.

9. **SUPERVISION OF FINANCIAL CONGLOMERATES:** In view of increased focus on empowering supervisors to undertake consolidated supervision of bank groups and since the Core Principles for Effective Banking Supervision issued by the Basel Committee on Banking Supervision have underscored consolidated supervision as an independent principle, the Reserve Bank had introduced, as an initial step, consolidated accounting and other quantitative methods to facilitate consolidated supervision. The components of consolidated supervision include, consolidated financial statements intended for public disclosure, consolidated prudential reports intended for supervisory assessment of risks and application of certain prudential regulations on group basis. In due course, consolidated supervision as introduced above would evolve to cover banks in mixed conglomerates, where the parent may be non-financial entities or parents may be financial entities coming under the jurisdiction of other regulators.

The financial landscape is increasingly witnessing entry of some of the bigger banks into other financial segments like merchant banking, insurance etc., which has made them financial conglomerates. Emergence of several new players with diversified presence across major segments and possibility of some of the non-banking institutions in the financial sector acquiring large enough proportions to have systemic impact make it imperative for supervision to be spread across various segments of the financial sector. In this direction, an inter-regulatory Working Group was constituted with members from RBI, SEBI and IRDA. The framework proposed by the Group will be complementary to the existing regulatory structure wherein the individual entities are regulated by the respective regulators and the identified financial conglomerates would be subjected to focussed regulatory oversight through a mechanism of inter-regulatory exchange of information. As a first step in this direction, an inter-agency Working Group on Financial Conglomerates (FC) comprising the above three supervisory bodies identified 23 FCs and a pilot process for obtaining information from these conglomerates has been initiated. The complexities involved in the supervision of financial conglomerates are a challenge not only to the Reserve Bank of India but also to the other regulatory agencies, which need to have a close and continued coordination on an on-going basis.

10. 'KNOW YOUR CUSTOMER' (KYC) GUIDELINES – ANTI MONEY LAUNDERING STANDARDS: Banks were advised in 2002 to follow certain customer identification procedure for opening of accounts and monitoring transactions of a suspicious nature for the purpose of reporting it to appropriate authority. These 'Know Your Customer' guidelines were revisited in the context of the recommendations made by the Financial Action Task Force on Anti Money Laundering standards and on Combating Financing of Terrorism. These standards have become the international benchmark for framing Anti Money Laundering and combating financing of terrorism policies by the regulatory authorities. Compliance with these standards both by the banks/ financial institutions and the country has become necessary for international financial relationships.

Detailed guidelines based on the Recommendations of the Financial Action Task Force and the paper issued on Customer Due Diligence for banks by the Basel Committee on Banking Supervision, with indicative suggestions wherever considered necessary, were issued to banks in November 2004. Banks were required to ensure that a proper policy framework on 'Know Your Customer' and Anti-Money Laundering measures is formulated and put in place with the approval of the Board within three months and be fully compliant with these guidelines before December 31, 2005. Compliance with the above is a significant challenge to the entire banking industry to fortify itself against misuse by anti-social persons/ entities and thus project a picture of solidarity and financial integrity of the Indian banking system to the international community.

11. **CORPORATE GOVERNANCE:** Banks are "special" as they not only accept and deploy large amount of uncollateralized public funds in fiduciary capacity, but they also leverage such funds through credit creation. Banks are also important for smooth functioning of the payment system. In view of the above, legal prescriptions for ownership and governance of banks laid down in Banking Regulation Act, 1949 have been supplemented by regulatory prescriptions issued by RBI from time to time. In this context, one must remember that profit motive should not be the sole criterion for business decisions. Flow of bank finance for productive purposes must always take priority over the granting of credit for speculative investment no matter how profitable the latter may be.

    If bank finance flows increasingly to finance speculative activities, it will be to the detriment of real productive investment for research, development and the production of real goods/ services.

    One might conclude that such uncontrolled flow would ultimately affect economic growth. Hence, funding of speculative activities must be subject to prudential limits, even though it might yield attractive returns. This will be a significant challenge to banks where the priorities and incentives might not be well balanced by the operation of sound principles of corporate governance. If the internal imbalances are not re-balanced immediately, the correction may evolve through external forces and may be painful and costly to all stakeholders. The focus, therefore, should be on enhancing and fortifying operation of the principles of sound corporate governance. Thus the Indian Banking Industry has to surmount the chanlleges ahead and vision 2020 is a productive transformed industry.

9

INDIAN BANKING - OPPORTUNITIES

The current economic situation provides a lot of opportunities as well as challenges to the existing banks. *It is up to the banks to leverage the opportunities to meet the challenges to the best of their abilities.* The past year witnessed a lot of turmoil in the Indian banking industry owing to the global financial crisis. The Reserve Bank of India (RBI), Ministry of Finance and other regulatory authorities have made several notable efforts to improve regulation in the sector. Many big banks operating in the market have made use of the changed regulations (viz., change in CRR and interest rate) to provide better options to potential and new customers. Adoption of new practices to cater to the demanding economy situation has enabled the banks to meet the changing customer requirements. Compared to other regional banks, over the last few years, Indian banks have performed favorably on growth, asset quality and profitability. The banking index has grown at a compounded annual rate of over 51% from April 2001 compared to the market index for the same period, which registered a growth rate of 27%.

The crisis that hit the financial services industry initially in the US and almost immediately in the entire world has moved our focus towards critical systemic issues—not only in the US banking business but also in India. Globally, these systemic issues are being tackled at the legislative and regulatory levels; in India, the solution to the systemic issues will require significant inputs and regulatory, industry and infrastructural interventions. To ensure survival, banks tried to quickly assess their liquidity reserves and capital position to check if they had any exposure to the failing global entities. Additionally, this check also meant a clear pulling down of new/additional credit outflow, unless and until their positions were clear. Over a short span of time, the situation resulted in banks totally stopping the outflow of new credit.

According to Indian Banks Association data, retail credit growth dropped drastically from 30% in 2007 to 10% in 2008, owing to increased pressure on existing loan portfolios and the fear of anticipated mass job losses which would result in high NPAs. Analysts and credit rating agencies in their reports showed marginal to moderate increases in NPLs in assets such as two-wheelers, commercial vehicles and unsecured loans. Growth in mortgages, which forms 50% of banks' retail portfolio, was also hit due to upward movement in interest rates, restriction on collection practices and soaring real estate prices.

Indian banks had to clean up their systems and practices to ensure stability in a recovering economy. Four challenges must be addressed before success can be achieved.

1. The market is witnessing haphazard growth, driven by new products and services, which include credit cards, consumer finance and wealth management on the retail side, and fee-based income and investment banking on the wholesale banking side. Continuous growth in these new products and services requires new skills in sales and marketing, credit, operations and, above all, a potential customer base to provide these offerings.
2. There will be no windfall treasury gains, which banks used to enjoy as a result of the decade-long secular decline in interest rates provided. This will expose the weaker banks and put them in trouble to a large extent.
3. Growing interest in India will encourage foreign banks

to set shop in India, thereby intensifying the competition for domestic and other existing players.

4. As India is experiencing demographic shifts resulting from changes in age profile and household income, now consumers will demand improved institutional capabilities and enhanced service levels from banks.

As has been mentioned earlier, in India, regulators need to play a major role in revolutionalizing and bringing about changes in the economy.

Of late, it has been realized that there is a need to create a market-driven banking sector, with ample stress on social development. *This requires dedicated efforts by the regulators in six important areas, which are as follows:*

1. Focus strongly on 'social development' by shifting from universal directed norms to an explicit incentive-driven system by introducing credit guarantees and market subsidies to encourage leading public sector, private and foreign players to leverage technology to innovate and profitably provide banking services to lower income and rural markets, thereby improving financial inclusion in the economy.
2. Like the biggest financial markets of the world, create a super regulator rather than having separate regulators for each and every participant in the financial services industry.
3. Focus on corporate governance and ensure that the same is improved by primarily focusing on board independence and accountability.
4. Speed up the process of creation of world-class supporting infrastructure (e.g., payments, Asset Reconstruction Companies (ARCs), credit bureaus, and back-office utilities) to enable the banking sector focus on core activities.
5. Undertake labor reforms, focusing on enhancing human capital, to help the public sector and old private banks compete with the newly established and much more efficient private banks and foreign banks entering the country.

Not only the regulators need to gear up, but even the banks need to pull up their socks and bring about some changes to support the reforms which the regulators aim to bring in:

6. Public sector banks need to improve certain areas of their work performance, viz., sales and marketing, service operations, risk management and the overall organizational performance ethic. Last but not the least is to enhance the human capital, which will be the single biggest challenge and definitely the most time-consuming one also.
7. What is true for public sector banks is also true for old private sector banks, as they have to also strengthen their basic skills. Additionally, they have to ensure their proactive participation in the Indian banking sector. This is of utmost importance to them, because the same will keep them up-to-date in this fiercely competitive market.
8. New private banks can achieve an altogether new height in their growth in the Indian banking sector by continuing to engineer new and differentiated business models to profitably, efficiently and effectively service segments like the rural/low income and affluent/HNI segments, and by keeping an eye open for the acquisition of small banks to grow and reach the next level of performance in their service platforms. Attracting, developing and retaining management capacity would be another critical factor for achieving this and would be the biggest challenge that these banks will have to face.
9. Foreign banks entering India will have to be innovative in their approaches to win the largest customer base and share of wallet and above all, to build a value-creating customer franchise in advance of regulations potentially opening up post 2009. At the same time, they need to be an active player in the game for potential acquisition opportunities, as and when they emerge, to ensure growth and establishment in India. They need to sustain

and maintain a long-term value-creation mindset, which will not be an easy task by any means.

Thus, banking in India involves the cooperation and participation of many stakeholders for the desired changes to be made in the existing system. Last year, during the economic slowdown, when the banking system globally went for a toss, the Indian banking industry emerged as a strong performer owing to the coordinated efforts of policy makers and the banks in bringing these policies to action for the best of the economy.

The Indian banking industry gathered the strength to sustain during such times through its huge deposit base, which is consistently on a growth path, central bank's proactive measures to steadily improve banks' balance sheet strength, and a demand in the economy for physical asset creation. These factors enabled the Indian banking sector to become stronger on the capitalization front and also ensure lower level NPAs and better spreads in the past one-and-a-half decade.

The strength provided through timely measures has helped the industry and the economy in many ways. Last year, the economy witnessed perhaps the biggest and positive impact of higher credit growth in infrastructure- related companies—power, telecom and others. However, it was partially compensated by the reduction in other funding sources such as private equity and foreign institutional investors.

The alarm will start ringing if the regulator decides to continue with the stimulus package for long. With dried-up liquidity and no borrowers (given the low credit growth), the banking system will continue to invest excessively in government securities, leading to fiscal deficit eventually.

However, an increase in domestic liquidity has had a cascading effect on the asset price inflation. According to a report by Tata Securities, the YTD growth in deposits is 9%, while the credit growth is only 5.4%, resulting in the banks' looking for other investment opportunities. The high liquidity with banks forced them to invest in the liquid funds of mutual funds, which in turn invested in commercial papers of corporates at a lower coupon— corporates would have otherwise borrowed at a higher cost from the banks for their working capital requirements.

The second half of the year, which is typically the time for maximum activity in the economy, usually witnesses a higher demand for bank credit, compared to the first six months of the financial year. The three broad segments of bank credit are: Capex and Infrastructure Credit; Working Capital Loans; and Consumer Loans.

It is expected that growth would be highest in the case of infrastructure credit and consumer loans. Additionally, it is also expected that the demand for working capital loans is likely to be low, as commodity prices (crude oil and metals) continue to be low, and thus companies will have to work with low working capital requirements on a yearly basis.

Infrastructure is expected to catalyze credit growth in the Indian economy. According to the allocations made by the authorities concerned, the planned outlay on infrastructure under the 11th Five Year Plan under the projected investment in infrastructure should be around Rs 4,500 bn per annum for the next three years. According to a report from Tata Securities, infrastructure as a percentage of total bank credit exists at 10.2% currently, and it is projected to grow at more than 40% y-o-y in the next three years.

Consumer demand has been very resilient. There has also been a rise in the purchasing power in smaller cities and rural areas, along with job stability in large cities and Pay Commission benefits. Research by Tata Securities suggests that secured retail loans in the mortgage and vehicle financing segments are seeing good demand and will drive the overall bank credit growth. The research also states that in the absence of a pickup in corporate working capital loans, banks are eager to grow the secured consumer loans portfolio.

It is expected that a price correction in the real estate market and gentle interest rates are factors which will promote growth in loan portfolios.

The downturn which the economy witnessed has discouraged the banks from having any exposure to unsecured consumer credit, and a revival in this segment is not expected to happen soon. According to a research report from Tata Securities, retail loans showed a CAGR of 22% during FY05-FY09. Within the retail segment, housing loans grew by 20% CAGR during the same period and consisted ~10% of the total bank credit. Thus, the banks, which had a big challenge on the unsecured loan front, had at the same time a bigger opportunity in the mortgage-backed security portfolio.

Abundant liquidity in the banking system during FY10 has been ensured through secular growth in deposits, low credit demand and prudent borrowing schedule issued by the government to maintain a balanced growth. According to a research report, despite the huge borrowings of Rs 4,510 bn by the government in FY10, the money held in reverse repo by banks remained considerably high. This will provide an opportunity to the banks to utilize the money in the most efficient and effective way to the benefit of both the customers and the economy as a whole, comprising various stakeholders.

Having talked about comfortable liquidity and the much-wanted stability in the banking system, one can expect that bond yields will remain in a higher range and would not fall significantly. Other reasons which are likely to support this fact includes:

- Lower than expected government borrowings
- Reduced global risk premium
- Higher credit growth

This brings another opportunity for the banks to earn higher income.

Besides the favorable condition for liquidity and high bond yield, it is expected that the Net Interest Margin (NIM) will not expand much. The banks need to have higher incremental CD ratio, improvement in spreads and stable yield on investments to improve NIMs. Banks are expected to have a low cost of deposits owing to a stable interest rate scenario and ample liquidity in the system.

Major Challenges which the Indian Banks face now a days are :

1. **CUSTOMER SERVICE:** It is no longer adequate for banks to provide only traditional banking services. Apart from providing the conventional banking services, banks have begun offering a bouquet of financial services to their clients, including cross selling of financial products. The ultimate aim is to offer a one-stop-shop for meeting varied customers' financial needs. Some banks have begun employing customer relationship management systems to not only retain the existing customers but also to attract new customers. The establishment of new private sector banks and foreign banks has rapidly changed the competitive landscape in the Indian consumer banking industry and placed greater demands on banks to gear themselves up to meet the increasing needs of customers. For the discerning current day bank customers, it is not only relevant to offer a wide menu of services but also provide these in an increasingly efficient manner in terms of cost, time and convenience. The Need for KYC (Know your Customers) cannot be neglected. RBI will take care of initiatives to encourage:
   - Greater degree of financial inclusion in the country;
   - Setting up of a mechanism for ensuring fair treatment of consumers; and
   - Effective redressal of customer grievances.
2. **BRANCH BANKING:** Traditionally banks have been looking to expansion of their branch network to increase their business. Against this background it is interesting

to observe that the new private sector banks as well as the foreign banks have been able to achieve business expansion through other means. It has been realized that it might not be necessary to establish a wider brick and mortar network to reach a wider population. Concepots of Narrow Banking, Universal Banking have to be elaborated.Another important area which requires critical attention is fee income. In the past few years, fee income has been the major contributor of revenue for private sector banks. Private sector banks have leveraged those areas to achieve the above, which public sector banks have not been able to, viz., transaction-related services and third party products sales, among others, to increase this non-fund based income.

Thus, we can very well say that the current situation has provided a lot of opportunities and challenges to the existing banks. Now, it is up to the banks as to how well they leverage the opportunities to meet the challenges to the best of their capacities.

3. **COMPETITION:** With the ever increasing pace and extent of globalisation of the Indian economy and the systematic opening up of the Indian banking system to global competition, banks need to equip themselves to operate in the increasingly competitive environment. This will make it imperative for banks to enhance their systems and procedures to international standards and also simultaneously fortify their financial positions.
4. **TECHNOLOGY:** A few banks which have impressive branch networks have not been able to meet their customers' expectations due to inefficiencies arising out of inadequate investment in technology and consequently faced an erosion of their market shares. The beneficiaries are those banks which have invested in technology. Another distinct advantage of use of technology is the ability to effectively use quantitative techniques and models which can enhance the quality of their risk management systems. Recognising the

benefits of modernising their technology infrastructure banks are taking the right initiatives. The challenge in this regard will be for banks to ensure that they derive maximum advantage out of their investments in technology and to avoid wasteful expenditure which might arise on account of:

a. Uncoordinated and piecemeal adoption of technology;

b. Adoption of inappropriate/ inconsistent technology and

c. Adoption of obsolete technology.

5. **CORE BANKING SOLUTIONS:** By Indian banks without assessing its scalability or adaptability to meet Basel II requirements has been implemented.

6. **IMPROVING RISK MANAGEMENT SYSTEMS:** Wrt Basle III norms apropos implementation of Basle II With the increasing degree of deregulation and exposure of banks to various types of risks, efficient risk management systems have become essential.

7. **IMPLEMENTATION TO IFRS:** Converse and roadmap ahead. Derivative activity in banks has been increasing at a brisk pace. While the risk management framework for derivative trading, which is a relatively new area for Indian banks (particularly in the more structured products), is an essential pre-requisite, the absence of clear accounting guidelines in this area is matter of significant concern. It is widely accepted that as the volume of transactions increases, which is happening in the Indian banking system, the need to upgrade the accounting framework needs no emphasis.

8. **TRANSPARENCY, CORPORATE GOVERNANCE, AND DISCLOSURES:** The disclosure requirements broadly covered the following aspects:

- Capital adequacy
- Asset quality

- Maturity distribution of select items of assets and liabilities
- Profitability
- Country risk exposure
- Risk exposures in derivatives
- Segment reporting
- Related Party disclosures

Thus the financial strength of individual banks, which are major participants in the financial system, is the first line of defence against financial risks. Strong capital positions and balance sheets place banks in a better position to deal with and absorb the economic shocks. Banks need to supplement this with sophisticated and robust risk management practices and the resolve to face competition without diluting the operating standards.

10

CRM in Banking - 7P'S of Marketing - A Case Study of ICICI Bank

7P's of Marketing are Product, Price, Place, Promotion, Process, Physical Evidence & People. This chapter highlights 7P's of Marketing with special reference to ICICI Bank.

10.1 PRODUCT MIX

1. DEPOSITS

ICICI Bank offers wide variety of Deposit Products to suit our requirements. Coupled with convenience of networked branches/ over 1800 ATMs and facility of E-channels like Internet and Mobile Banking, ICICI Bank brings banking at your doorstep.

Savings Account: ICICI Bank offers a power packed Savings Account with a host of convenient features and banking channels to transact through.

Senior Citizen Services: The Senior Citizen Services from ICICI Bank has several advantages that are tailored to bring more convenience and enjoyment in your life.

Young Stars: It's really important to help children learn the value of finances and money management at an early age. Banking is a serious business, but we make banking a pleasure and at the same time children learn how to manage their personal finances.

Fixed Deposits: Safety, Flexibility, Liquidity and Returns. A combination of unbeatable features of the Fixed Deposit from ICICI Bank.

Recurring Deposits: Through ICICI Bank Recurring Deposit you can invest small amounts of money every month that ends up with a large saving on maturity. So you enjoy twin advantages- affordability and higher earnings.

Roaming Current Account: Only Roaming Current Account from ICICI Bank travels the distance with your business. You can access your accounts at over 500 networked branches across the country.

Bank @ Campus: Thanks to bank@campus, child can now surf the Net and access all the details of his / her account at the click of a mouse! No need to visit the bank branch at all.

ICICI Bank Salary Account: is a benefit-rich payroll account for Employers and Employees. As an organization, you can opt for our Salary Accounts to enable easy disbursements of salaries and enjoy numerous other benefits too.

2. INVESTMENTS

Along with Deposit products and Loan offerings, ICICI Bank assists you to manage your finances by providing various investment options such as:

- ICICI Bank Tax Saving Bonds
- Government of India Bonds
- Investment in Mutual Funds
- Initial Public Offers by Corporate
- Investment in "Pure Gold"
- Foreign Exchange Services
- Senior Citizens Savings Scheme, 2004

3. ANYWHERE BANKING

ICICI Bank is the second largest bank in the country. It services a customer base of more than 5 million customer accounts through a multi-channel access network. This includes more than 500 branches and extension counters, over 1800 ATMs. Call Centre and Internet Banking.

Thus, one can access the various services ICICI Bank has to offer at anytime, anywhere and from anyplace.

4. LOAN

a. Home Loans

b. Personal Loans

c. Car Loans

d. Two Wheeler Loans

e. Commercial Vehicle Loans

f. Loans against Securities

g. Farm Equipment Loans

h. Construction Equipment Loans

i. Office Equipment Loans

j. Medical Equipment Loans

5. CARDS

a. Credit Card

b. Debit cum ATM Card

c. Travel Card

6. DEMAT SERVICES

ICICI Bank Demat Services boasts of an ever-growing customer base of over 7 lacs account holders. In their continuous endeavor to offer best of the class services to our customers we offer the following features:

- Digitally signed transaction statement by e-mail.
- Corporate benefit tracking.
- e-Instruction facility - facility to transfer securities 24 hours a day, 7 days a week through Internet Interactive Voice Response (IVR) at a lower cost.
- Dedicated specially trained customer care executives at their call centre, to handle all queries.

7. MOBILE BANKING

With ICICI Bank, banking is no longer what it used to be. ICICI Bank offers Mobile Banking facility to all its Bank, Credit Card and Demat customers. ICICI Bank Mobile Banking enables you to bank while being on the move.

8. NRI SERVICES

ONLINE MONEY TRANSFER facility available to NRIs worldwide through www.money2India.com at the click of a button!

Benefits:

- FREE Money transfers into accounts with over 30 banks in India
- Demand Drafts issued and payable at over 1250 locations in India
- ONLINE Tracking of the status of your funds
- SUPERIOR Exchange rates
- OFFLINE MONEY TRANSFER facility is also available across geographies through
- our local branches and in association with partner banks/ exchange houses.

10.2 PRICING MIX

The pricing decisions or the decisions related to interest and fee or commission charged by banks are found instrumental in motivating or influencing the target market.

The RBI and the IBA are concerned with regulations. The rate of interest is regulated by the RBI and other charges are controlled by IBA.

The pricing policy of a bank is considered important for raising the number of customers' vis-à-vis the accretion of deposits. Also the quality of service provided has direct relationship with the fees charged. Thus while deciding the price mix customer services rank the top position.

The banking organizations are required to frame two-fold strategies. First, the strategy is concerned with interest and fee charged and the second strategy is related to the interest paid. Since both the strategies throw a vice- versa impact, it is important that banks attempt to establish a correlation between two. It is essential that both the buyers as well as the sellers have feeling of winning.

Pricing Bank Products Starts With Three Basic Questions:

Q1. *What rate does the bank need to meet its financial objectives?*

The answer is, "it depends."

Some considerations for loan and deposit pricing are:

- ROA or ROE objectives
- Related income taxes
- Earning assets to total assets
- Equity-to-asset ratio
- Cost to service earning assets being funded or deposits funding an earning asset
- Pricing for the activities and risks associated with the product
- Rate tiers based on product balances
- Asset and liability mix

Another element to consider in the pricing of earning assets is the risk of loss. Most notably, this is relevant in loan pricing. Many banks assign a risk weighting to individual loans over a certain size or based on loan type and assign a credit risk charge based on those ratings.

Customer relationships are difficult to assign a value to in the pricing process. Customers will generally press for some price concessions in consideration of other relationships they have with the bank.

Asset and liability mix also impacts pricing results. Generally speaking, banks operating with higher loan-to-asset ratios are able to afford to pay more for deposits. Likewise, banks can afford to be more competitive on certain deposit products if they have fewer maturities in a particular timeframe or less total outstanding balances in a product line.

Q2. *What is the market rate for the core product?*

Customers have more distribution channels available to them today than at any other point in history. In the past 10 years, the number of bank locations has increased 20%. Of course, there are the mortgage bankers, the Internet, and a host of other financial service providers competing for your customer's loan and deposit business.

The point is, the competitive marketplace always ensures that if a financial institution is charging too much for loans or paying too little for deposits, its share of the market will likely dwindle as existing and prospective customers find alternative providers. You can do all the math you want to determine required pricing points, but if your pricing is uncompetitive, your market share will shrink.

Q3. *What would the bank have to do to sales and operations to make its rates the most competitive in its market?*

Pricing is a key issue for the associates who sell bank products to your customers. The fact is, lenders want the lowest rates, and people dealing with depositors want to pay the highest rates. You need the right balance of fee income, strategies to reduce operating costs, and a healthy asset and liability mix to change your required pricing.

10.3 PLACE

This component of marketing mix is related to the offering of services. The services are sold through the branches.

The 2 important decision making areas are: making available the promised services to the ultimate users and selecting a suitable place for bank branches.

The number of branches OF ICICI: 1900 in India and 33 in Mumbai.

LOCATION OF ATMS:

Why they select this place as branch?

- The selection of a suitable place for the establishment of a branch is significant with
- the view point of making place accessible.
- The safety and security provisions a
- Convenient to both the parties, such as the users and the bankers
- Infrastructure facility
- Near to station and located on s. v. road well crowded area.
- Market coverage

10.4 PROMOTION MIX

- **Advertising:** Television, radio, movies, theatres
- **Print media:** hoardings, newspaper, magazines
- **Publicity:** road shows, campus visits, sandwich man, Sponsorship
- **Sales promotion:** gifts, discount and commission, incentives,etc.
- **Personal selling:** Cross-sale (selling at competitors place),personalized service
- **Telemarketing:** ICICI one source Call center (mind space)

10.5 PROCESS

Flow of activities: all the major activities of ICICI banks follow RBI guidelines. There has to be adherence to certain rules and principles in the banking operations. The activities have been segregated into various departments accordingly.

Standardization: ICICI bank has got standardized procedures got typical transactions. In fact not only all the branches of a single-bank, but all the banks have some standardization in them. This is because of the rules they are subject to. Besides this, each of the banks has its standard forms, documentations etc. Standardization saves a lot of time behind individual transaction.

Customization: There are specialty counters at each branch to deal with customers of a particular scheme. Besides this the customers can select their deposit period among the available alternatives.

Number of steps: numbers of steps are usually specified and a specific pattern is followed to minimize time taken.

Simplicity: in ICICI banks various functions are segregated. Separate counters exist with clear indication. Thus a customer wanting to deposit money goes to 'deposits' counter and does not mingle elsewhere. This makes procedures not only simple but consume less time. Besides instruction boards in national boards in national and regional language help the customers further.

Customer involvement: ATM does not involve any bank employees. Besides, during usual bank transactions, there is definite customer involvement at some or the other place because of the money matters and signature requires.

10.6 PHYSICAL EVIDENCES

Physical evidence is the material part of a service. Strictly speaking there are no physical attributes to a service, so a consumer tends to rely on material cues. There are many examples of physical evidence, including some of the following:

- Internet/web pages
- Paperwork
- Brochures
- Furnishings
- Business cards
- The building itself (such as prestigious offices or scenic headquarters)

The physical evidences also include signage, reports, punch lines, other tangibles, employee's dress code etc.

Signage: each and every bank has its logo by which a person can identify the company. Thus such signages are significant for creating visualization and corporate identity.

Financial reports: The Company's financial reports are issued to the customers to emphasis or credibility.

Tangibles: bank gives pens, writing pads to the internal customers. Even the passbooks, chequebooks, etc reduce the inherent intangibility of services.

Punch lines: punch lines or the corporate statement depict the philosophy and attitude of the bank. Banks have influential punch lines to attract the customers.

Employee's dress code: ICICI bank follows a dress code for their internal customers. This helps the customers to feel the ease and comfort.

10.7 THE PEOPLE

All people directly or indirectly involved in the consumption of banking services are an important part of the extended marketing mix.

Knowledge Workers, Employees, Management and other Consumers often add significant value to the total product or service offering.

It is the employees of a bank which represent the organisation to its customers.

In a bank organization, employees are essentially the contact personnel with customer. Therefore, an employee plays an important role in the marketing operations of a service organisation.

To realize its potential in bank marketing, ICICI become conscious in its potential in internal marketing - the attraction, development, motivation and retention of qualified employee-customers through need meeting job-products. Internal marketing paves way for external marketing of services. In internal marketing a variety of activities are used internally in an active, marketing like manner and in a coordinated way.

The starting point in internal marketing is that the employees are the first internal market for the organization with basic objective to develop motivated and customer conscious employees. A service company can be only as good as its people. A service is a performance and it is usually difficult to separate the performance from the people. If the people don't meet customers' expectations, then neither does the service. Therefore, investing in people quality in service business means new services for current and future service line extensions.

11

RISK MANAGEMENT IN INDIAN BANKS

RISK MANAGEMNT AND BASLE II AFTERMATHS

11.1 INTRODUCTION

The Indian Financial System is tasting success of a decade of financial sector reforms. The economy is surging and has gathered the critical mass to convert it into a force to reckon with. The regulatory framework in India has sparked growth and key structural reforms have improved the asset quality and profitability of banks.

Growing integration of economies and the markets around the world is making global banking a reality. Widespread use of internet banking has widened frontiers of global banking, and it is now possible to market financial products and services on a global basis. In the coming years globalization would spread further on account of the likely opening up of financial services under WTO. India is one of the 104 signatories of Financial Services Agreement (FSA) of 1997. Thereby giving India's financial sector including banks an opportunity to expand their business on a quid pro quo basis.

As in different sectors, competition is driving growth in the banking sector also. The RBI requires all banks to comply with the standardized approach of the BASEL II accord by 31st March, 2019. The quantification and accounting of various risks would result in a more robust risk management system in the industry.

This paper attempts to project the implications of this transition and its effects on the internal operations of a bank followed by its effects on the banking industry and the economy.

11.2 RISK Management Scenario in the Future

Risk management activities will be more pronounced in future banking because of liberalization, deregulation and global integration of financial markets. This would be adding depth and dimension to the banking risks. As the risks are correlated, exposure to one risk may lead to another risk, therefore management of risks in a proactive, efficient & integrated manner will have be the strength of the successful banks. The standardized approach would be implemented by 31st March 2007, and the forward-looking banks would be in the process of placing their MIS for the collection of data required for the calculation of Probability of Default (PD), Exposure at Default (EAD) and Loss Given Default (LGD). The banks are expected to have at a minimum PD data for five years and LGD and EAD data for seven years.

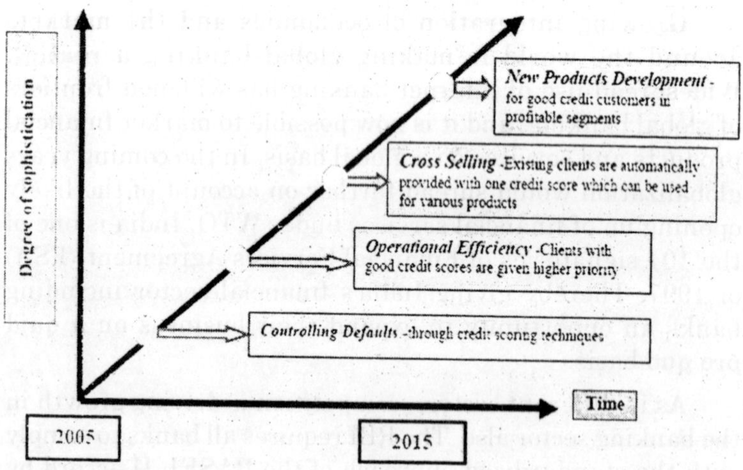

Figure 11.1 Strategic Coutinuum of Risk Scoring Models

Presently most Indian banks do not possess the data required for the calculation of their LGDs. Also the personnel skills, the IT infrastructure and MIS at the banks need to be upgraded substantially if the banks want to migrate to the IRB Approach.

Although many banks would be working towards the IRB Approach, the authors are of the opinion that RBI would have allowed a few banks to implement and follow the IRB Approach by the year 2019. Indian banks would be moving upward on the strategic continuum of risk scoring models as can be seen in the diagram on the previous page.

Risk Management Department's Role

The Risk Department would gain prominence within the banks as they would be playing an extremely critical role in the management of the risks of the bank. Streamlining of information and data flow through the Risk Department would be essential in calculation and management of risks.

11.2.1 Calculation of Risks and CAR

Calculation of risk would be an essential requirement in the banks as they would be in the process of calculating not only the Credit Risk but also the Market Risk and the Operational Risks that the bank would be facing. The capital to be set off for advances made by the bank would depend largely upon the fair and accurate calculation of these risks. In 2005 five credit risk models have received global acceptance as benchmarks for measuring stand-alone as well as portfolio credit risk. They are:

I. Altman's Z Score Model: Detailed in Chapter 13.4

II. Merton Model

III. KMV Model for measuring default risk - Chapter 13.1

IV. Credit Metrics - Chapter 13.2

V. Credit Risk+

These models would get more sophisticated and the

banks would have more options as other models would gain acceptance. For Market Risks the banks would be employing other models such as VaR, Monte Carlo Simulation etc. As for the Operational Risks the banks would be following internal risk frameworks in assessing significant operational risks and their mitigation.

11.2.2 Risk-Based Pricing

Risk-based Pricing is the technique of charging different interest rates from two different customers on the same type of loans, depending on the risk attributed to each of them. Under this method credit scores are calculated for individuals, taking into consideration various factors which are assumed to represent the individual's willingness and capacity to repay the loan installments. As the banks would be in the process of moving toward the IRB Approach they would be armed with the knowledge of the risks associated with the various types of exposures. This knowledge would help the banks in passing on the charge arising from higher credit risk to the customers. The authors are of the opinion that Risk-Based Pricing would be the norm of the banking industry in another ten years.

11.2.3 Technology (MIS)

Indian banks would invest in development of Information Systems as MIS would play an essential role in the calculation of LGD (Loss given Default), EAD (Exporment Default) and PD (Probability Default). As the banks are expected to integrate various financial services to provide a one-stop shop to the customers, MIS would be helpful to the banks in cross-selling and other marketing-related activities. The settings up of such systems are expected to reach completion by 2015 for most banks.

11.2.4 Strengthening of Treasury Operations

The spreads relating to core banking business of credit and deposit interest rates would narrow down. Also, if the bank enjoys low PD and LGD it would have larger amount of funds available to it, as its regulatory capital requirements would come down. The banks would have to search for alternative profit generating avenues in the form of float fund management, thereby strengthening their treasury operations, which will be a thrust area in the coming years.

11.2.5 Human Resource Development

More emphasis would be given to the human resources of the bank as Basel II would require banks to calculate and manage risks continuously. One of the key requirements of the new Accord is monitoring... the risk of direct or indirect loss resulting from inadequate or failed internal processes, people and systems... The composition of skills required to perform in the new environment would undergo a change.

This change will force banks to invest in educating its work force in various risk-scoring models and enabling them to acquire skills to tap the full potential that the market offers. The Operational Risk requirements of Basel II Accord extend deep into corporate procedures that may not seem obviously connected to financial risk management. HR systems, for example, must ensure that procedures and documents surrounding such tasks as staffing, education and system maintenance, are properly recorded and documented, and that organization charts and lines of responsibility can be tracked and reported as required. Banks would be required to address issues such as manpower planning, selection and deployment of staff and training them in Risk Management and Risk Audit. Hence, it is assumed that the banks that would have sound HR policies and practices in place.

11.2.6 Emphasis on Corporate Governance

In the future, there would be greater emphasis on corporate governance in banks because banking supervision cannot function as well if sound corporate governance is not in place and, consequently, banking supervisors have a strong interest in ensuring that there is effective corporate governance at every banking organization. Supervisory experience underscores the necessity of having the appropriate levels of accountability and checks balances within each bank.

11.3 BASEL II Effects on Banking Industry

The banking sector in will continue on the growth trajectory and would further integrate into the global financial system.

Consolidation

The trend in the Indian banking industry suggests that the industry is moving from a "large number of small players" towards a "small number of large players". There would be three reasons for the consolidation in the industry: -

i. Increased competition from foreign as well as domestic banks after deregulation and liberalization of the Indian banking industry. It would be very difficult for smaller banks to correctly price their loans and they would lose out on customers with low probability of default to larger banks, who would offer them lower interest rates and they would end up with customers with high probability of default, which would be offered higher interest rates by the larger banks. The only way the banks would be able to survive would be by growing in size, and mergers and acquisition would be the preferred path to growth. This trend has already started as can be seen by the spurt of mergers that have taken place during recent times (Times Bank and HDFC Bank (2000-01), ICICI Bank with Bank of Madura(2002) and subsequently with ICICI Ltd.(2002), Benares State Bank and BoB(2003), Global Trust Bank with Oriental bank of Commerce (2005).), Bank of Rajasthan with HDFC Bank (2009)

ii. To attain the benefits of IRB Approach like lower capital adequacy requirements, better image, etc., the banks would require investment in its risk management models as well as information systems. It could be difficult for a small sized bank to undertake these investments.

iii. Integration of financial services, for example insurance, brokering, consultancy etc. will take place making the banks a delivery channel for a host of financial products and services.

Increased Capital in the Market

The authors are of the view that in the future the banks would follow the strategy of low defaults and narrower spreads. This would bring down their CAR requirements, freeing up more funds that could be invested in the economy. Another point to be noticed is that the banks would have in place more sophisticated credit scoring models and they would be able to invest in more profitable and less risky avenues thereby improving the efficiency of the capital markets.

Systemic Risk

Although the banks would benefit by having more free funds available, taking a macro view of the system we might see the systemic risk going down. The rationale behind this statement is that the bank's risk models would have developed and become more sophisticated. They would not only take into account various characteristics of the borrower but also the future economic condition. The banks would become more robust and efficient thereby contributing to the reduction of systemic risk. The calculation of risk will be done by credit scoring models such as Altman's Z Score Model & Merton Model but in a more sophisticated and developed manner.

International Scope

With better utilization of capital, rollover of bank's funds through securitization and efficiency in operations, Indian banks would become competitive in the international markets. The consolidation of banks would give them the requisite size and compliance with the Basel II Accord would give them greater efficiencies in management thereby making them competent for the international market. As per Indian Banks' Association report "Banking Industry Vision 2010", there would be greater presence of international players in Indian financial system and some of the Indian banks would become global players in the coming years. So, one can envision Indian banks going global in search of new markets, customers and profits.

The following points provide further insight on the expected banking scenario. Although, not direct consequences of the BASEL norms these structural changes will be a fall-out of the reforms in the banking sector.

The implementation of the 2nd phase of the RBI's roadmap to reform in 2009, would allow foreign bank ownership of any local private bank, within an overall limit of 74%. These foreign banks would bring with them technological and management skills and improved efficiency.

RBI's role in the banking industry

RBI would be in the process of shifting to risk-based supervision (RBS) wherein the focus of its supervisory attention on the banks is in accordance with the risk each bank poses to itself and the system. The inceptions of RBS will require banks to reorient their original setup towards RBS and put in place an efficient Risk Management architecture, internal auditing focusing on risk, strengthening MIS and set up of compliance units.

Slimming and Trimming of the Indian Banks

Emphasis would be given to automation and outsourcing of different services would be done so as to enable the banks to tackle the increasing volumes of business effectively. Customer-Banker contact will be reduced to the bare minimum as it would be a paperless banking era, dominated by plastic money, electro-banking, and tele-banking.

11.4 BASEL II Effects on Economy

The Indian households have not shown great faith in the country's financial systems, this is shown by the enormous gold consumption that the country has. Indians possess around $200 Billion of gold, equal to nearly half of the country's bank deposits. The Indian government reckons that approximately $150 Billion is required over the next ten years to upgrade the country's infrastructure. The government has proposed to use its foreign-exchange reserves to finance these investments, but this would add only $3-$5 billion annually. Domestic savings are the only plausible source of extra funding.

The authors believe that this is due to the lack of transparency and household's perception of the Indian financial system as being weak. Basel II encourages more transparency and good corporate governance policies as disclosures are required to be made by the banks, under Pillar III (Market Discipline). This would help in gaining the trust of Indian households who would in turn increase their participation in the financial assets, which would benefit the country as the savings would be pooled to finance more important and productive investments.

There would be increased availability of funds for the rural markets as the banks would increase their penetration in the rural sectors. This would be done as the banks would have excess funds at hand, due to reduced Capital Adequacy Requirements by employing good credit risk models in place. Both the corporate and consumer clients would be enjoying decreased interest rates and increased availability of funds.

Conclusion

India's growth potential over the next 10 years sets the country at the forefront of the developing world. The authors firmly believe that Indian banks would capitalize on the opportunity available to them and the continuations of the reforms initiated over one decade ago will unleash their potential and bring India to a more advanced stage of development.

12

Credit Default Risk Modeling through Transition Matrix - A Case Analysis at IndusInd Bank Ltd

12.1 INTRODUCTION

Credit Risk

Credit risk is the largest and most elementary risk faced by banks. It essentially focuses on determining the likelihood of default or credit deterioration and how costly it will turn out to be if it does occur.

"**Credit Risk**" is defined as the probability / potential that the borrower or counter-party may fail to meet its obligations in accordance with agreed terms. It involves inability or unwillingness of a borrower or counter-party to meet commitments in relation to lending, trading, hedging, settlement and other financial transactions.

Credit risk is the risk of loss of principal or loss of a financial reward stemming from a borrower's failure to repay a loan or otherwise meet a contractual obligation. Credit risk arises whenever a borrower is expecting to use future cash flows to pay a current debt. Investors are compensated for assuming credit risk by way of interest payments from the borrower or issuer of a debt obligation.

Higher the perceived credit risk, higher will be the rate of interest that investors will demand for lending their capital. Credit risks are calculated based on the borrowers' overall ability to repay. This calculation includes the borrowers' collateral assets, revenue-generating ability and taxing authority (such as for government and municipal bonds).

Basel II requires banks to accurately measure credit risk to hold sufficient capital to cover it.

Credit risk is comprehensively managed, under the following broad categories.

- **Transaction Credit risk**
    - Risk based pricing exposure such as collaterals, limit, etc.
    - Risk Rating framework
    - Automation of appraisal process
    - Pricing framework for credit exposures
- **Portfolio Credit risk**
    - Analysis of composition
    - Management of Concentration risk
    - Portfolio level limit
- **Information and Analytical assistance**
    - Industry research reports – CRISIL
    - Industry research reports – Internal
    - Weekly Newsletter
    - Companies' data-base
    - 'Industry Risk Score' in Rating and Appraisal Models (RAM)
    - 'Business Risk Factors' in RAM

- **Risk-related Policies**
    - o Credit Risk Policy
    - o Bank Risk Policy
    - o Country Risk Policy
- **Basel II – Adoption**
    - o Ratings Migration
    - o PD, LGD and EAD Data

12.1.2 Sources of Credit Risk

Credit Risk can arise out of direct lending risk, contingent lending risk, issuer risk, pre-settlement risk and settlement risk, to name a few.

- **Direct lending risk** lies in products like loans and advances, overdrafts, bills discounted, etc. It is the risk that the dues may not be repaid on time. Direct credit risk is the risk of loss due to counterparty default on a direct, unilateral extension of credit, such as a loan, security, receivable or deposit. While these obligations are not perfectly fungible, they can usually be bought and sold in a secondary market and are considered somewhat marketable
- **Contingent lending risk** lies in products like letters of credit, guarantees, etc. It is the risk that contingent exposures get converted into actual obligations and that these obligations may not be repaid on time. Contingent credit risk is the risk of loss due to counterparty default on a possible future extension of credit. Though many credit-sensitive transactions have credit exposure on trade date, some might not carry any risk until some future point – if at all.
- **Issuer risk** is the risk of financial loss due to change in the credit rating of the issuer of a debt instrument. It is also the risk that the bank may not be able to sell the instrument within a predetermined holding period.

- **Pre-settlement risk** is the risk that a counter-party with whom the bank has a reciprocal agreement may fail before settlement of the contract e.g. in forwards, futures and options. As a result, the bank faces the risk of default on the settlement date and hence may have to undertake fresh transactions for covering the failed transactions, leading to replacement cost. The level of exposure varies throughout the life of the contract and the extent of losses will only be known at the time of default.
- **Settlement risk** (also known as Herstatt risk) is the risk that the bank delivers its part of the contract but the other bank does not fulfil its obligation. This risk arises out of time lags in settlement of one currency in one centre and the settlement of another currency in another time zone. Settlement risk is the risk of loss due to a default after a payment of foreign exchange or delivery of securities has been made to counterparty, but before an equivalent exchange has been received from the same counterparty. This risk comes from differences in settlement procedures, markets and time zones.

The bank should identify all sources of credit risk and monitor aggregated exposures to a borrower/counter-party on a **bank-wide basis.**

12.1.3 Components of Credit Risk

As per the existing Standardised approach, Risk Weight (RW) is assigned based on the "External Rating" of the borrowers for "Corporate" asset class and differential (concessional) risk weight of 75% is applicable for "Retail" exposures. Basel Committee taking into account the following elements has determined the risk weights:

- Frequency of Default (Probability of Default – PD)
- Severity of Default (Loss Given Default – LGD)
- Outstanding/modifiers for off balance sheet items (Exposure at Default)

- Maturity adjustment (M)

More advanced approaches provide banks with the following two options for measurement of credit risk:

1. Foundation – Internal Rating Based (FIRB) - Under the **foundation approach**, as a general rule, banks provide their own estimates of PD and rely on supervisory estimates for other risk components.
2. Advanced – Internal Rating Based (AIRB) - Under the **advanced approach**, banks provide more of their own estimates of PD, LGD and EAD, and their own calculation of M, subject to meeting minimum standards.

Ideally, the more suited approach shall be AIRB as under FIRB, the regulator provides LGD and EAD and it may not be appropriate to calibrate and benchmark these risk components to our portfolios.

AIRB is a highly data intensive approach and requires granular level information on all the aforesaid risk elements. The minimum number of years for which the historical data is to be collected, analysed, calibrated and validated for measurement of capital adequacy is specified below:

- PD: 5 yrs
- LGD and EAD: 7 yrs
- Maturity: Effective maturity based on cash flows

Basel II guidelines stipulates that the risk elements shall cover one full economic cycle so as to iron out the fluctuations in its measurement and computing capital adequacy in a more meaningful manner while possibly covering the economic downturn.

12.1.4 Credit Risk Management

The very foundation of credit risk management lies in the data it collects. The inputs needed at this stage are the obligor (borrower), facility (loan) and external ratings data. This is the first critical step in any loan process and all the necessary data about the obligor needs to be collected.

The next step is to develop rating models. The obligor has to be rated using an appropriate robust model. For example there are various models for a commercial & industry category obligor and a commercial real estate category obligor. The system must be robust and should correctly interpret the data collected by various sources. Also the rating system must be designed in a manner, which will be flexible enough to integrate with other existing and potential systems.

After developing the rating models, the credit risk management department has to calculate probability of default (PD), loss given default (LGD) and exposure at default (EAD). Using these three risk components, the department can then calculate the expected loss in amount as well as percentage.

The credit risk management team has a very vital task to perform. That is of designing a risk solution. This risk solution must be flexible enough because it will be required to interact with a variety of other systems. It must be robust enough to incorporate different types of risk models. It must be easy to manage so as to manage the entire credit risk lifecycle. It also needs to be stable enough to withstand back testing and validation. The risk solution must be adaptable, which means that it must be able to intake risk data from variety of other resources.

12.2 PROBABILTY OF DEFAULT

a. Default Rates

The default rate for a specified period is the number of defaults among rated entities during the period, expressed as a percentage of the total number of rated entities whose ratings were outstanding throughout the period. Default rates can be calculated at each rating level, and can be calculated over multiple periods.

b. Transition Rates

A transition rate measures the probability of a change in credit rating over a specified period. Transition rates can be calculated for the entire rated population, or can refer to a specified rating level.

For all debt market participants, accurate and reliable default and transition rates are critical inputs in formulating the following decisions:

1. ***Pricing of debt-*** Default and transition rates are critical inputs for the pricing of a debt instrument or loan exposure. Default probabilities associated with ratings help investors and lenders quantify credit risk in their debt exposures, and provide inputs on whether and how much to lend, and at what price.
2. ***Structuring and pricing of credit-enhanced instruments-*** The structuring, rating, and pricing of credit-enhanced instruments depend heavily on the default and transition rates of underlying borrowers and securities.
3. ***Credit risk measurement-*** Default and transition rates are key inputs for many quantitative risk assessment models. Investors in rated instruments can manage their risk exposures effectively if they have access to reliable default and transition rates. Transition rates are also important for debt funds that need to maintain a certain threshold level of credit quality in their portfolios, and for investors who are, because of regulations or otherwise, mandated to invest only in securities that are rated at a certain level or above.
4. ***Indicating the efficacy of the rating scale-*** CRISIL's credit ratings is an indicator of probability of default. If ratings are reliable, the default rates should decrease as one moves up the rating scale. Default and transition rates can therefore be used to validate rating scales and quantify rating stability.

The **Probability of Default** is the likelihood that a loan will not be repaid and fall into default. This PD will be calculated for each company who has taken a loan. The credit history of the counterparty and nature of the investment will all be taken into account to calculate the PD figures. Many banks will use external ratings agencies such as Standard and Poor. However, banks are also encouraged to use their own Internal Rating Methods as well.

Default risk is the uncertainty regarding a borrower's ability to service its debts and obligations. Default can be quantified by measuring Probability of Default (PD).

PD assumes a significant importance in commercial transactions since the lenders want compensation for the uncertainty around the likelihood of default and will demand a spread over the risk free interest rates.

There is a considerable variation in default probabilities across firms. Example AAA rated firm has approximately two in 10000 p.a. default probability, an A rated firm has five times higher the default probability i.e. 10 in 10000 and a CCC rated firm has a 200 times higher default probability. Hence, lenders demand a substantial spread for CCC rated firm vis a vis an A rated or AAA rated firm.

The current Basel II discussion focuses on the unexpected loss and excludes the expected loss from the risk weighting functions. As a consequence, provisions must be built in for the amount of expected loss according to internal loss data. The probability of default (PD) is now one of the key parameters in the calculation of expected losses.

c. Calculation Process

The following step will commonly be used:

- Analyze the credit risk aspects of the counterparty;
- Map the counterparty to an internal risk grade which has an associated PD
- Determine the facility specific PD. This step will give a

weighted Probability of Default for facilities that are subject to a guarantee or protected by a credit derivative. The weighting takes account of the PD of the guarantor or seller of the credit derivative.

- The related credit spread and valuation of the loan or bond is the next step.

Probability of Default (PD) for the "Other" segment: is derived from a credit scoring process for a new customer and behavioral scoring for existing business. The resulting PD is mapped to an internal risk grade.

(PD) of an Obligor can be derived from an Internal Rating model that is used and maintained within the business area responsible for the counterparty relationship. For the purposes of the Accord there will be one PD associated with each risk grade representing the probability of Default within a 1 year time period.

There are broadly two data sources used to compute obligor PD(Probability of Default):

– Internal data and model/ internal ratings
– External reference data/ external ratings

12.3 Measurement Methods

There are two approaches to measure default risk:

- *Stand – alone risk:* **Default probability**, the probability that the counterparty or borrower will fail to service its obligations
- *Portfolio risk*: **Default correlations**, the degree to which the default risks of the borrowers and counter parties in the portfolio are related.

Default rates or default risk are not directly observable from the data. Default risk measurement starts with the identification and measurement of risk drivers or risk indicators that best represent quantum of default risk. The risk drivers/ indicators are such that any changes in these factors are an indication of changes in the PD.

The next step is to model the risk factors to compute the default risk. The model may be quantitative or qualitative or both. The main problem is that for a model to work it has to be calibrated so that it is sensitive enough to signify changes in the PD. However, such calibration is difficult, primarily due to the following reasons:

Unexpected losses due to correlation: Borrowers default together since they are connected with each other as a supplier/ customer, competitor or partners or are subjected to a similar impact of the macroeconomic factors

Errors in PD measurement or estimation are also due to the following causes

- Incorrect selection of risk drivers/ indicators
- Drivers or indicators do not have the required sensitivity to the risk changes or have a lagging effect (eg. Rating provided by the external agencies lag behind the actual changes in the credit quality)
- Mapping or calibration error

This leads to the following two approaches to measure PD.

- ***Ex ante***: This is to measure the PD at the start of the period. This is Expected Loss (EL)
- ***Ex post***: This is to measure the default at the end of the period. This is realized loss.

It is easier to measure ex post PD. This simply represents the number of default compared to total number of exposures at the beginning of the period. The most difficult part is ex ante measurement of PD.

12.4 Risk Rating and Probability of Default

A rating is summary indicator of the credit quality or default rate. In general, it is an assessment of the borrower's probability to meet its obligations in accordance with the agreed terms.

Traditionally, the rating provided by the rating agencies does not only measure default risks but also other risk measures such as transition risk, loss severity and the financial strength of the obligor, in addition to default probability. In general, credit ratings are evaluated in terms of historical default rates, while other attributes are also important.

Time Horizon

The probability for a company to get into financial distress is dependent on the length of time under consideration. Default probabilities are estimated for each sub-portfolio of asset class over a certain time horizon, usually a year.

The time slices over which to measure the default rate: In general, the default is measured for one year. However, the criticism against this approach is that a one-year time horizon does not reflect the actual risks.

Factors Impacting the Choice of Time Horizon

- Time required to take loss mitigation action
- Gathering of default data
- New information from the obligor Time horizon for the model, which is being calibrated and required data reconciliation

Types of Time Horizon:

- Multiple time horizons, driven by the maturity of the facility
- Multiple time horizons, leading to a different set of PDs. The time horizons is driven by business cycle
- Averaging PDs over a complete business cycle to estimate a one-year default. The method is generally adopted by rating agencies
- One-time horizon/ one-year horizon for all the exposures.

Default rates are measured in terms of yearly rates. Yearly rates may be for one year or cumulative for many years. The many years horizon may be for assets to be held to maturity.

However, as a prudent measure, the Bank has been following lower exposure ceiling for single borrowers. The internally stipulated single borrower exposure ceiling is linked to the Credit rating of the borrower.

12.5 BANK PROFILE - IndusInd Bank Ltd A Case Study

MISSION

To position IndusInd Bank limited as a Top 3 performer in the new private bank space in 3 years measured by the 3 parameters of *Profitability, Productivity and Efficiency.*

HISTORY

IndusInd Bank derives its name and inspiration from the Indus Valley civilization - a culture described by National **Geographic** as 'one of the greatest of the ancient world' combining a spirit of innovation with sound business and trade practices.

Mr. Srichand P. Hinduja, a leading Non-Resident Indian businessman and head of the Hinduja Group, conceived the vision of IndusInd Bank - the first of the new-generation private banks in India - and through collective contributions from the NRI community towards India's economic and social development, brought the Bank into being.

The Bank, formally inaugurated in April 1994 by Dr. Manmohan Singh, Honorable Prime Minister of India who was then the country's Finance Minister, started with a capital base of Rs.1,000 million (USD 32 million at the prevailing exchange rate), of which Rs.600 million was raised through private placement from Indian Residents while the balance Rs.400 million (USD 13 million) was contributed by Non-Resident Indians.

A NEW ERA AT INDUSIND BANK

IndusInd Bank, which commenced its operations in 1994, caters to the needs of both Consumer & Corporate customers. It has a robust technology platform supporting multi - channel delivery capabilities. The Bank enjoys a patronage of 2 million customers and has a network of 224 branches and 533 ATMs spread over 180 geographical locations in 28 states and union territories across the country. The Bank also has Representative Offices in Dubai and London.

The Bank believes in driving its business through technology. It has multi-lateral tieups with other banks providing access to more than 21000 ATMs for its customers. It enjoys clearing bank status for both major stock exchanges - BSE and NSE – and three major commodity exchanges in the country - MCX, NCDEX, and NMCE. It also offers DP facilities for stock and commodity segments. The Bank has been bestowed with the mandate of being a Settlement Banker for tea auctions at Kolkata, Siliguri, Coonoor, Kochi, Coimbatore and Guwahati.In a pioneering initiative in 'Green Banking' project, the Bank became the first bank in Maharashtra to open a solar-power ATM. Subjects like sustainable development, social responsibility and climate change are fast becoming part of the corporate vocabulary and IndusInd is at the forefront of this change in the Indian banking sector.

The Bank received a series of awards commencing with the prestigious 'Technology Bank of the Year-2009' award in the private and foreign bank category from the Indian Banks' Association (IBA). It has also been recognized as the Bank with the Best Credit Quality in FE India's Best Banks, a publication brought out in support by Ernst & Young, reflecting the robustness of Bank's credit assessment systems.

Recently, CRISIL has reaffirmed its P1+ rating of IndusInd Bank's fixed deposits and certificates of deposit program. This reflects significant improvement in its asset quality.

The rating also factors in the Bank's resources and earnings profile, and capitalization levels. In a significant development for the Bank, credit rating agency ICRA Ltd. Has upgraded the long term ratings for its Tier II Bonds programme.

ICRA has upgraded the Lower Tier II Bonds rating of the Bank to LAA- (pronounced L double A minus) rating with stable outlook from LA+ (pronounced L A plus) rating with stable outlook. ICRA has also upgraded the Upper Tier II Bonds rating of IBL to LA+ rating with stable outlook from LA (pronounced L A) rating with stable outlook.

BRAND

IndusInd Bank understands its customers' money is not just money. It is the vehicle to realise their dreams! Hence, the bank aims to ensure that the customers' experience with the bank is pleasant and enriching. That they get value for their money, enabling them to lead a richer, fuller, content life... For this, the bank:

- Offers a new level of banking – better services, better understanding of unique needs and better management of finances
- Demystifies the banking process and makes it more accessible
- Apart from fulfilling traditional banking responsibilities, advises customers on how and where to use their money to get the best out of it
- Projects an image of being a young, energetic, modern bank with values of dynamism, confidence and progression

Further, as a banking partner, the bank also aims to help its customers discover how they can do more things with their money.

BUSINESS ACHIEVEMNETS:

- Received the prestigious 'Technology Bank of the Year-2009' award in the private and foreign bank category from the Indian Banks' Association (IBA).

- The State Forum of Bankers Clubs, Kerala, bestowed the "Excellence Award", as the second best new generation Bank in Kerala.
- Ranked No. 1 for "Credit Quality" amongst all banks in India by Financial Express and Ernst & Young study.

KEY BUSINESS HIGHLIGHTS AS ON 31.03.2010

- Net Interest Income (NII) was Rs. 886.41 crore as compared to Rs 459.03 crore in the corresponding period of the previous year, up 93%.
- Operating Profit for the 12-month period ended March 31, 2010 was Rs 703.89 crore as against Rs 368.25 crore in the corresponding period of the previous year, up 91%.
- Net Profit for the year ended March 31, 2010 was Rs 350.31 crore as against Rs
- 148.34 crore in the corresponding period of the previous year, recording a jump of 136 %
- The CASA (Current Accounts-Savings Accounts) ratio improved to 23.67 % as against 19.24% in 2008-09.
- The Net NPA of the Bank was 0.50% as compared to 1.14 % as on March 31, 2009.
- The Total Deposits of the Bank increased from Rs 22,110 crore as on March 31, 2009 to Rs. 26,710 crore as on March 31, 2010 recording a growth rate of 21% for the year.
- Total Advances for the year stood at Rs. 20551 crore, recording a growth of 30% as against Rs 15,771 crore recorded in the last year.
- The full year EPS works out to Rs 9.01 as against Rs 4.28 in the previous year.
- Net worth moves to Rs 2165.60 crore
- In Q4, FY 2009-10, the Bank raised Rs 420 crore through Tier II bond issue.

12.5.2 METHODOLOGY

In the credit risk management, quantification of the loss due to the movements in the market, given various possible scenarios various models can be applied to a portfolio as against stand alone assets. The commonly used covariance/ actuarial model/ macro economic default model help to mitigate counterparty credit risk. Transition matrix can help as against qualitative/ structural approaches.

TRANSITION MATRIX

Default probability is measured using risk factors. The change in the default probability or the volatility in PD is measured through Transition Matrix (TM) While PD measurement helps in measuring risk at the instrument level, PD volatility helps in measuring risk at the portfolio level. The likelihood of a customer migrating from its current risk-rating category to any other category within the time horizon is frequently expressed in terms of rating TM. TM is expressed in a Matrix form.

The transition matrix including probabilities to move from one rating to another rating represents the kernel of many credit risk and rating calculations. Following the requirements of Basel II financial engineers need software tools allowing for adjustment of transition matrices provided by rating agencies to the economic cycles and to generate transition matrices according to the local financial and economic conditions.

The generated transition matrixes are the basis for calculation of credit risk of counterparts using a set of internal (Credit Metrics, Credit Risk and Basel II Standard, Foundation and Advanced Approaches) evaluation models. The estimation of credit risk involve cumulative and marginal default probabilities for future periods used to calculate expected and unexpected losses (Credit VAR) within a multi-period credit exposure model. The results of transition matrix estimation of Data Supporter Module are used by Risk Evaluator to calculate credit risk of single counterparts and various aggregates based on sub portfolios, concern structures and other grouping criteria such as branches and countries.

One limitation of this method is the size of the pools. Most banks do not have large enough credit portfolios to be able to estimate PDs with accurate granularity. The smaller number of obligors, the more volatile the PD estimation will be.

Another limitation is given if PDs are calculated once a year (at year end), changes in the PDs cannot be foreseen in time. A monthly estimation and comparison of PDs on a year-to-year basis is therefore helpful to extend the time series and calculate the credit risk and expected losses on current data.

Using the method of pseudo-pooling, banks can compute transition probabilities or cumulated multi-year PD. For multi-year estimations, it is crucial that the pool remains "static" or "frozen" with respect to the obligors in it, so that the time period is equal for all the obligors in the respective pool. In other words, it will be incorrect – say 5-year PDs, if some obligors have been in the pool for 5 years and some for only 4 or 3 years. However to overcome this problem two types of pools are used-

Dynamic pool:

A dynamic pool of a year is a set of pool of companies where in the membership of the pool does not remain static/ constant but keeps on changing based on additions and withdrawals from the pool. Here the companies which withdraw or default in between will be considered and not be taken as addition or outstanding. That is why it is known as dynamic pool.

Unlike the static pool the ratings are not constant throughout the period. It will be dynamic or flexible in nature.

Static pool:

A static pool of a year is a set or pool of companies having an outstanding rating at the beginning of the year. The membership of the pool remains static /constant over a period of time. For a company to be included in a n year static pool, it has to be outstanding throughout that entire n years. Companies that withdraw or default in between will remain withdrawn of defaulted for the remaining years. A company that gets a rating subsequently, or recovers from default, is considered a new company in that static pool. A company that remains rated for more than one year is counted as many times as number of years over which it was rated. This assumes all ratings are kept current through an on going surveillance process.

Process of Static Pool

- The no of columns for static pools will depend upon the start year, end year and the minimum horizon.
- The software should count the number of rated accounts under each category, for a finalized assessment done between two particular dates.
- If there is any case, which has be clicked for "Default" the ratings of those accounts should not be included in the static pool. Similarly any withdrawn cases should also be excluded from the count.
- If there are more than 1 finalized assessment for a particular case the rating of that assessment which has the latest Assessment date should be considered for counting.
- After Static Pool we have to observe the behavior of the company i.e. the Transition of the company for the defined horizon.

12.5.3 QUESTIONS FOR DISCUSSION

Q1. With the opening up of credit default swaps in India by RBI, will the changing of the credit methodology and resorting to transition matrix in IndusInd bank would revive default loan portfolios?

Q2. Does the transition matrix model at IndusInd bank keeps in consonance with the base rate mechanism and deleting the BPLR concept?

Q3. In the recent days ballooning effect of the NPAs at the banks is a grave concern. IndusInd bank has a substantial NPA portfolio, does the probability of default model takes into account risk weights attached to the standard assets?

Q4. Discuss the credit risk portfolio matrix at IndusInd bank in the light of Basel II implementation commenting on the need for Basel III?

12.5.4 SUMMARY

Banks and financial institutions are lending to individual borrowers on an ongoing basis. Credit risk management is a vital link between the borrowers and the institution. Identifying, measuring, monitoring and control lead to credit risk mitigation. Correlation and volatility of credit portfolio have a direct effect on one or the other. Transition matrix for probability of default helps top to bottom approach of the ratings calculations.

It includes using credit risk, Basel II standards, foundation and advanced approaches and evaluation models. This model is a better model than value at risk (VAR) and it overlooks the limitations of VAR model (Delta method, historical simulation, Monte-Carlo method). This paper raises the awareness of VAR versus transition matrix in a heteroscedastic world within the framework for Basel II, accounting issues, tax issues. In case the limitations of this transition matrix can be improvised and the value of the credit event can be maximized it is worthwhile proposition to adopt transition matrix.

SCOPE

The scope of our study is to build a high quality portfolio in line with the Bank's risk appetite and strategy and to support sustainable business growth within this appetite. By building upon the model of transition matrix we have tried to identify, measure, monitor, manage and control risk effectively and to ensure that the Bank gets compensated for the risk assumed.

Diversifying the risk profile among different segments of Products, Geographies, Group etc in order to minimise the concentration risk and maximise returns and to maximize Bank's Risk-Adjusted Return by maintaining credit risk exposure within acceptable parameters..

OBSERVATIONS

The main findings of the project are:

- Bank uses a robust Risk rating framework for evaluating credit risk of the borrowers. The bank uses segment specific rating models equipped with transition matrix capabilities.
- The bank manages credit risk comprehensively; both at transaction level and portfolio level.
- Risks on various counter parties such as corporate, banks are monitored through counter-party exposure limits, governed by country risk exposure limits also in the case of international trades.
- The bank manages risk at the portfolio level too, with portfolio level prudential exposure limits to mitigate concentration risk.
- The bank has a well-diversified portfolio across various industries and segments.
- Retail and schematic exposures (which provide wider diversification benefits) account for as much as 45% of the total fund based advances
- The bank's corporate exposure is fully diversified across 85 industries, thus insulated from individual cycles.

ANNEXURES

ANNEXURE I

1. Rating Migrations Over A Period Of 4 Years For Capital Broker Model (B)

Customer ID	Year 1	Year 2	Year 3	Year 4
CAPITAL 1	B 2	B 3	B 3	B 3
CAPITAL 2	B 5	D	D	D
CAPITAL 3	B 1	B 1	B 1	B 1
CAPITAL 4	B 2	B 2	B 2	B 2
CAPITAL 5	B 3	B 2	B 2	B 2
CAPITAL 6	B 2	B 2	B 2	B 2
CAPITAL 7	B 7	B 7	B 6	B 7
CAPITAL 8	B 1	B 1	B 2	B 2
CAPITAL 9	B 2	B 2	B 2	B 2
CAPITAL 10	B 3	B 3	B 2	B 2
CAPITAL 11	B 7	B 7	B 7	B 7
CAPITAL 12	B 2	B 2	B 3	B 3
CAPITAL 13	B 4	W	W	W
CAPITAL 14	B 3	B 3	B 3	B 3
CAPITAL 15	B 2	B 2	B 2	B 2
CAPITAL 16	B 2	B 2	B 2	B 2
CAPITAL 17	B 8	B 8	B 8	B 8
CAPITAL 18	B 4	B 4	B 3	B 3
CAPITAL 19	B 2	B 2	B 2	B 2
CAPITAL 20	B 5	B 5	B 5	B 5
CAPITAL 21	B 3	B 3	B 3	B 3
CAPITAL 22	B 4	B 4	B 4	B 4

CAPITAL 23	B 2	B 2	B 2	B 3
CAPITAL 24	B 3	B 3	B 3	B 2
CAPITAL 25	B 4	B 4	B 3	B 3
CAPITAL 26	B 1	B 1	B 1	B 1
CAPITAL 27	B 4	B 5	B 5	B 5
CAPITAL 28	B 6	B 6	W	W
CAPITAL 29	B 5	B 5	B 4	B 4
CAPITAL 30	B 6	B 6	B 6	B 6
CAPITAL 31	B 3	B 3	B 3	B 3
CAPITAL 32	B 7	B 7	B 7	B 7
CAPITAL 33	B 1	B 1	B 1	B 1
CAPITAL 34	B 5	B 5	B 5	B 5
CAPITAL 35	B 4	B 4	B 4	B 5
CAPITAL 36	B 3	B 3	B 4	B 4
CAPITAL 37	B 6	B 7	D	D
CAPITAL 38	B 5	B 5	B 5	W
CAPITAL 39	B 8	D	D	D
CAPITAL 40	B 6	B 6	B 6	B 6
CAPITAL 41	B 6	B 6	B 6	B 6
CAPITAL 42	B 8	B 8	B 8	D
CAPITAL 43	B 3	B 3	B 3	B 3
CAPITAL 44	B 4	B 4	B 4	B 4
CAPITAL 45	B 1	B 1	B 1	B 1
CAPITAL 46	B 5	B 5	B 6	B 6
CAPITAL 47	B 7	D	D	D
CAPITAL 48	B 1	B 3	B 3	B 3
CAPITAL 49	B 1	B 1	B 1	B 1

CAPITAL 50	B 1	B 1	B 1	B 1
CAPITAL 51	B 1	B 1	B 1	B 1
CAPITAL 52	B 1	B 1	B 1	B 1
CAPITAL 53	B 1	B 1	B 1	B 1
CAPITAL 54	B 4	B 4	B 4	B 4
CAPITAL 55	B 4	B 4	B 4	B 4
CAPITAL 56	B 4	B 4	B 4	B 5
CAPITAL 57	B 4	B 4	B 4	B 4
CAPITAL 58	B 4	B 4	B 4	B 4
CAPITAL 59	B 4	B 4	B 4	B 4
CAPITAL 60		B 7	B 7	B 7
CAPITAL 61		B 7	B 7	B 8
CAPITAL 62		B 8	D	D
CAPITAL 63		B 5	B 5	B 5
CAPITAL 64			B 3	B 4
CAPITAL 65			B 8	B 8

ANNEXURE II

VALUES

Values Year 1 and Year 2

Count of Year 1	**Year 2**										
Year 1	B 1	B2	B 3	B 4	B 5	B 6	B 7	B 8	W	D	Grand Total
B 1	10		1								11
B 2		8	1								9
B 3		1	7								8
B 4				11	1				1		13
B 5					5					1	6
B 6						4	1				5
B 7							3			1	4
B 8								2		1	3
Grand Total	10	9	9	11	6	4	4	2	1	3	59

Values Year 2 and Year 3

Count of Year2	**Year3**										
Year 2	B 1	B 2	B 3	B 4	B 5	B 6	B 7	B 8	W	D	Grand Total
B 1	9	1									10
B 2	1	8									9
B 3		1	7	1							9
B 4			2	9							11
B 5				1	5	1					7
B 6						3			1		4
B 7						1	4			1	6
B 8								2		1	3
Grand Total	10	10	9	11	5	5	4	2	1	2	59

Values Year 3 and Year 4

Count of Year3	**Year4**										
Year 3	B 1	B 2	B 3	B 4	B 5	B 6	B 7	B 8	W	D	Grand Total
B 1	9										9
B 2		9	1								10
B 3		1	9	1							11
B 4				9	2						11
B 5					4				1		5
B 6						4	1				5
B 7							3	1			4
B 8								2		1	3
Grand Total	9	10	10	10	6	4	4	3	1	1	58

ANNEXURE III

PERCENTAGES

Count of Year1	Year2										
Year 1	B 1	B 2	B 3	B 4	B 5	B 6	B 7	B 8	W	D	Grand Total
B 1	90.91	0.00	9.09	0.00	0.00	0.00	0.00	0.00	0.00	0.00	100
B 2	0.00	88.89	11.11		0.00	0.00	0.00	0.00	0.00	0.00	100
B 3	0.00	12.50	87.50	0.00	0.00	0.00	0.00	0.00	0.00	0.00	100
B 4	0.00	0.00	0.00	84.62	7.69	0.00	0.00	0.00	7.69	0.00	100
B 5	0.00	0.00	0.00	0.00	83.33	0.00	0.00	0.00	0.00	16.67	100
B 6	0.00	0.00	0.00	0.00	0.00	80.00	20.00	0.00	0.00	0.00	100
B 7	0.00	0.00	0.00	0.00	0.00	0.00	75.00	0.00	0.00	25.00	100
B 8	0.00	0.00	0.00	0.00	0.00	0.00	0.00	66.67	0.00	33.33	100
Grand Total	90.91	101.39	107.70	84.62	91.03	80.00	95.00	66.67	7.69	75.00	800.00

Count of Year2	**Year 3**										
Year 2	B 1	B 2	B 3	B 4	B 5	B 6	B 7	B 8	W	D	Grand Total
B 1	90.00	10.00	0.00	0.00	0.00	0.00	0.00	0.00	0.00	0.00	100
B 2	11.11	88.89	0.00		0.00	0.00	0.00	0.00	0.00	0.00	100
B 3	0.00	11.11	77.78	11.11	0.00	0.00	0.00	0.00	0.00	0.00	100
B 4	0.00	0.00	18.18	81.82	0.00	0.00	0.00	0.00	0.00	0.00	100
B 5	0.00	0.00	0.00	14.29	71.43	14.29	0.00	0.00	0.00	0.00	100
B 6	0.00	0.00	0.00	0.00	0.00	75.00	0.00	0.00	25.00	0.00	100
B 7	0.00	0.00	0.00	0.00	0.00	16.67	66.67	0.00	0.00	16.67	100
B 8	0.00	0.00	0.00	0.00	0.00	0.00	0.00	66.67	0.00	33.33	100
Grand Total	101.11	110.00	95.96	107.22	71.43	105.95	66.67	66.67	25.00	50.00	800.00

Count of Year3	Year4										
Year 3	B 1	B 2	B 3	B 4	B 5	B 6	B 7	B 8	W	D	Grand Total
B 1	100.00	0.00	0.00	0.00	0.00	0.00	0.00	0.00	0.00	0.00	100
B 2	0.00	90.00	10.00		0.00	0.00	0.00	0.00	0.00	0.00	100
B 3	0.00	9.09	81.82	9.09	0.00	0.00	0.00	0.00	0.00	0.00	100
B 4	0.00	0.00	0.00	81.82	18.18	0.00	0.00	0.00	0.00	0.00	100
B 5	0.00	0.00	0.00	0.00	80.00	0.00	0.00	0.00	20.00	0.00	100
B 6	0.00	0.00	0.00	0.00	0.00	80.00	20.00	0.00	0.00	0.00	100
B 7	0.00	0.00	0.00	0.00	0.00	0.00	75.00	25.00	0.00	0.00	100
B 8	0.00	0.00	0.00	0.00	0.00	0.00	0.00	66.67	0.00	33.33	100
Grand Total	100.00	99.09	91.82	90.91	98.18	80.00	95.00	91.67	20.00	33.33	800.00

ANNEXURE IV

Average of 4 Years

Count of Year	Year										
Year	B 1	B 2	B 3	B 4	B 5	B 6	B 7	B 8	W	D	Grand Total
B 1	95.00	5.00	0.00	0.00	0.00	0.00	0.00	0.00	0.00	0.00	100.00
B 2	34.01	59.63	6.36	0.00	0.00	0.00	0.00	0.00	0.00	0.00	100.00
B 3	0.00	36.36	56.90	10.10	0.00	0.00	0.00	0.00	0.00	0.00	100.00
B 4	0.00	4.17	35.23	54.55	6.06	0.00	0.00	0.00	0.00	0.00	100.00
B 5	0.00	0.00	0.00	32.97	53.04	4.76	0.00	0.00	9.23	0.00	100.00
B 6	0.00	0.00	0.00	0.00	27.78	51.67	6.67	0.00	8.33	5.56	100.00
B 7	0.00	0.00	0.00	0.00	0.00	32.22	53.89	8.33	0.00	5.56	100.00
B 8	0.00	0.00	0.00	0.00	0.00	0.00	25.00	44.44	0.00	30.56	100.00
Grand Total	67.04	69.70	62.59	66.04	56.54	61.98	53.89	75.00	15.00	38.89	566.67

13

Credit Risk Models Applicable to Banks

Over the past decade the commercial banks have devoted internal models for risk management. Credit risk models in involve plenty of Cross - Sectional dimensional but scarce in time dimension. Various models are as below:

13.1 KMV MODEL

This model was developed by KMV Corporation based on Merton's (1973) analytical model of firm's value. This model uses stock prices and the capital structure of the firm to estimate its probability. The starting point of this model is the proposition that a firm would default only if its asset value falls below certain level (default point), which is a function of its liability. It estimates the asset value of the firm and its asset volatility from the market value of equity and the debt structure in the opinion theoretic framework. Using these two values, a metric (distance from default or DFD) is constructed that represents the number of standard deviation that the firm's asset value is away from the default point. Finally, a mapping is done between the default values and actual default rate, based on historical default experience. The resultant probability is called Expected Default Frequency (EDF).

Thus EDF is calculated in the following three steps:

- Estimation of asset value and asset volatility from equity value and volatility of equity return.

- Calculation of DFD as (Asset value – Default point) / (Asset value * Asset volatility)
- Calculation of expected default frequency.

13.2 CREDIT METRICS MODEL

Credit Metrics is a statistical model developed by J.P Morgan, the investment bank, in the year 1995 for internal use, but now it's being used all around the world by hundreds of banks including Indian banks like the ICICI bank. This model works on the statistical concepts like probability, means, and standard deviation, correlation, and concentrations.

Credit Metrics is a tool for assessing portfolio risk due to changes in debt value caused by changes in obligor credit quality. This model includes the changes in value caused not only by possible default events, but also by upgrades and down grades in credit quality, because the value of a particular credit varies with the corresponding credit quality.

Credit Metrics also assess the Value- at – risk (VAR) – the volatility of value- not just the expected losses. The model assesses the risk within the full context of a portfolio addressing the correlation of credit quality moves across obligors. This allows to directly calculating the diversification benefits or potential over concentrations across the portfolio.

The transition table for the various categories of bonds is determined and then joint probability for both these under different combinations. Then the NPV of the portfolio is determined for all the combinations and a probability distribution is constructed. These probabilities are actually an analysis of past migrations and same is the case with default probability. In the case of default a recovery rate is taken as the portfolio value. This distribution gives us 2 measures of credit risk: standard deviation and percentile level. This model has some limitations regarding the data availability but it doesn't require any changes as such for application in the Indian scenario.

13.3 VAR MODEL

This model is being used in some of the banks currently in India.

Value at risk (VAR) is a statistical risk measure, which is used extensively for measuring the market risk of portfolios of assets and/or liabilities.

Suppose a portfolio's value at risk is 2Mn$ with a 95% confidence level, then it means that the portfolio is expected to loose a maximum of 2Mn$ 95% of the times. The Value at risk is calculated by constructing a probability distribu-tion of the portfolio values over a given time horizon. The values may be calculated on the daily, weekly or monthly basis.

13.4 ALTMANN Z SCORE

Altman's Z score predicts whether or not a company is likely to enter into bankruptcy within one or two years. Edward Altman developed the model by examining 85 manufacturing companies in the year 1968. Later, additional "Z-Scores" were developed for private manufacturing companies (Z-Score - Model A) and another for general/service firms (Z-Score - Model B).

The Z-Score Bankruptcy-Predictor combines several of the most significant variables in a statistically derived combination. The algorithm has been consistently reported to have a 95 % accuracy of prediction of bankruptcy up to two years prior to failure on nonmanufac-turing firms as well. There have been many other bankruptcy predictors developed and published. However, none has been so thoroughly tested and broadly accepted as the Altman Z-Score.

The Altman Z-Score variables influencing the financial strength of a firm are: current assets, total assets, net sales, interest, total liability, current liabilities, market value of equity, earnings before taxes and retained earnings. The model can be used for a quick check about the health of a company. It however cannot be used for individuals.

The value of Z is given by the following equation:

$$Z = 0.012X1 + 0.014X2 + 0.033X3 + 0.006X4 + 0.999X5$$

Where,

X_1 = working capital/Total assets

X_2 = Retained earnings/Total assets

X_3 = Earnings before interest and taxes/Total assets

X_4 = Market value of equity/Book value of total liabilities

X_5 = Sales/Total assets

A "Z" value above 1.8 is supposed to be quite safe, while the value below 1.8 indicates a high probability of bankruptcy.

14

Basle II and Basle III

14.1 INTRODUCTION

The policy approach to financial sector in India is that the ultimate goal should be to conform to the best international standards and the process, the emphasis is on gradual harmonization with the international best practices.

In implementing Basel II, the RBI is in favor of gradual convergence with the new standards and best practices. The aim is to reach the best standards in a phased manner, taking a consultative approach rather than a directive one i.e. a consultative and participative approach has been adopted for both designing and implementing Basel II.The RBI has set up a steering committee to suggest migration methodology to Basel II. Based on recommendations of steering committee, in February 2005, the RBI proposed "draft guidelines" for implementing new capital adequacy.Before 1988, many central banks allowed different definitions of capital in order to make their country's bank appear as solid than they actually were.

In order to provide a level playing field the concept of regulatory capital was standardized in BASEL I. Along with definition of regulatory capital a basic formula for capital divided by assets was constructed and an arbitrary ratio of 8% was chosen as minimum capital adequacy. However, there were drawbacks in the BASEL I as it did not did not discriminate between different levels of risk. As a result a loan to an established corporate was deemed as risky as a loan to a new business. Also it assigned lower weight age to loans to banks as a result banks were often keen to lend to other banks.

BASEL II accord proposes getting rid of the old risk weighted categories that treated all corporate borrowers the same replacing them with limited number of categories into which borrowers would be assigned based on assigned credit system. Greater use of internal credit system has been allowed in standardized and advanced schemes, against the use of external rating. The new proposals avoid sole reliance on the capital adequacy benchmarks and explicitly recognize the importance of supervisory review and market discipline in maintaining sound financial systems. Basel II compliance and risk management in banks go hand in hand. The industry is gearing up to implement the standard. Under the current system, the balance sheet items, are assigned prescribed ratio (at present 9%) on the aggregate of the risk weighted assets and other assets on ongoing basis.

Basel II aims to build on solid foundation of prudent capital regulation, supervision and market discipline and to further risk and financial stability.Implementation of new framework will require substantial commitment on the part of field functionaries.

14.2 OBJECTIVES OF BASEL II

- To strengthen international banking systems
- Banks must attain solvency relative to their risk profile
- Supervisors should review each bank's own risk assessment & capital strategies
- Banks should maintain excess of minimum capital
- Regulators would intervene at an early stage
- Possibility of rewarding banks with better risk management systems.
- Each bank has suitable risk management framework and the expected level of capital

The primary *objectives* of the new Accord are (a) the promotion of safety and soundness of the financial system, (b) the enhancement of competitive equality and (c) the constitution of a more comprehensive approach to addressing risks. These *objectives* are sought to be attained *via* three cardinal principles: (a) minimum capital requirements, (b) supervisory review of capital adequacy and (c) effective use of market discipline.

14.3 THE BENEFITS OF BASEL II

✓ Improved risk management.

✓ Business expansion and better allocation of resources.

✓ More rational pricing.

✓ Higher credit ratings.

✓ Lower capital charges.

✓ Greater transparency.

✓ Stronger competitive position.

An overview of the Basel II accord is as under:

BASEL II		
PILLAR 1 **Minimum Capital Requirement**	**PILLAR 2** **Supervisory Review**	**PILLAR 3** **Market Discipline**
1. Capital for credit risk • Standardized approach • International Rating based approached - Foundation - Advanced 2. Capital for market risk • Standardized method - Maturity method - duration method 3. Capital for operational risk • Basic indicator approach • Standardized approach • Advanced measurement approach	1. Evaluation risk assessment 2. Ensure soundness and integrity of banks internal process to assess the adequacy of capital 3. Ensure maintenance of minimum capital 4. prescribed differential capital where necessary i.e. where internal processes are slack	1. Enhance disclosure 2. Core disclosure and supplementary disclosure 3. Semi annually submission

RBI expects banks to adopt the standardized approach for credit risk and basic indicator approach for operational risk. After adequate skills are developed both by banks and also by the supervisors, some of the banks may be allowed to migrate to the internal rating based (IRB) approach. On current indicators implementing of Basel II will require more capital for banks in India due to the fact that operational risk is not covered or captured under Basel I. The cushion available in the system, which at present has a capital to risk asset ratio (CRAR) of over 12% provides for some comforts but the banks are exploring various avenues for meeting capital requirements under Basel II.

The RBI on its part has issued policy guidelines enabling issuance of several instruments by the banks viz-**innovating perpetual debt instruments** (IPDI), perpetual non cumulative preference shares and hybrid debt instruments so as to enhance their capital raising options.

14.4 THREE-TRACK APPROACH FOR IMPLEMENTING BASE II IN INDIA:

In India, we have 85 commercial banks which account for about 78%(total assets) of the financial sector, over 3000 corporate banks which account for 9%and 196 RRB's which account for 3%. Taking in account the size, complexity of operations, relevance to the financial sector need to ensure greater financial inclusion the capital adequacy norms applicable to these entities have been maintained at different levels of stringency.

Given the differential risk appetite across banks and their business philosophies, it is likely that bank would self select their own approach, which in turn is likely to engender a stabilizing influence on the system as a whole. On first track, the commercial banks are required to maintain capital for both credit and market risks as per Basel I framework. The co operative banks on the second track, are required to maintain capital for credit risk as per Basel I framework and through surrogates for market risk. The Regional Rural Banks on the third track have a minimum capital requirement which is however, not par with Basel I framework. Consequently, we have a major segment of systematic importance on a full Basel I framework, a portion of minor segment partly on Basel I and smaller segment on a non Basel framework.

14.5 ISSUES AND CHALLENGES IN BASEL II IMPLEMENTATION IN INDIA

While there is no second opinion regarding the purpose, necessity and usefulness of the proposed accord-the techniques and methods suggested in the consultative document would pose considerable implementation challenges for the banks specially in developing country like India as follows :

1. Capital Requirement

The Basel II implementation will increase the level of capital to be maintained by banks as per their risk profile. Capital requirement for credit risk may go down due to adoption of more risk sensitive models; however the same will be offset by additional charge for operational risk plus increased capital for market risk. This partly explains the current trend of consolidation in the banking industry

2. Profitability

Competition among banks for highly rated corporate, needing lower amount of capital may exert pressure on already thinning interest rate speed. Further, huge implementation may also impact profitability for smaller banks

3. Risk management architecture

The new standards are amalgam of international best practices and call for introduction of advanced risk management system. It would be a daunting task to create the required level of technological architecture plus human skills cross the institution

4. Rating Requirement

For adopting the standardized approach, the banks require greater penetration of verdict rating agencies in

India. Also, rating in India is restricted to issue plus non issuers-encourage rating of issues would be a challenge.

5. Choice of alternative approaches

The new framework provides for alternative approaches for computation of capital requirement of various risks. Banks adopting IRB will be more sensitive resulting in high risk assets flowing to banks or standardized approach as they would require lesser capital for these assets. Hence the system as a whole may maintain lower capital than warranted plus become more vulnerable

6. Absence of historical database

The implementation of various approaches requires creation of historical database which is a time consuming process plus may require initial support from supervisor.

7. Supervisory Framework

The supervisory cadre has to be properly trained for understanding of critical issues for risk profiling of supervised entities and validating plus guiding development of complex IRB models

8. Corporate Governance Issues

The banks BOD has the responsibility for setting basic tolerance levels for various types of risks. It should ensure that management establishes a framework for assessing risks, develop a system to relate risks to the bank's capital levels and establish a method for monitoring compliance with Internal policies

9. Disclosure Regime

Pillar 3 purports to enforce market discipline through stricter disclosure requirements. However, this will only help the supervisory authorities, since the general public lacks the ability to comprehend and interpret the disclosed information. Also, too much disclosure may cause information overload and may even damage financial position of banks

10. Disadvantage for smaller banks

The new framework calls for revamping the entire management information system and allocation of substantial resources. Therefore, it may be out of reach for many smaller banks.

14.6 KEY CONCEPTS OF BASEL II

- ✓ Threats posed by risk prone asset held by the banks are to be counter balanced not only through holding prescribed minimum capital, but also be supplemented by effective supervisory review of capital adequacy plus accepted market discipline implying public disclosure. These constitute the three pillars of the Basel II accord
- ✓ The underlying implication of the new accord is greater risk sensitive. it embodies three principles of –flexibility, menu of approaches and incentives for better risk management
- ✓ Banks with advanced risk management tools would be permitted to use their own internal credit system for evaluating credit risk by process of internal based rating (IRB) approach. The use of this approach will subject to approval by the supervisory based on standards established by the committee
- ✓ The new accord intends to cover all types of risks to which banks are exposed in addition to credit risk.

	Basel II accord
Pillar 1	Specifies new standards for minimum capital requirements along with the methodology for assigning risk weights on the basis of credit risk + market risk + operational risk.
Pillar 2	Enlarges the role of banking supervisors give them power to review the bank's risk management system.
Pillar 3	Defines standards and requirements for higher disclosure by banks on capital adequacy, asst quality and other risk management processes

II. THE THREE PILLAR APPROACH

The capital framework proposed in the New Basel Accord consists of three pillars, each of which reinforces the other. The first pillar establishes the way to quantify the minimum capital requirements, is complemented with two qualitative pillars, concerned with organizing the regulator's supervision and establishing market discipline through public disclosure of the way that banks implement the Accord. Determination of minimum capital requirements remains the main part of the agreement, but the proposed methods are more risk sensitive and reflect more closely the current situation on financial markets.

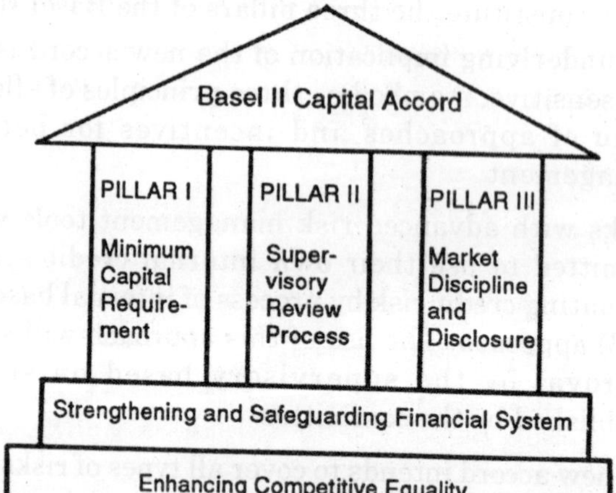

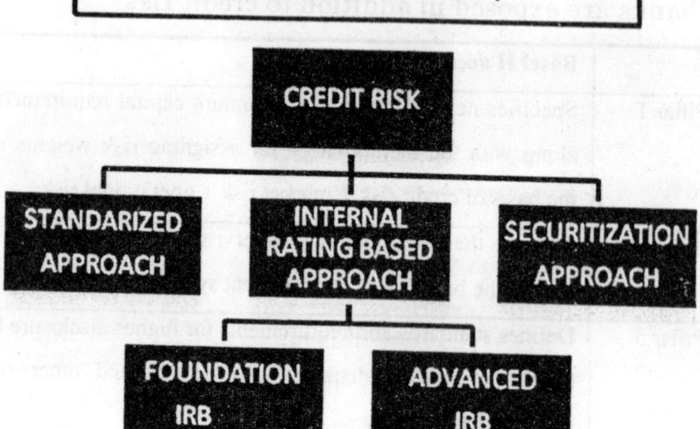

First Pillar: Minimum Capital Requirement

The first pillar establishes a way to quantify the minimum capital requirements. While the new framework retains both existing capital definition and minimal capital ratio of 8%, some major changes have been introduced in measurement of the risks. The main objective of Pillar I is to introduce greater risk sensitivity in the design of capital adequacy ratios and, therefore, more flexibility in the computation of banks' individual risk. This will lead to better pricing of Risks.

Capital Adequacy Ratio signifies the amount of regulatory capital to be maintained by a bank to account for various risks inherent in the banking system.

The Capital Adequacy ratio is measured as :

$$\frac{\text{Total Regulatory Capital } \textbf{(unchanged)}}{\text{Credit Risk + Market Risk + Operational Risk}} = \text{Bank's Capital (minimum 8\%)}$$

Regulatory capital is defined as the minimum capital, banks are required to hold by the regulator, i.e. *"The amount of capital a bank **must** have". It is the summation of Tier I and Tier II capital.*

1. Credit Risk:

The changes proposed to the measurement of credit risk are considered to have most far reaching implications. Basel II envisages two alternative ways of measuring credit risk.

The Standardized Approach

The standardized approach is conceptually the same as the present Accord, but is more risk sensitive. The bank allocates a risk-weight to each of its assets and off-balance-sheet positions and produces a sum of risk-weighted asset values. Individual risk weights currently depend on the broad category of borrower (i.e. sovereigns, banks or corporate). Under the new Accord, the risk weights are to be refined by reference to a rating provided by an external credit assessment institution that meets strict standards.

The Internal Ratings Based Approach (IRB)

Under the IRB approach, distinct analytical frameworks will be provided for different types of loan exposures. The framework allows for both a foundation method in which a bank estimate the probability of default associated with each borrower, and the supervisors will supply the other inputs and an advanced IRB approach, in which a bank will be permitted to supply other necessary inputs as well. Under both the foundation and advanced IRB approaches, the range of risk weights will be far more diverse than those in the standardized approach, resulting in greater risk sensitivity.

The Risk components include measures of :

a. Probability of default (PD)

b. Loss Given default (LGD)

c. Exposure at default (EAD)

d. Effective Maturity (M)

Proposed Risk weight Scale : MAPPING PROCESS :

Credit Assessment	AAA to AA-	A+ to A-	BBB to BBB-	BB+ to B-	Below B-	Unrated
Sovereign (Govt. central banks)	0%	20%	50%	100%	150%	100%
Claims on the banks						
Option I	20%	50%	100%	100%	150%	100%
Option 2 a	20%	50%	50 %	1005	150%	50%
Option 2b	205	20%	20%	505	150%	20%
Corporate	20%	100%	+0	150%		100%

Option 1 = Risk weights based on risk weight of the country

Option 2a =Risk weight based on assessment of individual Bank

Option 2b =Risk weight based on assessment of individual banks with claim of original maturity of less than 6 months

Retail Portfolio ==75%

Claims secured by residential property =35%

NPA's = If specific provision is less than 20% =150%

If specific provision is more than 20% =100%

2. Operational Risk:

Basel II Accord set a capital requirement for operational risk. It defines operational risk as "the risk of direct or indirect loss resulting from inadequate or failed internal processes, people and systems or from external events". Banks will be able to choose between three ways of calculating the capital charge for operational risk – the Basic Indicator Approach, the Standardized Approach and the advanced measurement Approaches.

The Second Pillar: Supervisory Review Process

The supervisory review process requires supervisors to ensure that each bank has sound internal processes in place to assess the adequacy of its capital based on a thorough evaluation of its risks. Supervisors would be responsible for evaluating how well banks are assessing their capital adequacy needs relative to their risks. This internal process would then be subject to supervisory review and intervention, where appropriate.

The Third Pillar: Market Discipline

The third pillar of the new framework aims to bolster market discipline through enhanced disclosure by banks. Effective disclosure is essential to ensure that market participants can better understand banks' risk profiles and the adequacy of their capital positions. The new framework sets out disclosure requirements and recommendations in several areas, including the way a bank calculates its capital adequacy and its risk assessment methods. The core set of disclosure recommendations applies to all banks, with more detailed requirements for supervisory recognition of internal methodologies for credit risk, credit risk mitigation techniques and asset securitization.

CREDIT ALLOCATION:

A. Credit Allocation For Market Risks:

Proposed Risk Weight Table

CREDIT ASSESSMENT	AAA TO AA-	A+ TO A-	BBB+ TO BBB-	BB+ TO B-	BELOW B-	UNRATED
Sovereign (Govt. & Central Bank)	0%	20%	50%	100%	150%	100%
Claims on Banks						
Option 1	20%	50%	100%	100%	150%	100%
Option 2a	20%	50%	50%	100%	150%	50%
Option 2	20%	20%	20%	50%	150%	20%
Corporate	20%	50%	100% to 150%			100%

Where:

Option 1 = Risk weights based on risk weight of the country

Option 2a = Risk weight based on assessment of individual bank

Option 2b = Risk weight based on assessment of individual banks with claims of original maturity of less than 6 months

Basic indicator approach states Operational risk and the calculation of capital charge.

Operational risk =

KBIA = ({(GI N *) } /N

KBIA = capital charge under Basic indicator approach

GI = gross Income,where positive over previous year

N = number of previous three years for which GI is positive

(i) All credit exposure were risk weighted 100%

(ii) Regulatory retail portfolio is defined and it carries a uniform risk weight of 75%.CRAR is 755 on retail Loans

(iii) Off Balance sheet items are first calculated and then risk weights are applied

B. Credit mitigation techniques–collateralized transactions

A collateralized transactions is one in which banks have a credit exposure and that exposure is hedged in whole or part by collateral posted by a counter party or by a third party on behalf of the counter party and banks have a specific lien on the collateral and the requirement of legal certainty as mentioned here in above are met.

Overall framework and minimum conditions

1. In addition to the general requirements for legal certainty, the legal mechanism by which collateral is pledged or transferred must ensure that the bank has a right to liquidate or take legal possessions of it, in a timely manner in the event of default, insolvency or bankruptcy.

   Reserve bank has further advised that they must take all steps necessary to fill those requirements under the law applicable to the bank's interest in the collateral for obtaining and maintaining an enforceable security interest.

2. In order for collateral to provide protection, the credit quality of the counterparty and the value of the collateral must not have a material positive correlation. Under this comprehensive approach,when taking collateral banks will need to calculate their adjusted exposure to a counter party for capital adequacy purposes in order to take account of that collateral. The adjustments in the value of collateral is called haircut. The application of haircut will produce volatility adjusted amount for both exposure and collateral. The volatility adjusted amount for exposure is higher than the exposure and the volatility adjusted for the collateral is lower than the collateral.

Eligible financial collaterals are:

The following are the eligible financial collateral instruments:

1. Cash
2. Gold
3. Security issue by central and state government

4. Indira vikas patra, Kisan Vikas patra and NSC
5. Life Insurance Policies
6. Debt securities rates by recognized Credit rating agency
7. Debt securities rates by not recognized Credit rating agency
8. Undertaking of collective investments in transferable sec and mutual funds

Haircuts is an estimation of potential losses for calculating amount of exposure to the counter of collateral received

RBI has advised two ways of calculating the haircuts.

1. Standard supervisory haircuts using parameters set by committee and
2. Own estimate haircuts using internal estimate of market price volatility

RBI has advised that the banks in India will use standard haircuts for the exposure as well as collateral.

For the Calculation of the Capital requirement in the collatorised transactions, exposure amount after risk mitigation is calculated :

E* = ma { 0,(E(1+Hc)-(1-Hc-Hfx)} E*=exposure after risk mitigation, E=Current value of exposure, Hc=Haircut appropriate to collateral received Hfx = Haircut appropriate for Currency mismatch between exposure and collateral

CAPITAL RISK MITIGATION AT A BANK

A Bank has an exposure towards a Term Loan facility of Rs 100. The Tenor of the loan is 1 Year. The Bank has received debt security, (Collateral) rated A+. There is no maturity mismatch between the exposure and the collateral. The Collateral received by the Bank qualifies the recognition under the Credit Risk mitigation. The exposure will be calculated as follows :

E=Rs100 Hz= Rest 0 C =Rs100 haircut appropriate to collateral 1 yr haircut = 1% =0.01 Haircut for mismatch between currency mismatch (Collateral & exposure) Hfx =8% 0.08

E = Max{0,(100*(1+0)-100*(1-0.01-0,08)}

Max (0, {100-100*(0.91)}

Max (0,{100 - 91}

Max(0,9) = 9

Exposure Value after Risk Mitigation will be Rs 9

C. Credit Mitigation Techniques

A range of guarantees are recognized under Basel 2 accord. The detailed operational guidelines for guarantee eligible for being treated as a CRM are as under:

a) A guarantee must represent a directly claim on the protection provider and must be explicitly referenced to specific exposures or a pool of exposures.

b) A guarantec must be irrevocable

c) The guarantee must be unconditional

d) On the quality default/nonpayment of the counterparty, the bank may in timely manner pursue the guarantor for on monies outstanding under the documentations governing the transactions.

e) The guarantee is an explicitly documented obligation assumed by the guarantor.

f) The guarantee covers all types of the payments the underlying obligor is expected to make under the documentation governing the transaction.

RBI has issued detailed guidelines for computation of capital charge on Market Risk. The guidelines seek to address the issues involved in computing capital charge for interest rate related instruments in the trading book, equities in the trading book and foreign exchange risk (including gold and precious metals) in both trading and banking book. Trading book will include:

- ✓ Securities included under the Held for trading category
- ✓ Securities included under the Available for Sale category

- ✓ Open gold position limits
- ✓ Open foreign exchange position limits
- ✓ Trading position in derivatives and derivatives entered into for hedging trading book exposures.

As per the guidelines, minimum capital requirement is expressed in terms of two separately calculated charges:

a) Specific Risk and
b) General Market Risk

CONCLUSIONS & RECOMMENDATIONS

A. Implementation of Basel II = A Retrospective Approach

Implementation of Basel II is likely to improve the risk management systems of banks as the banks aim for adequate capitalization to meet the underlying credit risk plus strengthen the overall financial system of the country

It is apparent that advantage lies in favor of encouraging central banks/banking sector regulators to implement Basel II framework at their own pace plus in a manner appropriate to their economies, banking systems and supervisory mechanisms. In India, banks are likely to comply with the Basel II norms by March 2007.

In the short term, Indian commercial banks may need to augment their regulatory capitalization levels in order to comply with Basel II. However, in the long term, they would derive benefits from improved operations and credit risk management practices. As the deadline of implementing Basel II approaches, the Indian banking is still preparing to solve the risk puzzle for a more transparent and free risk financial base

a) The Standardized approach yields little in linking Capital to risk while the IRB approach looks complex to implement and is difficult to monitor.The Banks adopting IRB approach will be more risk sensitive than the Banks on the Standardized approach,since even a small change in degree of risk might translate into a large impact on capital requirement for IRB Banks

b) For the Banks adopting the Standardized Approach, the relative capital requirement would be less for the same exposure and would be inclined to assume the exposures to high risk clients, which were not financed by IRB Banks. As a result, high risk assets could flow towards bank on Standardized approach which needs to maintain lower capital on these assets. Hence, the system as a whole may maintain lower capital than warranted.

Keeping in view of the above, we suggest a Centralized Rating based (CRB) approach where RBI dictates a rating scale and asks the Banks to rate borrowers according to the centralized scale. RBI thus would be able to monitor and control their capital sufficiency's in relation to risk much more effectively.The Banks would thus by CRB approach have their own Rating Scales in consultation with RBI and use them as a reference tool.

SUMMARY

The challenges in implementation of Basle II norms are:

(i) Costly Database Creation and Maintenance Process:

The most obvious impact of BASEL II is the need for improved risk management and measurement. It aims to give impetus to the use of internal rating system by the international banks. More and more banks may have to use internal model developed in house and their impact is uncertain. Most of these models require minimum 5 years bank data which is a tedious and high cost process as most Indian banks do not have such a database

(ii) Additional Capital Requirement:

In order to comply with the capital adequacy norms we will see that the overall capital level of the banks will raise a glimpse of which was seen when the RBI raised risk weight ages for mortgages and home loans in October 2004. Here there is a worrying aspect that some of the banks will not be able to put up the additional capital to comply with the new regulation and they may be isolated from the global banking system.

(iii) Large Proportion of NPA's:

A large number of Indian banks have significant proportion of NPA's in their assets. Along with that a large proportion of loans of banks are of poor quality. There is a danger that a large number of banks will not be able to restructure and survive in the new environment. This may lead to forced mergers of many defunct banks with the existing ones and a loss of capital to the banking system as a whole.

(iv) Relative Advantage to Large Banks:

The new norms seem to favor the large banks that have better risk management and measurement expertise. They also have better capital adequacy ratios and geographically diversified portfolios. The smaller banks are also likely to be hurt by the rise in weight age of inter-bank loans that will effectively price them out of the market. Thus banks will have to restructure and adopt if they are to survive in the new environment.

(v) Increased Pro-Cyclicality:

The appropriate question is not then whether Basel II introduces pro-cyclicality but whether it increases it. The increased importance to credit ratings under Basel II could actually imply that the minimum requirements could become pro-cyclical as banks are required to raise capital levels for loans in times of economic crises.

(vi) Low Degree of Corporate Rating Penetration:

India has as few as three established rating agencies and the level of rating penetration is not very significant as, so far, ratings are restricted to issues and not issuers. While Basel II gives some scope to extend the rating of issues to issuers, this would only be an approximation and it would be necessary for the system to move to ratings of issuers. Encouraging ratings of issuers would be a challenge.

(vii) Cross Border Issues for Foreign Banks:

In India, foreign banks are statutorily required to maintain local capital and the following issues are required to be resolved;

- Validation of the internal models approved by their head offices and home country supervisor adopted by the Indian branches of foreign banks.
- Date history maintained and used by the bank should be distinct for the Indian branches compared to the global data used by the head office
- capital for operational risk should be maintained separately for the Indian branches in India

B. Compliance to Basle II norms for Indian Bank :

(a) Better position to fight with primary three risks which they face namely – Credit, Market and Operational.

(b) Put Indian Banks on equal footing to that of International Banks and help to improve credibility.

14.7 BASEL III

Basel Committee's proposals to strengthen global capital and liquidity regulations with the goal of promoting a more resilient banking sector. The objective of the Basel Committee's reform package is to improve the banking sector's ability to absorb shocks arising from financial and economic stress, whatever the source, thus reducing the risk of spillover from the financial sector to the real economy.

Sudden changes in asset quality and value can quickly wipe out bank capital. Where short-term wholesale liabilities fund longer-term assets, failure to roll over short-term financial paper, or a 'run' on deposits, can force de-leveraging and asset sales. Banking crises associated with such changes are often systemic in nature, arising from the interconnectedness of financial arrangements: banks between themselves, with derivative counterparties and with direct links to consumption and investment spending decisions. In history, banking crises have been associated with major economic disruption and recessions. It is for this reason that policy makers regulate the amount of capital that banks are required to hold, and require high standards of corporate governance, including liquidity management, accounting, audit and lending practices.

14.7 (A). Summary of Proposed Changes in Basel III

- First, the quality, consistency, and transparency of the capital base will be raised.
    - o Tier 1 capital: the predominant form of Tier 1 capital must be common shares and retained earnings.
    - o Tier 2 capital instruments will be harmonized.
    - o Tier 3 capital will be eliminated.
- Second, the risk coverage of the capital framework will be strengthened.
    - o Strengthen the capital requirements for counterparty credit exposures arising from banks' derivatives, repo and securities financing transactions.
    - o Raise the capital buffers backing these exposures.
    - o Reduce procyclicality and
    - o Provide additional incentives to move OTC derivative contracts to central counterparties (probably clearing houses).
    - o Provide incentives to strengthen the risk management of counterparty credit exposures.
- Third, the Committee will introduce a leverage ratio as a supplementary measure to the Basel II risk-based framework.
    - o The Committee therefore is introducing a leverage ratio requirement that is intended to achieve the following objectives:
        - Put a floor under the build-up of leverage in the banking sector
        - Introduce additional safeguards against model

risk and measurement error by supplementing the risk-based measure with a simpler measure that is based on gross exposures.

Fourth, the Committee is introducing a series of measures to promote the build up of capital buffers in good times that can be drawn upon in periods of stress ("Reducing procyclicality and promoting countercyclical buffers").

- o The Committee is introducing a series of measures to address procyclicality:
  - Dampen any excess cyclicality of the minimum capital requirement;
  - Promote more forward looking provisions;
  - Conserve capital to build buffers at individual banks and the banking sector that can be used in stress; and
- o Achieve the broader macroprudential goal of protecting the banking sector from periods of excess credit growth.
  - Requirement to use long term data horizons to estimate probabilities of default,
  - downturn loss-given-default estimates, recommended in Basel II, to become mandatory
  - Improved calibration of the risk functions, which convert loss estimates into regulatory capital requirements.
  - Banks must conduct stress tests that include widening credit spreads in recessionary scenarios.
- o Promoting stronger provisioning practices (**forward looking provisioning**):
  - Advocating a change in the accounting standards towards an expected loss (EL) approach (usually, *EL amount* := LGD*PD*EAD)

Fifth, the Committee is introducing a global minimum **liquidity standard** for internationally active banks that includes a 30-day liquidity coverage ratio requirement underpinned by a longer-term structural liquidity ratio.

- The Committee also is reviewing the need for additional capital, liquidity or other supervisory measures to reduce the externalities created by systemically important institutions.

17.7.2 B. NEED OF BASEL III

Capital regulations under Basel I came into effect in December 1992 (after Development and consultations since 1988). The aims were: first, to require banks to maintain enough capital to absorb losses without causing systemic problems, and second, to level the playing field internationally (to avoid competitiveness Conflicts). A minimum ratio of 4% for Tier 1 capital (which should mainly be equity less goodwill) to risk-weighted assets (RWA) and 8% for Tier 1 and Tier 2 capital (certain subordinated debt etc).

A 'revised framework' known as Basel II was released in June 2004 (BCBS, 2004) after many issues with Basel I, most notably that regulatory arbitrage was rampant (Jackson, 1999). Basel I gave banks the ability to control the amount of capital they required by shifting between on-balance sheet assets with different weights, and by securitising assets and shifting them off balance sheet – a form of disintermediation. Banks quickly accumulated capital well in excess of the regulatory minimum and capital requirements, which, in effect, had no constraining impact on bank risk taking.

14.7.3 Basel I and II fail to stop global crisis

As the centrepiece for capital regulation to avoid crises the Basel approach has failed in its 1st and 2nd formulations and the world is still dealing with the after effects of the greatest financial crisis since the Great Depression.

Pillar 1 of the Basel II system defines minimum capital to buffer unexpected losses. Total RWA are based on a complex system of risk weighting that applies to 'credit'.

'market' (MR) and 'operational' risk (OR), which are calculated separately and then added:

RWA= {12.5(OR+MR) + 1.06*SUM [w (i) A (i)]} (1)

Where: w (i) is the risk weight for asset i; and A(i) is asset i; OR and MR are directly measured and grossed up by 12.5 for 8% equivalence; and credit risk is the sum of the various asset classes, each weighted by its appropriate risk weight. A scaling factor applied to this latter term, estimated to be 1.06 on the basis of QIS-3 data (but subject to change), was envisaged for the transition period, which was supposed to start for most countries in January 2008. Banks were to be able to choose between: first, a simplified approach (for smaller institutions without the capacity to model their business in risk terms) by using the fixed weights; second, an approach based on external ratings; and third, an internal ratings-based (IRB) approach for sophisticated banks, driven by their own internal rating models.

The simplified Basel II approach is more 'granular' than Basel I, but retains its basic features. It is striking in light of the financial crisis that the simplified approach shows the Basel Committee cutting the risk weight to mortgages by some 30% (from 50% to 35%) and much more in the sophisticated version. The weight for lending between banks was only 20% under Basel 1, kept the same under the simplified Basel II, and is likely to be cut by 20 to 30% under the sophisticated approach.

Complex modelling

The IRB approach requires banks to specify the probability of default (PD) for each individual credit, its loss-given-default (LGD), and the expected exposure at default (EED). This requires highly- complex modeling and aggregation, and offers banks with the necessary expertise the possibility of deriving more risk- sensitive weights. This approach requires the approval of the bank's supervisor.

PROBLEMS WITH PILLAR 1

- ***No concentration penalty in Pillar 1: Portfolio invariance***

The risk weighting formulas in the Basel capital regulations are based on a specific mathematical model, developed by the Basel Committee, which is subject to the restriction that it be 'portfolio invariant'; that is, the capital required to back loans should depend only on the risk of that loan, not on the portfolio to which it is added (Gordy, 2003). This is convenient for additivity and application across countries. But it has an important disadvantage: it does not reflect the importance of diversification as an influence on portfolio risk.

Thus the minimum capital requirements associated with any type of loan due to credit risk simply rise linearly with the holding of that asset type, regardless of the size of the exposure (that is, appropriate diversification is simply assumed). This means that it does not penalize portfolio concentration (as might occur for example under a quadratic rule applied to deviations from a diversified benchmark; see below). Concentration issues are left to supervisors in Pillar 2.

- ***No country-specific risk: Single global risk factor***

For the mathematical model underlying the Basel approach (I or II), each exposure's contribution to value-at-risk (VaR) is portfolio invariant only if: *(a)* dependence across exposures is driven by a single systemic risk factor – a global risk factor, since it is supposed to apply to global banks operating across countries; and *(b)* each exposure is small (Gordy,2003). What we know of the sub-prime crisis is that it originated in the US housing market (regional sector risk in this framework) and exposures were quite large.

Of the two conditions for invariance, by far the most important is the requirement of a single risk factor that applies to all participants. Almost prophetically, Gordy (2003) says:

A single factor model cannot capture any clustering of firm defaults due to common sensitivity to these smaller scale components of the global business cycle. Holding fixed the state of the global economy, local events in, for example, France are permitted to contribute nothing to the default rate of French obligors. If there are indeed pockets of risk, then calibrating a single factor model to a broadly diversified international credit index may significantly understate the capital needed to support a regional or specialized lender.2

- ***CDS destroys notions of ex ante risks in the specific financial institutions;***

The Basel risk-weighting approach in fact encourages portfolio concentrations in low-weighted assets like government bonds, mortgages and lending between banks – there is always an incentive to economise on capital and expand business into lower-weighted areas. Unfortunately, this approach evolved at the same time as did the market for credit default swaps (CDS). Prior to the CDS contract it was not possible to go short in credit, unlike in other markets. The credit markets were "incomplete". The CDS contract created the potential for complete markets in credit. The banks were able to transform the buckets of risk themselves with derivatives, thus undermining the fundamental idea of capital weights, without having to trade as much on the underlying securities on primary markets (favouring assets with low-risk weights).

This issue is about promises in the financial system. If regulations treat promises differently in different sectors, then with complete markets in credit, the promises will be transformed into those with the lowest capital charges.

- ***Contagion and counterparty risk as hallmarks: Bank capital market activities***

In many ways the main hallmarks of the global financial crisis were the contagion and counterparty risks. Both of these arose from banks involving themselves in capital market activities for which they did not carry sufficient capital. Securitisation and its warehousing on and off-balance sheet proved to be a major problem. In the US, Variable Interest Entities (VIEs) to which banks are linked had to be consolidated onto balance sheets if banks became insolvent or if liquidity of funding became problematic. This was completely missed in the capital regulations. Similarly, counterparty risk became a major issue with the failures of Lehman Brothers and AIG. In the latter case, the banks exposed relied on public compensation to ensure that the crisis did not make them insolvent.

- ***The capital regulations are pro- cyclical: Pro-cyclicality***

The Basel system is known to be pro-cyclical. There are many reasons for this. The most basic reason is that judgments tend to underestimate risks in good times and overestimate them in bad times. More specific factors include:

- Leverage ratios depend on current market values (and are therefore high in good times and low in bad times). If asset values do not accurately reflect future cash flows, pro-cyclicality results;
- Banks' risk measurements tend to be point-in-time and not holistic measures over the whole cycle;
- Counterparty credit policies are easy in good times and tough in bad; and
- Profit recognition and compensation schemes encourage short-term risk taking, but are not adjusted for risk over the business cycle.

Capital regulation under previous Basel regimes did nothing to counter this pro-cyclicality. Banks can control their RWA via regulatory arbitrage and by varying bank capital more directly via dividend and share buyback policies (high dividends and buybacks in the good times and vice versa).

- ***Estimation of PD, LGD and EAD***

The IRB approach of the revised framework actually institutionalises this pro- cyclicality by making banks themselves responsible for estimating Probability of Default (PD), Loss Given Default (LGD) and Exposure at Default (EAD), which are all a function of the cycle, and are led by the stock market, asset values and other financial variables. Private bankers cannot predict future asset prices and future volatility events. The simplified system changed nothing relative to Basel I, and the external ratings based approach still used credit ratings, which are notoriously pro-cyclical.

- ***Subjective inputs***

  Risk inputs are subjective. Some prices are of the over-the-counter variety and are not observable, nor do they have appropriate histories for modelling purposes. Banks can manipulate inputs to reduce capital required. For these sorts of reasons, the Basel Committee envisaged that Pillar 2 would deal with risks not appropriately covered in Pillar 1.3

- ***Unclear and inconsistent definitions***

  The main problems here have been the definition of capital.

  - Regulatory adjustments for goodwill are not mandated to apply to common equity, but are applied to Tier 1 and/or a combination of Tier 1 and Tier 2.
  - The regulatory adjustments are not applied uniformly across jurisdictions opening the way for further regulatory arbitrage.
  - Banks do not provide clear and consistent data about their capital.

This means that in a crisis the ability of banks to absorb losses is compromised and different between countries – exactly as seen in the crisis.

Pillars 2 and 3

Pillar 2 relates to the supervisory review process. With stress testing and guidance from supervisors, banks can be made to hold capital for risks not appropriately captured under Pillar 1. Building buffers in this way requires supervisors to be forward looking, that is, to keep up with changes in market structure, practices and complexity. This is inherently difficult. Supervisors may be even less likely to be able to predict future asset prices and volatility than private bankers. Furthermore, supervisors have smaller staff (per regulated entity) and are mostly less well paid. If supervisory practices lag the policy makers will be ineffective in countering defects in Pillar 1.4 Pillar 2 is not likely to be effective in a forward-looking way.

In this respect it is worth noting (see below) that the UK Financial Services Authority (FSA), which is one of the best staffed and most sophisticated of supervisors, signed off on Northern Rock to be one of the first banks to go to the Basel II IRB approach, understanding fully that this would reduce their capital significantly, immediately prior to the sub-prime crisis. More recently, the Lehman use of repo 105 to disguise leverage in its accounts was not hidden from supervisors – it appears they did not fully appreciate what they were looking at (Sorkin, 2010).

Markets just aren't Efficient

Pillar 3 relies on disclosure and market discipline that will punish banks with poor risk management practices. Underlying this is an efficient markets notion that markets will act in a fully rational way. At the level of markets, the bubble at the root of the sub-prime crisis, and crises before it, suggest the systematic absence of informational efficiency. The whole pro-cyclicality debate concerning the Basel system is premised on the idea that asset prices do not reflect future cash flows accurately.

'Basel III' Proposals for Reform

Trading Book Market Risk Changes:

Basel II, to all intents and purposes, never came properly into effect. In July 2009 the Basel Committee already adopted changes that would boost capital held for market risk in the trading book portfolio (see MR in equation 1 above) – in essence applying a multiplier of 3 to VaR specific risk and to stressed VaR risk in the calculation (BCBS, 2009a). The quantitative impact study has shown, oddly, that the average capital requirement for banks in the study would rise by 11.5%, but the median would only rise by 3.2% (BCBS, 2009b). More capital of course is to be welcomed. The consultative document issued by the Basel Committee in December 2009 aims to fix some of the problems noted above.

Aim:

1. *To raise the quality, consistency and transparency of the capital base Common equity is good*

Tier 1 capital will consist of going concern capital in the form of common equity (common shares plus retained earnings) and some equity-like debt instruments which are both subordinated and where dividend payments are discretionary. Criteria for Tier 2 capital will also be tightened (subordinate to depositors, five-year minimum maturity and no incentives to redeem). After a quantitative impact study, it is proposed to fix minima for common equity as a percentage of RWA, and similarly for Tier 1 capital and total capital. It is proposed to abolish Tier 3 capital.

As far as improving the definition of capital is concerned, the report stresses that equity is the best form of capital, as it can be used to write off losses. Not included in (to be deducted from) common equity are:

- **Goodwill** This can't be used to write off losses.
- **Minority interest** That if a company takes over another with a majority interest and consolidates it into the balance sheet, the net income of the 3rd party minorities can't be retained by the parent as common equity.
- **Deferred tax assets (net of liabilities)** These should be deducted if they depend on the future realization of profit (not including tax pre-payments and the like that do not depend on future profitability).
- **Bank investments in its own shares.**
- Bank investments in other banks, financial institutions and insurance companies – all cross-share holdings and

investments in sister companies, all holdings if a bank's position in another institution is 10% or more, and an aggregation adjustment of all holdings that amount to more than 10% of common equity. The aim here is to avoid double counting of equity.

- **Provisioning shortfalls**
- **Other deductions** Such as projected cash flow hedging not recognised on the balance sheet that distorts common equity; defined benefit pension holdings of bank equity; some regulatory adjustments that are currently deducted 50% from Tier 1 and 50% from Tier 2 not addressed elsewhere.

2. *Enhancing risk coverage*

One major problem in the crisis was the failure of the Basel approach to capture on and off balance sheet risks (related Special Purpose Vehicles (SPVs) for example). Going forward, it is proposed that banks:

a. *Use "stressed" inputs*

- Must determine their capital requirement for counterparty credit risk using stressed inputs, helping to remove pro-cyclicality that might arise with using current volatility-based risk inputs.
- Must include capital charges (credit valuation adjustments) associated with the deterioration in the creditworthiness of a counterparty (as opposed to its outright default).

b. *Wrong-way risk*

- Implement a Pillar 1 capital charge for wrong-way risk (transactions with counter parties, especially financial guarantors, whose PD is positively correlated with the amount of exposure). Adjusting the multiplier applied to the exposure amount identified as wrong way risk will do this.

c. Correlation multiplier

- Apply a multiplier of 1.25 to the asset value correlation (AVC) of exposures to regulated financial firms with assets of at least $25bn, (since AVC's were 25% higher during the crisis for financial versus non- financial firms). This would have the effect of raising risk weights for such exposures.

d. Margining periods

Will be required to apply tougher (longer) margining periods as a basis for determining regulatory capital when they have large and illiquid derivative exposures to a counterparty.

e. Centralised exchange incentives

Will qualify for a zero risk weight for counterparty risk exposure if they deal with centralised exchanges (that meet certain criteria): hence creating an incentive to use centralised exchanges (since higher charges will apply for bilateral OTC derivatives).

The Committee is also trying to improve the usefulness of external ratings in the above recommendation, and so proposes to require banks to assess these ratings with their own internal processes.

3. Leverage ratio 'Backstop' leverage ratio

The introduction of a leverage ratio is intended to help to avoid the build-up in excess leverage that can lead to a deleveraging 'credit crunch' in a crisis situation. The Committee refers to this as a 'backstop' measure for the risk-based approach.

It is proposing a simple leverage ratio based on Tier 1 capital, with a 100% treatment to all exposures net of provisions, including cash and cash-like instruments. Certain off-balance sheet exposures will be included with a 100% credit conversion factor, and written credit protection will be included at its notional value. It is proposed that there be no netting of collateral held and no netting off-balance sheet derivative exposures (more akin to IFRS treatment than to GAAP).

4. Pro-cyclicality

The Basel Committee places considerable emphasis on the role of pro- cyclical factors in the crisis resulting from mark-to-market accounting and held to maturity loans; margining practices; and the build-up of leverage and its reversal amongst all financial market participants. The following ideas are proposed to deal with this:

- To dampen the cyclicality of the minimum capital requirement the committee is looking to focus on longer-term calibration of the probability of default in the modelling of risk; the use of Pillar 2 supervisory override is also being recommended when necessary.

5. Forward-looking provisioning

The Committee will promote forward-looking provisioning by strongly supporting the IASB principles to base it on the 'expected' (rather than the current 'incurred') losses of banks' existing portfolios. It also proposes to deduct from bank capital any shortfall in these provisions (*i.e.* to expected losses) to provide an incentive against under-provisioning.

6. Buffers are very important

Very importantly, the Committee is proposing that banks hold buffers of capital above the regulatory minimum – large enough that they remain above the minimum in periods of significant sector-wide downturns.

Furthermore, when the buffers are run down banks would be required to build them again by reducing discretionary dividend distributions, buybacks and staff bonus payments.

- The Committee is proposing that the buffer system might be used in a macro prudential framework to help restrain credit growth when it is perceived as excessive – the buffer would rise and fall in a countercyclical manner.

14.7.5 CHALLENGES WITH THE BANKING INDUSTRYWHICH BASLE III FACES IN CURRENT ERA

- With the feature of additional capital requirements, the overall capital level of the banks will see an increase. But, the banks that will not be able to make it as per the global system.
- Another biggest challenge is re-structuring the assets of some of the banks would be a tedious process, since most of the banks have poor asset quality leading to significant proportion of NPA. This also may lead to Mergers & Acquisitions, which itself would be loss of capital to entire system.
- The new norms seem to favor the large banks that have better risk management and measurement expertise, who also have better capital adequacy ratios and geographically diversified portfolios. The smaller banks are also likely to be hurt by the rise in weightage of inter-bank loans that will effectively price them out of the market. Thus, banks will have tore-structure and adopt if they are to survive in the new environment.
- Since improved risk management and measurement is needed; it aims to give impetus tothe use of internal rating system by the international banks. More and more banks mayhave to use internal model developed in house and their impact is uncertain. Most of thesemodels require minimum historical bank data that is a tedious and high cost process, asmost Indian banks do not have such a database.
- The technology infrastructure in terms of computerization is still in a nascent stage inmost Indian banks. Computerization of branches, especially for those banks, which have their network spread out in fa r-flung areas, will be a daunting task. Penetration of information technology in banking has been successful in the urban

areas, unlike in the ruralareas where it is insignificant.

- Experts say that dearth of risk management expertise in the Asia Pacif ic region will serve as a hindrance in laying down guidelines for a basic framework for the new capital accord.
- An integrated risk management concept, which is the need of the hour to align market, credit and operational risk, will be difficult due to significant disconnect between business, risk managers and IT across the organizations in their existing set-up.
- Implementation of the Basel II will require huge investments in technology. According to estimates, Indian banks, especially those with a sizeable branch network, will need to spend well over $ 50-70 Million on this.

14.7.6 EFFECTIVE DATES OF DISCLOSURES (CONCLUSION)

The notification states that the earliest dates of making application by banks and likely approval by the regulator for implementing internal models approach for market risk are April 1, 2010 and March 31, 2011 respectively. The earliest dates of making application by banks and likely approval by the regulator for implementing the standardized approach for operational risk are April 1, 2010 and September 30, 2010 respectively. The earliest dates of making application by banks and likely approval by the regulator for implementing advanced measurement approach for operational risk are April 1, 2012 and March 31, 2014 respectively.

The earliest dates of making application by banks and likely approval by the regulator for implementing internal ratings-based approaches for credit risk (foundation- as well as advanced IRB) are April 1, 2012 and March 31, 2014 respectively.

As per the circular released by the Indian regulator on April 27, 2007 on the new capital adequacy framework, foreign banks operating in India and Indian banks having operational presence outside India have migrated to the simpler approaches available under the Basel II framework since March 31, 2008. Other commercial banks have also migrated to these approaches from March 31, 2009. Thus, the standardized approach for credit risk, basic indicator approach for operational risk and the standardized duration approach for market risk (as slightly amended under Basel II framework) have been implemented for the banks in India.

The latest notification issued by the regulator states that the banks, at their discretion, would have the option of adopting the advanced approaches for one or more of the risk categories, as per their preparedness, while continuing with the simpler approaches for other risk categories, and it would not be necessary to adopt the advanced approaches for all the risk categories simultaneously. However, the banks should invariably obtain prior approval of the Reserve Bank of India for adoption of any of the advanced approaches.

A. Tier I Capital	***Basle II***	***Basle III***
Tier I Capital Ratio	4%	6%
Core Tier I Capital Ratio	2%	4.5%
B. Counter Cyclical Capital Buffer		
	Basle II	Basle III
No Counter Cyclical Capital Buffer		Yes
Framework-	2013-2019	0-2.5% on T.I of common equity after deductions

15

NPA MANAGEMENT

I. Loan Portfolio Risks Management in Banking Business – Non- Performing Assets Management in Indian Context – (An Empirical Study of Andhra Bank)

15.1 INTRODUCTION

The Banking Industry is currently dependent upon the financial growth and stability of the economy. The primary functions of lending funds to various sectors have ceased to generate Income / Principal repayment. The R.B.I. has already suggested various Income recognition and prudential norms thereby telling the banks "critical performance areas". Non – recovery of the loan assets has increased the strain on the banks' network and eroding the net worth considerably. Thus the banks' credit is considered to be a catalyst to the economic growth of the country and any bottlenecks in the smooth flow of the credit / mounting of the N.P.A.s is bound to create adverse repercussions on the economy.

Since the N.P.A.s have galloped in the Indian Banking System, with the introduction of the new, stronger foreclosure laws [SARFAESI (The Securitization and Reconstruction of Financial Assets and Enforcement of Security Interests)] the gross N.P.A. levels have fallen in the Public Sector Banks. Management / Resolution of the N.P.A.s include the SARFAESI Act; One time settlement scheme, setting up of the C.D.R. (Corporate Debt Restructuring) mechanism, Restructuring / Stripping the sale of assets are the plausible remedial regulations for timely comparison of the recovery of 'Asset based lending' versus 'Income based Lending'.

A. NPA the Present Scenario

The current domestic economic slowdown, coupled with the impact of global recessionary trends on liquidity, has raised concerns of rising NPAs (non-performing assets) in the Indian banking system Whilst credit demand has diminished to some extent in recent months, banks are also exercising greater caution now than a few months earlier in lending to Small and Medium Enterprises, auto, textile and other stressed sectors. Sectors such as textiles and real estate were among the first to be affected by the slowdown and there has already been some restructuring of repayment terms to banks. The impact of the slowdown on small borrowers was likely to be more pronounced, due to their small scale of operations coupled with sluggish revenue growth, lower capacity utilization, shrinking margins and / or lengthening working capital cycles, have severely dented borrowers' financial strength and flexibility.

International rating agency, Moody's Investors Service, has changed its fundamental credit outlook for the Indian banking system to 'negative' from 'stable', reflecting the deceleration of the Indian economy in the context of the global financial turmoil and an increasingly bleak economic outlook, which, combined with higher loan delinquency rates, indicates a potential weakening in the asset quality of Indian banks.

Moody's negative credit outlook for the Indian banking system expresses the rating agency's view on the likely future direction of fundamental credit conditions in the industry over the next 12 to 18 months. Moody's stress- test of the India banks' asset quality suggests that their financial profiles are likely to come under pressure, which could trigger negative rating actions. Moody's also downgraded Delhi-based Oriental Bank of Commerce (OBC) as the bank has relatively low capacity to raise tier-1 capital in order to absorb potential losses from a future deterioration in asset quality. OBC's government shareholding is close to the required minimum of 51%. The rating agency concluded that, compared with other similarly rated banks in India, OBC appears vulnerable to the possibility an acute asset quality stress. The ongoing deterioration of credit quality will hit the small and medium banks more than the big banks like State Bank of India, and ICICI Bank.

In this context, bankers are currently evaluating how far the issue of rising non-performing assets can be a drag on their balance sheets assuming that there is no change in the global economic environment until the end of the first half of 2009-10. Various analysis show that gross NPAs in the banking industry will jump to 4.7% in 2009-10 from current levels and they will peak at 5.0% of total advances in 2010-11. At the end of 2007-08, the gross advances of Indian banks stood at Rs 25 lakh crore, the gross NPAs were at Rs 56,400 crore and net NPAs were posted at Rs 24,700 crore. While the gross NPA ratio was 2.3%, the net NPA ratio stood at 1.0% of total advances.

Possible reasons for the high amount of NPAs among the public sector banks are a large quantum of loans disbursed in the agriculture sector, as 50 per cent of the bank's branches are in rural and semi-urban areas. Due to continuous drought, several of these loans had become bad accounts. Another reason could be the increase in interest rates in the banking industry over the last few years, which in turn led to an increase in monthly repayments. Maximum rise of 266 per cent in net NPAs was witnessed by Punjab National Bank in Q3, 2007-08, followed by Centurion Bank of Punjab with an increase by 125 per cent, ICICI Bank (77 per cent), Vijaya Bank (49 per cent), HDFC Bank (37.46 per cent) and State Bank of India (25 per cent).

Another reason for increase in NPA could be RBI guidelines to commercial banks to classify a loan for financing an infrastructure project as a non-performing asset (NPA) even if the interest dues are being serviced; the project is classified as an NPA. This will create a problem in the coming years if the project has not begun operation one year after the date on which the project was originally expected to be completed.

Public Sector Bank have urged the government to ask the Reserve Bank of India (RBI) to outline flexible norms for recognizing defaults on lending to infrastructure projects, given delays in project implementation, such as delay in obtaining statutory and regulatory clearances, land acquisition and ongoing litigation, which were beyond the promoter's control. The representation assumes significance as investments required for development of infrastructure in the country over the next five years are estimated to be over $500 billion.

15.2 Rationale of the study:

NPA management is a matter of concern to the entire banking industry. What one has to see is the background of an NPA and its origination. A lot of NPAs result from lack of proper monitoring and control. There are NPAs which occur due to factors beyond the control of the borrower. Sometimes, NPAs occur due to diversion of funds by the borrower. But ultimately, effective monitoring and control will definitely restrict the NPAs. Instead of getting into action after the accounts have turned into NPAs, what banks are planning to do is take a standard account and closely monitor it to see that slippages do not occur.

Banks are strengthening the Risk Management System at all levels from doing due diligence on the borrower, monitoring loans accounts .and upgrading weak accounts. Similarly, the recovery mechanism is implemented effectively improving the scoring system and rating model in order to reduce the rate of adverse selection is also another step in this direction. NPAs need constant monitoring. The system exists, but it was not followed strictly. It needs to be strengthened at every level. Banks have to monitor each and every account very closely to find out the strengths and weaknesses of the borrower and the likely areas of slippages on a regular basis. The balance sheet will help the banker only to some extent. But more than that, bank must know the man behind the figures and statements of the balance sheet. Banks are in the process of devising more innovative methods based on the experiences they have had in NPA management.

Banks need to understand and appreciate the actual credit requirements of the borrower. Of course, it should be need-based. Under financing would damage the unit of a borrower. This is what is happening in the SSI sector across the country. For effective NPA management, rehabilitation exercise becomes very important. It is not that when the account shows sickness, bank should drop the borrower. After all, the bank is a partner in the borrower's business. Merely filing a recovery suit does not help Bank. Of course, if the credibility of the borrower is in doubt, such as he is trying to cheat or defraud the bank, bank has no other way than go ahead with recovery procedures.

15.3 *Review of literature*:

Non performing assets are an inevitable burden on the banking industry. Hence the success of banks depends upon methods of managing NPAs and keeping them within tolerance level. The problem of NPAs has been studied over the years to bring insight into the problem of NPAs, its cause and solution.

The Pricewaterhouse Coopers Limited (2002) carried out a study of NPA incidence in India and NPA management by Indian Banking Industry. The study reveals that though Indian banking industry has achieved significant progress in NPA management but much still needs to be done in areas such as credit risk management, identification and correction of NPA problem in a time bound manner.

According to Muniappan (2002) there are many internal and external factors affecting NPAs. The internal factors highlighted are diversion of funds, taking up new projects, promoting associate concerns, time/cost overrun during the project implementation stage while external factors are economic growth rate, growth rate of other countries, general price level etc.

Ranjana Kumar (2000) has highlighted legal hurdles as the major cause of delay in recovery of bank loans and has suggested speedy resolution of the large number of pending suits against defaulters to overcome the weakness in the legal framework. The study concludes that an effective monitoring and control, aided by proper legal reforms would change the contours of NPA in banking at par with international standards and build resilience for a stronger and vibrant financial system to realize the objective of the reform measures implemented so far.

Rajaraman Indira and Vasishtha (2002) in their empirical study proved that significant bivariate relationship exists between non performing loans of public sector banks and the inefficiency on the side of the borrowers. This is very relevant in today's context as there is a pressure on Small Manufacturing Enterprises (SMEs) as many of them are unable to repay their advances in the current scenario. Banks need to adjust their risk management mechanisms to face the situation and avoid slippage of standard asset to NPA.

Das A and Ghosh S (2003) established relationship between non performing loans of India's public sector banks in terms of various indicators, such as asset size, credit growth and macroeconomic condition, and operating efficiency indicators. The study also covers private as well as foreign banks operating in India.

Pradeep Singh (2007) has thrown light on the banking sector reforms especially in the area of NPA management with special reference to Securitization and Reconstruction of Financial Assets and Enforcement of Security Interest bill (2002), establishment of Asset Reconstruction Companies (ARCs) in India and operational procedure of ARCs.The study includes non performing loans of Public sector, old private sector, new private sector and foreign bank groups over the period of 2000-2005.The study concludes that to face global challenges and to maintain the liquidity and profitability it is essential to maintain the NPA with lower level and efficiently realization (before they become bad debts) is essential. In this respect SARFAESI act and ARCs can play a vital role for the management of NPA in Indian banking environment.

Gourav Vallabh, Anoop Bhatia and Saurabh Mishra (2007)has adopted an empirical approach to the analysis of Non performing Assets of public, private and foreign sector banks in India. A model consisting of two prime parameters; macroeconomic factors and bank specific parameters has been used to observe the NPA behavior of three groups of banks. The study concludes that NPA of private banks is most sensitive to capital adequacy ratio; hence banks maintaining higher capital do better in terms of maintaining lower level of NPA. While NPA of public sector banks is more sensitive to macroeconomic factors. The empirical analysis depicts negative relationship between NPA of private as well as public sector banks with priority sector lending.

15.4 Objectives of the study:

This study focuses on the following major objectives:

- To conceptualize NPAs and their impact on the liquidity of banks.
- To analyze the factors attributable to NPAs in public sector banks.
- To analyze relationship between Net N.P.A. as % of Net Advances and Operating Profits as %Working Funds, return on Assets, priority sector and non-priority sector lending by public sector banks in India.
- To suggest a benchmark model for public sector banks for effective NPA management.

15.5 Research Methodology

(A) Variables:

(i) Non Performing Assets:

An asset, including a leased asset, becomes non-performing when it ceases to generate income for the bank. A non-performing asset is a loan or advance where:

- Interest and / or installment of principal remain overdue for a period of more than 90 days
- The account remains 'out of order' in respect of an Overdraft/Cash/Cash Credit (OD/OC).
- The bill remains overdue for a period of more than 90 days in the case of bills purchased and discounted.
- A loan granted for short duration crops will be treated as NPA, if the installment of principal or interest thereon remains overdue for two crop seasons.
- A loan granted for long duration crops will be treated as NPA, if the installment of principal or interest thereon remains overdue for one crop season.
- Banks should classify an account as BNPA only if the interest charged during any quarter is not serviced fully within 90 days from the end of the quarter.

(ii) Net NPA as percentage of net advances

Net Non Performing Assets (NPAs) are gross NPAs' net of provisions on NPAs and suspense account. Net NPA is obtained by deducting items like interest due but not recovered, part payment received and kept in suspense account etc., from Gross NPA.

(iii) Operating profit as percentage of working funds

Operating profits as percentage of working funds

= operating income - operating expenses /working funds *100.

Operating Income is fee and commission based income

while operating expenses are Establishment expenses, Rent, Taxes & lighting, printing and stationary, advertisement and publicity, depreciation and insurance.

(iv) Return on Assets

Return on Assets (ROA) is net profit expressed as a percentage of total assets, is widely accepted as an indicator of profitability of a bank, providing a measure of the efficiency of profit generation of the assets of the bank. Since profitability reflects quality of assets of a bank, we may construe that ROA is a qualitative measure of the business of a bank.

(v) Priority sector and non priority sector lending by public sector banks of India

The priority sector comprises of:

Agriculture, Small scale industries, Small road and water transport operators, Small business, Retail trade, Professional and self-employed persons (borrowing limit not exceeding Rs.10 lakh of which not more than Rs.2 lakh for working capital; in the case of qualified medical practitioners setting up practice in rural areas, the limits are Rs 15 lakh and Rs 3 lakh respectively and purchase of one motor vehicle within these limits can be included under priority sector),Education (educational loans granted to individuals by banks), Housing [both direct and indirect – loans up to Rs.5 lakhs (direct loans up to Rs 10 lakh in urban/ metropolitan areas), Loans up to Rs 1 lakh and Rs 2 lakh for repairing of houses in rural/ semi-urban and urban areas respectively], Consumption loans (under the consumption credit scheme for weaker sections),Micro-credit provided by banks either directly or through any intermediary; Loans to self help groups(SHGs) / Non Governmental Organizations (NGOs) for on lending to SHGs, Loans to the software industry (having credit limit not exceeding Rs 1 crore from the banking system), Loans to specified industries in the food and agro-processing sector having investment in plant and machinery up to Rs 5 crore, Investment by banks in venture capital (venture capital funds/ companies registered with SEBI).Other remaining heads are covered under non-priority sector.

(B) Data Source:

The financial figures for financial years 2006,07 and 08 of twenty public sector banks of India has been collected from Balance sheet of respective banks, Reserve Bank of India Database, various journals of Indian Banking Association.

(C) TOOLS OF ANALYSIS USED

Method used for empirical analysis of NPA and its impact on liquidity of banks Karl Pearson's Coefficient of correlation has been done with respect to operating profit as % of working funds, Return on Assets and lending to priority as well as non priority sector lending by Public sector banks in India.

15.6 Observation and Analysis:

Expansion of credit is a must for a country like India. But as mentioned above, high credit growth may lead to high NPAs. Policymakers, therefore, face the dilemma as to how to minimize such risks that arise from dilution in credit quality, while still allowing bank lending to contribute to higher growth and efficiency.

Asset Classification:

Banks are required to classify non-performing assets further into following three categories based on the period for which the asset has remained non-performing and the reliability of the dues.

- Sub-standard Assets: With effect from 31.03.2005, a sub-standard asset would be one which has remained NPA for a period less than or equal to 12 months.
- Doubtful Assets: With effect from 31.03.2005, a doubtful asset would be one which has remained in the sub-standard category for a period of 12 months.
- Loss assets: A loss asset is one where loss has been identified by the bank or internal or external auditors or the RBI inspection but the amount has not been written off wholly.

The classification of assets and provisioning norms as per the extant guidelines and as detailed above could be summarized as depicted in the following table.

Classification of Assets	Description	Provisioning Norms
Standard Assets	Otherwise known as performing assets	0.40% on standard assets 0.25% on direct advances to agriculture and SME 1.00% on personal loans, capital market exposures, residential houses beyond Rs. 20 lacs and commercial real estate
Sub-standard Assets	NPAs up to a period of 2 years	10 % on total outstanding irrespective of security coverage/ guarantee. The unsecured portion will attract additional provision of 10 percent.
Doubtful Assets	NPAs over two years	100 % shortfall in the securities and 20%/30%/50%100% depending upon the age of the asset
Loss Assets	NPAs in which there was little/ negligible realizable value of security	100% of balance outstanding

Reasons for NPAs in Banks

An account does not become an NPA overnight. It gives signals sufficiently in advance that steps can be taken to prevent the slippage of the account into NPA category. An account becomes an NPA due to causes attributable to the borrower, the lender and for reasons beyond the control of both.

Attributable to the Borrower / Project

The following is a list of factors attributable to the borrower, which could account for the borrower's accounts becoming non-performing assets:

- Financial losses for two years consecutively.

- Poor management and marketing strategy, poor assessment of demand, over capacity for the product, lack of commitment, entering a declining market, price war, etc.
- Diversion of funds within and outside the business or project. Sometimes funds are diverted for another project.
- Differences and disputes among promoters/directors.
- The bandwagon effect. People with little experience in the field enter a profession just because others have succeeded recently. This is common in the construction, real estate and hospitality industries.
- High cost base evidenced by labor costs, low productivity, distribution costs, raw material cost, high reorganization cost.
- Inadequate financial control demonstrated by poor debt management/structure.
- Inadequate information which is demonstrated by the following - poorly prepared budgets or no budgets, no costing/unit costs, limited analysis/planning for stocks, capital expenditure not planned/budgeted.
- Time and cost overrun due to poor supervision and control over the project by the promoters.
- Increasing low margin sales, debtor provisions, currency losses, creditor pressure, and short-term debt. Emphasis on cash sales with little regard for profit.
- Borrowing to pay operational expenses like electricity, wages, etc.
- Recurrence of problems previously resolved.
- Maintenance of expensive offices/keeping premises in a continuous state of neglect.
- Short term loans / ad hoc loans/excess over limits continuing beyond due date.
- Qualified audit opinion.
- Unable to comply with loan covenants.
- Liquidity ratios reveal deteriorating trends.
- Increase in creditors days outstanding.

- Speculative investments
- However, there are also external factors over which the borrower has no control and these could also lead to non-performing assets. These external factors could include:
- Delay in financial closure.
- Delay in realization of receivables.
- Exchange rate fluctuations.
- Depressed capital market.
- General recession in the particular industry.
- Changes in personal habits of promoters/key people.

Fraud is also a contributory factor to cases of NPAs. The following are all signs of fraud that need to be recognized in order to prevent NPAs.

- Sales/inventory/assets overstated, liabilities understated.
- Audits cease.
- Abnormally large fund transfers.
- Significant cash balances in non-interest earning accounts.
- Management overrides internal controls.
- Sale of assets to related parties.
- Unusual supplier relationships.
- Staff working unusually long working hours.

Attributable to the Bank

- Deficiency in credit assessment and monitoring system.
- Improper valuation of securities at the time of appraisal of loans.
- Failure in verification of end use of the loans and improper follow-up of and inadequate periodical verifications.
- Inadequacy/ deficiency insecurity creation/ documentation at the time of disbursal of loans.
- Laxity in taking timely corrective measures when an asset emits 'distress signals'.
- Delay in decision making regarding rendering of further assistance.

- Excess/short lending.
- Non-adoption of appropriate" resolution strategy" for tackling of NPA accounts.
- Managerial deficiencies or incompetence of the borrowers.
- Delay in implementation of the projects leading to cost escalation.
- Diversification/siphoning of funds.
- Willful default of the borrower.

External / Others

- Lack of demand for the product in market and downward trend in sales.
- Increase in rate of interest.
- Delay in implementation of rehabilitation programmes.
- Borrower friendly legal environment for recovery of defaulted loans.
- Change in the overall economic environment of the country.

Net N.P.A. as % of Net Advances of Public Sector Banks (2007 -08)

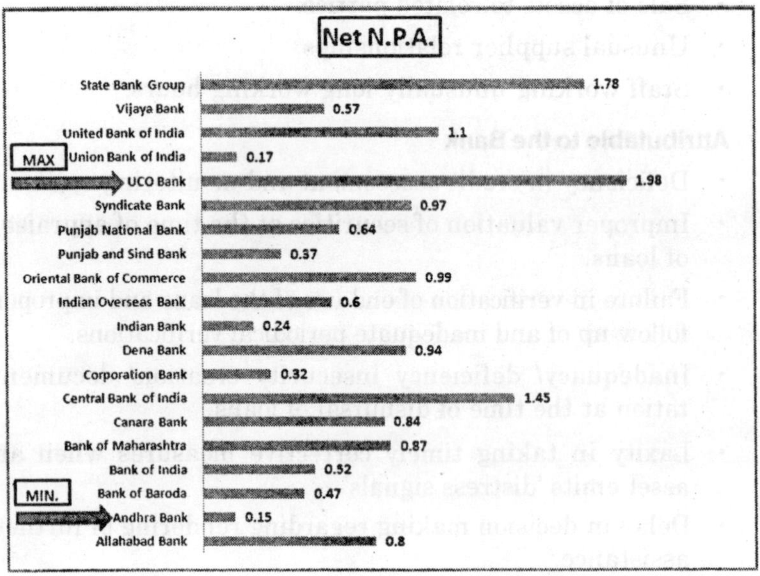

It is evident that Net NPA as % of Net Advances of Andhra Bank is at minimum 0.15 % and Maximum is of UCO Bank at 1.98 %. The second best performer in NPA Management is Union Bank of India while second highest NPA is of State Bank of India may be attributable to SBI's huge size. At the same time Corporation Bank and Indian Bank are better performers in NPA management.

Correlation between Net N.P.A. as % of Net Advances and Operating Profits as %Working Funds (2007 - 08)

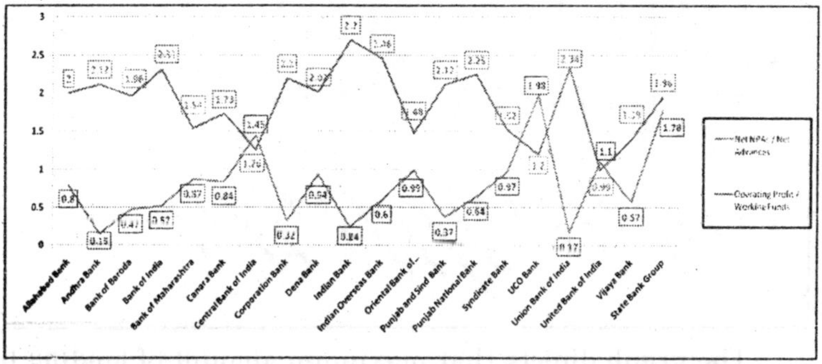

Corrleation between Net NPA as percentage of Net Advances and operating profit as % of working funds depicts that there is a high degree of negativ ecorrelation between the two variables. The statisitcal analysis reveals that decreasing Net NPA as % of Net advances by 1 percent will increase operating profit as % of working funds by 0.6551 percent.

Correlation between Net N.P.A. as % of Net Advances and Return on Assets (2007 - 08)

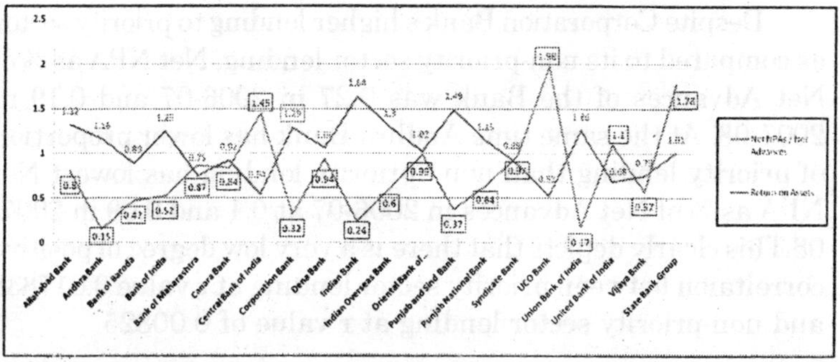

There is a very high degree of negative correlation between Net NPA as % of Net Advances and Return on Assets. The graph revelas that by decreasing Net NPA as % of Net Advances by 1 % increases Return on Assets of the Bank by 0.6675 percent.

Priority and Non-priority sector Lending by Public Sector Banks in India

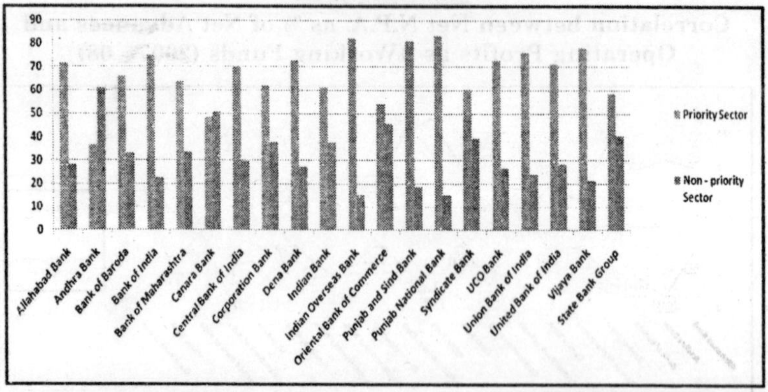

The graph dipicts that maximum amount of lending to priority sector incurred is by Punjab National Bank, then by Punjab and Sind Bank but highest Net NPA as % of Net Advnaces is of UCO Bank not only in 2007-08 but also in 2006-07. Also, Canara Bank and Oriental Bank of Commerce diffrence between lending to priority sector and non –priority sector lendingis not much but Net NPA as % of Net Advances of Canara Bank was 0.56 in 2006-07 and 0.5 in 2007-08 and of Oriental Bank of Commerce it was 0.29 and 0.59 in 2006-07 and 2007-08.

Despite Corporation Bank's higher lending to priority sector as compared to its non-priority sector lending, Net NPA as % of Net Advances of the Bank was 0.27 in 2006-07 and 0.19 in 2007-08. At the same time Andhra Bank has lower proportion of priority lending than non –priority lending has lowest Net NPA as % of Net Advances in 2006-07 at 0.1 and 0.09 in 2007-08.This clearly depicts that there is a very low degree of positive correltaion between priority sector lending at r value 0.017838 and non-priority sector lending at r value of 0.00825.

PART II A CASE STUDY OF ANDHRA BANK

Benchmark in Asset Management of Public Sector Banks

Present Scenario of NPAs in Public Sector Banks in India

S. No.		Gross NPA/Total Assets (%) 2006-07	2007-08	Net NPA/Total Assets (%) 2006-07	2007-08
	1	2	3	4	5
	Scheduled Commercial Banks	1.46	1.3	0.58	0.57
	Public Sector Banks	1.6	1.34	0.62	0.59
	Nationalized Banks	1.64	1.25	0.53	0.44
1	Allahabad Bank	1.62	1.22	0.65	0.48
2	Andhra Bank	0.84	0.66	0.1	0.09
3	Bank of Baroda	1.46	1.1	0.35	0.27
4	Bank of India	1.48	1.08	0.45	0.33
5	Bank of Maharashtra	2.1	1.59	0.71	0.53
6	Canara Bank	0.9	0.78	0.56	0.5
7	Central Bank of India	2.77	1.9	0.94	0.86
8	Corporation Bank	1.18	0.88	0.27	0.19
9	Dena Bank	2.37	1.48	1.16	0.56
10	Indian Bank	0.97	0.69	0.18	0.14
11	Indian Overseas Bank	1.36	0.98	0.31	0.36
12	Oriental Bank of Commerce	1.97	1.41	0.29	0.59
13	Punjab & Sind Bank	1.32	0.44	0.35	0.22
14	Punjab National Bank	2.09	1.67	0.45	0.38
15	Syndicate Bank	1.75	1.65	0.44	0.58
16	UCO Bank	2.01	1.84	1.34	1.22
17	Union Bank of India	1.82	1.34	0.59	0.1
18	United Bank of India	1.93	1.4	0.79	0.56
19	Vijaya Bank	1.33	0.91	0.34	0.32
20	State Bank of India	1.76	1.78	0.93	1.03

The table depicts among all other public sector banks Andhra Bank has minimum gross NPA to total Assets in 2006-07 as well as in 2007-08. Not only has this Andhra Bank had minimum Net NPA to total assets in 2006-07 and 2007-08.

The Success Story of Andhra Bank

Gross and Net NPAs of Andhra Bank

Particulars	March 2002	March 2003	March 2004	March 2005	March 2006	June 2006
Gross NPAs as % to Gross Advances	5.26	4.89	4.60	2.46	1.94	1.91
Net NPAS AS % TO Net Advances	2.45	1.79	0.93	0.28	0.24	0.07
Provision Coverage Ratio	54.22	64.23	80.16	88.22	87.20	95.49
Slippage Ratio*	2.90	2.51	2.61	1.18	0.88	0.10

*Slippage Ratio is the ratio of total fresh NPAs added during the year to the total Standard Assets at the beginning of the year.

The table depicts increase in the provision coverage from 54.22 % in March2002 to 87.20% by 2006 and the same has further increased to 95.49 % by June 30, 2006.Another positive feature is that the slippage ratio is continuously decreasing and has come to 0.10 percent during June 2006. The declining trend is still continued and the outcome is the ratio of Net NPA to Total Assets is lowest of Andhra Bank in 2007 as well as in 2008 amongst all Nationalized Banks.

Prime Financial Indicators of Andhra Bank as on March'2008

Interest Income / Working Funds	Non-Interest Income / Working Funds	Operating Profit / Working Funds	Return on Assets	Business per Employee	Profit per Employee
8.61	1.17	2.12	1.16	626.53	4.3

Banks are faced with the problem of increasing liquidity in the system. Further, Reserve Bank of India (RBI) is increasing the liquidity in the system through various rate cuts. Banks can get rid of its excess liquidity by increasing its lending but, often shy away from such an option due to the high risk of default. Hence to ensure that asset quality is maintained as suggested by RBI, Andhra Bank has made the stipulated provisions of 1% in respect of standard advances on specific sectors much before the stipulated date of March 31, 2008 besides providing the stipulate percentages under SME, agriculture and other sectors. Priority sector lending in March 2008 by Andhra Bank was 36.67% and Non priority sector lending was 60.84%.

The Success Mantra of low Net NPA and Gross NPA of Andhra Bank:

- Strategic Planning to arrest and attack the NPAs right from the incipient stage by evolving a system of identification of assets as Potential NPAs.
- Constant monitoring of Standard Assets closely to prevent its slippage to NPAs
- Overdue and irregularities in accounts are identified as PNPAs (Potential NPA accounts) and such accounts are closely monitored.
- The irregularities/recovery of overdue are attended in time bound manner to arrest slippage into NPA category.
- Formation of Asset Recovery Team of group of officers to pay thrust on recovery of dues in NPA and technically written –off accounts. It consists of DLNO (district level nodal officers) who are effectively used by Zonal Offices for recovery and follow up of NPA and technically written off accounts in the districts allotted to them. These Nodal Officers meet NPA borrowers personally along with Branch Managers for settlement of accounts on terms acceptable to the bank.
- A Comprehensive Corporate Compromise Policy (CCCP) has been framed to settle the dues of borrowers by

encouraging negotiated settlements through compromise and expediting their disposal as a legitimate tool.

- High Value NPA accounts are reviewed periodically by the chairman and Managing Director /Executive Director through Tele/Video Conferences and efforts are made to settle them by negotiation and persuasion.
- Special Recovery Drive Campaign has been launched to recover dues of small NPA and written off accounts of below Rs one lakh.
- NPA borrowers with outstanding balance of Rs. 50.00 lakh and above are called at Head Office and negotiations are arranged with Chairman and Managing Director/Executive Director and General / Regional Managing Director for settlement of dues.
- Whenever normal course of persuasion for recovery of dues failed, action is initiated under SARFAESI Act. With the enactment of the Securitization and Reconstruction of Financial Assets and Enforcement of Security Interest Act, 2002, banks can issue notices to the defaulters to pay up the dues and the borrowers will have to clear their dues within 60 days. Once the borrower receives a notice from the concerned bank and the financial institution, the secured assets mentioned in the notice cannot be sold or transferred without the consent of the lenders.

The main purpose of this notice is to inform the borrower that either the sum due to the bank or financial institution is paid by the borrower or else the former will take action by way of taking over the possession of assets. Besides assets, banks can also takeover the management of the company. Thus the bankers under the aforementioned Act will have the much needed authority to either sell the assets of the defaulting companies or change their management.

It is very much evident that Andhra Bank form very beginning took steps for creating awareness among the staff at branches on the concept of Income Recognition, Asset Classification and Provisioning. The Bank proceeded with the motto" Pay back to help you back". Another important milestone in the success path was management of NPAs through accelerated recoveries and containment of loan delinquency to bring strength and resilience in the banking system.

15.7 CONCLUSIONS AND RECOMMENDATIONS:

It can be concluded that an account does not become an NPA overnight. The account emits enough amber signals of the impending problems which the banker should be alert to catch these signals to quickly analyze, react and take corrective action.

It has been analyzed that there is a 0.017838 degree and 0.008251 degree of positive correlation between Net NPA as percentage of Net Advances and Priority sector lending and non priority sector lending respectively of public sector banks. But the Ratio of Operating Profit to Working Funds is 0.65507; Return on Assets is 0.68748, Business per employee is 0.32304 and Profit per employee is 0.636904 degree negatively correlated to Net NPA as % of Net Advances. Hence this clearly brings to notice that the school of thought that Priority Sector contributes more for NPA portfolio is a myth as there is a very low level of positive correlation between Priority sector lending and Net NPA as percentage of Net Advances. It can further be justified by considering Corporation Bank's Priority Sector lending of 62.02 percent of total lending but still Net NPA as percentage of Net Advances is 0.32 percent lower than Oriental Bank of Commerce with 54.25 % lending to Priority Sector but Net NPA as percentage of Net Advances is 0.99 percent quite higher than Corporation Bank.

The impact of NPAs on different financial parameters is:

- Current profit of the bank will decline with provisioning requirement and it also affects accretion of capital fund. Operating Profit to Working Funds decrease by ρ.65507 percent on increase in Net NPA as percentage of Net Advances by one percent.
- The total size of interest income will decline as income is

only recognized on receipt basis.Increase in Net NPA as percentage of Net Advances decreases Interest Income to working funds by -0.40489.

- Recycling of fund will be restricted and asset liability mismatch will be widened.
- NPAs reduce the earning capacity of assets and badly affect Return on assets of the bank. Return on Assets decreases by -0.68748 with increase in Net NPA as percentage of Net Advances.
- Higher Provisioning requirement on mounting NPA is adversely affecting capital adequacy by 0.42718 percent decrease in CRAR by one percent increase in Net NPA as percentage of Net Advances and also banks profitability decrease by -0.63904.
- Since NPA is taken in to consideration for total advances and average income assets, these show less worth than actual.
- Cost of Capital will increase due to NPA and require Economic Value Added(EVA= Net Operating profit after deducting tax and cost of capital)

It can be concluded that as present environment is fraught with risks of various kinds and dimensions, a tested and sound credit-risk model has to be put in place to have proper perception of the risk in a proposal and decide on the acceptability or otherwise and to take mid-course correction in respect of existing accounts. Though total elimination of NPAs is not possible in banking business as elements of risk is an inseparable ingredient, especially in the present context of the externalities fraught with risk. But, by effective management, its incidence can only be minimized.

The adage' prevention is better than cure' or 'a stitch in time saves nine', hold good in the monitoring of credit portfolio and arresting fresh generation of NPAs is equally important as recovery of NPA. In a banking system, NPA is inevitable and cannot be totally eliminated. What needs to be done is to arrest fresh accretion and contain it to the barest minimum by preventing slippage through effective proactive steps and that too at the right time.

Recommendations:

- Arresting slippage of accounts through relentless monitoring and focus on the continuous viability of the borrowing concern with improved asset classification is must. At the same time all accounts in the Standard category should not be taken for granted and should be subjected to periodical and in-depth review in a systematic manner through a sound adequate loan review mechanism in place.
- Categorization of standard accounts into A, B, C based on actual recovery of interest and installments due, will help a focused and strengthened monitoring.
- Banks should ensure that they should move with speed and charged with momentum in disposing off the loss assets. This is because as uncertainty increases with the passage of time, there is all possibility that the recoverable value of asset also reduces and it cannot fetch good price. If faced with such a situation than the very purpose of getting protection under the Securitization Act, 2002 would be defeated and the hope of seeing a must have growing banking sector can easily vanish.
- Bank should adhere to "Know Your Customer" norms for identification of borrower, guarantor and verification of their addresses to minimize the risk of default in case of housing sector lending. In respect of agricultural advances, recovery camp should be organized during the harvest season.
- Ongoing monitoring of bank's borrowers is important to understand the primary cause of corporate decline and to be able to identify the symptoms of a potential distress situation. Loan Officers and staff should be alert and diligent for signs of borrower distress. It is essential to identify signs of distress which diminish the Borrowers capacity to repay debt. Early recognition followed by appropriate action is essential if the bank is to minimize NPAs.
- Loan Workout Unit should be created which should be

exclusively responsible for managing non-performing and under performing loans to maximize the recovery value from a portfolio of distressed loans, through the employment of an equitable and professional workout process.

APPENDIX

Net N.P.A.; OPERATING PROFIT; RETURN ON ASSETS (2007 - 08)

Sr. No.	Name of the Bank	Net NPAs/ Net Advances	Operating Profit/ Working Funds	Return on Assets
1	Allahabad Bank	0.8	2	1.32
2	Andhra Bank	0.15	2.12	1.16
3	Bank of Baroda	0.47	1.96	0.89
4	Bank of India	0.52	2.31	1.25
5	Bank of Maharashtra	0.87	1.54	0.75
6	Canara Bank	0.84	1.73	0.92
7	Central Bank of India	1.45	1.26	0.54
8	Corporation Bank	0.32	2.2	1.29
9	Dena Bank	0.94	2.02	1.06
10	Indian Bank	0.24	2.7	1.64
11	Indian Overseas Bank	0.6	2.46	1.3
12	Oriental Bank of Commerce	0.99	1.48	1.02
13	Punjab and Sind Bank	0.37	2.12	1.49
14	Punjab National Bank	0.64	2.25	1.15
15	Syndicate Bank	0.97	1.52	0.88
16	UCO Bank	1.98	1.2	0.52
17	Union Bank of India	0.17	2.34	1.26
18	United Bank of India	1.1	0.99	0.68
19	Vijaya Bank	0.57	1.39	0.75
20	State Bank Group	1.78	1.96	1.0
	'r' value		-0.6551	-0.6875

Note: Independent Variable: Net NPAs / Net Advances

Dependent variable: Operating Profit / Working Funds; Return on Assets

Net N.P.A.; PRIORITY; NON - PRIORITY SECTOR LENDING (2007 - 08)

Sr. No.	Name of the Bank	Net NPAs/ Net Advances	Priority Sector	Non-Priority Sector
1	Allahabad Bank	0.8	71-78	28.17
2	Andhra Bank	0.15	36.67	60.84
3	Bank of Baroda	0.47	65.88	33.56
4	Bank of India	0.52	75.13	22.61
5	Bank of Maharashtra	0.87	63.92	33.8
6	Canara Bank	0.84	48.71	50.7
7	Central Bank of India	1.45	70.28	29.69
8	Corporation Bank	0.32	62.02	37.98
9	Dena Bank	0.94	72.51	27.46
10	Indian Bank	0.24	61.06	37.56
11	Indian Overseas Bank	0.6	82.1	15.14
12	Oriental Bank of Commerce	0.99	54.25	45.75
13	Punjab and Sind Bank	0.37	81.26	18.74
14	Punjab National Bank	0.64	83.2	15.21
15	Syndicate Bank	0.97	60.23	39.66
16	UCO Bank	1.98	72.95	26.89
17	Union Bank of India	0.17	75.96	24.04
18	United Bank of India	1.1	71.42	28.58
19	Vijaya Bank	0.57	78.16	21.15
20	State Bank Group	1.78	58.49	40.88
	'r' value		0.017838	0.008251

Note: Independent Variable: Net NPAs / Net Advances

Dependent variable: Priority Sector; Non - Priority Sector Lending

16

CREDIT PROPOSAL

Rationalistic view and Assessment of a Long Term Credit Proposal for Consortium Banking –
A Research on Juslification of Viability Report at Punjab National Bank

16.1 INTRODUCTION

The availability of infrastructure facilities is imperative for the overall development of any country. Today, there is a need to focus on enhancing the quantity as well as improving the quality of infrastructure services provided in India.

Infrastructure development was a sector that received enthusiastic attention from the early days of Indian liberalization. India was the promised land, with an abundance of large projects at various stages of conceptualization – a hundred or so power projects, scores of telecom projects, many infrastructure deals. A decade later, the enthusiasm has ebbed considerably and several projects lie by the wayside, for want of debt or equity.

Developers are tired, and seem to be willing to give the promised land a pass for the time being. Some part of this exhaustion may be well founded, but myth and exaggeration have contributed to some degree as well, in creating an investor-unfriendly image. This article attempts to provide an insider's perspective.

The truth is that India needs infrastructure and there are deals to be done. Foreign investment (whether debt or equity) is welcomed with open arms, and restrictions are reduced literally on a daily basis. More importantly, there are local resources available.

The Indian institutions both source and provide long-term funds. Money for 10 or 12 years is available. The bond market for long-term infrastructure projects is developing, albeit slowly. Indian developers and financiers are developing sophistication in financing techniques. They understand risk. They understand limited resource finance.

Some can even match expertise with the best in the world. A professional community of advisers – legal, financial and sector experts – has also emerged. The legal system, albeit slow in resolving disputes, is as sophisticated as any in the world. There is truly a rule of law. The basics exist. As in the early and mid-nineties, one would have expected the streets to be lined with eager financiers and advisors

A key area of reform Yates to the new proposals on payment security. The mega power project policy was announced a few years ago. The Hirma, Pipavav and Ennore power projects were listed for this purpose. The mega project status conferred special benefits including tax benefits and preferred payment security through escrow or other arrangements. Like the 'D' Project, these are also monster-sized projects and are moving in a stop-start fashion. In the absence of credible payment structures, these mega projects are not bankable.

True that with the intervention of the Power Trading Corporation (PTC), the ability to sell the power to more than one state should, in theory, spread the risk. But neither the credit standing of PTC nor the states in question have inspired the requisite confidence. The crux will be the innovation of a payment security structure. Amongst the options explored include the creation of a charge on the Consolidated Fund of India, or of the state

Government, direct payment instructions to the Reserve Bank (to debit state revenues), creating an overriding legislative charge on state revenues from particular sources of tax.

The constitutional efficiency of these is a matter of debate and there is little precedent. Clearly these are long-haul projects and will undergo several fits of activity before they reach their final outcome.

The salient features of project finance are as follows:

A. The lenders finance the project looking at the creditworthiness of the project, not the creditworthiness of the borrowing party. The repayment of the loans is made from the earnings of the project.

B. Project financing is also known as "limited recourse" financing as the borrower has a limited liability. The security taken by the lenders is largely confined to the project assets.

While project financing questions are some of the important issues facing firms engaging in International business activity. Extremely important issues Yate to firms' debt financing. In the corporate finance Literature, starting with Myers (1977), a number of pieces have evaluated the choice of borrowers or Different types of debt by firms.

While corporate finance issues are important, in India the nature of institutions that has Governed the process of fund raising from banks, and the process of obtaining funds from domestic or overseas locations, has been critical. The institutional characteristics of India have been all encompassing, idiosyncratic, important in influencing firms' behavior, and have had the ability to engender or retard growth of firms.

Feasibility Study: A Schematic Diagram

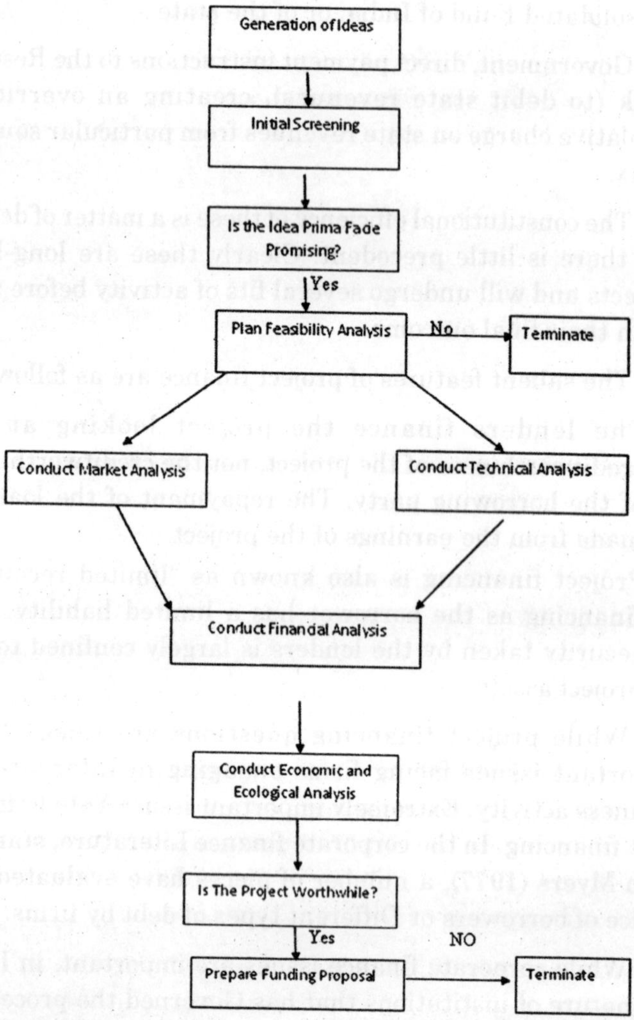

Steps in Term Loan Appraisal can be summarized as follows: Procedure:

1 Submission of loan application: The borrower submits an application mentioning comprehensive information about the project covering following aspects:

- Promoter's background
- Particulars of the industry
- Particulars of project (capacity, process, technical arrangements, management, location, land and buildings, plant and machinery)
- Cost of the project
- Means of financing
- Marketing and selling arrangement
- Profitability and cash flows
- Economic considerations
- Governmental consents

2. Initial processing of loan application
3. Appraisal of the proposed project
4. Issue of letter of sanction
5. Acceptance of terms and conditions by borrowing unit
6. Execution of loan agreement
7. Creation of security
8. Disbursement of loans
9. Monitoring

16.2 Project appraisal:

Financial institutions appraise a project from the marketing, technical, financial, economic and managerial angles.

Market appraisal: importance of potential market appraisal cannot be ignored

- Examine the reasonableness of demand projections by utilizing the findings of available surveys, industry associations projections and independent market surveys
- Assess the adequacy of marketing infrastructure in terms of promotional effort, distribution network, transport facilities

- Knowledge, experience and expertise of key marketing personnel

Technical appraisal:

- Product mix
- Capacity
- Process
- Engineering know how
- Raw materials and consumables
- Location and site
- Building
- Plant and equipments

Financial appraisal:

- Estimation of capital cost
- Reasonableness of estimation of working results
- Adequacy of rate of return
- Appropriateness of financing pattern

Economic appraisal: the economic appraisal looks at project from large social point of view

Managerial appraisal: in order to judge the managerial capabilityof promoters:

- Resourcefulness
- Understanding
- Commitment

The power sector provides one of the most important inputs for the development of a country and availability of viable and inexpensive power is critical for its sustainable economic development. To sustain GDP growth rate of around 9-10 %, it is imperative that the power sector also grows at the same rate.

Indian power sector has grown significantly in size and capacity since independence with the installed capacity of power generation having increased by around 80 times, electricity generation by nearly 140 times and the total length of transmission lines by over 135 times. Generation capacity, which was only 1,362 MW at the time of independence, has increased to over 1,41,500 MW. Even after the considerable growth in the power sector infrastructure and the supply of electricity, many parts of the country continue to face severe power shortages as consumption by commercial and industrial consumers has been increasing at much faster rate than electricity supply.

The per capita annual consumption of electricity in India is one of the lowest in the world at approximately 660 kWh, when compared to the estimated per capita annual consumption of over 1,200 kwh in China and nearly 13,000 kwh in the United States of America. In terms of per capita consumption, India does not rank even in the top 100 countries of the world, whose weighted average per capita consumption exceeds 5,700 kwh (nearly 10 times India's per capita consumption). The low per capita consumption is a result of the low penetration of electricity at the household level. The Census 2001 reveals that only 55.8 % of the households in India have access to electricity, which varies between 87.6 % of urban households and only 43.5 % of rural households.

Here we are analyzing a firm involved in power production and the issuance of debt to such a firm, which is new in the market, thus cannot have a credit rating, faces the complexity of debt.

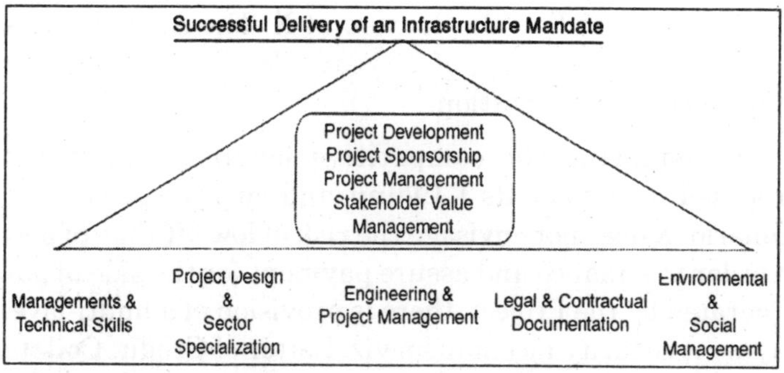

The proposal falls under the powers of MC on account of exposure.

X Power Ltd (XYZ) was incorporated by PFC for selection of developer for the X Ultra Mega Power Project (UMPP). X became a wholly owned subsidiary of Y Power pursuant to the selection of Y Power as the successful bidder and subsequent to execution of a Share Purchase Agreement between PFC, X and Y Power.

X is setting up a pit-head coal based power plant with a capacity of 3960 MW (6 x 660 MW).X has been awarded this project, the first pit head UMPP, through a competitive bidding process, for long term supply of power to the procurer States, conducted under UMPP initiative of MoP, Government of India.

The total land requirement for the Power Plant, mining and supporting facilities is 4,316 hectares excluding the land requirement for Resettlement & Rehabilitation (R&R). Out of this, mining requires 2,965 hectares of land. The area required for Power Plant is spread across land owned by private parties (Private Land) and Government (Government Land) and land in the forest area (Forest land). The Company is in advanced stage of completing land acquisition for the project.

PPA dated August 7, 2007 has been signed amongst X and 14 Procurers from 7 States for sale of power corresponding to a contracted capacity of 3722.40 MW (total generation capacity of 3960 MW less auxiliary power consumption) at Bus Bar located at X. The Agreement is to be effective for a period of 25 years (Initial Term) from the COD of the Power Station.

Considering the competitive levelised tariff of the proposed project at Rs.1.19/unit and current power deficit scenario, X does not envisage the risk of low off-take of power. In order to enhance and assure payment for the sale of power generated by the Project, there is provision of a multi-layered payment security mechanism viz. Letter of Credit, Collateral Agreement by a Default Escrow Agreement and provisions for third party sales in case of default.

REASONS FOR REQUIREMENT OF LONG TERM DEBT:

1. This is the 1st UMPP based on captive coal based power project, awarded through competitive bidding guidelines, hence would have early mover advantage over other UMPPs which are proposed by MoP. Since it becomes a new sort of a project shareholders may not invest a 100% and thus a need for long term debt arises.
2. Y, the parent company has already raised, raised Rs.11000 Crores through an Initial Public Offer (IPO), which would be utilised to part-finance the construction and development of the power projects being implemented through its SPVs including the proposed project. Therefore, the promoters' contribution for part-financing the proposed project is considered to be fully tied-up and thus a requirement of long term debt is inevitable.
3. Infusing a long term debt also ensures proper governance as banks and other financial institutions have their say in the participation and executive decision making thereby ensuring that these projects act and perform like competitive business organization and not like government undertakings responsible for infrastructure development of the country.

In this paper the authors have tried to evaluate and understand the credit rating, the returns and risk associated with the project and the considerations that the bank are supposed to keep in mind while evaluating the project. Also a statistical tool has been applied on the estimated cash flows and finding out the FCFF (Future cash flow to firm) and then applying a model on the same to evaluate the profitability of the project.

16.3 Objectives:

1. To evaluate a loan proposal (long term debt) for a major bank and the factors considered therein by any bank.
2. To understand the intricacies involved in credit evaluation and loan proposal of a private sector giant and what influences the same.

3. To better understand the sector of power and gas production and how does a bank evaluate these projects on the basis of cash flow, balance sheet ratios, profitability computations and DSCR calculations
4. For ascertaining the limitations in such term loan appraisals and what more factors could be involved more to formulate this process as a more effective one.
5. To understand the future expectations and returns associated with the grant of the loan proposal for the same and the gains of the bank involved therein.

16.4 Methodology:

A. The proposal is about a private newly formed leveraged company involved in the production of gas and power for a term loan proposal of 6.87% (proposed) of the total cost of the project which is Rs.19400 Crores. The debt to equity ratio is 3:1. The repayment period is 50 % of the Rupee Debt Facility in 40 equal quarterly installments from the end of the moratorium period. Balance debt (i.e. 50 % of the total Rupee Debt) shall be payable by a single bullet installment at the end of 10 years.

The Name of the Borrower and BO & Controlling Office M/s XYZ Limited and the Asset Classification is not available as this is a New Company. The present credit rating of the company is "B" and the company is not yet rated by any external agency. The business activity is supposed to produce 3960 MW (6 x 660MW) pithead coal based ultra mega power project (Power Project) and development of coal mines ("Mine Project"). Since the company is already leveraged these are the details of the same. The Company has appointed SBI Capital Markets as the sole arranger for syndicating/ arranging the total Long Term Debt of Rs.14550 Crores (Rupee Term Loan Rs.8075 Crores and ECA/ECBs Foreign Currency Loan of Rs.6475 Crores) for the project.

Canara Bank has provided a Bank Guarantee facility of Rs.187.31 Crores. The company also maintains current accounts for meeting the project requirements.

Besides the Company has also received sanction of Rs.11718 Crores from various Banks/FIs as per details given below:

Banks And Sanctioned Amount (In Rs Cr)

Bank / FI	Amount in Crs 2009
SBI	3200
IIFCL	400
Andhra Bank	200
Union Bank	200
Power Finance Corporation	1770
Rural Electrification Corporation	1342
United Bank of India	200
Corporation Bank #	200
IIFCL (UK)	2156*
LIC #	800
IDBI #	500
Axis Bank #	750
Total	11718

*USD 440 Million

A first charge on all the Project's bank accounts including but not limited to the Trust & Retention Account (TRA) (including DSRA) opened in a designated bank, where all cash inflows from the Project shall be deposited and all proceeds shall be utilized in a manner and priority to be decided by the lenders. The appointment of the Trustee for operating the above account shall be subject to the approval of the Lenders;

B. Credit Rating by agencies {CRISIL/ICRA/CARE/FITCH INDIA} with purpose of such rating.

Since it is new account rating from external agencies has not been got done. However we have proposed a condition that Company should get it self rated from any of the external agencies to comply with Basel II norms. Thereafter, the rating should be obtained and furnished to the lenders at least at annual intervals.

C. Details of Working Capital Limits from the Consortium/ Multiple Banking

Canara Bank has provided a Bank Guarantee facility of Rs.187.31 Crores. The company also maintains current accounts for meeting the project requirements. However the Company has estimated working capital requirements from FY 2011-12 for which provisions for margin and working capital has been provided in cost of finance. The Company will tie up working capital requirement at that time.

Present proposal is for sanction of:

i. Term Loan of Rs.1000 Crores to part finance 3960 MW (6 x 660 MW) pithead coal based ultra mega power project and development of coal mines

ii. Sanction of NFB (ILC/FLC/BG) limit of Rs.1000 Crores within the proposed Term Loan of Rs.1000 Crores.

iii. Approval of other issues.

D. Sources of Promoters' Contribution and the time schedule as to when the funds will be brought.

Based on the debt equity ratio of 75:25, the Promoter's contribution is estimated at Rs. 4,850 crore which would comprise Equity Share Capital and quasi equity. The entire promoter's contribution would be brought in by Y Power.

The Promoter proposes to contribute its share in a combination of equity share capital and quasi equity (in the form of subordinated unsecured debt/ preference shares). Of the total Promoter's contribution, upto 50 % could be infused by way of quasi-equity which would not be repaid during the currency of Senior Loan but would carry interest during the commercial operation period, subject to compliance of all financial covenants and restrictive payment conditions.

Further, the Promoter would also expressly waive any rights they have regarding instituting legal proceedings for winding up and dissolution of the Company.

A suitable undertaking has been stipulated for a) infusion of remaining equity and b) financing of cost overrun, if any (subject to a cap of 5 % of the envisaged Project Cost), by promoters through their own contribution.

The Company would be permitted to raise subordinated, unsecured loans by securitizing future CER receivables to the extent of 5% of total Project Cost. To this extent, the sub-debt to be infused by Promoter, by way of Promoter's Contribution, would be reduced. The terms of such subordinated loans shall be subject to the approval of the Lead Bank.

E. Long Term Debt

Debt requirement of the Project of Rs. 14,550 crore is proposed to be arranged through a mix of Rupee Term Loan (RTL) and foreign currency loan from various sources viz. Commercial Banks, Export Credit Agencies and Multilateral Agencies etc.

X proposes to arrange Rs. 8,075 crore of RTL comprising of PFC/FI Tranche of Rs. 3500 crs. and remaining from other Indian Banks. The long term foreign currency loan of Rs. 6,475 crore (equivalent to about US$ 1.50 billion) is proposed to be tied up with IIFCL (UK) for around US$ 500 million and remaining amount of US$ 1000 million from other foreign banks. The Company also proposes to avail Buyer's credit of Rs. 1,720 crore from international market which will be converted to RTL at the end of the construction period.

The maximum door-to-door tenure of the RTL facility other than PFC Tranche would be for 15 years (4.50 years of construction period from financial closure, 0.50 years of moratorium period and repayment of 10 years (40 Quarterly Instalments of 1.25 % each). At the end of 15 years a bullet repayment of 50 % of the term loan shall be made, which would be refinanced at the end of that period.

It is also envisaged that PFC tranche would have a door-to-door tenure of around 20 years (4.50 years of construction period from financial closure, 0.50 years of moratorium period and repayment of 15 years (60 Quarterly Instalments of 1.67 % each).

It may be mentioned that initially the Company would tie-up higher RTL (about Rs. 11,000 crore) with an option to substitute up to 35 % of this higher total rupee debt by way of ECB / ECA / FCL within 36 months of the signing of the loan documents with the Rupee Loan Senior Lenders and correspondingly the amount of rupee loan sanctioned would be reduced.

F. Financial Viability:

The Financial viability of the project has been established with respect to the tariff quoted and margin available for debt servicing. Based on the detailed assumptions as indicated in the Information Memorandums, the cost of generation of power for the X Project needs to be viewed in the light of the following

The cost profile of X Power Project has certain advantages in terms of higher GCV of coal, lower cost of coal mining and minimal transportation cost (being a pit head power project), which if converted into the monetary benefits would provide an additional saving of over Re 1 to the company per unit of power. This means that the effective tariff for the project is above Rs. 2.30 per unit.

As mentioned above, there is enough margin available in the power tariff for servicing the debt (interest & principle amounts) ie. around Rs. 46-57 paise after project COD is achieved in March 2013. Hence, it may be concluded that though the tariff profile for sale of power is competitive, it provides satisfactory financial results to make the project viable.

Risk structure in project finance:

Most project finance structures are complex. The risks in the project are spread between the various parties; each risk is usually assumed by the party, which can most efficiently and cost-effectively control or handle it.

- The Group has proven track record of flawless project execution capabilities; hence to leverage the same Y Power is currently implementing / developing 13 power projects having aggregate capacity of 28,200 MW (including the X Project). The Group has evolved through integrated value chain in various segments of power sector business. Y Infra has experience in other areas of power sector like transmission and distribution viz. distribution licensee in Mumbai, Delhi and Orissa (distributes over 5000 MW power – largest by private power sector utility) and transmission line network.

- Environment Clearance from Ministry of external affairs for the X UMPP has already been obtained in November, 2006.
- Equity requirement of the Project is estimated to be Rs. 4,850 crore, which would be brought in entity by Y Power out of the proceeds mobilized through IPO.
- The objects of the issue had identified the funding requirement of the projects which would be part-financed through the IPO proceeds. X is one of the Projects so identified. Hence, the envisaged equity contribution has already been raised by Y Power.
- X would seek disbursement of funds only after promoter's contribution to the extent of 20 % has been infused.
- Full tariff charges shall be recoverable at normative availability of 80 %. In case the same is not achieved, full tariff charges shall not be recovered thereby impacting debt servicing.
- All the generation projects of Y Power are currently enjoying availability in excess of 90 %.
- Impact of non-achievement of normative availability up to 5 % has been analyzed and the debt servicing has been found to be satisfactory.
- Escalation in O&M costs may impact the financials. Impact of the same has been analyzed and debt servicing has been found to be satisfactory.

16.5 FCFF Evaluation (Free Cash Flow for the Firm)

This is a measurement of a company's profitability after all expenses and reinvestments. It's one of the many benchmarks used to compare and analyze financial health.

A positive value would indicate that the firm has cash left after expenses. A negative value, on the other hand, would indicate that the firm has not generated enough revenue to cover its costs and investment activities. In that instance, an investor should dig deeper to assess why this is happening - it could be a sign that the company may have some deeper problems.

The above table shows FCFF (Future cash flow to firm) calculation that the firm have a present value 13,745.6 Crores of all the projected cash flows (from 2012- 2024), where as the loan sanctioning amount is the just 8,075 Crores of RTL. Therefore if see the net present value of this project:

Net present value = PV of all projected cash flows – Loan sanction

= 13,745.6 – 8,075

= 5670.64354

As the npv is coming positive therefore it is a lucrative project for the bank that's why the bank should sanction the loan amount to the company.

Conclusions and recommendations

1. Banks need to assess their appraisal and delivery methods for extending credit. Norms Yating to eligibility, security, margin and loan to value ratio should be strictly adhered to as dilution of lending standards (to maintain value as competition increases) will degenerate the banking system.
2. With the estimated projected rate of return and the back up of a powerful organisation the bank feels feasible to grant the loan to the company. Also it will be an oppurtunity for the bank to understand the sector more carefully and evaluate more projects and build an expertise in the same.
3. The research also brings about in light the various measures which are available for evaluation of the projects or companies which are Yatively new, the projected cash

flow method, the profitability analysis and various ratios available for the project. Although all methods have their own limitation but to come at a conclusion all should be taken into perspective.

4. The power sector in India is vastly expanding and it becomes a social duty for the public sector banks to grant loans for infrastructure development and thus provide public utility. These factors along with environmental consideration for the same is a very crucial and social responsibility issue for the bank.

Limitations:

1. The evaluation of the project is done on the basis of cash flow estimation and various ratios, but since the project and the companies are new the economic scenario and demand for the factors of production and supply side should also be kept in consideration while evaluating a project.
2. The prices and the cost assumed for the units of power produced in the (ror) plant and supplied is assumed as constant over a long period of time which is almost impractical and is a factor bank should seriously look into.
3. It is impossible to ascertain the kind of returns to be associated with these sort of projects as they are at a very naïve stage in Indian economy and also the risk associated with the same. Since the bank has also to decide the repayment period and wave off period and these are important considerations for the same.
4. Banks should emphasis on quality of assets rather than on volume of business. The comparatively less served segments of the economy should be carefully granted loans and advances. Banks should follow in a more rigorous manner the Know Your Customer (KYC) guidelines. It is desirable that all banks should make full use of the information of potential borrowers that may be available with Credit Information Bureau (India) Limited (CIBIL) so as to avoid defaults in loan repayments at a future date.

ANNEXURE:

A) Projected Profit & Loss Account (upto Refinance) (In Crores)

Profit & Loss Account	2012	2013	2014	2015	2016	2017	2018	2019	2020	2021	2022	2023	2024
Electricity Generated (Million Units)	1177	16591	29144	29347	29428	29347	29347	29347	29428	29347	29347	29347	29428
Revenue													
Revenue From Sale of Power	82	1156	3796	3841	3847	3837	3837	3835	3844	3828	3826	3824	3835
Revenue from Carbon Credits	7	92	158	158	159	159	159	159	160	160	160	59	-
Interest on O&M Res. & Cash Bal.	-	-	26	21	26	28	25	26	32	32	37	32	28
Total Revenue	89	1248	3979	4020	4032	4024	4022	4021	4035	4020	4024	3915	3863
Expenditure													
Fuel Cost	32	306	544	562	578	540	562	579	623	817	760	776	837
O&M Expense	51	174	264	287	299	310	323	336	350	363	378	393	410
Insurance Premium	15	48	56	58	60	62	64	67	69	71	74	76	79
Total Expenditure	98	528	863	906	937	912	950	982	1042	1252	1211	1245	1326

A) Projected Profit & Loss Account (upto Refinance) (In Crores)

PBDIT	(9)	720	3116	3113	3095	3112	3072	3039	2993	2769	2812	2670	2537
Interest													
Interest on Loan	64	879	1605	1516	1414	1312	1210	1107	1005	902	800	707	612
Interest on WC	1	14	39	40	40	41	41	42	42	44	44	45	45
Interest on Quassi Equity / sub debt	-	-	279	279	279	279	279	279	279	279	279	279	279
Total Interest	66	893	1923	1834	1733	1631	1530	1428	1326	1224	1123	1030	937
PBDT	(75)	(173)	1193	1279	1362	1480	1542	1611	1667	1544	1689	1640	1601
Depreciation	40	567	985	985	985	986	986	986	987	987	988	988	989
PBT	(115)	(740)	209	294	376	495	556	625	680	557	701	651	612
Tax	-	-	24	33	43	56	63	71	77	63	79	74	69
Deferred Tax	(39)	(251)	47	67	85	-	-	-	-	-	-	-	-
PAT	(76)	(488)	138	194	248	439	493	554	603	494	622	577	543

B) Projected Cash Flow statement (upto refinance).

(Rs. in Crores)

Profit & Loss Account	2012	2013	2014	2015	2016	2017	2018	2019	2020	2021	2022	2023	2024
Electricity Generated (Million Units)	1177	1659 1	2914 4	2934 7	2942 8	2934 7	2934 7	2934 7	2942 8	2934 7	2934 7	2934 7	2942 8
Revenue													
Revenue From Sale of Power	82	1156	3796	3841	3847	3837	3837	3835	3844	3828	3826	3824	3835
Revenue from Carbon Credits	7	92	158	158	159	159	159	159	160	160	160	59	-
Interest on O&M Res. & Cash Bal.	-	-	26	21	26	28	25	26	32	32	37	32	28
Total Revenue	89	1248	3979	4020	4032	4024	4022	4021	4035	4020	4024	3915	3863
Expenditure													
Fuel Cost	32	306	544	562	578	540	562	579	623	817	760	776	837
O&M Expense	51	174	264	287	299	310	323	336	350	363	378	393	410
Insurance Premium	15	48	56	58	60	62	64	67	69	71	74	76	79
Total Expenditure	98	528	863	906	937	912	950	982	1042	1252	1211	1245	1326

PBDIT	(9)	720	3116	3113	3095	3112	3072	3039	2993	2769	2812	2670	2537
Interest													
Interest on Loan	64	879	1605	1516	1414	1312	1210	1107	1005	902	800	707	612
Interest on WC	1	14	39	40	40	41	41	42	42	44	44	45	45
Interest on Quassi Equity / sub debt	-	-	279	279	279	279	279	279	279	279	279	279	279
Total Interest	66	893	1923	1834	1733	1631	1530	1428	1326	1224	1123	1030	937
PBDT	(75)	(173)	1193	1279	1362	1480	1542	1611	1667	1544	1689	1640	1601
Depreciation	40	567	985	985	985	986	986	986	987	987	988	988	989
PBT	(115)	(740)	209	294	376	495	556	625	680	557	701	651	612
Tax	-	-	24	33	43	56	63	71	77	63	79	74	69
Deferred Tax	(39)	(251)	47	67	85	-	-	-	-	-	-	-	-
PAT	(76)	(488)	138	194	248	439	493	554	603	494	622	577	543

Computation of Fcff

Term	1	2	3	4	5	6	7	8	9	10	11	12	13
Profit & Loss Account	2012	2013	2014	2015	2016	2017	2018	2019	2020	2021	2022	2023	2024
Total Revenue	89	1248	3979	4020	4032	4024	4022	4021	4035	4020	4024	3915	3863
Total Expenditure	98	528	863	906	937	912	950	982	1042	1252	1211	1245	1326
Depreciation	40	567	985	985	985	986	986	986	987	987	988	988	989
Ebit	-49	153	2131	2129	2110	2126	2086	2053	2006	1781	1825	1682	1548
Tax(11.25%)		17.2125	239.7375	239.5125	237.375	239.175	234.675	230.9625	225.675	200.3625	205.3125	189.225	174.15
Ebit(1-tax)	-49	135.7875	1891.263	1889.488	1872.625	1886.825	1851.325	1822.038	1780.325	1580.638	1619.688	1492.775	1373.85
Depreciation	40	567	985	985	985	986	986	986	987	987	988	988	989
Fcff	-9	702.7875	2876.263	2874.488	2857.625	2872.825	2837.325	2808.038	2767.325	2567.638	2607.688	2480.775	2362.85
P.V. of fcff(11.91%)	-8.04218	561.1594	2052.21	1832.672	1628.024	1462.5	1290.704	1141.436	1005.171	833.3832	756.3063	642.9255	547.193
Total	13745.6												

Note: Tax rate is calculated on the basis of tax given in the projected profit and loss account

For calculating PV of the FCFF IRR has Considered as WACC

17

FOREIGN EXCHANGE RISK MANAGEMENT: PROCESS AND NECESSITY

Firms dealing in multiple currencies face a risk (an unanticipated gain/loss) on account of sudden/unanticipated changes in exchange rates, quantified in terms of exposures. Exposure is defined as a contracted, projected or contingent cash flow whose magnitude is not certain at the moment and depends on the value of the foreign exchange rates. The process of identifying risks faced by the firm and implementing the process of protection from these risks by financial or operational hedging is defined as foreign exchange risk management. This paper limits its scope to hedging only the foreign exchange risks faced by firms.

17.1 Kinds of Foreign Exchange Exposure

Risk management techniques vary with the type of exposure (accounting or economic) and term of exposure. Accounting exposure, also called translation exposure, results from the need to restate foreign subsidiaries' financial statement into the parent's reporting currency and is the sensitivity of net income to the variation in the exchange rate between a foreign subsidiary and its parent. Economic exposure is the extent to which a firm's market value, in any particular currency, is sensitive to unexpected changes in foreign currency. Currency fluctuations affect the value of the firm's operating cash flows, income statement, and competitive position, hence market share and stock price. Currency fluctuations also affect a firm's balance sheet by changing the value of the firm's assets and liabilities, accounts payable, accounts receivables, inventory, loans in foreign currency, investments (CDs) in foreign banks; this type of economic exposure is called balance sheet exposure. Transaction Exposure is a form of short term economic exposure due to fixed price contracting in an atmosphere of exchange-rate volatility. The most common definition of the measure of exchange-rate exposure is the sensitivity of the value of the firm, proxies by the firm's stock return, to an unanticipated change in an exchange rate. This is calculated by using the partial derivative function where the dependant variable is the firm's value and the independent variable is the exchange rate.

The most important exposures are:

- Transaction
- Translational
- Economic

A. Transaction Exposure

Transaction exposure materialises when, and as soon as, a contractual obligation arises in a currency other than your reporting currency ie. the booking of a transaction at one rate of exchange whereas the eventual receipt or payment of cash comes in at a different rate of exchange. The exposure may well not appear immediately or ever in the accounting records. Transaction exposure can be considered short term economic exposure. For example, consider goods sold by a UK manufacturer at an invoice price of Swfr 500,000 at a time when the FX rate is Swfr 1.90 to £1.00; payment is due in 90 days. After 90 days by the rate is Swfr 2.00 to £1.00 (ie. sterling has strengthened). The value of the sale initially recorded in the books of the manufacturer was £263,157.89 but they receive only £250,000. This is called a closed exchange as it has been completed. An open exchange is a transaction across two currencies which has not yet been completed.

Consider the effect of exchange rate movements on UK company profits given a difference between the currency of costs and the currency of profits: If the costs in £'s (Home) and the income is in the overseas currency ie. ($) and the current rate is $2/£1.

a. £ weakens ® $1/£1 therefore income increases in £'s value.
b. £ Strengthening ® £3/£1 income decreases in £'s value.

The increase in volatility of all currencies has made transaction exposure very dangerous, but it is comparatively easy to identify because it is specified and discrete being linked with individual items of business. It may also be used to describe transactions which are confidently expected to be booked soon, and transactions which are forecast, as long as the forecast is a reasonably close one. There is a point in time - not clearly definable - when 'transaction' exposures merge into 'economic' exposures. In general, transaction exposures are relatively easy to identify. For example, a US company exporting to a German customer in Deutchsemarks has a transaction exposure to the US dollar/Deutchsemark exchange rate on the money they are due to receive for sales they have already made. Similarly, a French importer is at risk if sterling rises and they have invoices to pay in sterling. Transaction exposures arise on cash movements, including dividends and interest as well as sales and purchases, and affect the profit and loss account in a very direct way.

Transaction exposure is by its nature of uncertain timing, and its cover should not be considered in a static or item by item manner. The exposure in an on-going business is ever evolving - changing day by day or even hour by hour - as business is won, orders are placed, payables paid, receivables received, or cover taken. It is not often that the treasurer can say at any particular time that they have covered all their foreign exchange exposure. It is more efficiently covered by taking a broader, overall and forward looking view. Companies usually try to determine the net amount of inflows and outflows in each currency and determine the overall exposure to those currencies.

Protective measures to guard against transaction exposure involve entering into foreign currency transactions whose cash flows exactly offset the cash flows of the transaction exposure.

- Protective measures include:
- forward contracts
- price adjustment clauses
- currency options
- borrowing and lending in the foreign currency
- invoice in home currency

B. Translational Exposure

Translational exposure is the risk of the net worth of a company changing because of the fluctuating home valuation of assets and liabilities denominated in foreign currencies. It arises from converting a multinational's overseas subsidiaries translated from local currency to home currency prior to consolidation with the parent's financial statements. This may include foreign currency loans and investments. If the subsidiary's balance sheet is unchanged from one year-end to the next, the subsidiary is unaffected. However, the group may not due to movements on foreign currency. For example, at a particular time, a UK company has an Australian subsidiary which has a net worth of A$6m and is in the parent company's book at £4m because the exchange rate used was A$1.5 = £1. But in the due course of time when the exchange rates change to A$2 = £1 then the Australian subsidiary will be valued in the accounts of its parent at £3 (A£6m @ A$2 = £1). In Australia the unit is still worth A$6. Nothing has changed. It is still generating its normal profit, but looked at in sterling terms it has lost 25% of its worth. If we wish to protect against this risk we must consider selling Australian dollars.

Translation exposure does not represent real movements of cash between different currency systems, but can clearly impact both the consolidated profit and loss account and the consolidated balance sheet. The balance sheet effects are often dismissed as illusory since they have no cash impact. However the level of assets and liabilities can effect financial ratios calculated using balance sheet figures which causes practical problems where the company has restrictions on its level of borrowings placed by covenants. Translational exposure can be managed by fully, matching assets and liabilities in the overseas currency, whenever possible, But this may result in losing control of consolidated gearing. There is also the problem of trying to match assets to liabilities in countries where there are no sophisticate capital markets or in other cases a perfect match is not necessarily desirable. Companies have attempted to get round this problem by either using grouping currencies together and using a proxy currency or a basket currency.

If currency values change foreign exchange translation gains or losses may result. Assets and liabilities that are translated at the current (post change) exchange rate are considered to be exposed; these translated at a historic (pre change) exchange rate will maintain their home currency values and hence are not exposed.

Translation exposure is the difference between exposed assets and exposed liabilities. A greater amount of exposed assets than liabilities will give rise to a positive exposure while a greater amount of liabilities than assets will give rise to a negative exposure.

The amount of translation exposure depends on the degree of foreign involvement of a multinational's overseas subsidiaries, the location of these foreign subsidiaries and the correlation between that currency and the home currency and the methods for accounting for the translation. Controversies among accountants centre on which assets and liabilities are exposed and on when accounting derived FX gains and losses should be recognised.

Companies have at least three available methods for managing their translation exposure:

- Adjusting fund flows
- Entering into forward contracts
- Exposure netting

Basic hedging strategy for reducing translation exposure is to increase hard currency (likely to appreciate) assets and decrease soft currency (likely to depreciate) assets, while simultaneously decreasing hard currency liabilities and increasing soft currency liabilities. Thus if devaluation appears likely, the basic hedging strategy would be:

- Reduce level of cash
- Tighten credit terms to decrease accounts receivable
- Increase local currency borrowing
- Delay accounts payable
- Sell the weak currency forward

But activities not automatically valuable. If the market recognises the likelihood of currency appreciation, this recognition will be reflected in the costs of various hedging techniques. Hedging exchange risk costs money and the costs need to be scrutinised like any other purchase of insurance.

C. Economic Exposure

The definition of 'economic' and 'competitive' exposures varies, and is less important than the underlying concepts. A 'transaction' exposure is one which is readily identifiable in the currency in which it arises. Once the exposure is uncertain, or not genuinely in the currency in which the transaction is settled, it is usually called an 'economic' exposure rather than a transaction exposure.

The longer term change in value relationship between two currencies gives rise to ECONOMIC exposure. It is the most subtle and insidious of all the types of exposure, and has the potential to ruin a company, but to do it in a very surreptitious manner. It arises when it is thought that future cash flows will be affected by changing exchange rates. Economic exposure can thus be thought of as the extent to which the present value of future cash flows are affected by exchange rate movements. Transaction exposure is a subset of economic exposure. However economic exposure is taking place on a continuing basis, it has no time limit, nor a defined direction of movement. It is simple to spot the influence of the expected change in exchange rates on forecasted sales columns. But the significance of changes in the value of competitors' currencies, which appear unrelated to your operations, should not be underestimated. It is important to appreciate a competitor's ability to take a greater market share or larger profit because changing exchange rates have moved in their favour.

The term 'economic' exposure may be used to describe any exposure which is forecast to become a transaction exposure in due course - although if the forecast can be made fairly accurately, this would often be regarded rather as a transaction exposure. The simplest example is when a forecast transaction does not occur. Next year's sales budget for example (as opposed to next week's) can only be an estimate. If we forecast sales in pesetas of 500 million but only achieved 300 million, the difference of 200 million is an exposure which we expected but which never occurred. It could therefore have been unwise to hedge the whole exposure.

Another example is where the currency underlying the economics of the goods or service is not the same as the currency of payment. Suppose for example that a company is paying for fuel in French Francs but the price of the fuel in the medium term is linked to the US dollar - because that is the currency in which oil is traded internationally. The fuel purchases which have already been invoiced but not paid clearly represent a French Franc risk - a transaction exposure. But future purchases represent a US dollar risk - an economic exposure. If the dollar strengthens, the cost will rise, so that the company must buy dollars if it wishes to hedge against this risk.

Economic exposures relate directly to the competitive position for a firm within the ever more global trading community. For example, both Jaguar and Porshe sell cars to the US market where they compete at the luxury end. Both clearly have an economic exposure to the level of the US dollar against their home currencies. They also have because of the cost base in their manufacturing territories, an economic exposure to the £/DM rate. As mentioned at the outset, an economic exposure to FX rates can exist for an indigenous industry. Many examples can be cited from the early 1980s when the relative strength of sterling gave importers sufficient incentive to undermine UK producers who had, hitherto, strong positions in their domestic market. This type of economic exposure is very difficult to analyse.

17.2 Necessity of managing foreign exchange risk

A key assumption in the concept of foreign exchange risk is that exchange rate changes are not predictable and that this is determined by how efficient the markets for foreign exchange are. Research in the area of efficiency of foreign exchange markets has thus far been able to establish only a weak form of the efficient market hypothesis conclusively which implies that successive changes in exchange rates cannot be predicted by analysing the historical sequence of exchange rates. However, when the efficient markets theory is applied to the foreign exchange market under floating exchange rates there is some evidence to suggest that the present prices properly reflect all available information.

This implies that exchange rates react to new information in an immediate and unbiased fashion, so that no one party can make a profit by this information and in any case, information on direction of the rates arrives randomly so exchange rates also fluctuate randomly. It implies that foreign exchange risk management cannot be done away with by employing resources to predict exchange rate changes.

17.3 Hedging as a tool to manage foreign exchange risk

There is a spectrum of opinions regarding foreign exchange hedging. Some firms feel hedging techniques are speculative or do not fall in their area of expertise and hence do not venture into hedging practices. Other firms are unaware of being exposed to foreign exchange risks. There are a set of firms who only hedge some of their risks, while others are aware of the various risks they face, but are unaware of the methods to guard the firm against the risk. There is yet another set of companies who believe shareholder value cannot be increased by hedging the firm's foreign exchange risks as shareholders can themselves individually hedge themselves against the same using instruments like forward contracts available in the market or diversify such risks out by manipulating their portfolios.

There are some explanations backed by theory about the irrelevance of managing the risk of change in exchange rates. For example, the International Fisher effect states that exchange rates changes are balanced out by interest rate changes, the Purchasing Power Parity theory suggests that exchange rate changes will be offset by changes in relative price indices/inflation since the Law of One Price should hold. Both these theories suggest that exchange rate changes are evened out in some form or the other. Also, the Unbiased Forward Rate theory suggests that locking in the forward exchange rate offers the same expected return and is an unbiased indicator of the future spot rate. But these theories are perfectly played out in perfect markets under homogeneous tax regimes. Also, exchange rate-linked changes in factors like inflation and interest rates take time to adjust and in the meanwhile firms stand to lose out on adverse movements in the exchange rates.

The existence of different kinds of market imperfections, such as incomplete financial markets, positive transaction and information costs, probability of financial distress, and agency costs and restrictions on free trade make foreign exchange management an appropriate concern for corporate management. (Giddy and Dufey, 1992) It has also been argued that a hedged firm, being less risky can secure debt more easily and this enjoy a tax advantage (interest is excluded from tax while dividends are taxed). This would negate the Modigliani-Miller proposition as shareholders cannot duplicate such tax advantages. The MM argument that shareholders can hedge on their own is also not valid on account of high transaction costs and lack of knowledge about financial manipulations on the part of shareholders.

There is also a vast pool of research that proves the efficacy of managing foreign exchange risks and a significant amount of evidence showing the reduction of exposure with the use of tools for managing these exposures. In one of the more recent studies, Allayanis and Ofek (2001) use a multivariate analysis on a sample of S&P 500 non-financial firms and calculate a firms exchange-rate exposure using the ratio of foreign sales to total sales as a proxy and isolate the impact of use of foreign currency derivatives (part of foreign exchange risk management) on a firm's foreign exchange exposures. They find a statistically significant association between the absolute value of the exposures and the (absolute value) of the percentage use of foreign currency derivatives and prove that the use of derivatives in fact reduce exposure.

17.4 Foreign Exchange Risk Management Framework

Once a firm recognizes its exposure, it then has to deploy resources in managing it. A heuristic for firms to manage this risk effectively is presented below which can be modified to suit firm-specific needs i.e. some or all the following tools could be used.

- **Forecasts:** After determining its exposure, the first step for a firm is to develop a forecast on the market trends and what the main direction/trend is going to be on the foreign exchange rates. The period for forecasts is typically 6 months. It is important to base the forecasts on valid assumptions. Along with identifying trends, a probability should be estimated for the forecast coming true as well as how much the change would be.

- **Risk Estimation:** Based on the forecast, a measure of the *Value at Risk* (the actual profit or loss for a move in rates according to the forecast) and the *probability* of this risk should be ascertained. The risk that a transaction would fail due to *market-specific problems4* should be taken into account. Finally, the Systems Risk that can arise due to inadequacies such as reporting gaps and implementation gaps in the firms' exposure management system should be estimated.

- **Benchmarking:** Given the exposures and the risk estimates, the firm has to set its limits for handling foreign exchange exposure. The firm also has to decide whether to manage its exposures on a cost centre or profit centre basis. A cost centre approach is a defensive one and the main aim is ensure that cash flows of a firm are not adversely affected beyond a point. A profit centre approach on the other hand is a more aggressive approach where the firm decides to generate a net profit on its exposure over time.

- **Hedging:** Based on the limits a firm set for itself to manage exposure, the firms then decides an appropriate hedging strategy. There are various financial instruments available for the firm to choose from: futures, forwards, options and swaps and issue of foreign debt. Hedging strategies and instruments are explored in a section.

- **Stop Loss:** The firms risk management decisions are based on forecasts which ar but estimates of reasonably unpredictable trends. It is imperative to have stop loss arrangements in order to rescue the firm if the forecasts turn out wrong. For this, there should be certain monitoring systems in place to detect critical levels in the foreign exchange rates for approp iate measure to be taken.

❖ **Reporting and Review:** Risk management policies are typically subjected to review based on periodic reporting. The reports mainly include profit/ loss status on open contracts after marking to market, the actual exchange/ interest rate achieved on each exposure, and profitability vis-à-vis the benchmark and the expected changes in overall exposure due to forecasted exchange/ interest rate movements. The review analyses whether the benchmarks set are valid and effective in controlling the exposures, what the market trends are and finally whether the overall strategy is working or needs change.

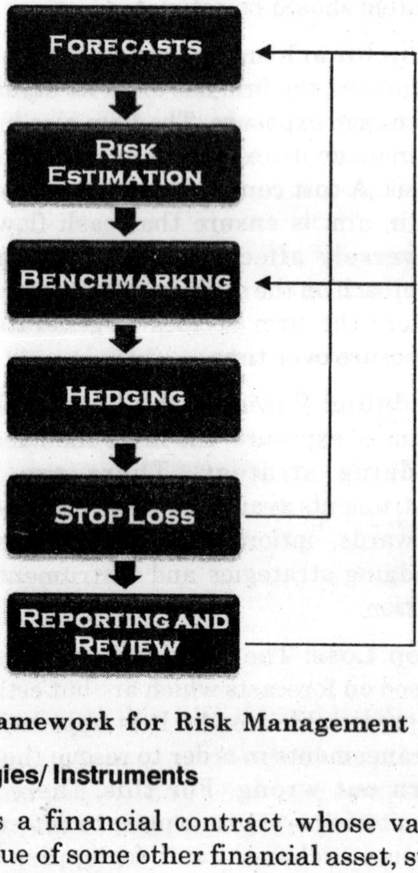

Figure 1: Framework for Risk Management

17-5 Hedging Strategies/ Instruments

A derivative is a financial contract whose value is derived from the value of some other financial asset, such as a stock price, a commodity price, an exchange rate, an interest rate, or even an index of prices. The main role of derivatives is that they reallocate risk among financial market participants, help to make financial markets more complete. This section outlines the hedging strategies using derivatives with foreign exchange being the only risk assumed.

❖ **Forwards:** A forward is a made-to-measure agreement between two parties to buy/sell a specified amount of a currency at a specified rate on a particular date in the future. The depreciation of the receivable currency is hedged against by selling a currency forward. If the risk is that of a currency appreciation (if the firm has to buy that currency in future say for import), it can hedge by buying the currency forward. E.g if RIL wants to buy crude oil in US dollars six months hence, it can enter into a forward contract to pay INR and buy USD and lock in a fixed exchange rate for INR-USD to be paid after 6 months regardless of the actual INR-Dollar rate at the time. In this example the downside is an appreciation of Dollar which is protected by a fixed forward contract. The main advantage of a forward is that it can be tailored to the specific needs of the firm and an exact hedge can be obtained. On the downside, these contracts are not marketable, they can't be sold to another party when they are no longer required and are binding.

❖ **Futures:** A futures contract is similar to the forward contract but is more liquid because it is traded in an organized exchange i.e. the futures market. Depreciation of a currency can be hedged by selling futures and appreciation can be hedged by buying futures. Advantages of futures are that there is a central market for futures which eliminates the problem of double coincidence.

Forecasts

Risk Estimation

Benchmarking

Hedging

Stop Loss

Reporting and review

Futures require a small initial outlay (a proportion of the value of the future) with which significant amounts of money can be gained or lost with the actual forwards price fluctuations. This provides a sort of leverage. The previous example for a forward contract for RIL applies here also just that RIL will have to go to a USD futures exchange to purchase standardised dollar futures equal to the amount to be hedged as the risk is that of appreciation of the dollar. As mentioned earlier, the tailorability of the futures contract is limited i.e. only standard denominations of money can be bought instead of the exact amounts that are bought in forward contracts.

- **Options:** A currency Option is a contract giving the right, not the obligation, to buy or sell a specific quantity of one foreign currency in exchange for another at a fixed price; called the Exercise Price or Strike Price. The fixed nature of the exercise price reduces the uncertainty of exchange rate changes and limits the losses of open currency positions. Options are particularly suited as a hedging tool for contingent cash flows, as is the case in bidding processes. Call Options are used if the risk is an upward trend in price (of the currency), while Put Options are used if the risk is a downward trend. Again taking the example of RIL which needs to purchase crude oil in USD in 6 months, if RIL buys a Call option (as the risk is an upward trend in dollar rate), i.e. the right to buy a specified amount of dollars at a fixed rate on a specified date, there are two scenarios. If the exchange rate movement is favourable i.e the dollar depreciates, then RIL can buy them at the spot rate as they have become cheaper. In the other case, if the dollar appreciates compared to today's spot rate, RIL can exercise the option to purchase it at the agreed strike price. In either case RIL benefits by paying the lower price to purchase the dollar.

- **Swaps:** A swap is a foreign currency contract whereby the buyer and seller exchange equal initial principal amounts of two different currencies at the spot rate. The buyer and seller exchange fixed or floating rate interest payments in their respective swapped currencies over the term of the contract. At maturity, the principal amount is effectively re-swapped at a predetermined exchange rate so that the parties end up with their original currencies. The advantages of swaps are that firms with limited appetite for exchange rate risk may move to a partially or completely hedged position through the mechanism of foreign currency swaps, while leaving the underlying borrowing intact. Apart from covering the exchange rate risk, swaps also allow firms to hedge the floating interest rate risk. Consider an export oriented company that has entered into a swap for a notional principal of USD 1 mn at an exchange rate of 42/dollar. The company pays US 6months LIBOR to the bank and receives 11.00% p.a. every 6 months on 1st January & 1st July, till 5 years. Such a company would have earnings in Dollars and can use the same to pay interest for this kind of borrowing (in dollars rather than in Rupee) thus hedging its exposures.

- **Foreign Debt:** Foreign debt can be used to hedge foreign exchange exposure by taking advantage of the International Fischer Effect relationship. This is demonstrated with the example of an exporter who has to receive a fixed amount of dollars in a few months from present. The exporter stands to lose if the domestic currency appreciates against that currency in the meanwhile so, to hedge this, he could take a loan in the foreign currency for the same time period and convert the same into domestic currency at the current exchange rate. The theory assures that the gain realised by investing the proceeds from the loan would match the interest rate payment (in the foreign currency) for the loan.

17.6 Choice of hedging instruments

The choice of hedging instruments is very scant. Among the available studies, Géczy et al. (1997) argues that currency swaps are more cost-effective for hedging foreign debt risk, while forward contracts are more cost-effective for hedging foreign operations risk. This is because foreign currency debt payments are long-term and predictable, which fits the long-term nature of currency swap contracts. Foreign currency revenues, on the other hand, are short-term and unpredictable, in line with the short-term nature of forward contracts. A survey done by Marshall (2000) also points out that currency swaps are better for hedging against translation risk, while forwards are better for hedging against transaction risk. This study also provides anecdotal evidence that pricing policy is the most popular means of hedging economic exposures. These results however can differ for different currencies depending in the sensitivity of that currency to various market factors. Regulation in the foreign exchange markets of various countries may also skew such results.

An Example of Hedging Using Forward Agreement

Assume that a Malaysian construction company, Bumiways just won a contract to build a stretch of road in India. The contract is signed for 10,000,000 Rupees and would be paid for after the completion of the work. This amount is consistent with Bumiways minimum revenue of RM1,000,000 at the exchange rate of RM0.10 per Rupee. However, since the exchange rate could fluctuate and end with a possible depreciation of Rupees, Bumiways enters into a forward agreement with First State Bank of India to fix the exchange rate at RM0.10 per Rupee. The forward contract is a legal agreement, and therefore constitutes an obligation on both sides. The First State Bank may have to find a counter party for this transaction – either a party who wants to hedge against the appreciation of 10,000,000 Rupees expiring at the same time or a party that wishes to speculate on an upward trend in Rupees. If the bank itself plays the counter party, then the risk would be borne by the bank itself. The existence of speculators may be necessary to play the counter party position. By entering into a forward contract Bumiways is guaranteed of an exchange rate of RM0.10 per Rupee in the future irrespective of what happens to the spot Rupee exchange rate. If Rupee were to actually depreciate, Bumiways would be protected. However, if it were to appreciate, then Bumiways would have to forego this favourable movement and hence bear some implied losses. Even though this favourable movement is still a potential loss, Bumiways proceeds with the hedging since it knows an exchange rate of RM0.10 per Rupee is consistent with a profitable venture.

An Example of Hedging with Put Options

Consider our Bumiways example. Instead of having already won the contract to build the road in India, let's however assume that it is in the process of bidding for the contract, as is common in real-life. Bumiways wants a minimum acceptable revenue of RM1,000,000 after hedging costs, but Bumiways need to quote a bid price now. In this instance, Bumiways would only face the exchange rate risk contingent upon winning the bid. Due to this contingency, options fare a better hedging tool compared with forwards or futures. Assume it is now July and the results of the bidding will be known in September. The following September options quotes are available today:

RM0.10 call @ RM0.002

RM0.10 put @ RM0.001

The size of each Rupee contract is 2,000,000 Rupees.

The following is how Bumiways would make its hedging strategy:

1. Buy puts or calls? Since the Bumiways would receive Rupees in the future if it won the contract, its risk is a depreciation of Rupees. Therefore, it should buy puts.
2 What should be the bid amount? To answer this question

we need to compute the effective exchange rate after incorporating the premium, i.e. RM0.10 minus RM0.001 which equals RM0.099. Now the bid amount is computed as RM1,000,000/RM0.099, which equals 10,101,010 Rupees.

3. How many put contracts should it buy to protect against the depreciation in Rupees? To answer this, just take the bid amount and divide by the contract size, i.e. 10,101,010/ 2,000,000 equals 5.05. Since fractions of contracts are not allowed and we don't overhedge, 5 contracts are sufficient with some portion being unhedged. However, to guarantee a minimum revenue of RM1,000,000 we cannot tolerate imperfections in hedging. Therefore in this example we should go for 6 contracts.
4. What is the cost of hedging? Cost of hedging is computed as follows: 6 contracts x 2,000,000 per contract x RM0.001 equals RM12,000. This cost of hedging is the maximum loss possible with options.

In September, Bumiways would have known the outcome of the bid. By then also the Rupee might have appreciated or depreciated. Lets assume the Rupees either appreciates to RM0.20 or depreciates to RM0.05 per Rupee. The following are the four outcomes possible and their cash flow implications.

The below example illustrates how options can be used to guarantee a minimum cash flow on contingent claims. In case the bid is won, a minimum cash flow of RM1,000,000 is guaranteed while allowing one to still enjoy a favourable movement if it does take place. If the bid is lost, the maximum loss possible is the premium paid.

Determinants of Hedging Decisions

The management of foreign exchange risk, as has been established so far, is a fairly complicated process. A firm, exposed to foreign exchange risk, needs to formulate a strategy to manage it, choosing from multiple alternatives.

Possible Cash Flow Outcomes of Hedging using Options

	Rupee Depreciates to RM0.05	Rupee Appreciates to RM0.20
Bid Won	Exchange the 10.101.010 Rupees @RM0.05 = RM505,050.50 Plus profit from options 6 x 2,000,000 x (RM0.10-RM0.05) = RM600,000 Less cost of hedging = RM12,000 Net Cash flow = RM1,093,050 (which guarantees the minimum revenue of RM1,000,000)	Exchange the 10,101,010 Rupees @RM0.20 = RM2,020,202 Puts options not worth exercising, therefore let them just expire. Less cost of hedging = RM12,000 Net Cash flow = RM2,008,202 (In this case the option allows Bumiways to enjoy a favourable movement)
Bid Lost	In this case Bumiways would not receive the bid amount. But however it could still exercise its rights and realize its profit from puts. Profit from options 6 x 2,000,000 x RM0.05 = RM600,000 Less cost of hedging = RM12,000 Net Cash flow = RM578,000	This is the worst case that can happen. Bid lost and also the put option position ends up being not profitable. Bumiways loses the premium paid = RM12,000. This is the maximum loss possible.

This section explores what factors firms take into consideration when formulating these strategies.

Production and Trade vs. Hedging Decisions

An important issue for multinational firms is the allocation of capital among different countries production and sales and at the same time hedging their exposure to the varying exchange rates. Research in this area suggests that the elements of exchange rate uncertainty and the attitude toward risk are irrelevant to the multinational firm's sales and production decisions *(Broll,1993)*. Only the revenue function and cost of production are to be assessed, and, the production and trade decisions in multiple countries are independent of the hedging decision.

The implication of this independence is that the presence of markets for hedging instruments greatly reduces the complexity involved in a firm's decision making as it can separate production and sales functions from the finance function. The firm avoids the need to form expectations about future exchange rates and formulation of risk preferences which entails high information costs.

Cost of Hedging

Hedging can be done through the derivatives market or through money markets (foreign debt). In either case the cost of hedging should be the difference between value received from a hedged position and the value received if the firm did not hedge.

In the presence of efficient markets, the cost of hedging in the forward market is the difference between the future spot rate and current forward rate plus any transactions cost associated with the forward contract. Similarly, the expected costs of hedging in the money market are the transactions cost plus the difference between the interest rate differential and the expected value of the difference between the current and future spot rates. In efficient markets, both types of hedging should produce similar results at the same costs, because interest rates and forward and spot exchange rates are determined simultaneously.

The costs of hedging, assuming efficiency in foreign exchange markets result in pure transaction costs. The three main elements of these transaction costs are brokerage or service fees charged by dealers, information costs such as subscription to Reuter reports and news channels and administrative costs of exposure management.

Factors affecting the decision to hedge foreign currency risk

Research in the area of determinants of hedging separates the decision of a firm to hedge from that of how much to hedge. There is conclusive evidence to suggest that firms with larger size, R&D expenditure and exposure to exchange rates through foreign sales and foreign trade are more likely to use derivatives. *(Allayanis and Ofek, 2001)* First, the following section describes the factors that affect the decision to hedge and then the factors affecting the degree of hedging are considered.

- **Firm size:** Firm size acts as a proxy for the cost of hedging or economies of scale. Risk management involves fixed costs of setting up of computer systems and training/hiring of personnel in foreign exchange management. Moreover, large firms might be considered as more creditworthy counterparties for forward or swap transactions, thus further reducing their cost of hedging. *The book value of assets is used as a measure of firm size.*

- **Leverage:** According to the risk management literature, firms with high leverage have greater incentive to engage in hedging because doing so reduces the probability, and thus the expected cost of financial distress. Highly levered firms avoid foreign debt as a means to hedge and use derivatives.

- **Liquidity and profitability:** Firms with highly liquid assets or high profitability have less incentive to engage in hedging because they are exposed to a lower probability of financial distress. *Liquidity is measured by the quick ratio, i.e. quick assets divided by current liabilities). Profitability is measured as EBIT divided by book assets.*

❖ **Sales growth**: Sales growth is a factor determining decision to hedge as opportunities are more likely to be affected by the underinvestment problem. For these firms, hedging will reduce the probability of having to rely on

Table 1: Evidence of Derivative use for Hedging FX Risk in Indian Firms

Instruments	Currency(mn)	Rs (Cr)	Nature of exposure
Reliance Industries			
Currency Swaps		1064.49	Earnings in all business are linked to USD. The key input, crude oil is purchased in USD. All export revenues are in foreign currency and local prices as well
Options Contracts		2939.76	
Forward Contracts		5764.10	
Maruti Udyog			
Forward Contracts	6411 (INR-JPY) 70 ($-INR)		Import Royalty payable in Yen and Exports Receivables in dollars.
Currency Swaps	124.70 (USD-INR)		Interest rate and forex risk.
Mahindra and Mahindra			
Forward Contracts	350 (INR-JPY) 2 (INR-EUR) 27.3 ($-INR)		Trade payables in Yen and Euro and export receivables in dollars.
Currency Swaps	5390 (JPY-INR)		Interest rate and foreign exchange risk.
Arvind Mills			
Forward Contracts	152.98 ($-INR) 2.25 (GBP-INR) 5 (INR-$)	703.67 21.88	Most of the revenue in either in dollars or Linked to dollars due to export.
Options Contracts	122.5 ($-INR)	547.16	
Infosys			
Forward Contracts	119 ($-INR)	529	Revenues denominated in these currencies.
Options Contracts Range barrier options	4 ($-INR) 8 (INR-$) 3 ($-INR) 3 (Eur-INR)	18 36 971	
Tata Consultancy Services			
Forward Contracts	15 (Eur-INR) 21 (GBP-INR)	265.75	Revenues largely denominated in foreign currency, predominantly USS, GBP, and Euro, other currencie include Australian $, Candian $, South African Rand, and Swiss Franc
Options Contracts	830 ($-INR) 47.5(Eur-INR) 76.5(Gbp-INR)	4057	
Ranbary			
Forward Contracts		2894.589	Exposed on acconts receivable and loans payable. Exposure in USD and Jap Yen
Dr. Reddy's Labs			
Forward Contracts	398 ($-INR) 11 (Eur-$)		Foreign currency earnings through export currency requirements for settlement of liability for import of goods.
Options Contracts	30 (EUR-$)		

Note:

1. $INR Forward contract denote Selling of USD forwards to convert revenues to INR IRN-$ Forward contracts denote buying of USD forwards to meet USD payment obligations.
2. $-INR Option contract are put options to sell USD, INR-$ are call options to buy USD

external financing, which is costly for information asymmetry reasons, and thus enable them to enjoy uninterrupted high growth. *The measure of sales growth is obtained using the 3-year geometric average of yearly sales growth rates.*

As regards the degree of hedging Allayanis and Ofek (2001) conclude that the sole determinants of the degree of hedging are exposure factors (foreign sales and trade). In other words, given that a firm decides to hedge, the decision of how much to hedge is affected solely by its exposure to foreign currency movements.

Conclusions

Derivative use for hedging is only to increase due to the increased global linkages and volatile exchange rates. Firms need to look at instituting a sound risk management system and also need to formulate their hedging strategy that suits their specific firm characteristics and exposures.

In India, regulation has been steadily eased and turnover and liquidity in the foreign currency derivative markets has increased, although the use is mainly in shorter maturity contracts of one year or less. Forward and option contracts are the more popular instruments. Regulators had initially only allowed certain banks to deal in this market however now corporate can also write option contracts. There are many variants of these derivatives which investment banks across the world specialize in, and as the awareness and demand for these variants increases, RBI would have to revise regulations.

For now, Indian companies are actively hedging their foreign exchanges risks with forwards, currency and interest rate swaps and different types of options such as call, put, cross currency and range-barrier options. The high use of forward contracts by Indian firms also highlights the absence of a rupee futures exchange in India. However, the Dubai Gold and Commodities Exchange in June, 2007 introduced Rupee- Dollar futures that could be traded on its exchanges and had provided another route for firms to hedge on a transparent basis. There are fears that RBI's ability to control the partially convertible currency will be subdued by this introduction but this issue is beyond the scope of this study. The partial convertibility of the Rupee will be difficult to control if many exchanges offer such instruments and that will be factor to consider for the RBI.

Accordingly, Reserve Bank of India in the Annual Policy Statement for the Year 2007-08 proposed to set up a Working Group on Currency Futures to study the international experience and suggest a suitable framework to implement the proposal, in line with the current legal and regulatory framework.

18

Foreign Exchange Management = Key Concerns

18.1 INTRODUCTION

The foreign exchange or forex market is one of the largest and most liquid financial markets in the world with a daily transaction of almost 1.5 trillion U.S. dollars. Banks, financial institutions and individual investors, therefore, have huge potential of economic gain as well as losses.

Foreign exchange risk is a potential gain or loss that occurs as a result of a change in exchange rate. In order to minimize the possibility of financial loss, every investor needs to adopt some forex risk management measures.

For minimizing forex risk, one must remember few basic points:

1. Value of a currency changes frequently affecting firms and individuals engaged in international transactions
2. Assets, liabilities, and cash flows are affected through changes in the exchange rates.

Foreign exchange risk is the possibility of a gain or loss to afirm that occurs due to unanticipated changes in. exchange rate.For example, if an Indian firm imports goods and pays inforeign currency (say dollars), its outflow is in dollars; thus it is exposed to foreign exchange risk. If the value of the foreigncurrency rises (i.e., the dollar appreciates), the Indian firm has to pay more domestic currency to get the required amount of foreign currency.

The advent of the floating exchange rate regime, since the early 1970s, has heightened the interest of MNCs in developing techniques and strategies for foreign exchange exposure management. The primary goal is to protect corporate profits from the negative impact of exchange rate fluctuations.However, the goals and techniques of management vary depending on whether the focus is on accounting exposure or economic exposure.Foreign exchange risks, therefore, pose one of the greatest challenges to a multinational company. These risks arise because multinational corporations operate in multiple currencies.Infact, many times firms who have a diversified portfolio find that the negative effect of exchange rate changes. on one currency are offset by gains in others i.e. exchange risk isdiversifiable.

Types of Exposure:

There are mainly three types of foreign exchange exposures:

1. Translation exposure
2. Transaction exposure
3. Economic Exposure

A. Translation Exposure

- T*ranslation exposure*, also called accounting exposure, arises because financial statements of foreign subsidiaries – which are stated in foreign currency – must be restated in the parent's reporting currency for the firm to prepare consolidated financial statements.
- Translation exposure is the potential for an increase or decrease in the parent's net worth and reported net income caused by a change in exchange rates since the last translation.
- The accounting process of *translation*, involves converting

these foreign subsidiaries financial statements into home currency-denominated statements.

- ❖ Two basic methods for the translation of foreign subsidiary financial statements are employed worldwide:
  - The *current rate method*
  - The *temporal method*
- ❖ Regardless of which method is employed, a translation method must not only designate at what exchange rate individual balance sheet and income statement items are remeasured, but also designate where any imbalance is to be recorded (current income or an equity reserve account)

1. Current Rate Method

- ❖ The *current rate method* is the most prevalent in the world today.
- ❖ Assets and liabilities are translated at the current rate of exchange.
- ❖ Income statement items are translated at the exchange rate on the dates they were recorded or an appropriately weighted average rate for the period.
- ❖ The biggest advantage of the current rate method is that the gain or loss on translation does not pass through the income statement but goes directly to a reserve account (reducing variability of reported earnings).

2. Temporal Method

- ❖ Under the *temporal method*, specific assets are translated at exchange rates consistent with the timing of the item's creation.
- ❖ This method assumes that a number of individual line item assets such as inventory and net plant and equipment are restated regularly to reflect market value.
- ❖ Gains or losses resulting from remeasurement are carried directly to current consolidated income, and not to equity reserves (increased variability of consolidated earnings).

3. Monetary / Non-monetary Method

- ❖ If these items were not restated but were instead carried at historical cost, the temporal method becomes the *monetary/non-monetary* method of translation.
- ❖ Monetary assets and liabilities are translated at current exchange rates.
- ❖ Non-monetary assets and liabilities are translated at historical rates.
- ❖ Income statement items are translated at the average exchange rate for the period.
- ❖ Dividends (distributions) are translated at the exchange rate on the date of payment.
- ❖ Equity items are translated at historical rates.

Managing Translation Exposure

- ❖ The main technique to minimize translation exposure is called a *balance sheet hedge*.
- ❖ A balance sheet hedge requires an equal amount of exposed foreign currency assets and liabilities on a firm's consolidated balance sheet.
- ❖ If this can be achieved for each foreign currency, net translation exposure will be zero.
- ❖ These hedges are a compromise in which the denomination of balance sheet accounts is altered, perhaps at a cost in terms of interest expense or operating efficiency, to achieve some degree of foreign exchange protection.

B. Transaction Exposure

- ❖ *Transaction exposure* measures changes in the value of outstanding financial obligations incurred prior to a change in exchange rates but not due to be settled until after the exchange rates change.
- ❖ Thus, this type of exposure deals with changes in cash flows that result from existing contractual obligations.

- Transaction exposure arises from:
- Purchasing or selling on credit goods or services whose prices are stated in foreign currencies.
- Borrowing or lending funds when repayment is to be made in a foreign currency.
- Being a party to an unperformed foreign exchange forward contract.
- Otherwise acquiring assets or incurring liabilities denominated in foreign currencies.

Suppose a U.S. firm, Trident, sells merchandise on account to a Belgian buyer for:

- €1,800,000 payment to be made in 60 days.
- S_0 = $0.9000/€
- The U.S. seller expects to exchange the €1,800,000 for $1,620,000 when payment is received.
- *Transaction exposure arises because of the risk that the U.S. seller will receive something other than* $1,620,000.
- If the euro weakens to $0.8500/€, then Trident will receive $1,530,000
- If the euro strengthens to $0.9600/€, then Trident will receive $1,728,000

Thus, exposure is the chance of either a loss or a gain

C. Operating Exposure

- *Operating exposure,* also called *economic exposure, competitive exposure,* and even *strategic exposure* on occasion, measures any change in the present value of a firm resulting from changes in future operating cash flows caused by an unexpected change in exchange rates.

Measuring the operating exposure of a firm requires forecasting and analyzing all the firm's future individual transaction exposures together with the future exposures of all the firm's competitors and potential competitors worldwide

- ❖ Operating exposure is far more important for the long-run health of a business than changes caused by transaction or accounting exposure.
- ❖ Operating exposure is inevitably subjective, because it depends on estimates of future cash flow changes over an arbitrary time horizon.
- ❖ Planning for operating exposure is a total management responsibility because it depends on the interaction of strategies in finance, marketing, purchasing, and production.
- ❖ An expected change in foreign exchange rates is not included in the definition of operating exposure, because both management and investors should have factored this information into their evaluation of anticipated operating results and market value.
- ❖ From an investor's perspective, if the foreign exchange market is efficient, information about expected changes in exchange rates should be reflected in a firm's market value.
- ❖ Only unexpected changes in exchange rates, or an inefficient foreign exchange market, should cause market value to change. Plausible Questions Are:
- ❖ Where is the company selling?
- ❖ Who are the key competitors?
- ❖ How sensitive is demand to price?
- ❖ Where is the company producing?

Where are the company's inputs coming from?

- ❖ Volvo produces most of its cars in Sweden, but buys most of its inputs from Germany.
- ❖ The U.S. is an important export market for Volvo.
- ❖ Volvo management believed that a depreciating Swedish

krona versus the $ and an **appreciating** Swedish krona versus the DM would be beneficial to Volvo.

- But researchers found that statistically:

  A ***depreciating*** krona relative to the Deutschemark improved Volvo's cash flow!

These results reflect the fact that Volvo's major competitors are the German firms BMW, Mercedes and Audi.

- **Audits/Scenario Analysis**: Qualitative examination of the separate elements of a firm's operating cash flow and anticipating its sensitivity to real exchange rate changes.
- **Statistical Approach**: Regress changes in firm value on changes in exchange rates to obtain a quantitative assessment of sensitivity.
  - Presumption is that changes in the value of a firm's public securities measures the effect of exchange rate changes. (measure of aggregate exposure)
- Pass Through – can the company pass the price increase on to the customer?
- This depends on the product and the level of competition in the market.
- For low-quality goods, price competition is usually intense, so no one company can change prices.
- For high-quality goods, there may be room to increase prices and not effect demand.
- Use of Marketing Strategies
- Market Selection
- Pricing Strategy/Product Strategy
- Promotional Strategy
- Use of Production Management
- **Input mix**
- Plant Location & Shifting production among plants
- Raising Productivity (i.e. lowering costs)
- Financial Hedging techniques may also be used

18.2 Necessity of managing foreign exchange risk

A key assumption in the concept of foreign exchange risk is that exchange rate changes are not predictable and that this is determined by how efficient the markets for foreign exchange are. Research in the area of efficiency of foreign exchange markets has thus far been able to establish only a weak form of the efficient market hypothesis conclusively which implies that successive changes in exchange rates cannot be predicted by analysing the historical sequence of exchange rates.(Soenen, 1979). However, when the efficient markets theory is applied to the foreign exchange market under floating exchange rates there is some evidence to suggest that the present prices properly reflect all available information.(Giddy and Dufey, 1992).

This implies that exchange rates react to new information in an immediate and unbiased fashion, so that no one party can make a profit by this information and in any case, information on direction of the rates arrives randomly so exchange rates also fluctuate randomly. It implies that foreign exchange risk management cannot be done away with by employing resources to predict exchange rate changes.

18.3 Foreign Exchange Risk Management Framework

Once a firm recognizes its exposure, it then has to deploy resources in managing it. A heuristic for firms to manage this risk effectively is presented below which can be modified to suit firm-specific needs i.e. some or all the following tools could be used.

Forecasts: After determining its exposure, the first step for a firm is to develop a forecast on the market trends and what the main direction/trend is going to be on the foreign exchange rates. The period for forecasts is typically 6 months. It is important to base the forecasts on valid assumptions. Along with identifying trends, a probability should be estimated for the forecast coming true as well as how much the change would be.

Risk Estimation: Based on the forecast, a measure of the *Value at Risk* (the actual profit or loss for a move in rates according to the forecast) and the *probability* of this risk should be ascertained. The risk that a transaction would fail due to *market-specific problems4* should be taken into account. Finally, the Systems Risk that can arise due to inadequacies such as reporting gaps and implementation gaps in the firms' exposure management system should be estimated.

Benchmarking: Given the exposures and the risk estimates, the firm has to set its limits for handling foreign exchange exposure. The firm also has to decide whether to manage its exposures on a cost centre or profit centre basis.A cost centre approach is a defensive one and the main aim is ensure that cash flows of a firm are not adversely affected beyond a point. A profit centre

approach on the other hand is a more aggressive approach where the firm decides to generate a net profit on its exposure over time.

Hedging: Based on the limits a firm set for itself to manage exposure, the firms then decides an appropriate hedging strategy. There are various financial instruments available for the firm to choose from: futures, forwards, options and swaps and issue of foreign debt. Hedging strategies and instruments are explored in a section.

Stop Loss: The firms risk management decisions are based on forecasts which are but estimates of reasonably unpredictable trends. It is imperative to have stop loss arrangements in order to rescue the firm if the forecasts turn out wrong. For this, there should be certain monitoring systems in place to detect critical levels in the foreign exchange rates for appropriate measure to be taken.

Reporting and Review: Risk management policies are typically subjected to review based on periodic reporting. The reports mainly include profit/ loss status on open contracts after marking to market, the actual exchange/ interest rate achieved on each exposure, and profitability vis-à-vis the benchmark and the expected changes in overall exposure due to forecasted exchange/ interest rate movements. The review analyses whether the benchmarks set are valid and effective in controlling the exposures, what the market trends are and finally whether the overall strategy is working or needs change.

VARIOUS NEW HEDGING PRODUCTS

DESCRIPTION	POSITIVES	NEGATIVES
Forwards – a customized contract where MFI and bank agree to exchange local currency for foreign currency on a specified date(s), for specified amount(s). at a specified price.	• Customized contracts • Readily available	• Typical maximum length of 1 year • Imperfect coverage (for example, using a series of 1-year forwards on a 5-year loan protects principal only)
Swap – an MFI trades its foreign currency payment stream obligation to another institution in exchange for the other's local currency payment stream obligation.*	• More customized/fuller coverage (matches debt obligation cash flows) • Longer tenors • Flexible application	• Needs appropriate match • Exotic currencies might be more difficult • Large minimum amount required
Futures – a standardized, transferable, exchange-traded contract requiring the holder to exchange a specified amount of currency for another, at a specified price, on a specified future date; i.e., a standardized, transferable, exchange-traded forward contract.	• Can be less expensive • Can be sold in the market by unwinding hedge • Can spread among many contracts which allows for diversification of counterpart risk to MFI • Margin calls	• Available only in 20 currency markets. (Some countries do trade locally, e.g., Columbia.) • Rigid; has preset maturity dates and amounts • Extensive requirements; needs to match situation • Requires management
Option – contract with a bank giving MFI the option, but not the obligation, to buy a foreign currency for a specific price at/or over a given period of time.**	• Limits worst case scenario • MFI maintains control and choice whether to use or not	• A premium is paid for the option even if not used • Does not eliminate all losses, but can minimize them • Limited availability • Complicated • Requires monitoring

A. SPOT

Definition:

Spot refers to the price of one currency in terms of another. For example, USD/CAD means that 1 USD equals 1.1250 CAD (Canadian Dollars)

Market Conventions:

A spot price is quoted as a spread between the BID (level where the bank buys the underlying currency) and the OFFER (level where the bank sells the underlying currency). The underlying currency is the first one in the currency pair. For example, if USD/CAD is 1.1250 - 1.1260, Scotiabank buys USDs at 1.1250 against CAD and sells USDs at 1.1260 against CAD.

CAD Settlement:

Spot transactions settle one business day after the transaction date for USD/CAD and in two business days for all other currency pairs.

Advantages:

- Exporters benefit from domestic currency devaluation.
- Importers benefit from domestic currency appreciation.
- No transaction cost.
- Simple/Easy to monitor changes in the market.

Disadvantages

- Exporters are vulnerable to domestic currency appreciation.
- Importers are vulnerable to domestic currency depreciation.
- Monitoring is required in order to transact at a favorable rate

B. Forward Outright Contracts

Definition:

A forward outright is the price of one currency in terms of another for settlement on a date other than spot. In other words, the spot rate is adjusted by accounting for the interest rate differential between two currencies.

Market Conventions:

Swap points are also quoted as BID and OFFER, and are added to the spot component to obtain the *All In Forward.*

For example:

Spot USD/CAD:	1.1250	1.1260
3 month forwards:	-.0032	-.0031
All In forward outright=	1.1250 -.0032 1.1218	1.1260 -.0031 1.1229

Settlement:

Forward outrights settle at the predetermined future date.

Advantages

- Complete protection from adverse currency moves
- No transaction costs
- Simple to monitor
- Simple to unwind (very liquid).

Disadvantages

- Loss of opportunity gains resulting from favorable currency moves.
- Liability from both parties to transact.

C. SWAPS

Definition:

A contract to exchange two currencies at one time (T1), in order to exchange back to each investor's original position at some future date (T2), for a predetermined price.

Market Conventions:

Swaps are quoted similar to outright forwards as BID / OFFER spread on swap points. However, it is the Far Date that is priced (T2)"

Example: A holder of US Dollars agrees to "sell and buy" US Dollars against CAD from Scotia. This means a sale of USD at T1 and is accompanied by a purchase of USD at T2 for a predetermined price.

Settlement:

Swaps settle at the near date and the far date. However, if the near end matches the maturity of a previous contract, it is only the resulting gain or loss that is cash settled.

Advantages

- Allows a position to be "rolled" so that settlement is postponed.
- Circumvents the money market
- Simple to unwind (very liquid).

Disadvantages

- Cash settlement must take place against any transaction maturing on the near date.

Examples:

Question1: Consider 2 companies rated AAA and BBB.

	FIXED RATE	FLOATING RATE
AAA	10%	L+0.50%
BBB	115	L+0.75

Both are planning to raise a loan of $ 1 MIO. AAA is interested in raising loan under floating rate. BBB is interested in raising loan under fixed rate. An intermediary brings them on at able and a n interest SWAP is arranged. The benefit of the SWAP is to be shared equally by 3 parties. Find the net interest burden (%) for AAA and BBB

Solution 1.

If no SWAP is arranged, Total interest cost to both parties if they borrow as per their plan

AAA L + 0.5

BBB 11% TOTAL L + 11.50 % == A

If Swap is arranged AAA should borrow on a fixed basis and BBB on a floating. The total interest Cost in this situation is

AAA 10%

BBB - L+0.75%

TOTAL —L+10.75 % —B

Savings on the Interest cost – A-B =(L+11.50) - (L+10.75%) = 0.75%

Since savings is to be distributed equally i.e 0.25 each

NET INTEREST BURDEN = Cost under Own Choice – Share in saving

FOR AAA (L+0.5) -0.25 = L+0.25 FOR BBB == (11-.25 = 10.75)

AAA has a Comparative advantage in the fixed rate market but wants to borrow at a floating rate. This provides the basis for a SWAP

QUESTION 2. Two Companies want to borrow. Company X in Euro money market at the floating rate and company Y in Euro Bond Market at a fixed rate.

Company X	T Percent	L+0.25
Company Y	T +1.50 Percent	L+0.75
Advantage of Co , X over Co Y	1.50Percent	0.50Percent

A bank comes between two Companies as Mediator and charges 0.20 Percent as margin. rest being divided equally. Show the net cost both to the Companies X & Y

SOLUTION OF THE SWAPS :

SWAP through Bank:

A bank comes between the two companies as a mediator since it may not be easy for the companies to find the counter parties. This role is played by the bank which of course, makes a gain in the in bargain for the services rendered. The swap operation is shown below:

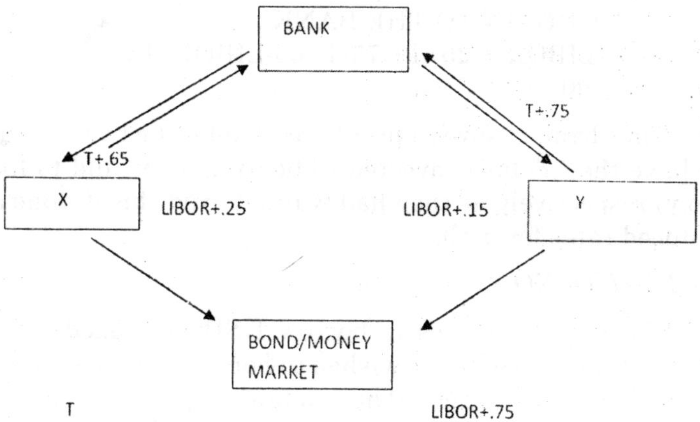

1. Co X:
   - PAYS T% TO THE BOND MARKET
   - PAYS LIBOR+.25%TO THE BANK
   - RECEIVES T+.65% FROM THE BANK

{1.50-0.20=1.30/2=0.65}

NET COST TO THE Co X = T +LIBOR+.25-T-0.65
=LIBOR-0.40=======COMPANY X

2. Co Y:
   - PAYS LIBOR+.75% TO THE EURO MONEY MARKET
   - PAYS T+.75% TO THE BANK
   - RECEIVES LIBOR +.15% FROM THE BANK

   NET COST TO THE Co Y

   = LIBOR +.75+T+.75-LIBOR-.15
   = T+1.35================== COMPANY Y

3. BANK:
   - RECEIVES LIBOR+.25% FROM Co X
   - RECEIVES T+.75 % FROM Co Y
   - PAYS T+.65 TO CO X
   - PAYS LIBOR +.15 TO CO Y

NET GAIN TO THE BANK
= LIBOR +.25+T+.75-T-.65-LIBOR-.15
= .20

Thus bank receives a profit but enables the two company to have their debts converted to floating (co x) and to fixed (co y) respectively as they had wanted. And this is done ast reduced rates for both.

QUESTION NO 3.

Company X wishes to borrow USD at a fixed rate of Interest and Company Y wishes to borrow Japanese Yen at a fixed rate of interest. The amount required by the two Companies is the same at Current Foreign Exchange rate. Design a SWAP that will net a Bank, acting as an Intermediary, 50 basis point per annum

	YEN %	DOLLARS %	YEN INTEREST	DOLLAR INTEREST
Company X	5.0	9.6	6	10.6
Company Y	6.5	10	7.5	11.0

SOLUTION

Let x be the spread in the yen market (in this case 150basis points 6.5-5) and let y be the spread in the dollar market (40 basis points,10-9.6).the total gain available is x-y = 1.5-0.40 i.e 110 basis points. The bank will take 50 basis points, so that leaves 60 basis points to be divided equally among the two companies i.e 0.30. Therefore x must end up paying 10.3% (10.6 – 0.30) in dollars and y must end up paying 7.2% (7.5- 0.30) in yen.

X	Pay 6% yen to outside lenders
	Pay 10.3% in dollars to the bank in swap
	Receive 6% in yen from the bank in swap
Total	10.3% in dollars
Y	Pay 11% in dollars to outside lenders
	Pay 7.2% to bank in swap
	Receive 11% in dollars from bank in swap
Total	7.20 % in yen

The bank profits of 50% comes from receiving 7.2% in Yen and giving 6% in yen and gaining 120 basis points in yen,while receiving 10.30 %and giving 11% in dollars. Thus losing 70 Basis points in Dollars. Also the final exchange of principa. [illegible]l expose X & Y to the exchange rate risk, but not the B[illegible]k

D. OPTIONS

Definition:

An option gives the holder the right but not the obligation, to buy or sell an underlying asset at a predetermined price at or until a certain time. It differs from a forward contract in that it is not an obligation to transact. An option provides insurance from adverse currency movements.

Market Conventions & Language:

Strike price: The predetermined price agreed to by both counterparties, i.e. the protection level. Expiry date: The date on or up to which the option may be exercised, i.e. decision deadline (by 10:00am New York Time).

Value date: The date on which settlement occurs.

American style: The option can be exercised at any time up to the expiry date.

European style: The option can be exercised only on the expiry date. The standard form for Over The Counter (OTC) options.

At the Money: An option is "At the Money" when the strike price equals the underlying forward price.

In the Money: An option is "In the Money" when the strike price is below the underlying forward price for a call and above the underlying price for a put.

Out of the Money: An option is "Out of the Money" when the strike price is above the underlying forward price for a call and below the underlying price for a put.

Types of Options:

Call: The holder has the right, but not the obligation to purchase the underlying asset at the strike price.

Put: The holder has the right, but not the obligation to sell the underlying asset at the strike price.

Example: Exporter with USD based sales wants to protect receivables against a CAD rally, purchases a CAD Call (USD Put), at a predetermined strike price, expiry and premium. Importer with USD expenses wants to protect payables against a weakening CAD, sells a CAD Call (USD Put), at a predetermined strike price, expiry and premium.

Settlement:

The protection lasts until the expiry date and settlement takes place one business day following exercise.

Advantages

- Complete protection against adverse currency moves.
- Complete gains from beneficial moves.

Disadvantages

- A premium has to be paid.

E. ZERO COST COLLARS

Definition:

A zero cost collar consists of the simultaneous purchase of one option and sale of another at different strikes, both for the same amount, for the same time frame. In this way complete protection against adverse currency moves beyond a certain level is paid for by giving up gains beyond a second (more favorable) rate.

Market Conventions & Language:

Zero Cost Collars are also called Risk Reversals, Range Forwards, Tunnels, Caps and Floors.

Example:

Exporter with USD based sales wants to protect receivables against a CAD rally, purchases a CAD Call (USD Put) and sells a CAD Put (USD Call) for the same expiry date and for the same amount, at "zero cost". Importer with USD expenses wants to protect payables against a weakening CAD, sells a CAD Call (USD Put) and buys a Cad Put (USD Call) for the same expiry and for the same amount, at "zero cost".

Settlement:

The protection lasts until the expiry date and settlement takes place one business day following exercise.

Advantages

- Complete protection against adverse currency moves beyond the floor level.
- Zero transaction cost.
- Complete gains from beneficial moves up to a limit.

The zero cost collar hedging strategy

The Ceylon Petroleum Corporation got into a ground breaking agreement with the Standard Chartered Bank earlier this year. The agreement was to provide upside price protection to the CPC from escalating crude oil price in a spot market. This agreement was a trailblazer initiative that introduced the concept of commodity hedging using Derivative instruments for the first time in Sri Lanka. By introducing hedging, the CPC created a precedent in Sri Lanka. However, despite having a hedge model in place to provide upside price protection the CPC had to increase the retail fuel prices in the recent months. Rationally, these recent price increases from a laymen's analysis, potentially disputes and questions the very validity of the hedging process.

Given due regards to the recent price revision, this article intends to discuss the validity of commodity hedging as it would apply as a measure introduced to guarantee price and provide protection in a volatile market.

Validity of the Price Guarantee Mechanism:

The process of seeking price protection in a volatile spot market by taking an opposite position in the Derivatives market is known as Hedging. Hedging is an integral part of any operation that is sensitive to adverse movement in interest rates, foreign exchange rates, commodity prices (Agricultural / energy) and precious metal prices. In recent years, globally, all energy trading operations — oil producers, refineries, airlines — given the high oil prices introduced hedging as a measure to insulate from adverse commodity price movements/volatility.

Financial instruments referred to as Derivatives facilitate the hedging process. Derivative instruments can be exchange traded or that are traded over the counter between two counter parties. Futures and Options are Exchange traded while Over the Counter (OTC) Derivatives are customized trades. For the most part,

Success of a hedge model is contingent upon the selection of the - *Correct Instrument (Futures, Options, and SWAPS)

*Strategy (Asian Option, Average Price Commodity SWAP).This article intends to take a closer look at the Zero Cost Collar strategy used by Standard Charted Bank to provide a price protection to the Ceylon Petroleum Corporation.

What is a Zero Cost Collar?

"Zero Cost Collar" or a "Costless Collar" is an Option trading strategy that is used in the short term to seek protection from short term market volatility forecasts.

Transaction Basics: A Zero Cost Collar strategy combines the sale of a Put Option and the purchase of a Call Option. Put Option gives the holder the right to sell the underlying product ie. commodity at a strike price(capped price) that is pre determined. Call Option gives the holder the right to buy the underlying product at the strike price that is pre determined. In a situation where the protection seeker wants protection from increasing spot market prices, as illustrated above the Option premium collected by the sale of the Put Option with a lower strike price (capped sale price) will fund the purchase of a Call Option with a higher strike price(capped purchase price). For the most part, due to the inverse relationship between the strike price and the Option premium with a wide spread between the Put Option and the Call Option, the limited proceeds from the sale of the Put Option will only fund a Call Option with a relatively higher purchase price of the underlying commodity thereby compromising the potential benefits.

Zero Cost Collar, essentially creates a position of a "Synthetic Futures". Futures contracts "locks & guarantees" the purchase / sale price for forward delivery. Extreme downside participation is given up for partial benefits from upside participation. Effectively, the Zero Cost Collar will pay off once the spot market price exceeds the Call Option strike price (=call capped price). The Put Option will expire worthless. However, if the spot market price drops below the Put Option Strike price (=put caped price) the Zero Cost Collar strategy will not allow any participation in the down side.

The above is an illustration of a Zero Cost Collar strategy. When the spot market price moves over and above the strike price of the Call Option, the Call Option will be exercised and the difference between the strike price and market price will be received by the Zero Cost Collar buyer. Meanwhile, if the spot market price is below the strike price of the Put Option, the Zero Cost Collar buyer cannot participate in the lower spot market price. As long as the spot market price moves between the Put option strike price and the Call Option strike price, there will be no pay backs. However, the moment, the spot market price moves beyond the Call Option strike price, the Call Option will pay back.

Over a long period of time, the sport market prices can move significantly. The price pendulum can move from one extreme to the other. Given the implied volatility of the spot market price movement, Zero Cost Collar is a strategy that will be effective only on the short term. If used on a long term basis, the benefits will be minimal since the strategy effectively creates a synthetic futures position due to the put option locking in the future delivery price even when the spot market price drops below the Put Option strike price.

There is a trade of in any situation. It is said that you get what you pay for. Zero Cost Collar is a protection seeking strategy virtually for free. This is akin to getting an auto insurance policy free without any premium payments. But how good is that policy going to be? Obviously, it will provide the policy holder the bear minimum. By the same token, a Zero Cost Collar while being a relatively cost effective process of seeking limited upside protection gives up the potential to participate in the downside price movement. Given the above matrix of the Zero Cost Collar structure, the better alternative to the Zero Cost Collar is a basic Call Option strategy that will provide upside protection for the upfront payment of a premium.

This strategy will allow the Call Option holder to participate in the downside of the market price movement. The Option premium is an investment and not be seen as an expense. As long as the Option Premium is perceived as an expense, potential benefits of the hedge will be compromised by not getting into hedging and seeking a price protection.

I. FORWARD CONTRACT

- Cash market transaction in which a seller agrees to deliver a specific cash commodity to a buyer at some point in the future. Unlike futures contracts (which occur through a clearing firm), cash forward contracts are privately negotiated and are not standardized. Further, the two parties must bear each other's credit risk, which is not the case with a futures contract. Also, since the contracts are not exchange traded, there is no marking to market requirement, which allows a buyer to avoid almost all capital outflow initially (though some counterparties might set collateral requirements). Given the lack of standardization in these contracts, there is very little scope for a secondary market in forwards. The price specified in a cash forward contract for a specific commodity. The forward price makes the forward contract have no value when the contract is written. However, if the value of the underlying commodity changes, the value of the forward contract becomes positive or negative, depending on the position held. Forwards are priced in a manner similar to futures. Like in the case of a futures contract, the first step in pricing a forward is to add the spot price to the cost of carry (interest forgone, convenience yield, storage costs and interest/dividend received on the underlying). Unlike a futures contract though, the price may also include a premium for counterparty credit risk, and the fact that there is not daily marking to market process to minimize default risk. If there is no allowance for these credit risks, then the forward price will equal the futures price.

A forward contract—or forward—is an OTC derivative. In its simplest form, it is a trade that is agreed to at one point in time but will take place at some later time. For example, two parties might agree today to exchange 500,000 barrels of crude oil for USD 42.08 a barrel three months from today.

A forward contract is specified with four variables:

- The underlier,
- The notional amount *n*,
- The **delivery price** *k*, and
- The settlement date on which the underlier and payment will be exchanged.

In our example, oil is the underlier. The notional amount is 500,000 barrels. The delivery price is USD 42 per barrel. The settlement date is the actual date three months from now when the oil will be delivered in exchange for a total payment of USD 21.04MM.

The party who receives the underlier is said to be long the forward. The other party is short.

At settlement, the forward has a market value given by

$$n(s - k)$$

where s is the spot price of the underlier at settlement. This formula derives from the fact that, at settlement, the long party is paying a delivery price k for an underlier then trading at price s. The difference between those two prices, multiplied by the notional amount, is the market value of the forward.

Torwards have linear payoffs. This is depicted in Exhibit 1. Compare with the options payoffs depicted in the article *options spreads*.

Payoff of a Long or Short Forward

Exhibit 1

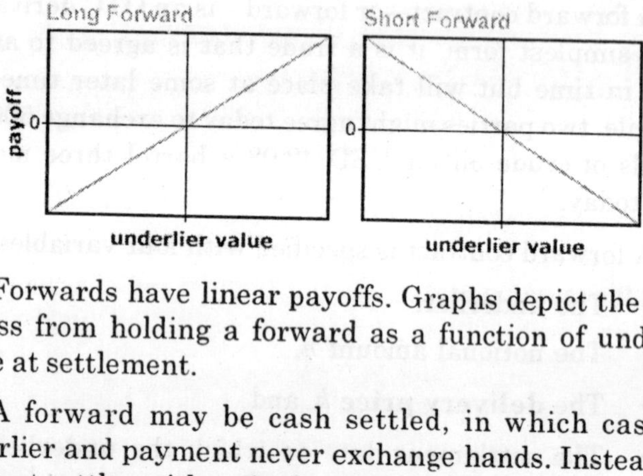

Forwards have linear payoffs. Graphs depict the profit or loss from holding a forward as a function of underlier value at settlement.

A forward may be cash settled, in which case the underlier and payment never exchange hands. Instead, the contract settles with a single payment for the market value of the forward at settlement, as given by If the market value is positive, the short party pays the long party. If it is negative, the long party pays the short party.

Suppose the forward in our oil example were cash-settled. On the settlement date three months from today, no oil would change hands, and there would be no payment of

USD 21.04MM. If the spot price at settlement were, say, USD 47.36, then the forward would settle with a single payment of made by the short party to the long party.

$$500{,}000(47.36 - 42.08) = \text{USD } 2.64\text{MM}$$

Forward are generally quoted as delivery prices, which are called forward prices. Forward prices fluctuate with market conditions. When a forward is entered into, the contract's delivery price is set equal to the quoted forward price. That delivery price then remains fixed until the forward settles. For example, a dealer might quote a three-month oil forward at 41.25/41.29. Those are the bid and offer forward prices. If a counterparty accepts the offer price for 500,000 barrels, then the delivery price on that contract will be USD 41.29.

Issues such as the time value of money, short-term supply and demand, market expectations of future spot prices and cash-and-carry arbitrage tend to make forward prices diverge from spot prices, but relevant factors vary from one market to the next. A graph of forward prices for different maturities is called a forward curve. Exhibit 2 shows the forward curve for West Texas intermediate crude oil on September 15, 2005.

Forward Curve for WTI Crude

Exhibit 2

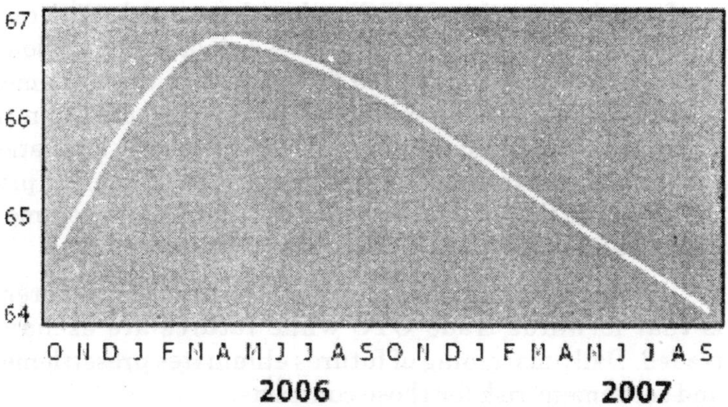

Forward curve for West Texas intermediate (WTI) crude oil on September 15, 2005. Prices are USD per barrel.

Forwards are a convenient vehicle for hedging or speculation. For example, an airline can conveniently hedge its fuel costs by purchasing jet fuel several months forward. The hedge eliminates price exposure, and it doesn't require an initial outlay of funds to purchase the fuel. The airline is hedged without having to take delivery of or store the jet fuel until it is needed. It doesn't even have to enter into the forward with the ultimate supplier of the jet fuel. If the forward is cash settled, the hedge can be put on with any counterparty.

Prior to settlement, a forward has a market value given by

$$dn(f - k)$$

where f is the current forward price and d is the discount factor. Returning to our oil example, suppose it is now a month until the contract settles, one-month Libor is 2.18, and the one-month forward price for oil is USD 45.16. Then and the forward has market value

$$(.9981)\ 500{,}000\ (45.16 - 42.08) = \text{USD } 1.54\text{MM}$$

There are active forward markets on a variety of commodity, energy and financial underliers. These include forward markets for coffee, cocoa, cotton, natural gas, oil and electricity. The largest forward market is the interbank foreign exchange forward market. Forward rate agreements (FRAs) are cash-settled forwards on short-term loans. Forwards entail market risk, presettlement risk and settlement risk. With cash-settled forwards, there can also be a risk of manipulation of the underlier price index used for calculating the settlement value. This has been a problem in energy markets when the paper market dwarfed the physical market. In such a situation, a small physical transaction performed at an off-market price could impact the settlement value of a far greater volume of paper transactions.

Forwards are similar to futures. The primarily difference is that forwards trade OTC while futures are exchange traded. Daily margining of futures eliminates presettlement and settlement risk for those contracts.

SECTION C

BANKING OBJECTIVE QUESTIONS WITH SOLUTIONS

19

BANKING OBJECTIVE QUESTIONS

I. CURRENT RATES

A. Latest Rates

Bank Rate :6.0% Repo Rate –6.25% Reverse Repo rate –5.25%

CRR 6.0% SLR -25.0%

B. Exchange rates (RBI reference Ratio)

INR / 1 USD	: 45.2200
INR / 1 Euro	: 59.9900
INR / 100 Japanese YEN	: 54.0300
INR / 1 Pound Sterling	: 71.4114

C. Lending / deposit rates

Base Rate	: 7.50%-8.00%
Savings Bank Rate	: 3.5%
Savings Bank Rate	: 3.5%
Deposit Rate	: 7.00%-8.00%

II. SAMPLE TEST

Q1. Star Series of notes relate to:

a currency notes of various denominations

b mutilated notes/ defective priting

c bank notes of various denomination

d counterfeit or fake notes

Q2. *Which of* the following cheques will be paid by the paying bank, if otherwise in order:

a cheque dated Jan 12, 2010, presented for payment on Mar 22, 2010. It is signed by agent who died on Feb 28, 2010

b cheque dated Jan 12, 2010signed by Secy. of a Club authorized to sign cheque appointed on Jan 15, 2010.

c Cheque dated Dec 26, 2009signed by the agent and presented on Jan 25, 2009 when bank has information about the death of the account holder.

d Cheque dated 20 November, 2009 presented for payment on Nov 30, 2009.

Q3. With regard to sale and purchase of NPA by banks which of the following is correct:

a selling bank can sell an NPA which is at least 15 months' NPA

b selling bank can sell an NPA on without recourse basis

c asset classification with the buyer bank shall be standard for one year

d buyer bank can sell the NPA after retaining it for 24 months

Q4. Which of the following is not correct in the following cases:

a Spend now and pay later refers to credit cards

b hot listing refers to restrictions put on use of a lost credit card

c point of sale refers to merchant establishments that provide service against credit card

d debit cards relate to loans and credit cards relate to deposit accounts

Q5 Which of the following relationship between bank and customer is not correct:

a in case of pledge – pawnee and pawner

b in case of locker – lessor and lessee

c in case of garnishee order receipt – debtor and creditor

d in case of currency chest with RBI – bailor and bailee

Q6. A firm has networking capital of Rs.90000. With its current ratio at 3:1, what is the amount of current assets:

a Rs.135000 b Rs.90000

c Rs.45000 d Rs.180000

Q7. A bill of exchange is drawn by M/s Kasturi Lal and Sons on M/s Shiva Traders in consideration of purchase of goods, Mr. Shayam Kumar being its payee. Shayam Kumar endorsed the bill in favour of Mr. Shanti Prakash who had endorsed it in blank. It is stolen by Mr. Sudhir Phatke, an employee of Shanti Prakash and delivered to M/s Dyal Traders for value, but it is dishonoured on presentation for payment. From whom can M/s Dyal Traders recover the amount on the bill?

a From Mr. Shanti Prakash b From M/s Shiva Traders

c From M/s Kasturi Lal & Sons

d From Shyam Kumar

e From all the above

Q8. New Delhi branch of Modern Bank issued a fixed deposit of Rs.3 lac for 5 years in the name of Mr. S Subramaniam who raises a loan of Rs.50000 against the FDR with a view to meet exigencies at a later stage. He comes for addition of the name of his son, as he is not keeping good health for few months.

a the request of the depositor will be accepted being a genuine reason b the request will be accepted since the addition is for the his son's name

c the request will be accepted since the FDR is to mature after long time

d the request cannot be accepted till the loan is outstanding

e any of the above

Q9. A Hindu soldier gives an oral will while he is fighting on Indo-Pak border. Such wills are called:

a oral will b invalid will

c privileged will d unprivileged will

e a and c

Q10. A month back the dollar-rupee rate was Rs.39.90 per dollar. Now it is Rs.40.10 per dollar. Who among the following is the gainer:

a who exports b who imports

c who has to make outward remittance

d who moves for a visit abroad

e none of the above

Q11 FILL IN THE BLANKS

(a) Commercial banks have implemented Basle II wef _ ___/____/ 2010_. Extension is upto_____.

(b) Capital Adequacy Ratio = Capital Funds / _______x100

(c) Tier II of the Capital Funds Contains _______, _______

(d) Pillar II of Basle Accord Contains _____Role

(e) Indian Parliament Passed __________2002 for prevention of Money Laundering

(f) Name any 5 Retail Banking Products ________, ____________, ____________, ____________,

(g) An FD payable to Either of Survivor for Rs 25,000 is in name of A & B.Receipt is lost and a duplicate is issued on the basis of indemnity. Later A Comes with Original FD on date of maturity. Will the bank Pay —YES // NO

(h) CRR refers to ______________and refers minimum cash to be kept with _________by Banks. At present CRR is _________

(i) A nomination can be accepted in favour of a Minor —YES / NO

Q12 Name Five Functions of Reserve bank Of India

(a) ______________________________

(b) ______________________________

(c) ______________________________

(d) ______________________________

(e) ______________________________

Q13 Expand the following terms :

(a) ALCO ______________________________

(b) BIFR ______________________________

(c) CAMELS ______________________________

(d) CAR ______________________________

(e) CP ______________________________

Q14 Tick the Correct Answer

(i) Transferable L/c can be transferred

(a) Any no. of times (b) Only 2 times

(c) 5 Times (d) Only Once

(ii) Who among the following would be natural guardian of a Hindu Minor widow

(a) Her mother (b) Her father

(c) Her father in law

(d) her Mother in law if father in law also expired

(iii) A banker shouldnot pay the Cheques drawn by a customer who has been sent to jail for

(a) rape (b) Criminal Liabilty

(c) Insolvency (d) Both a and b

(iv) Garnishee Order is in the name of the partner in firm. It will

(a) Apply to all Partners

(b) Apply to Firm's account

(c) Not apply to Firm's Account

(d) None of the above

(v) Natural Guardian of an adopted Minor will be

(a) adoptive father (b) _Real Father

(c) As declared by the Court (d) a or c

(vi) What is the timeperiod during which the cheque can be presented u/s138 ofNI Act –

(a) Before the Bank fails

(b) Before the drawer makes stop Payment of Cheque

(c) During the validity of the Cheque

(d) Maximum within 6 months of date of issue

(e) c and d

Q15 Fill in the Blanks

(i) Instruments of Monetary Control at RBI include ____________, ____________, ____________,

(ii) The Reserve Bank of India was established on ____________________.

(iii) CACS Foreign Banks ______________________

(iv) New Banks and Branch licensing is under_____Act _____.

(v) Development Banking is financing _______assessed for _____and involves _______,DCF,_________NPV

(vi) Failure to maintain SLR by Bank will attract penalty interest from RBI __ percent p.a above Bank rate for that day on the shortfall or _percent above bank Rate for the Concerned days of default on the shortfall

(vii) Foreign L/Cs are subject to UCP _________ issued by _________

(viii) As per Banking regulation act 1949 Banking defines as ________for Lending or_____repayable on ______

(ix) Name three functions of Commercial banking

(x) Differentiate between Pledge and Hypothecation

(xi) Three Criteria for Banks to enter Insurance sector are –minimum Net worth Rs——Cr,_______ _____,___________________________

(xii) FEMA 2000

(a) Replacement of____________Act

(b) Consists of_________Articles

(c) Describes New Definition of Spouse as ______________which is at par with NRI

(d) What is Capital Account Transactions________ __________.

(xiii) Amounts eligible to take Foreign Exchange

(a) For Medical, Hospitalization, Immigration, Real Estate buying,Education_______________ USD ___________

(b) For receiving Gifts from NRI in USD ______ and for sending Gifts abroad USD - ______

(c) Under BTQ as Tourist permitted to carry USD - ____________ per calendar year provided to & fro Air tickets are there and journey to Commence within ________ days

(d) Permitted to carry coins and keep them for numismatic purposes – USD ______

(xiv) ____ Banks were nationalized on 19th July 1969 and -______ banks nationalized on 15th April 1980.

(xii) Expand

(a) EFT ____________________

(b) PMS ____________________

(c) ATM ____________________

(d) BPLR __________

(e) Prevailing bank rate is ______________, ____________

III.(i) A. D ____________________

(ii) DRI____________________

(iii) CRAR____________________-

(iv) LDB ____________________

(v) NOF____________________

(vi) PTLR____________________

(vii) ROA____________________

(viii) ROANW ____________________

(ix) YTM ____________________

(x) CHIPS ____________________

(xi) SWIFT ____________________

(xii) Pillar I, Pillar II,Pillar III in Basle II Norms are ____________________, __________, ________

(xiii) CD ____________________

Analyse the problems Answers Given

1. Interest in NPA account will be recognized as income after : : it becomes due and received
2. A is having SB account as well as Overdraft Account with debit balance with the bank. Bank will adjust the account after using _____. : right of set off
3. X is having loan account duly guaranteed by Mr. & Mrs. Y. They are having a an FDR for Rs.40,000/- with maturity value of Rs.57010/-. X defaulted in repayment of Loan and bank on maturity adjusted the loan account of X with the maturity value of FDR and credited the balance to SB Mr. Y and Mrs.Y. Mr. and Mrs.Y objected to this adjustment since the loan is time barred. : bank had right of set off which it has correctly used (presuming that notice had been given doing so
4. XYZ and ABC are two firms having the same partners in both the partnership firms. One firm is having debit balance and other firm is having credit balance in their accounts. Whether bank can exercise right of set off in this case. : partners being same, this can be done
5. A solicitor is having two accounts with the bank. One in personal name and other in clients name. One Cheque is presented in 'clearing' in clients account. In the meantime, garnishi order is served on the solicitors' account. Whether Bank will pay this cheque presented in the clearing. : cheque will be paid, since it relates to client account, which the solicitor has opened in fiduciary capacity.
6. Mr. D is having one overdraft account with us. He is also having three other accounts with us, (namely) his personal SB Account, Joint account with his wife and one u/gship account with his son. Bank can use right of set off in which of these accounts. : right available in personal SB account
7. Mr. Seth is having C/A with us. He has appointed his son 16 years of age, as his agent.Can the minor operate this account after this? : since he is agent, be can operate it

8. A minor 16 years of age, is having an FDR of Rs.10000 with the bank. He requested for before-maturity payment. Can bank allow before maturity payment. : bank can accept the request of the minor

9. In case a minor is appointed as a nominee for a term deposit and death of the depositor takes place: payment can be obtained by the guardian of the minor on his behalf

10. After the death of locker holder his daughter comes to the bank with the key to operate the account. What is the course of action that will be suggested by the bank? : get a letter of administration

11. Vehicle loan financed by banks are registered with RTA with the sole objective of : : Getting the charge in favour of the bank so that borrower can not sell the vehicle without permission of the bank.

12. A company is having stock of Rs.20 Lacs stored at its godown. It is insured for Rs. 10 Lacs. Co. has sent stocks for Rs.4 Lacs for processing at some distant place where it gets destroyed at the place of processing by fire. What amount of claim will be admissible. : nil

13. Pari passu charge in case of a consortium advance by banks to a big borrower means which of the following:: each bank will have pro-rata charge on the security in the ratio of their outstanding within the limits approved by the consortium

14. A endorsed a cheque in favour of B and B endorsed it to C who just signs the cheque. The cheque is stolen by D, who endorsed the cheque in favour of Ashok (an old creditor of the D) for valid consideration. Ashok took the payment of the cheque. In this case Ashok is liable to whom: : he is not liable to any one since he is holder in due course

15. Corporate Bank receives a cheque written in three different inks and three handwritings. : the cheque will be paid

16. A firm had a current ratio of 2:1 and its current liabilities at Rs.15 lac. What will be the amount of net working capital of the firm? : Rs.15 lac

17. How many working directors are there with a Nationalised Bank : 2

18. LC where the packing credit can be allowed to exporter: Red Clause

19. How many times a transferable LC can be transferred: once

20. Where on the strength of one LC another LC can be established

21. Amount ceiling for reporting under KYC : Rs.10 lac summation

22. Cheque written in different scripts (say Gujarati and English) : Valid. It will be paid

23. In Hypothecation, with whom is the possession or ownership : Borrower

24. Model Bank issued an FDR in the name of Mr. X and his wife W. Mrs W comes to the bank and request for premature payment to meet the expenses on treatment of Mr. X who is admitted to one hospital and cannot sign, because of fractured hands: payment can be made after verifying the facts and after obtain thumb impression of Mr. X in the hospital, witnessed by the attending Doctor

25. Mr. X and Y are having a joint account in which they have nominated Mr. A. On death of Mr. X, Mr A approaches the bank for payment : being nominee, payment would be made to A payment would be made to Y and legal heirs of X

26. Stop payment instruction received from a Coparcener for a cheque issued by Karta : Bank will not accept

27. Mr. Banerjee, a permanent resident of Kolkata raises a loan of Rs.10 from the bank in Delhi. He has a house in

Mumbai and another in Chennai. To secure the loan, he offers equitable mortgage of house in Mumbai. The mortgage can be created (a) in Kolkata only being is permanent residence (b) in Chennai or Mumbai only being presidential towns (c) in Delhi being National Capital (d) Chennai, Mumbai or Kolkata and if Delhi is notified town, in Delhi also:

(a) a, b and d is correct (b) a, b and c correct

(c) a to d all correct (d) only d is correct

28. One rupee note bears the signatures of:

a: Governor RBI.

b: Secy. Ministry of Finance

c: Prime Minister of India

d: Finance Minister. e President of India

29. There is an FDR of A and B but A dies before its maturity. B also dies one week after his death. FD amount is payable to:

a: Legal heirs of A b: Legal heirs of B

c: Legal heirs of A and B

d: legal heirs of the person who died later e None of the above.

30. Interest and principal can be repatriated by an NRI, in the following accounts ?

a FCNR b NRE

c EEFC d a & b

e all the above

20

ANSWERS

1. (b)
2.
3. (d)
4. (d)
5. (d)
6. (a)

Current Assets – Current Liabilities = Net Worth

AC/CL = 3: 1 3CL = CA.

3CL – CL = 90,000 ∴ CA = 90,000 + 45000

2CL = 90000 = ! 35,000

CL = 45000

7. (e)
8. (d)
9. (c)
10. (a)
11. (a) 31 / 3 / 2010
    (b) Risk Weighted Average
    (c) Undisclosed income + Revaluation Reserves + Provisions + Hybrid Debt + Subordinated Debt (Long team unsecured loans)

(d) Supervisory

(e) POMLA

(f) Educational Loan, SME Loans, Housing Loan, Vehicle Loan, Consumer Loans, Loans to Boutiques/ working women.

(g) No

(h) Cash Reserve Ratio, RBI, 6.0

(i) No

(d) o

12. 1. Ussue Notes & coins (Except are Rupee Note)
    2. Custuction of foreign Currency
    3. Regulator of the banks
    4. Banker's to the Government and Banker's to the Banks.
    5. Credit controller

13. (a) Asset Liability Committee
    (b) Board for Industrial Financial Reconstruction
    (c) Capital Adequacy, Management effectiveness, Earnings, Liquidity, Systems and Control
    (d) Capital Adequacy Ratio
    (e) Commercial Paper

14. (i) d
    (ii) c
    (iii) c
    (iv) c
    (v) a
    (vi) e

15. (i) CRR, SLR, Repo rate, Reverse Rapo rate
    (ii) 1st April 1935

(iii) Capital Adequacy, Asset Quality, Compliances System and Controla

(iv) Banking Regulation Act, 1949

(v) Agriculture, IRR, ARR

(vi) 3%, 5%

(vii) 600, International Chamber of Commerce (ICC)

(viii) Accepted, Borraving, Demano

(ix) 1. Receiving deposits

2. Receiving Loans

3. Discounting Bill of Exchange, issuing Letter of Credit and Bank Guarantee

(x) Pledge and Hypothecation (Pg 76 of Toor)

(xi) 500 cr, Capital Adequacy 10% Three Years Continous Profit, Good track record of the Subsidiaries

(xii) (a) FEMA

(b) 49

(c) PIO (Person of Indian Region)

(d) Change Asset and Liabilities as laid in schedule I ând schedule II of FEMA

(xii) (a) 1 Lakh USD per Calendar Year 2000.

(b) 2 Lakh 50 thousand, 5,000 (as Inividual)

(c) 3000 currency notes and USD 7000 traveller cheque per person per calendar Year

(d) No Limit

(xiv) 14, 7

(xv) (a) Electronic Fund Transfer

(b) Portfolio management Scheme

(c) Automated Teller Machine

(d) Benchmark Prime Lending Rate

21

COMMITTEEES IN BANKING

1. VERMA COMMITTEEE ON WEAK BANKS-SOLVENCY, EARNING CAPACITY AND PROFIT
2. NARSIMHAN COMMITTEE -1991 –1ST AND 2ND — REDUCTION OF SLR & CRR IN PHASED MANNER, INTEREST RATE DEREGULATION, CAPITAL ADEQUACY, TRANSPARENCY, RESTRUCTURING OF THE BANKS
3. DR GADGIL –AGRICULTURAL FINANCE
4. P.L. TANDON- FOLLOW UP OF THE BANK CREDIT
5. K.B. CHORE REVIEW OF CASH CREDIT SYSTEM
6. DAMLE COMMITTEE ——MICR INTRODUCTION
7. RANGARAJAN COMMITTEE—COMPUTERISATION IN BANKS/ BANK MECHANISATION
8. MARATHE COMMIITTEE –CREDIT AUTHORIZATION SCHEME –FAST TRACK
9. GS PATEL ——ORGANISATION & MANAGEMENT OF STOCK EXCHANGES
10. KÁLYANSUNDARAM COMMITTEE —— FACTORING SERVICES
11. GOIPORIA COMMITTEE ——CUSTOMER SERVICE
12. DAVE COMMITTEE —— MUTUAL FUNDS

13. RAJA CHELLIAH ———TAX REFORMS
14. GHOSH COMMITTEE – FRAUDS & MALPRACTISES IN BANKS
15. SHETTY COMMIITTEE ——– CONSORTIUM BANKING
16. JILANI COMMITTEE — INSPECTION IN BANKS
17. SS TARAPORE COMMITTTEE – CONVERTABILITY OF INDIAN RUPEE
18. MS VERMA COMMITTEE — MEASURES OF WEAK BANKS
19. SS KOHLI COMMITEEE — WILLFUL DEFAULTERS
20. LAKSHMI NARAYANAN COMMITTEE — CONSORTIUM BANKING

22

ABBREVIATIONS IN INDIAN BANKING

AD	Authorized Dealer
ADB	Asian Development Bank
ADR	American Depository Receipt
AFS	Annual Financial Statement
AGM	Annual General Meeting
ASSOCHAM	Associated Chambers of Commerce and Industry of India
ATM	Automated Teller Machine
BIS	Bank for International Settlements
BoP	Balance of Payments
BSCS	Basel Committee on Banking Supervision
BSR	Basic Statistical Returns
CAD	Capital Account Deficit
CC	Cash Credit
CD	Certificate of Deposit
CD	Ratio Credit Deposit Ratio
CP	Commercial Paper
CPI	Consumer Price Index
CRAR	Capital to Risk Weighted Asset Ratio

CRR	Cash Reserve Ratio
DD	Demand Draft
DICGC	Deposit Insurance and Credit Guarantee Corporation of India
DRI	Differntial Rate of Interest Scheme
ECS	Electronic Clearing Scheme
EEFC	Exchange Earners Foreign Currency
FDI	Foreign Direct Investment
FII	Foreign Institutional Investor
FIMMDA	Fixed Income Market and Derivatives Association of India
FRN	Floating Rate Note
G-Sec	Government Securities
ICICI	Industrial Credit and Investment Corporation of India
ISDA	International Swaps and Derivative Association
ISO	International Standards Organization
KVIC	Khadi & Village Industries Corporation
LAF	Liquidity Adjustment Facility
M1	Narrow Money
M3	Broad Money
MA	Moving Average
MT	Mail Transfer
MTM	Mark-To-Market
OD	Over Draft
OLTAS	OnLine Tax Accounting System
OMO	Open Market Operations
RDBMS	Relational Database Management System

RFC	Residents Foreign Currency
RLA	Recoveries of Loans & Advances
RoCs	Registrars of Companies
RWA	Risk Weighted Asset
SDR	Special Drawing Right
SEBI	Securities and Exchange Board of India
SGL	Subsidiary General Ledger
SHGs	Self-Help Groups
SLR	Statutory Liquidity Ratio
SRWTO	Small road & Water Transport Operators (Retail Banking)
TBs	Treasury Bills
TT	Telegraphic Transfer
VC	Venture Capital
YTM	Yield to Maturity

23

Banking Questions with Answers

- When Ombudsman's award is accepted by the customer, the bank is to implement the award within : 30 days.
- Real Time Gross settlement system takes care of which risk : Systemic risk and settlement risk
- Under SARFAESI Act 2002 the banks give notice for payment of due amount to the borrower / owner of charged assets within ___ days, otherwise action will be initiated u/s 13(2) of the Act : 60 days
- The minimum & maximum period of certificate of deposit is : 7 days, 12 months
- Banks print cheque books having similar particulars. The format of cheque is prescribed by which Act : It is a practice
- Which crossing takes away the feature of assumption of defective free title available to the transferee : Not negotiable
- Bearer uncrossed cheque can be paid to whom : To the bearer
- What is NOSTRO: A bank's account abroad with another bank
- On, other than a negotiable instrument, what is the time period for payment of stamp duty, if the document is executed outside India : 3 months
- FCNR (B) deposit can be accepted by banks in ____ currencies : 6
- Statutory Liquidity Ratio provisions for banks are as per Section _____ of _____ : 24, Banking Regulation Act 1949

- An NRI can open a joint account with a resident in case of ___ accounts : Non-resident Ordinary.
- What type of charge is applicable on loan against term deposits in a bank : Assignment
- Garnishee Order is not applicable on : Un-used cash credit or overdraft limit
- The facility of nomination is not available to Trust account because it is _____ account : Non-individual
- A person wants to open an account which his wife should be able to operate only after his death. What type of account he should open : Former or survivor
- In case of a jointly operated joint account, the nominee can obtain payment, when : none of the account holder is alive
- The long term liability to tangible net worth ratio implies: Long term solvency of the firm or capacity of the firm to pay long term debt.
- Current ratio implies : Capacity of the firm to pay current liabilities.
- Working capital requirement of a firm is required to be met through : Short term sources and surplus of long term sources over long term uses
- Star series notes relate to : Defective notes
- Who cannot become a partner as per Supreme Court judgement : HUF
- A company wants to electronically pay the dividend to large no. of its shareholders, which include small amounts also : Electronic Clearing Services – Credit (ECS-Credit)
- The terms used for hiding money to avoid tax is : Money laundering
- A cheque is written in different hand-writings and different inks : It will be paid
- Opening of non-resident accounts by _____ has been allowed by RBI : RRBs

- Bailment of goods by a person to another person, to secure a loan is called : Pledge
- When mortgage is created by a person by deposit of title deed orally, it is called ____ mortgage : Equitable
- Which crossing is not a general crossing : When name of bank is written within or without parallel lines.
- Buy now and pay later is the facility available under : Credit card
- A financial statement that provides information regarding where the funds have come and where these have been used, is called : Funds flow statement
- Who can open NRE account : NRI
- A mandate holder for a current account has died and a cheque signed by him is presented for payment after his death : The cheque shall be paid, if not dated subsequent to date of death or prior to the date of mandate.
- The true owner of a cheque has been deprived his right by collection of the cheque for a different person. This is called : Conversion
- A bank branch receives a counterfeit note of Rs.1000, which customer wants back. What the bank should do : To be impounded and not to be returned in any circumstances.
- Banks provide term loans and deferred payment guarantee to finance capital assets like plant and machinery. What is the difference between these two : Outlay of funds.
- Islamic banking has the features of : Conservative banking
- Which among the Muslims, Christians, Budhists & Jains is not a minority community : Jain
- For the purpose of creation of equitable mortgage, the place for deposit of the title deed is notified by : State Govt.

- For FCNR (B) deposits, the exchange risk is born by : Bank, accepting such deposit.
- As per recent RBI/Govt. guidelines, pensioners can open account jointly with: with spouse, to be operated as either or survivor.
- Housing loan is part of the priority sector advance, with a maximum amount of : Rs.20 lac.
- Which of the following forms will be used for allowing exemption to a depositor aged 61 years : Form 15 G
- A cheque signed by an agent is presented for payment, after his death. What will the paying bank do : Cheque will be paid in normal course if it is not dated subsequent to date of his death.
- NRE term deposit can be accepted by banks for a period of: 1 to 3 years.

: Financial inclusion

- Customer day is observed by banks on ____ th of the month : 15
- Minimum no. of days for which term deposit can be made by banks : 7 days
- A retail trader in other than essential goods is financed by the bank. What is the maximum amount of such loan that can be classified under priority sector : Rs.20 lac.
- What type of bench mark is used for lending in banks "Base rate
- The format of cheque is prescribed in which Act : It is only a practice.
- The amount in a cheque is written differently in words and figures and amount written in words is higher of the two : Amount written in words will be paid.
- While paying a bearer cheque, signatures are obtained on the back side of the cheque. Why ? : As evidence of payment
- Bank note which is misprinted by RBI is replaced by issuing a ________ note : Star series

- Current ratio indicates : Capacity of a firm to meet it current liabilities.
- What is the right of nominee in case of term deposit that has not matured : To obtain premature payment and not raise loan against the security of such term deposit
- Preshipment credit is available in which type of letter of credit : Red clause
- The quarterly financial results of companies and banks are to be declared / published under directions provided by : SEBI
- RBI injects liquidity through : Repo
- Collateral security in case of PMRY advances is exempt up to : Loan of Rs.5 lac in case of industry projects per borrowal account and Rs.2 lac for business/servicing per borrower.
- Legal status of nominee is that of a : Trustee for legal heirs
- M, a minor admitted for benefits in a firm wants to withdraw from the firm on attaining majority. How much time is available to him to do so : 6 months from date of majority or 6 months from date of information to him that he was admitted for benefits, whichever is later.
- Who cannot be a partners (a) HUF (b) illiterate (c) Blind person (d) company : HUF
- Money to be deposited by A in the account of B. A has informed that B has become insane : can be deposited with consent of the family members (i.e. guardian)
- Mortgagee enjoys the income of the mortgaged property in case of which mortgage : Usufructuary
- Hypothecation becomes pledge : when goods are given for possession to the bank, by the borrower.
- There is excess cash with the cashier while closing the cash balance in the evening. It is to be deposited in : Sundries account (credit balance).

- Which document is required to be attested (witnessed) (a) mortgage deed (b) pledge agreement (c) Hypothecation agreement : Mortgage deed
- In India is (a) above 40000 (b) above 50000 (c) above 60000 (d) above 70000 : Above 70000
- A, B and C want to open a joint account with the provision that after death of any of them, the money should not be paid to any legal heir, what mode of operation should be opened : Either or any of them
- ECB can be raised under automatic approval by (a) companies (b) firms : Companies
- Borrowing power of Board of Directors is described in: Articles of Association.
- Doctorine of Ultravires borrowing relates to : Borrowing by a company for an activity, which it is not authorized to undertake as per its Memorandum of Association
- Net working capital is Rs.80000. Current ratio is 3:1. The current assets are : 120000
- Right to retain goods is called : Lien
- For obtaining loan against shares, the Charge on shares: Lien
- A director of the bank wants to raise loan from your bank against (a) FDR of other bank (b) share of same bank(c) surrender value of Life Policy. Loan can be given against : Surrender value of Life Policy.
- Bill of lading, Railway Receipt are negotiable instruments under (a) NI Act (b) Sec 3 of Transfer of Property Act (c) Sec 137 of Transfer of Property Act (d) Sale of Goods act : C
- Keeping goods in safe custody is as per provisions of (a) NI Act (b) Indian Partnership Act (c) Indian Contract Act : C
- No dues certificate in case of agricultural advances is exempted up to a loan of: Rs.50000

- Liability of a coparcener in case of loan raised by HUF is : Restricted to his share in HUF property/assets
- In KYC guidelines, the small account where simple KYC is applicable are those account where the amount deposited in the account is restricted to (a) Rs.50000 (b) Rs.1 lac : Rs.1 lac
- In case of SMEs, the registration is mandatory in case of (a) medium enterprises in servicing (b) small manufacturing enterprises (c) manufacturing medium enterprises : C
- What is the maximum amount of loan for obtaining guarantee under CGTMSE of SIDBI : Rs.50 lac
- A company has been sanctioned cash credit-pledge limit. Internal auditor finds that charge has not been registered with Registrar of Companies in time. In how much time it is to be done : In case of pledge, not required.
- Loan system of credit delivery is not applicable in case of : Software industry
- To sell an NPA, the account must remain in the books of seller bank : for 24 months as NPA
- One of these is an indirect rate (a) one \$ = Rs. 39.56 (b) one pound = Rs. 89.56, (c) one yen = Rs. 0..30 (d) Rs.100 = \$ 2.60 : D
- Which crossing is not recognized by NI Act (a) Special (b) payee's account (c) not negotiable : B
- Which among the following can open an Resident Foreign Currency account (a) NRI (b) Resident (c) Erstwhile NRI now resident (d) none : C
- A partner wants to retire from the firm XYZ. He has to (a) get consent of other partners (b) has implied authority to retire (c) has to give public notice (d) can retire when desired by him by giving notice to other partners : A : C
- The limitation period u/s 138 of NI Act begins from : Date of cause of action

- A cheque is issued by a company as "pay yourselves". A clerk from the company comes and signs on behalf of the company and requests for preparation of a demand draft: Cannot be prepared.
- CRR & Bank rates are :6.00 & 6.00
- Repo rate is..............and reverse repo rate is...............: 6.25% & 5.25%(2/111/2010)
- A cheque passed in a current account of an Un Registered Firm having insufficient balance allow OD in the account without any instructions from the Firm. Bank has an FD, whether bank can recover the amount of OD allowed in the account from the proceeds of FD? : Yes
- Whether Minor can nominate? no
- TDS not deducted what is the penalty and for what period: Bank to pay the amount with interest @ 1% p.m. simple
- What is the position of a Nominee ? : The money will be paid to nominee after death of depositor

24

Problems in Banking

1. X and Y have been maintaining a saving bank account operated jointly. A cheque is presented in their account and is paid. Later on Y claims that he did not sign such cheque and his signatures have been forged. The signature of X, however are genuine. What is the liability of the bank and X. **{JOINTLY AND SEVERALLY}**

2. Mr. X having a current account with the bank issued a cheque of Rs.12500 in favour of a TV dealer to make the payment of a TV set purchased by him. When the cheque was presented to the bank for payment through clearing, it was observed that the account had balance of Rs.15300 including an amount of Rs.7600 representing a cheque sent for clearing by the bank. The bank returned the cheque stating 'insufficient funds'. When the fact came to the notice of the customer he objected and claimed that the amount of cheque was credited to the account on that day and the amount of cheque sent in clearing was also credited to bank's account on the same day. He requested the bank to pay him the amount of loss as he is facing a case u/s 138 of NI Act. What is the position of the bank.**{BANK NOT LIABLE AS ISF {insufficientFunds}}**

3. Mr. Goverdhan Lal purchased a demand draft from Lucknow branch of Punjab National Bank in the name of his son who was to visit Puri, in Orissa in connection with his admission in a professional college there. The

boy carried the DD with a view to use it, in case he gets admission. In a test conducted by the college for which he sought admission, he was declared successful and was asked to deposit the fee within 24 hours. Next day being Saturday, the boy went to the drawee branch of the bank to get the DD encashed. However, the bank did not pay the DD on the ground that the advice has not been received from the issuing branch. When the payee explained the urgency, he was told that the DD cannot be paid unless the advice is received as only a few days back a fraud has taken place in the branch in a similar situation. What is the right of the payee, under the circumstances. **{BANK 100% Liable}**

4. Mr. Y having a current account with Corporation Bank had drawn an uncrossed bearer cheque of Rs.32000, reading as 'Pay to Corporate Bank OR bearer', to get a demand draft issued and sent his servant to get the demand draft prepared. The servant however, presented the cheque across the counter and obtained the cash payment and ran away with the money. When the customer came to know about this, he asked the bank to restore the amount as bank should not have made the payment in cash when bank was payee of the cheque, although it was a bearer. The bank on the other hand, insisted that it was a bearer cheque and bank was not negligent in making the payment of the cheque. What is the liability of the bank, in your view **{ BANK LIABLE IN TERMS OF KYC}**

5. Dehradun Branch of Commercial Bank has been given huge deposit and credit targets by its Head Office on the basis of growth rate in the past. But the branch has been far behind the targets and the branch manager is under pressure from HO to ensure that targets are achieved. There are a large no. of loan accounts where cash credit facilities have been sanctioned, but due to seasonality factors, these facilities are not availed by the borrowers,

at the time of annual closing. In order to meet the targets, the branch manager plans to obtain request letters from these borrowers to debit their accounts and place the amount for a week or 10 days in current accounts of these firms. He gives assurance to the borrowers that bank will not charge interest on the debit balance, to the extent of balance in the current account. Such action was resorted to in the past also, by the branch. **{BRANCH HEAD LIABLE MALPRACTICE }**

25

PRACTICE QUESTIONS

1. Internal rate of return is: A discount rate, at which the net present value of a project is Zero.
2. Cheque is issued by a company as "pay yourselves". A clerk from the company comes and signs on behalf of the company and requests for preparation of a demand draft
3. The limitation period u/s 138 of NI Act begins from
4. Govt. shareholding in public sector banks cannot be below
5. A loan document is signed by one partner on June 15, 2007, by 2nd partner on June 21 and by 3rd partner on June 29. The period of limitation will start from
6. Which crossing is not recognized by NI Act (a) Special (b) payee's account (c) not negotiable
7. A company has been sanctioned cash credit-pledge limit. Internal auditor finds that charge has not been registered with Registrar of Companies in time. In how much time it is to be done
8. Bill of lading, Railway Receipt are negotiable instruments under (a) NI Act (b) Sec 3 of Transfer of Property Act (c) Sec 137 of Transfer of Property Act (d) Sale of Goods act
9. Right to retain goods is called
10. Borrowing power of Board of Directors is described in: Articles of Association//Memorandum

11. Which document is required to be attested (witnessed) (a) mortgage deed (b) pledge agreement (c) Hypothecation agreement : Mortgage deed
12. Who cannot be a partners (a) HUF (b) illiterate (c) Blind person (d) company
13. RBI injects liquidity through CRR/REPO/Reverse REPO/ None of the above
14. Preshipment credit is available in which type of letter of credit : Red clause //Green Clause // Transferable // Back to Back LC
15. Full form of BCBS : Basel Committee For Banking Supervision
16. Formula of DSCR : (Net profit + depreciation + interest on long term loans) / Installment of Long term loans + interest on long term loans
17. Pillar III of Basel-II related to
18. Whether Minor can nominate
19. The amount in a cheque is written differently in words and figures and amount written in words is higher of the two. Which is to be paid
20. Weaker persons of the society available deposit and loan services from banks, which is called : Financial inclusion
21. Which among the Muslims, Christians, Buddhists & Jains is not a minority community
22. A person wants to open an account which his wife should be able to operate only after his death. What type of account he should open : Former or survivor// Either OR Survivor
23. Real Time Gross settlement system takes care of which risk : Systemic risk and settlement risk
24. A customer of your branch Mrs. Neelam, has both a saving bank and current account. She issues a cheque for Rs.12500 from the saving bank account, in favor of a local consumer goods dealer. The balance in the saving

bank account, however, is Rs.9870 only, but the current account has balance amounting to Rs.6500. What would you do with the cheque?

25. Expand SARFAESI : Securitization & Reconstruction of Finance Assets and Enforcement of Security Interest Act 2002

SAMPLE PAPER I

Course Title:- Financial Management of Banking & Insurance Companies

Duration: 2 hrs **Max. Marks: 60**

Q1. Please Answer the following : {10 +10+6=26}

(A) Choose the right answer :

(i) The charge on moveable to be created would be charge known as (a) Pledge (b) Hypothecation (c) Mortgage (d) Setoff

(ii) Mr. Ram Kumar, a Hindu and father of a minor Sham Kumar converts himself to a Mohammedan Called Abdul Hamid . What is the status of the guardian- (a) Remains Natural Guardian (b) Ceases to be Natural Guardian

(c) Remains Guardian if Hindu mother does not object to (d) None of the above

(iii) How many times a Locker can be operated (a) Once a day (b) Once a week (c) 50 times in a year (d) No restrictions

(iv) In accepting articles for safe custody , the nomination facility is available under which of the following : (a) NI ACT 1881 (b) Banking Regulation Act 1949 (c) RBI Act 1934 (d) Indian Contracts Act 1872

(v) Describe Section 131(statutory protection of Collecting Banker),Section 10 (Payment in due Course) of NI Act 1881. **{10}**

(B) List any 4 Assumptions of Black Scholes Option Pricing Generalised Model used by a Treasury of a Bank . Suppose a Corporate wants to book a call option with Treasury of Standard Chartered Bank Mumbai for Rs 10 Crores . The following information is available : Spot Price (S)= 30, Exercise Price (X)=30 , t=Option Period = 3 Months Forward , Rate of Interest (r) = 10% . The Standard deviation is 0.30 . Please calculate the value of the Option ? d1 =0.24 Nd1=0.5948, d2 =0.09 Nd2= 0.5359 **{10}**

(C) Mr. X having a current account with the bank issued a cheque of Rs.15000 in favour of a TV dealer to make the payment of a TV set purchased by him. When the cheque was presented to the bank for payment through clearing, it was observed that the account had balance of Rs.20600 including an amount of Rs.5600 representing a cheque sent for clearing by the bank. The bank returned the cheque stating 'FEP (Funds Expected , Present Again) and also EA (Exceeds Arrangement). When the fact came to the notice of the customer he objected and claimed that the amount of cheque was credited to the account on that day and the amount of cheque sent in clearing was also credited to bank's account on the same day. He requested the bank to pay him the amount of loss as he is facing a case u/s 138 of NI Act. What is the position of the bank. **{6}**

Q2. Write analytical notes on any One(1) of the following:

(i) Attachment Order and Garnishee Order with examples

(ii) Banc assurance and the recent tie ups with the Insurance Companies by the banks with theories and examples

(iii) What is Mortgage . Describe Equitable Title Deeds vs Usufructuary type of Mortgages **{5}**

Q3. Discuss in detail the Insurance Regulatory and Development Authority Act (IRDA) stating its role and functions in the Insurance Business What do you understand by Reinsurance , Proximate Cause in Marine Insurance ,Insurable interest . Doctrine of subrogation in an Insurance Policy **{5}**

Q4. Write short notes on any Three of the following {8x 3=24}

(a) Comment on the Micro finance schemes and Indian Banking scenario with examples. Discuss the role of Self Help Groups and the need of their financing in terms of micro credit.

(b) Is there any Offence for the Dishonour of Cheques under the Negotiable Instruments Act in the commercial practice? If so, describe the various sections under law in view of any two decided cases.

(c) Profitability parameters of the Indian Banks

(d) Enumerate the salient features of the Balance sheet of a Bank. List the various schedules and comment on the Auditors Report. What improvements would you suggest?

(e) What is a Commercial Paper? Which are all the institutions permitted by the RBI to issue Commercial Paper in the Indian Money markets? What are the RBI guidelines relating to the issue of Commercial Paper? How is the Yield of a Commercial paper is calculated if the Price is given?

SAMPLE PAPER II

Course Title:- Financial Management of Banking & Insurance Companies

Duration: 2 hrs **Max. Marks: 60**

Q1. Please Answer the following: A.10+B.5+C.10=25}

(A) (i) A Bill Of Exchange is dated 31.08.2007 and is payable 3 Months after date . It is presented on September 02,2007 and is accepted by the drawee on September 03,2007 . What will be its due date ?

(ii) Describe the terms Negative Lien and General Lien in Banking

(iii) What is Garnishee Order . How is it different from Attachment Order

(iv) A loan document is signed by one partner on June 30, 2007, by 2nd partner on July 21 , 2007and by 3rd partner on July 29,2007The period of limitation will start from which date ?

(v) Who among the following would be natural guardian of a Hindu Minor widow (a) Her mother (b) Her father (c) Her father in law (d) her Mother in law if father in law also expired **{10}**

(B) Mr. Ramesh having a current account with Indian Bank had drawn an uncrossed bearer cheque of Rs.50,000, reading as 'Pay to Indian Bank OR bearer', to get a demand draft issued and sent his driver to get the demand draft prepared. The driver however, presented the cheque across the counter after convincing the Branch Manager and obtained the cash payment and ran away with the money.

When the customer came to know about this, he asked the bank to restore the amount as bank should not have made the payment in cash when bank was payee of the cheque, although it was a bearer. The bank on the other hand, insisted that it was a bearer cheque and bank was not negligent in making the payment of the cheque. What is the liability of the bank, in your view or is permissible under the normal Banking practice and under the provisions of NI Act , 1881 **{5}**

(C) Write the Black Scholes Formula for European Call Option Pricing stating the terms used . **{10}**

Assume that on November 22,2007 the customer approaches the Treasury of a Bank and requests to compute fair price value an <u>European call option</u> expiring on 21, December,2007 on X stock and the stock does not pay dividends and further : S=Rs92 , X=Rs95 ,t=50days or 50/365 =0.137 of a year as option expires on 21.12.2007, r=7.12% p.a , S.D =3.5%. Please Compute as per Black-Scholes Model. N(d1) as per tables=0.4570 and N(d2)=0.4061

Q2. Write Short Notes on any Two (2) of the Following giving Examples :

(i) Banc assurance and the recent tie ups with the Insurance Companies by the banks with theories and examples

(ii) Money Market Instruments in Indian banking System . List any 5 Money Market instruments . State as to how the Price of a certificate of deposit is calculated if the yield and number of days of maturity are given

(iii) IRDA ACT and functions of IRDA . What are the basic principles of Insurance . Explain Reinsurance. **{5x2=10}**

Q3. Discuss the provisions Criminal liability for Dishonour of Cheques? Please state in light of the sections 138 to 147 of The Negotiable Act 1881 with latest decided judgments and cases.

OR

Q3. Give an Analysis of the Scheduled Commercial bank. What are the salient features in the Bank balance Sheet? Comment on the Auditors Report and the need for improvements **{10}**

Q4. Write short notes on any three (3) of the following

(a) Micro finance

(b) Universal banking

(c) N.P.A Management and Securitisation Act

(d) K.Y.C. (Know Your Customer) Guidelines in Banking

(e) Retail Banking

(f) Non fund based business in a Bank

(g) Describe Section 131(statutory protection of Collecting Banker), Section 10 (Payment in due Course) of NI Act 1881 **{5x3=15}**

OR

Q. Give an overview of the Scheduled Commercial Bank. What are the salient features in the Bank in [illegible] sector? Comment on the [illegible] Report and the need for improvements (10)

Q. Write short notes on any three (3) of the following:

(a) Micro Finance

(b) Universal Banking

(c) NPA Management and Securitization Act

(d) K.Y.C. (Know Your Customer) guidelines in Banking

(e) [illegible] based [illegible]

(f) Describe Section 131 Statutory Protection of Collecting Banker/Section 10 (Payment in due Course) of NI Act 1881 [illegible]

SAMPLE PAPER III

Answer all Questions:

Q1. Fill in the Blanks **20**

(A) (a) Commercial banks will be implementing Basle II wef _ ___/____/ 200_

(b) Capital Adequacy Ratio = Capital Funds /______ ×100

(c) Tier II of the Capital Funds Contains ______, ____________

(d) Pillar II of Basle Accord Contains ___ _Role

(e) Indian Parliament Passed ____________2002 for prevention of Money Laundering

(f) Name any 5 Retail Banking Products ________, ______________, ______________, ______________, ______________

(g) An FD payable to Either of Survivor for Rs 25,000 is in name of A & B .Receipt is lost and a duplicate is issued on the basis of indemnity. Later A Comes with Original FD on date of maturity . Will the bank Pay ---YES // NO

(h) CRR refers to ______________and refers minimum cash to be kept with ________by Banks. At present CRR is _________

(i) A nomination can be accepted in favour of a Minor ---YES / NO

B. Expand :

(I) ALCO --

(II) BIFR ______________________________

(III) CAMELS ______________________________

(IV) CAR ______________________________

(V) CP ______________________________

Q2. Write short notes on any Two of the following

(a) Basle II in Indian Banking and its implementation

(b) Recent Mergers & Amalgamations in Indian Banks

(c) N.P.A Management in Indian Banks

(d) Retail banking in India **{10x2 =20 }**

Q3. Discuss the provisions Criminal liability for dishonour of Cheques? Please state in light of the sections 138 to 147 of The Negotiable Act 1881 with latest decided judgments and cases. **{20}**

Q4. Write Analytical Notes on any two of the following with one case example **{20}**

(a) Banc assurance and the recent Insurance business taken up by the Banks

(b) FEMA vs FERA and the Anti Money laundering measures in Banking.

(c) Recent IT /Technology products and developments in Indian Banking

(d) Universal, Narrow and Unit Banking

Q5. Write short notes on any two of the following giving suitable examples :--------- **{20}**
Insurable Interest in Life business

(i) Assignment and Indemnity

(ii) Reinsurance

(iii) General Principles of Insurance **(5x2=10)**

(b) Describe the Insurance regulatory and Development Authority Act 1999 listing the duties, powers and functions of the Authority. **(10)**

INDEX